'Mixed Race' Studies

A Reader

'Mixed Race' Studies is one of the fastest growing, as well as one of the most important and controversial areas in the field of 'race' and ethnic relations. Bringing together pioneering and controversial scholarship from both the social and the biological sciences, as well as the humanities, this Reader charts the evolution of debates on 'race' and 'mixed race' from the nineteenth to the twenty-first century. This collection adds a new dimension to the growing body of literature on the topic and provides a comprehensive history of the origins and directions of 'mixed race' research as an intellectual movement. It is divided into three main sections:

- Tracing the origins: miscegenation, moral degeneracy and genetics.
- Mapping contemporary and foundational discourses: 'mixed race', identities politics and celebration.
- Debating definitions: multiraciality, census categories and critiques.

Each section begins with a brief editorial guide to the readings, and includes revision 'probes' (study questions) for each reading, as well as suggestions for further reading. 'Mixed Race' Studies: A Reader is an invaluable resource for examining the complexities and paradoxes of 'racial' thinking across space, time and disciplines.

Jayne O. Ifekwunigwe is Reader in Anthropology at the University of East London, where she teaches a course on comparative 'mixed race' studies.

'Mixed Race' Studies

A Reader

Edited and introduced by

Jayne O. Ifekwunigwe

Routledge
Taylor & Francis Group

LONDON AND NEW YORK

First published 2004
by Routledge
11 New Fetter Lane, London EC4P 4EE

Simultaneously published in the USA and Canada
by Routledge
29 West 35th Street, New York, NY 10001

Routledge is an imprint of the Taylor & Francis Group

© Editorial matter and selection 2004 Jayne O. Ifekwunigwe;
the contributors and publishers for their chapters

Typeset in Perpetua and Bell Gothic by RefineCatch Ltd, Bungay, Suffolk
Printed and bound in Great Britain by TJ International Ltd, Padstow, Cornwall

British Library Cataloguing in Publication Data
A catalogue record for this book is available from the British Library

Library of Congress Cataloging in Publication Data
Ifekwunigwe, Jayne O.
Mixed race studies : a reader / [edited by] Jayne O. Ifekwunigwe.
     p. cm.
   Includes bibliographical references and index.
     1. Racially mixed people.   2. Miscegenation.   3. Ethnicity.
   4. Ethnic relations.   5. Race relations.

HT1523.M59 2004
305.8′00973–dc22   2004042765

ISBN 0–415–32163–8 (hbk)
ISBN 0–415–32164–6 (pbk)

For past, present and future cohorts of AN234 (Rules of Métissage ('Racial') Mixing: Anthropological Perspectives on 'Race', Status and Colour) students at the University of East London, from whom I (re)learn every time I teach.

Contents

PART TWO
Mapping contemporary and foundational discourses: 'mixed race', identities politics and celebration

PART THREE
Debating definitions: multiraciality, census categories and critiques

The census and categories

Multiraciality and critiques

Preface

'*Mixed Race' Studies: A Reader* is the partial by-product of countless provocative exchanges I have had with colleagues, students and friends over a thirteen-year period in seminars, at international conferences and symposia, in the classroom, and during informal social gatherings or conversations. There are far too many to mention each by name. However, I will acknowledge a few kindred minds and spirits, who, in varying ways and during different phases of the 'birthing process', have provided inspiration, encouragement, support or respite when 'rethinking "mixed race" ' was on the verge of becoming a 'mind-exploding exercise' (apologies in advance to anyone I may have inadvertently omitted):

Minelle Mahtani, April Moreno, David Parker, Miri Song, Peter Aspinall, Katya Azoulay, Monica Russel y Rodriguez, Glenn D'Cruz, Yasmine Khan, Yasmin Alibhai-Brown, Naomi Zack, Maria Root, Paul Spickard, Patricia Hill Collins, Steven Robins, Sean Jacobs, Colin Samson, Stephen Small, Ben Carrington, Mark Christian, Heidi Mirza, Tunde Jegede, Joanne Ramsey, Andrew Ward, Onyekachi Wambu, Bisi Silva, Caroline and Catherine Naysmith, Folake Shoga, Galina Chester, Maya Jobarteh, Annmarie Shadie, Eleanor Grant, Peter Luff, Thea Shaw, Mahesh/ Manjula Shah, Tony Day, Frank Hodder, Gary Andrews, Don Bebel and Fiston. My colleagues at the University of East London have also been incredibly supportive, in particular, Barbara Harrison, Head of the School of Social Sciences; Tim Butler, Head of Research for the School of Social Sciences; Lionel Sims, Subject Area Coordinator for Anthropology; Diane Ball, Anthropology Administrator; Merl Storr, Phil Cohen, Abiola Ogunsola, Mike Rustin, Dean of the former Faculty of Social Sciences; and Mike Thorne, Vice-Chancellor. Members of my transnational family have always been my most loyal and my biggest fans, and for this I am forever in their debt, particularly to my uncle/aunt in Birmingham (UK), and to my parents in Los Angeles, who during many a transatlantic phone call listened patiently and attentively while I dramatically recounted the numerous pitfalls encountered along the way. A special thank-you is also extended to the twenty-five courageous women and men in Bristol (UK), who participated in my earlier research on 'mixed race', identities, families and memories. In so doing, they provided the catalyst for my long-standing engagement with comparative 'mixed race' studies.

This Reader has been in the 'delivery room' for quite a long time, and has been a much more challenging discursive exercise than writing a book, chapter or article on 'mixed race' studies. As I view the light at the end of the proverbial tunnel, I now know what veteran editors meant when they asked: 'Are you really sure that you want to edit a Reader?' This project was originally commissioned by Mari Shullaw, then Senior Editor in Sociology at Routledge. She has since moved on to pastures new. Yet I remain indebted to her for embracing this 'brainchild', and for shrewd editorial assistance and boundless patience when this book had to be placed on a back burner to accommodate other publication commitments or unforeseen setbacks. Thanks also to her editorial assistant James McNally. However, the most gratitude is extended to Gerhard Boomgaarden, who is the current Senior Editor in Sociology at Routledge. With humour, understanding and enthusiasm as his compass, he has been an excellent navigator. Of course, I must also thank the rest of the dynamic Routledge publishing team including editorial assistant Lizzie Catford. Finally, I am grateful to Routledge's anonymous academic referees, who helped wittle down the scope of this unwieldy project to a manageable size.

Acknowledgements

The publishers would like to thank the following for permission to reprint their material. The editor would also like to thank all of the authors she contacted who kindly gave their permission to reprint edited extracts of their work.

Alfred A. Knopf for permission to reprint Melville Herskovits, 'The Amalgam He Represents and His Significance for the Study of Race', from *The American Negro*, New York: Alfred A. Knopf, 1928, pp. 3–4, 74–76. *The American Negro* by Melville Herskovits, copyright 1928, Alfred A. Knopf Inc, and renewed 1956 by Melville J. Herskovits. Used by permission of Alfred A. Knopf, a division of Random House, Inc.

American Anthropological Association for permission to reprint 'American Anthropological Association Statement on "Race"', Arlington, VA: Executive Board of the American Anthropological Association, 1998, pp. 1–4. Reprinted by permission of the American Anthropological Association from *Anthropology News*, Volume 39, 1998.

American Association for the Advancement of Science for permission to reprint William B. Provine, 'Geneticists and the Biology of Race Crossing', *Science*, 182 (4114), 1973, pp. 790–796. Reprinted with permission from William B. Provine, 'Geneticists and the Biology of Race Crossing', *Science*, 182 (4114), 1973, pp. 790–796, copyright 1973, American Association for the Advancement of Science.

Anthropological Quarterly for permission to reprint Paul Brodwin, 'Genetics, Identity and the Anthropology of Essentialism', *Anthropological Quarterly*, 75(2), 2002, pp. 323–330.

aunt lute books for permission to reprint Gloria Anzaldúa, '*La concienca de la mestiza*: Towards a New Consciousness', from *Borderlands/La Frontera: The New Mestiza*, San Francisco: aunt lute books, 1987, pp. 77–80, 82–83. From

Borderlands/La Frontera: The New Mestiza, copyright 1987, 1999, Gloria Anzaldúa. Reprinted by permission of aunt lute books.

Cambridge University Press and Paul Rich for permission to reprint Paul Rich, 'The "Half-Caste" Pathology', from *Race and Empire in British Politics* (2nd edn), Cambridge: Cambridge University Press, 1990, pp.120–121, 130–135.

Doubleday for permission to reprint Lisa Jones, 'Is Biracial Enough? (Or, What's This About a Multiracial Category on the Census?: A Conversation)', from *Bulletproof Diva: Tales of Race, Sex and Hair*, New York: Doubleday, 1994, pp.56–62. From *Bulletproof Diva: Tales of Race, Sex and Hair* by Lisa Jones, copyright 1994, Lisa Jones. Used by permission of Doubleday, a division of Random House, Inc.

Elsevier for permission to reprint Peter Aspinall, 'The Conceptualisation and Categorisation of Mixed Race/Ethnicity in Britain and North America: Identity Options and the Role of the State', *International Journal of Intercultural Relations*, 27, 2003, pp.289–292. Reprinted from *International Journal of Intercultural Relations*, 27, Peter Aspinall, 'The Conceptualisation and Categorisation of Mixed Race/Ethnicity in Britain and North America: Identity Options and the Role of the State', pp.289–292, copyright 2003, with permission from Elsevier.

Itabari Njeri and the Miriam Altshuler Literary Agency for permission to reprint extracts from Itabari Njeri, *The Last Plantation: Color, Conflict and Identity: Reflections of a New World Black*, New York: Houghton Mifflin, 1997, pp.216–221, 226–229, 234–236. Reprinted by permission of Miriam Altshuler Literary Agency, on behalf of Itabari Njeri, copyright 1997, Itabari Njeri.

McGraw-Hill Education for permission to reprint Edward Byron Reuter, 'The Hybrid as a Sociological Type', from *Race Mixture: Studies in Intermarriage and Miscegenation*, New York: McGraw-Hill Education, 1931, pp.183–185. Edward Byron Reuter, *Race Mixture*, copyright 1931, McGraw-Hill Education. Reproduced with permission of McGraw-Hill Companies.

Office for National Statistics (http://www.statistics.gov.uk) for permission to reprint 'Census 2001 – Ethnicity and Religion in England and Wales', 2002, pp.1–4. Source: National Statistics website: http://www.statistics. Reproduced with permission of the Crown copyright 2003.

Palgrave Macmillan for permission to reprint Mark Christian, 'Assessing Multiracial Identity', from *Multiracial Identity: An International Perspective*, London: Macmillan Press, 2000, pp.104–107, 111–113, 115–119.

Pantheon Books for permission to reprint Danzy Senna, 'The Mulatto Millennium', in Claudine Chiawei O'Hearn (ed.) *Half and Half: Writers on Growing Up Biracial and Bicultural*, New York: Pantheon Books, 1998, pp.12–13, 22–27. 'The Mulatto Millennium', copyright 1998, Danzy Senna from *Half and Half: Writers on Growing up Biracial and Bicultural* by Claudine Chiawei O'Hearn, copyright 1998, Claudine Chiawei O'Hearn. Used by permission of Pantheon Books, a division of Random House, Inc.

Pluto Press for permission to reprint Charlie Owen, 'Mixed Race in Official Statistics', in David Parker and Miri Song (eds) *Rethinking 'Mixed Race'*, London: Pluto, 2001, pp.146–151; Minelle Mahtani and April Moreno, 'Same Difference: Towards a More Unified Discourse in "Mixed Race" Theory', in

David Parker and Miri Song (eds) *Rethinking 'Mixed Race'*, London: Pluto, 2001, pp.71–75.

Pluto Press and Rutgers University Press for permission to reprint Frank Füredi, 'Crossing the Boundary: The Marginal Man', from *The Silent War: Imperialism and the Changing Perception of Race*, copyright Frank Füredi, London: Pluto, and New Brunswick, NJ: Rutgers University Press, 1998, pp.138–139, 144–145, 149–152. Frank Füredi, *The Silent War: Imperialism and the Changing Perception of Race*, copyright 1998, Frank Füredi. Reprinted by permission of Rutgers University Press.

Routledge for permission to reprint Clarence Lusane, 'Made in America, Perfected in Germany: The Nazi Sterilization Program Against Blacks', from *Hitler's Black Victims*, 2003, New York: Routledge, pp.134–143. Copyright 2003 from *Hitler's Black Victims* by Clarence Lusane. Reproduced by permission of Routledge/Taylor & Francis Books, Inc; Jayne O. Ifekwunigwe, 'Let Blackness and Whiteness Wash Through: Competing Discourses on Bi-racialization and the Compulsion of Genealogical Erasures', from *Scattered Belongings: Cultural Paradoxes of 'Race', Nation and Gender*, 1999, London/New York: Routledge, pp.183–187, 190–191. Copyright 1999 from *Scattered Belongings: Cultural Paradoxes of 'Race', Nation and Gender* by Jayne O. Ifekwunigwe. Reproduced by permission of Routledge/Taylor & Francis Books, Inc.

Sage Publications, Inc for permission to reprint Maria P.P. Root, 'Within, Between, and Beyond Race', in Maria P.P. Root (ed.) *Racially Mixed People in America*, Thousand Oaks, CA: Sage, 1992, pp.3–11. Maria P.P. Root, 'Within, Between, and Beyond Race', in Maria Root (ed.) *Racially Mixed People in America*, pp.3–11, copyright 1992, Sage Publications. Reprinted by permission of Sage Publications; Paul R. Spickard, 'The Illogic of American Racial Categories', in Maria P.P. Root (ed.) *Racially Mixed People in America*, Thousand Oaks, CA: Sage, 1992, pp.18–23, copyright 1992, Sage Publications. Reprinted by permission of Sage Publications.

Taylor & Francis (http://www.tandf.co.uk) and Lewis R. Gordon for permission to reprint the elaborated version of 'Critical Mixed Race?', from *Social Identities*, 1(2) 1995, which appears as 'Race, Biraciality, and Mixed Race', from *Her Majesty's Other Children: Sketches of Racism from a Neocolonial Age*, Lanham, MD: Rowman and Littlefield, 1997, pp.56–57, 62–67.

Temple University Press for permission to reprint Naomi Zack, 'Black, White, and Gray', from *Race and Mixed Race*, Philadelphia: Temple University Press, 1993, pp.167–172. From *Race and Mixed Race*, by Naomi Zack. Reprinted by permission of Temple University Press. Copyright 1993, Temple University Press. All Rights Reserved; G. Reginald Daniel, 'The New Millennium: Toward a New Master Racial Project and Epilogue: Beyond Black or White: A New United States Racial Project', from *More Than Black?: Multiracial Identity and the New Racial Order*, Philadelphia: Temple University Press, 2002, pp.172–175, 189–194. From *More Than Black?: Multiracial Identity and the New Racial Order* by G. Reginald Daniel. Reprinted by permission of Temple University Press. Copyright 2002, Temple University Press. All Rights Reserved.

University of California Press for permission to reprint William S. Penn, 'Introduction', from William S. Penn (ed.) *As We Are Now: Mixblood Essays on Race and Identity*, Berkeley: University of California Press, 1997, pp.1–3, 6–8. William S. Penn, 'Introduction', from William S. Penn (ed.) *As We Are Now: Mixblood Essays on Race and Identity*, copyright 1997, The Regents of the University of California; George G. Sanchez, 'Y tú ¿qué? (Y2K): Latino History in the New Millennium', from Marcelo Suárez-Orozco and Mariela Páez (eds) *Latinos: Remaking America*, Berkeley: University of California Press, 2002, pp.50–56. George G. Sanchez, 'Y tú ¿qué?: Latino History in the New Millennium', from Marcelo M. Suárez-Orozco and Mariela M. Páez (eds) *Latinos: Remaking America*, Berkeley: University of California Press, copyright 2002, The Regents of the University of California.

University of Minnesota Press and Kimberly TallBear for permission to reprint Kimberly TallBear, 'DNA, Blood and Racializing the Tribe', *Wicazo Sa Review*, 18(1), 2003, pp.88–93, 98–99. Copyright 2003, University of Minnesota Press.

US Census Bureau (http://www.census.gov) for permission to reprint Elizabeth M. Grieco and Rachel C. Cassidy, 'Overview of Race and Hispanic Origin: Census 2000 Brief', March 2001, pp.1–10.

Every effort has been made to trace the copyright holders and to seek authors' consent. If any have been inadvertently overlooked, at the first opportunity, the publishers will be pleased to make the necessary arrangements.

Notes on terminology

Throughout this Reader, the variable presentation of terms used to define, describe and name people of 'mixed race' is in keeping with the preferred use of the individual authors. This diversity reflects the social evolution of the term from its pathological roots as a derogatory 'racial' category (i.e. 'half-caste', 'racial hybrid', mulatto) to its contemporary usage as a political emblem of identification and empowerment (i.e. 'mixed race', biracial, multiracial, mixed parentage, mixed heritage). Such variation in terminology also highlights the problems associated with subsuming the many and varied individuals/communities who identify and/or who are identified as 'mixed race' under one umbrella term. Their particular histories are complex. Although, at times comparable, the social, cultural and political processes which have given rise to their presence are specific.

Why do I use the term 'mixed race'?

In previous publications,[1] I have invoked the doubly appropriated conceptual term *métis(se)* as a shorthand analytical stand-in response to what I believed were the inadequacies of the myriad and at times ambiguous terms deployed to name individuals with differently racialized parents. The term *métis(se)* is a 'French-African', in particular Senegalese, reappropriation of the continental French *métis(se)*. In translated continental French, *métis(se)* is synonymous with the derogatory English 'half-caste' and 'half-breed'. However, in French-African contexts, linguistic inform-ants Senegalese comparative literature professor Samba Diop and Senegalese/ Congolese ethnomusicologist Henri-Pierre Koubaka suggest that alternative transla-tions of *métis(se)* both include and transcend Black/White discourses and in so doing encompass diasporic convergences across ethnicities, cultures, religions and nationalities.[2] For example, one is considered *métis(se)* if one has a Wolof parent and a Mandinka parent – two distinct Senegambian cultural groups, two different languages.

By redeploying this term in English milieux, my intention was to decentre 'race'[3] as a primary identity marker and to clear space for the *interplay* of other hierarchically positioned signifiers such as ethnicity, religion, sexuality, locality, generation, gender and social class. Although the deprivileging of 'race' remains both an important critical theoretical and research objective, I now believe that the term *métis(se)* does not sufficiently do this important job. My research has taught me that parents, carers, practitioners, educators, policy makers, academics and 'mixed race' individuals themselves are all hungry for a uniform but not essentialist term which carves out a space for the naming of their specific experiences without necessarily reinscribing and reifying 'race'. Using a French-African term in an English context, even if simply for discursive analyses, could be perceived as potentially exoticizing and further marginalizing 'mixed race' subjectivities. Another self-critique is that the double linguistic othering of *métis(se)* downplays the fact that scattered and ambiguous belongings also characterize the lived realities of other members of designated minority ethnic and diasporic groups such as English-born children of continental African or African Caribbean immigrant parents in general, and those who have been 'transracially' adopted and/or fostered in particular. Furthermore, one could argue that partially deflecting the attention away from what I call the popular folk concept of 'race'[4] to other forms of identification and stratification diminishes the significant and potent function institutionalized racism plays in the maintenance of privilege and power for some and disadvantage and discrimination for others. Finally, in attempting to construct a new lexicon, I am perpetuating a fictional history which ignores the ways in which the social processes of 'racial' mixing are themselves old.

Rather, as the selected readings in this collection illustrate, it is the localized and temporal reinterpretations of the designated status of the children of such 'inter-minglings' that keep shifting. In other words, in the case of African American communities, or for my purposes, African Caribbean communities in England, the legacy of slavery as both a mode of economic exploitation as well as a strategy for the diversification of African *and* European descent groups means that to be 'mixed race' is constitutive of the genealogies of most just 'black' *or* just 'white' families. Hence, although the previously outlined conceptual motivation underpinning my temporary deployment of *métis(se)* – that of rupturing allegedly stable racialized faultlines – has not changed, I now problematize the utility and potential application of this or any other mediating term.[5]

The unanswered conundrum, which will be explored at length in *'Mixed Race' Studies*, is twofold. First, how do we create textual and conceptual space for the contestation and construction of complex and multilayered identities without either reproducing a South African apartheid typology or promoting what a friend and colleague Donovan Chamberlayne critically refers to as 'I amism': 'I am not "black" or "white", I am just me'?[6] Second, how do we create political alliances forged from shared marginal status while also acknowledging the varied and inherently hierarchical power dynamics within, between and among such disparate and differently racialized groups? For example, in 'whiteness'-centred societies such as Britain or the USA, those who can pass for 'white' face a different set of psychosocial challenges than those individuals whose non-'whiteness' is visibly marked.

So why 'mixed race'? Although as problematic as *métis(se)*, my reviving the term 'mixed race' is a necessary, deliberate and discursive political intervention. Unlike *métis(se)*, 'mixed race' is a term that is part and parcel of the English vernacular. Unlike 'mixed parentage' and 'mixed heritage' which retreat from a racialized discourse, someone with white Scottish and white Welsh parents could claim to be both 'mixed parentage' and 'mixed heritage'. To be 'mixed race' presumes differently racialized parentage. Therefore, for purposes of critical discussion, I use the term 'mixed race' to describe individuals who according to popular folk concepts of 'race' and by known birth parentage embody two or more worldviews or, in genealogical terms, descent groups. These individuals may have physical characteristics that reflect some sort of 'intermediate' status *vis-à-vis* their birth parents. More than likely, at some stage, they will have to reconcile multiple cultural influences. The degree of agency afforded a 'mixed race' individual is contingent in part upon local folk 'readings of their phenotype' in relation to systems of categorization and classification that may reinforce eighteenth- and nineteenth-century 'race' science fiction. By phenotype, I mean the visible physical markers of genetically inherited traits such as skin colour, hair texture and colour, eye shape and colour, general facial features, and body structure. In addition to the social meanings of phenotype, social class, gender, generation and locality are also important variables.

Moreover, as the chosen extracts in Parts two and three of this Reader will reveal, it is contradictory racialized perceptions of physical differences that frequently determine and undermine the lived experiences of those who, as active agents, identify as and/or are socially designated as 'mixed race'. These social applications of the term 'mixed race' highlight the paradoxes of kin and colour, and pinpoint the problems of reinscribing a term predicated on the bases of scientifically dubious criteria.

NOTES

1   Ifekwunigwe, Jayne O. (1997) 'Diaspora's Daughters, Africa's Orphans?: On lineage, Authenticity, and "Mixed Race" Identity', in H. Mirza (ed.) *Black British Feminism*, London: Routledge, pp.127–153; Ifekwunigwe, Jayne O. (1999a) *Scattered Belongings: Cultural Paradoxes of 'Race', Nation and Gender*, London: Routledge; Ifekwunigwe, Jayne O. (1999b) 'Old Whine, New Vassals: Are Diaspora and Hybridity Postmodern Inventions?', In P. Cohen (ed.) *New Ethnicities, Old Racisms*, London: Zed Books, pp.180–204.; Ifekwunigwe, Jayne O. (1999c) 'When the Mirror Speaks: The Poetics and Problematics of Identity Construction for Métisse Women in Bristol', in R. Barot, H. Bradley and S. Fenton (eds) *Ethnicity, Gender and Social Change*, London, pp.206–222.

2   Samba Diop, personal communication, 1993/1998; Henri-Pierre Koubaka, personal communication, 1993.

3   In these notes as well as in both my Introduction to the Reader and the introductory remarks before each part, I have placed 'race', 'mixed race', 'black' and 'white' in quotations to highlight their unstable and contested natures and the ways in which their local meanings vary across time and space.

4   A potent dynamic social and cultural imaginary, the naturalization of which attaches symbolic meanings to real or manufactured physical differences. These create, explain, justify and maintain social inequalities and injustices; and perpetuate differential access to privilege, prestige and power.

5   Ifekwunigwe, Jayne O. (2001) 'Re-membering "Race": On Gender, "Mixed Race" and Family in the English-African Diaspora', in D. Parker and M. Song (eds) *Rethinking 'Mixed Race'*, London: Pluto Press, pp.42–65.; Ifekwunigwe, Jayne O. (2002) '(An)Other English City: Multiethnicities, (Post)modern Moments and Strategic Identifications', Special Issue on Cities and Ethnicities, *Ethnicities*, 2(3): 321–348.; Ifekwunigwe, Jayne O. (2003) 'Scattered Belongings: Reconfiguring the "African" in the English-African Diaspora', in K. Koser (ed.) *New African Diasporas*, London: Routledge, pp.56–70.

6   Donovan Chamberlayne, personal communication, 1996.

INTRODUCTION
Rethinking 'mixed race' studies

■ Jayne O. Ifekwunigwe

Setting the scene: 'mixed race' subjects as artefacts of the past and beacons of the future

IN THE AUTUMN OF 1993 I was living in Berkeley, California, where I was putting the finishing touches to my Ph.D. dissertation, which was later published as *Scattered Belongings: Cultural Paradoxes of 'Race', Nation and Gender* (Ifekwunigwe 1999). Late one evening, I made my usual run to the local 7–11 convenience store for a fix of a vice I had acquired while writing: forty-four ounces of a healthy cocktail of *aspartame*-laced diet sodas – caffeine-free Diet Coke, Diet Coke, Diet Pepsi. Before leaving the shop I completed my second ritual, which entailed perusing the news-stand for any relevant headlines. Staring back at me was a special issue of *Time* magazine. It had a red cover. In the foreground was a head shot of a very attractive woman. By her face, the copy read: 'Take a good look at this woman. She was created by a computer from a mix of several races. What you see is a remarkable preview of. . . .' Underneath her face and the title of the special issue were the words: 'The New Face of America: How Immigrants are Shaping the World's First Multicultural Society.' In the background, and in a fashion eerily reminiscent of photographs of ranked 'races' found in turn-of-the-twentieth-century books on 'race' science (Günther 1927), was a portion of a photographic grid. In its entirety, the photographic grid represented the forty-nine computer-generated recombinant images, or 'morphies' as they are called based on the name of the software package *Morph 2.0* used, and depicted probable facial features of the seven women and seven men's potential offspring. Those of you who have been tracking the surgical 'morphing' of Michael Jackson will be interested to know that the application of an earlier version of this program was responsible for the special effects in his *Black or White* video (1991).

On the inside cover of this special issue, the managing editor James Gaines (1993:2) had written:

> The woman on the cover of this special issue of Time does not exist –
> except metaphysically. Her beguiling if mysterious visage is the product
> of a computer process called morphing – as in metamorphorsis, a striking
> alteration in structure or appearance. When the editors were looking for
> a way to dramatize the impact of interethnic marriage, which has
> increased dramatically in the US during the latest wave of immigration,
> they turned to morphing to create the kind of offspring that might result
> from seven men and seven women of various ethnic and racial back-
> grounds . . . The highlight of this exercise in cybergenesis was the creation
> of the woman on our cover, selected as a symbol of the future, multiethnic
> face of America. A combination of the racial and ethnic features of the
> women used to produce the chart, she is: 15% Anglo-Saxon, 17.5%
> Middle Eastern, 17.5% African, 7.5% Asian, 35% Southern European,
> and 7.5% Hispanic.

Given America's recent checkered past as it pertained in certain instances to legal sanctions prohibiting 'interracial' marriage and mating (Nakashima 1992), *Time's* intervention was perreceived by some as progressive and bold (Nash 1999, Sanchez 2002). However, *Time* magazine's cyber-'experiment' also exemplified the dangerous ways in which confused media, such as the active imaginations of Madison Avenue advertising executives, induce fantasies about a future replete with 'interracial' cyborgs (Haraway 1991).

We have chosen to reproduce this image as the cover for *'Mixed Race' Studies: A Reader* as a graphic way to illustrate (dis)continuities in historical and con-temporary thinking about 'mixed race' which is still both sexualized and gendered:

> The cover photo was a 'composite' picture of America's racial future – a
> lovely young woman, only ever-so-slightly oriental, only ever-so-slightly
> brown. It is revealing, but not surprising, that *Time's* editors chose to
> computer simulate a woman's face, not a man's face, and that the 'racial
> mixing' that produced the *Time* composite American was essentially a
> pretty, young white woman.
>
> (Nagel 2003: 23)

What was striking to me then and now is the presumption that the 'races' being 'mixed' are themselves discrete and pure (Phoenix and Owen 2000, Texeira 2003). Moreover, there is a collapsing of the constructs of 'race', nationality, ethnicity, and culture (Burroughs and Spickard 2000). The image of immigrant as interloper is also propagated. One need only stroll down the streets of Honolulu, Hawaii, Liverpool, England, Cape Town, South Africa or Rio de Janeiro, Brazil, for examples, to be reminded of the obvious: these heralded acts of so-called transracial transgression actually transpired long before they were re-invented by the American (and British) media (Gerzina 1995, Hudson 1996). And this very old story continues . . .

Global *Masala*:[1] a broader thematic and comparative introduction

> Stereotyping according to races runs deep, however, even in science, having once been thought to represent deep biological divisions between the peoples of the world. For decades, *Homo sapiens'* global divergences were assumed to be the vestiges of million-year old cleavages in our family tree. Race has a profound biological meaning, it was reckoned. Recent acceptance of the Out of Africa theory has changed that perspective – for it has been shown we are indeed all Africans under the skin, and that our differentiation into Eskimos, Bushmen, Australians, Scandinavians, and other populations has merely been a coda to the long song of human evolution.
>
> (Stringer and McKie 1996: 181)

By using palaeontological (bones), archaeological (stones) and genetic (DNA) evidence, proponents of the explosive 'Out of Africa' thesis challenged 'multi-regionalism' (i.e. that modern human diversity is a result of simultaneous and separate evolutionary processes in different parts of the world: Wolpoff and Caspari 1997) and proved that all modern humans are descendants of a small group of Africans, who 100,000 years ago migrated 'Out of Africa' from what is now present-day Ethiopia, Kenya and Tanzania (Stringer and Andrews 1988). As such, genetic variations, which are evident in contemporary populations, are attributable not to 'racial' differences but to natural selection in the forms of differential evolutionary adaptation to local environmental pressures (Darwin 1859, Dawkins 1976, Knight 1991, Knight *et al.* 1995). As I paraphrase: '*We are all African, only some of us have been "away" longer than others.*' That said, for as long as modern humans have populated the earth and migrated within and across continents, intergroup mating and marriages have been inevitable and commonplace (Gist and Dworkin 1972). As such, it is argued that there are no discrete or pure biological 'races' (Jones 1996, Rose *et al.* 1984). In fact, there is more variation within a group that is *socially designated* as a 'race' than between groups *socially designated* as different 'races'. That is, the genetic differences between the so-called 'races' is minute:

> On average, there is a 0.2% percent difference between any two ran-domly chosen people on the Earth. Of that diversity, 85% will be found within any local group of people. More than half (9%) of the remaining 15% will be represented by difference between ethnic and linguistic groups within a given race. Only 6% represents differences between races. That's 6% of 0.2%. In other words, race accounts for a miniscule 0.012% difference in our genetic material.
>
> (Hoffman 1994:4)

Yet, despite this statistically insignificant genetic variance, it is *the popular folk concept of 'race'*[2] which persists in the collective imagination of societies organized on the basis of 'race'/colour hierarchies. Paraphrasing Senegalese anthropologist Cheik Anta Diop (1991): in these societies, differential 'readings' and 'rankings' of phenotypes (physical expressions of genetic inheritances) are the major determinants of the qualitative nature of intergroup relations. In his provocative essay 'Mixing Bodies and Cultures: The Meaning of America's Fascination with Sex between "Orientals" and "Whites" ', Yu (1999: 459) corroborates:

> An awareness of the physical markers of biology is still part of American consciousness, and so there remains a masked connection between bodies and culture. It is only because of our fine-tuned awareness of bodily difference that our fascination with intercultural sex and marriage makes sense. As long as Americans connect cultural difference with physical difference, we shall equate the racial with the cultural, and we shall remain fascinated with the idea of sex across racial boundaries.

This 'fascination' explains the persistence of particular popular representations of 'interracial' sexualities (Small 2001), but this is not the primary focus of the Reader. Instead, the impetus behind the compilation of this collection is what I call the ultimate paradox of 'mixed race' studies (Coombes and Brah 2000). That is, the text explores why popular and academic interest in the idea of 'mixed race' persists – and in fact continues to grow – despite the fact that 'biological' explanations for 'racial' differences have long been discredited (Zack 2001).

Not since the nineteenth-century Victorian era, when pseudoscientific treatises on the presumed social pathology of the 'racial' hybrid abounded, has there been such an academic interest in 'mixed race' studies (Johnson 2003, Parker and Song 2001, Winters and DeBose 2003). That said, the intellectual content and social and political contexts of contemporary scholarship are very different. Rather than being objects of the scientific gaze (as speaking subjects) scholars, many of whom identify as 'mixed race' or 'multiracial',[3] have deployed the idea that 'race' is a social construct that shifts across space and time (Camper 1994, Erasmus 2001, O'Hearn 1998). In so doing, they seek to validate 'mixed race' as a legitimate psychosocial and political category (Root 1996, Zack 1995).

Over the past decade, and particularly in North America, theoretical, empirical and biographical work on 'mixed race' that addresses the fluidity, dynamism, complexity and practices of identity politics has flourished (Spickard 2001). In the twenty-first century, a body of writings is emerging which talks back to the resurgent literature that gave birth to the 'multiracial' nomenclature and its contested politics. By critically engaging with either the problematics or the possibilities of 'multiracial' activism, expression and ideology, this latest phase signals the emergence of a critical discourse on 'mixed race' and 'multiraciality' from which there are no signs of retreat (Alibhai-Brown 2001, Ali 2003, Olumide 2002).

This empirical and experiential celebration and contestation of 'mixed race' and 'multiraciality' is by no means unified or essentialist. At the beginning of this Reader, in 'Notes on Terminology', I address the important issue of 'hierarchies within' as an impediment to 'mixed race' unity. The most interesting debates have emerged from different conceptualizations of the canon. For example, conceptual and political disagreements over the categories 'mixed race', biracial' and 'multiracial' stem from the dominance of binary *biracialized*[4] 'black'/'white' paradigms in US and British 'racial' discourses (Park and Park 1999). The emphasis on socially designated 'black/white' mixes is said to exclude those who are socially designated and identify as dual minority 'mixes' that do not include 'black'/'white' and neglect certain individuals who claim triple or more 'mixes' (Waters 2000). As Mahtani and Moreno (2001: 67) assert:

> In the recent explosion of writings about multiraciality, we have seen a plethora of discussions about white/black crossings and white/Asian crossings (and we want to remind you that we are using these terms very suspiciously). But we worry that we have not yet seen a great deal of discussion about people who are of dual minority mixes, or who are not part white.

This binarism also overlooks the important fact that conceptions of 'race', 'mixed race' and social status are historically, geographically and culturally specific, and hence do not travel easily (D'Cruz 1999, Erasmus 2000, Torres and Whitten 1998). The American 'one drop rule', which subsumes anyone with at least one known African ancestor under the heading 'black' whether or not they also have European and/or Native American ancestry, differs remarkably from the more fluid notion of 'race', colour and social hierarchy in Brazil, wherein ascribed gradations between 'black' and 'white' are varied and many (Daniel 2000, Twine 1998, Winant 1999). In a British context, 'black' as a collective 'multiracial' identification does not perform the same intellectual, political or cultural labour as it did in previous decades (Alexander 1996, Gilroy 1987, Mirza 1997, Modood 1988). The fact that the Irish 'have become white' in the late twentieth and early twenty-first centuries (Ignatiev 1995), along with recent racialized class and ethnic conflicts in the north of England as well as the current European/American rhetorical 'clash of civilizations' (Huntington 1996), are all powerful indicators of the ways in which 'blackness'/'non-whiteness' and 'whiteness' are shifting (Jacobson 1998, Ware and Back 2002), and are thus unstable signifiers of exclusion and inclusion (Bonnett 2002, Hall 2000, Hesse 2000).

A broader historical and geographical vantage point also highlights the crosscutting ways in which the global processes and erotic projects of slavery, imperialism and diaspora(s) have created similar shifts in the local making, management and regulation of status and power as articulated through the everyday discourses and practices of 'race', 'mixed race' and social hierarchies (Fernández 1992, Hodes 1999, Huhndorf 1997, Nagel 2003). Building on Frederickson's (2001: 2) three pillars (European expansion and colonization of the non-Western world, slavery, and a colour code determining status), which he constructs to explain the similar historical processes underpinning manifestations of racism in Brazil, South Africa and the USA, I have formulated *Four global pillars of 'racial' mixing.*[5] These pillars provide a framework, which will enable students to compare the different social outcomes in specific geographical contexts of similar historical processes (Christian 2000, Davis 1991, Stonequist 1937, Wolfe 1999). Put simply, in the past and in different parts of the world, were 'mixed race' communities 'socially engineered'? How were these 'ethnographic events' (Wolfe 1999) examples of global economic *and* erotic projects? Were the grand ideologies of scientific racism mere rationalizations for European greed in the form of scrambles for indigenous riches (i.e. slaves as property, land, cotton, gold, diamonds, sugar)? Did European (i.e. British, Portuguese, Spanish, Dutch, French or German) colonizers differ in their attitudes towards 'interracial' mixing (Fernández 1992, Twine 1998, Winant 1999)? In what ways does the past inform contemporary 'mixed race' and 'multiracial' debates?

In other words, although similar global economic and political processes of domination and resistance have contributed to similar social inequities in different societies across time and space, there were and still are social, cultural and political variations in the rules determining the social status of the offspring of 'interracial' unions (Rogers 1944/1972, 1952/1980). In his book *Who is Black?*, James Davis (1991) refers to different rules or statuses, which determine the social position not only of mulattos but also of other 'mixed race' offspring. In the first status position, the individual occupies a lower status than either of her or his parents, such as Anglo-Indians in India. In the second status position, the individual achieves a higher status than either parent, such as the *mestizos* of Mexico. In the third status position, the individual is a member of an intermediate group, which acts as a buffer between the 'white' minority and the 'black' majority, as was the case with 'coloureds' in South Africa. The fourth status position is not fixed, but rather is said to be negotiated on the basis of social class and colour, such as in Brazil. The fifth status position is also variable, but operates independently of socially designated 'racial' signifiers as in Hawaii. The sixth status position also known as 'the one drop rule' dictates that the individual occupies the same position as the lower status parent, such as in the USA. The seventh status group entitles the individual to the position of an assimilated minority, i.e. individuals in the USA with 'partial' Native American, Filipino, Japanese or other 'racially distinctive minority ancestry other than Black'. The specific requirements for membership in the seventh status group suggest that according to social engineers, in the popular imagination, 'black' African ancestry still represents the ultimate in genealogical degeneration (Christian 2000, Gordon 1995).

However, in the past ten years, many of these designations have shifted. A Black Power Movement in Brazil has inspired more mulattos to identify as 'black' (dos Santos 1999, da Silva 1999, Hanchard 1999). In the USA, a 'Mixed Race' Movement has emerged, wherein 'mixed race' children, many born after 1967 when legalization which prohibited 'interracial' marriages was eradicated, are asserting a distinct 'multiracial' identity separate from 'one drop rule' 'black' (J.M. Spencer 1997, R. Spencer 1999). In post-apartheid South Africa, there is tension between 'coloureds' who wish to retain their 'buffer' identity and those who are reclaiming African or 'black' identifications (Erasmus 2001). These dynamic geographical

FOUR GLOBAL PILLARS OF 'RACIAL' MIXING

POLITICAL ECONOMIC/POWER – PRODUCING

1 European expansion, settler-colonization, and imperialisms

Began in 1500, led, in certain instances, to the development of settler colonies which displaced, marginalized or subordinated indigenous peoples, i.e. North America (Nash 1999), Latin America (Wade 1997), South Africa (Hendricks 2001) and Australia (Wolfe 1999).

2 Slavery

The importation of 'non-European' slaves (and, in certain instances, indentured labourers) to meet local labour needs and to perform work that the settlers and planters were unwilling to do, i.e. the Caribbean, Brazil and the Southern United States in the case of the transatlantic slave trade, which contributed to the economic development of Europe and North America and the underdevelopment and depopulation of continental Africa (Rodney 1972, Shepherd and Beckles 2000, Williams 1944) or the transindian oceanic slave trade in the case of the Cape Colony in South Africa (Marx 1998, Shell 1994).

STRUCTURAL/STATUS – DEFINING

3 'Race'/colour hierarchies

'White' European supremacy and 'indigenous' or 'non-white' inferiority assumed and backed up by nineteenth-century 'race' science. Although, in specific ethnographic contexts, the cultural and historical constructions of 'race' and colour varied depending on the social and political needs of the ruling elite, who were frequently outnumbered, which in turn determined the differential status of 'mixed race' communities, i.e. Anglo-Indians in British colonial India (Hawes 1996) as a 'buffer group' in a tripartite system or the attempts to 'assimilate' both *Métis* in former French and Dutch South East Asian colonies (Stoler 2000) and 'half-caste' Aborigines in the settler-(post)colony of Australia (Wolfe 1999).

4 Gender hierarchies

'White' European/American men were positioned at the top, 'white' European/American women were positioned beneath them, followed by 'non-white' men. 'Non-white' women were positioned at the very bottom and as such were subjected to sexual exploitation which frequently culminated in the creation of 'mixed-race' offspring, whose own status was determined by prevailing 'race'/colour codes (Kempadoo 1999, Nagel 2003), i.e. relatively speaking, the more 'privileged' position of mulatta women during plantation slavery in the Americas (Bodenhorn 2002, Shepherd 2000).

and cultural groupings represent diverse outcomes to a common heritage of slavery, colonialism, miscegenation and racial discrimination. The dynamic concepts of 'interracial' mixing and 'mixed race' highlight the contested nature of 'race' as a 'scientific' idea which attaches hierarchical meanings to physical differences. Differentially informed by structural factors such as gender, generation, social class, locality, colour and sexuality, these social hierarchies create, explain, justify and maintain social inequalities and injustices, and perpetuate differential access to privilege, prestige and power (Twine 1997).

Sketching three 'ages' of 'mixed race' studies

As Robert Young argues eloquently in *Colonial Desire*, it is the nineteenth-century marriage of discourses on biology and culture which lends so much weight to the contemporary persistence of the idea of 'hybridity' as the sexual transgression of so-called pure 'racial' boundaries: ' "hybrid" forms (. . . miscegenated children) were seen to embody threatening forms of perversion and degeneration and became the basis for endless metaphoric extension in the racial discourse of social commentary' (Young 1995:5). I call this first phase the modern '*Age of Pathology*'. As I keep expounding, these false conceptions of 'racial' purity and pollution defy the established scientific fact that there are no discrete genetically homogeneous 'races', which means there are no pure 'races' (Fisher 1995, Hannaford 1996).

Nevertheless, one of the many personal, political and categorical terms which emerges from this false belief in 'racial' homogeneity is 'mixed race' (Rose *et al.* 1984, Spickard 1989, Tizard and Phoenix 1993). As previously mentioned, the 1990s witnessed a publishing explosion in the form of pioneering compilations on 'mixed race' populations in the USA, i.e. *Racially Mixed People in America*, edited by Root (1992), *The Multiracial Experience*, also edited by Root (1996), and *American Mixed Race*, edited by Zack (1995). I refer to this second phase as the (post)modern '*Age of Celebration*' (Parker and Song 2001) or what Teresa Brennan (1993), reinvoking Lacan, would refer to as the 'Era of the Ego'. Here authors, many of whom themselves identify as 'mixed race', recognize the persistence of objectifying and damaging perspectives on 'mixed race' in the present (Azoulay 1997). At the same time, they argue in favour of 'actor-centred' conceptual approaches which presume that processes of identity formation are fluid, shifting, contingent, situational and complex (Goldberg 1995). In my 'Notes on terminology', I also suggest that it was at this particular historical moment that an 'Iamism' discourse was born. For example: 'I am not Asian or "white", I am just me.'

More recently, other anthologies have been published in the USA including *Mixed Race America and the Law* edited by Johnson (2003) and *New Faces in a Changing America: Multiracial Identity in the Twenty-first Century* edited by Winters and DeBose (2003). *Rethinking 'Mixed Race'*, edited by Parker and Song (2001), is more 'transatlantic' in focus and incorporates contributions by British scholars. In the late twentieth/early twenty-first century a third phase has evolved. I refer to this as the post-(post)modern '*Age of Critique*', wherein 'multiraciality' is replacing 'mixed race' as the dominant paradigm (Nakashima 1996), and scholars continue to grapple with unresolved tensions between identification and categorization and structure and agency, i.e. the tangle of census terminology or the political limitations of a 'Multiracial' Movement (Aspinall 1997, Colker 1996, Cose 1997, Morning 2003, Nobles 2002).

The evolutionary focus of '*Mixed Race' Studies: A Reader*, which is organized on the basis of these three 'ages' of 'mixed race' studies (the age of pathology, the age of celebration and the age of critique), each of which has different agendas and theoretical underpinnings, makes it an ideal companion text for previous foundational works and more recent synthetic anthologies. This outline of the three 'ages' of 'mixed race' studies is to provide a broader theoretical context for the selected extracts, which comprise the remainder of the Reader. In so doing, I hope to facilitate readers' understanding of and engagement with processes of knowledge production and contestation as they pertain to 'mixed race' studies (Gilroy 2000). Since the historical starting point of this collection differs from its predecessors, here below I have created specific textual space for the 'retracing' of the first 'age' (Stocking 1982, 1987).

The age of pathology: miscegenation and moral degeneracy

> Mixed race people of all backgrounds and histories have tended to have similar characteristics attributed to them. The most common designation imposed on mixed race people of all ancestries is the inference that they are fragmented beings. Words such as 'mulatto' and 'octoroon' have referred to those having origins in Africa, while for Native Americans, 'mixblood' or 'halfbreed' is more commonly used . . . among US Latinos, 'mestizo' refers to Indian/White mixes. For those with mixed origins among Asians, the Hawaiian derived 'Hapa' is used. . . . Regardless of the reference, however, all of these terms perpetuate the notions of blood divisions that can be quantified in fractional terms, and in a race-conscious society, serve to reinforce the ideology that the mixed race individual is somehow less than a whole person.
>
> (Mengel 2001: 101)

Of one species, human populations are capable of interbreeding across generations and reproducing offspring who can in turn interbreed. However, in the eighteenth and nineteenth centuries, now discredited evolutionary theories emerged which maintained that distinct 'races' existed that could be ranked differentially on the bases of heredity, physical characteristics and intelligence (Malik 1996, Wolpoff and Caspari 1997). The architects of this 'racial' hierarchy positioned 'white' Europeans at the top and other 'non-Europeans' on intermediate rungs of this evolutionary ladder:

> Such blatant pseudoscience was meant to establish a theoretical framework that ordered and explained human variety, as well as to distinguish superior races from inferior ones. In this racial hierarchy, Indians were in competition with African-Black Americans as the lowest 'race of mankind,' in what was referred to as 'the great chain of being' by Eurocentric social scientists.
>
> (Jaimes 1995: 134)

Any interbreeding across 'racial' borders was said to threaten the assumed purity and supremacy of the 'white race'. In the Introduction to her compelling edited collection, *Sex, Love, Race: Crossing Boundaries in North American History*, Hodes suggests that it is the dynamics of this 'racial' hierarchy that are responsible for the dominance of 'black'/'white' discourses on 'race' (and 'mixed race') in North America: 'This reflects the persistence of a vision of "race" in North America that refers largely (or only) to those of European and African ancestries, and in turn, the reflection of that vision within the academy' (1999: 2). When both making selections and writing this Introduction, an ongoing challenge I have faced is how to incorporate this dominant *biracialized* viewpoint while also including other interwoven historical formations of 'race' and 'mixed race' in a fashion that is not perceived as fragmented (Mahtani and Moreno 2001, Park and Park 1999). As such, the particular recounting of the 'age of pathology' in this Introduction is informed primarily by my own particular research area, which is 'black/white' 'mixed race' in the English-African diaspora and the American-African diaspora (Ifekwunigwe 1999, 2001, 2002). However, as excerpts in this Reader will demonstrate, 'racial' ideologies of the time were applied in similar and different ways across all 'mixed race' groups (Root 2003).

Amalgamation was the initial term used to describe sexual reproduction – within or outside the context of marriage – involving individuals who were presumed to belong to distinct 'races', especially those sociologically and biologically designated as 'black' or 'white'. With the publication of his pamphlet *Miscegenation: The Theory of the Blending of the Races Applied to the American White and Negro* in 1864, David Goodman Croly introduced the word 'miscegenation', which he thought sounded more scientific than amalgamation. He combined two Latin words *miscere* (to mix) and *genus* (race) to create miscegenation. Along with hybridization, miscegenation and amalgamation are terms used interchangeably. 'Black'-'white' miscegenation dates back to the sixteenth century and the beginning of the transatlantic slave trade, wherein West Africans were forcibly removed from their homelands and sold as chattel slaves to work on plantations in the Southern USA, the Caribbean and Brazil. In societies whose economies were originally dependent on the exploitation of 'non-white' slaves, miscegenation between slave women and their slave masters contributed to the viability of the labour force. The different laws and rules instituted to manage 'mixed race' offspring born during and after the abolition of slavery would form the bases of contemporary 'racial' politics and conflicts (Williamson 1995). Going back to the four global pillars again, in the Americas in general and the USA in particular, clearly there have been similar processes of 'miscegenation' at work in the formation of interwoven Native American (Huhndorf 1997, Jaimes 1995, Katz 1986, 1993, Krupat 1999, Wilson 1992), Asian American (Nakashima 1992, Williams-León and Nakashima 2001, Yu 1999) and Latino/Chicano (Alcoff 1995, Anzaldúa 1987, Bost 2003, Fernández 1992) 'mixed race' communities.

Historical origins of miscegenation

The biological distinction between varieties and species was the intellectual precursor to the major scientific debate of the nineteenth century over whether human 'races' were of one species, *monogenesis*, or separate species, *polygenesis*. The potential fertility of mulattos, the term used to describe the offspring of sexual unions between 'black' slaves and 'white' Europeans or Americans, was used to defend both *monogenesis* and *polygenesis*. Biologist Carolus Linnaeus suggested that successful reproduction of fertile mulatto offspring was proof positive in support of same species status. American physician and natural historian Samuel Morton (1850) introduced the concept of biological hybridity to the separate origins discussion. He accepted that mulattos were fertile, but provided evidence which he claimed proved that mulatta women had difficulty bearing children. He speculated that if mulattos reproduced exclusively with each other, over generations, their offspring's fertility would diminish to the extent that they would all die out. This he concluded proved that 'whites' and 'blacks' were not varieties of a single 'race' but an entirely separate species. One of Morton's opponents was John Bachman (1850), who maintained that it was virtually impossible for hybrids to be 'relatively sterile' as Morton claimed. Bachman insisted that not only were mulattos as fertile as so-called pure 'races', but that he could provide evidence of successful intermarriage and procreation among mulattos across five generations. He also opposed the idea put forward by Morton and his colleague Agassiz that there was a natural and moral repugnance between so-called races which functioned as a social barrier. Having awarded 'black' Africans same-species status, Bachman justified ownership of slaves on the contested grounds that they were an inferior variety of the species.

Josiah Nott and George Gliddon (1854), who were both students of Morton, asserted that individuals without at least one 'white' ancestor were uncivilized and lacked the alleged superior mental capacity of their 'white' European and American counterparts. The theory of unilateral hybridity put forward by French anthropologist Paul Broca (1864) endorsed sexual relations between 'white' men and 'black' women on the grounds that such a union would produce not only fertile offspring but children who would more closely approximate their 'white' father's supposed 'racial' superiority. Sexual unions between 'black' men and 'white' women were thought to produce sterile children. What may be described as 'racial' enhancement was practised by 'white' slave masters in the form of sexual exploitation of 'black' and mulatta slave women in the antebellum American South, pre-emancipation Brazil and South Africa as well as the Caribbean. In keeping with the contradictions of patriarchy, while the sexual exploits of the majority 'white' male in the Americas, the Caribbean and other imperial locales were neither policed nor disparaged, their female counterparts were not awarded the same 'liberties'. These contradictory social relationships between masters and slaves were formed based on the regulation and control of domestic arrangements. Gender- and 'race'-specific sexual restrictions were imposed, which meant that 'white' men had unlimited sexual access to 'white', 'black' and mulatta women:

> professors and medical doctors offered scientific evidence that 'race mixture' contaminated Europeans, biologically and culturally, and gave rise to a population of mixed origins that was physically inferior and psychologically unstable. . . . At the same time, the vigour with which

> White men opposed 'race mixture' officially, especially for men of
> colour, was exceeded only by the fervour with which they practised it
> privately.
>
> (Small 2001: 120)

As 'white' women were considered symbols of virtue and morality, sexual liaisons
between 'black' men and 'white' women were forbidden. During and after slavery
in the USA, 'black' men could receive violent punishment just for looking in the
direction of a 'white' woman:

> American discourses of ethnosexual danger most often are articulated as
> threats to the purity and safety of white women by sexually menacing
> nonwhite men. This is especially ironic since white men have posed con-
> stant and serious threats of sexual violence against women of all colors
> throught United States history.
>
> (Nagel 2003: 23)

Legal and social categories were constructed which determined hierarchies
and maintained 'racial' boundaries between 'whites' and 'non-whites', citizens and
subjects, illegitimate children and heirs. The links among 'race', gender, sexuality
and power were particularly strong in the plantations of Southern USA (Hernton
1988). The 'one drop rule' was instituted in order to keep the offspring of 'white'
male plantation owners born to enslaved 'black' women under their control for
sexual and economic exploitation. The 'one drop rule of social hypodescent' dictated
that one known African ancestor made a person 'black' (Williamson 1995). The
system ensured that 'mixed race' children of 'white' male slave owners were
automatically disinherited and became 'black' slave labourers.

Racial degeneracy, the rise of eugenics, and anti-miscegenation legislation

With his theory of evolution by natural selection, Charles Darwin, author of *The
Origin of Species: The Preservation of Favoured Races in the Struggle for Life*,
published in 1859, had been instrumental in silencing proponents of polygenesis.
Evolution by natural selection was based on change. Random variations within populations provided the basis for adaptation to changing environmental circumstances.
Social Darwinism, the application of Darwinian theory to society, assumed that
'races' were fixed and distinct. Social Darwinists also differed from Darwin in their
understanding of the concept of fitness. For Darwin, the fitness of a population was
measured by the number of offspring produced. Social Darwinists believed that there
was a natural hierarchy of 'races', which was maintained by the distribution of
'races' according to fitness.

These ideas gained prominence during the late nineteenth century and altered
'interracial' relations throughout the British Empire, in the USA and in Brazil
(Degler 1971, Harris 1980, Hyam 1990). In the early twentieth century, Darwin's

cousin Francis Galton coined the term 'eugenics'. The scientific mission of the Eugenics Movement was the eradication of inferior and unfit 'races' and the elevation of superior 'races', based on the belief that intelligence, criminality and other social traits were in and of themselves determined exclusively by heredity (Kelves 1995). The foundation of eugenics was the idea of 'racial' degeneracy, which was belief in the deterioration of an allegedly superior 'race' via miscegenation (Kohn 1996). 'Racial' degeneracy was thought to be prevented by four means: selective breeding of the fit 'races' with each other; social segregation of the fit and unfit 'races', and at times, legal sanctions against miscegenation; sterilization; and, in certain instances, physical extermination of those deemed unfit.

In the inter-war period, the campaign of selective breeding to ensure 'racial' hygiene and purity culminated in the Nazi Experiment and Hitler's Final Solution (Hitler 1925/1992). In addition to ordering the extermination of those considered unfit, such as Jews, Gypsies, homosexuals and the mentally disabled, Hitler demanded the forced sterilization of German women who gave birth to non-Aryan children including Afro-Germans, who were themselves involuntarily sterilized (Lusane 2003, Opitz *et al.* 1986). In studies of miscegenation in inter-war Britain, 'white' women who were married to 'black' men and/or had children with them were described as 'immoral and of below average intelligence' (Rich 1990). In Liverpool and Cardiff, two British cities with large 'mixed race' communities, associations were established for the 'Welfare of Half-Caste Children', who were perceived as a moral problem and as a threat to the presumed 'racial' purity of the nation.

Although an informal colour bar and 'racial' conflict persist in certain British cities, statutory laws were never enforced to segregate 'races' nor to prohibit 'inter-racial' marriages and sexual relationships. This was not the case in the Jim Crow Southern USA. The belief was that increased contact would lead to increased mixing which would in turn lead to the social and moral degeneracy of the allegedly pure 'white' races (Ferber 1998). In the Southern USA of the 1890s through to the 1960s, separate but unequal 'black' and 'white' social institutions existed. Jim Crow was a post-slavery caricature of a 'black' man as happy and humble, which then became the label for the form of government-sanctioned racism known as Jim Crow segregation. By 1915, 'the one drop rule' had become firmly entrenched in the collective American conscience. On a state-by-state basis, laws maintaining the 'white/black' power imbalance were implemented for virtually every social institution: housing, property ownership, inheritance, voting rights and privileges, education, health and marriage. Anti-miscegenation laws were put in place to make 'interracial' marriage and sexual relations criminal offences. On 12 June 1967, with the Loving Decision, the Supreme Court deemed anti-miscegenation laws unconstitutional (Brown and Douglas 2003). Federal law superseded state laws. It took individual states longer to remove these statutes from their books. In 1883, Alabama introduced anti-miscegenation law, but did not overturn this until March 1999, which indicates the ways in which earlier views on miscegenation still manifest themselves in contemporary attitudes towards 'race', sexuality and gender (Talty 2003). In fact, 'black' Americans were given civil and voting rights before they were given the right to marry across the colour line.

Moral degeneracy theorists provided fuel for opponents of 'racial' mixing. Social scientists also formulated theories to explain the alleged 'social maladjustment' of children who were already born as a result of these 'forbidden' unions. In the USA, the most popular approach adopted by sociologists of 'race' relations and propagated in the inter-war period was 'problem'-oriented. Building on Weberian theory, Simmel's idea of the 'stranger' and Park's earlier and broader work on 'the marginal man', Stonequist (1937: 50) developed his *Marginal Man* thesis:

> The status and role of a particular mixed blood group can be taken as an index of the larger race problem and in turn the development of the mixed blood class reacts back upon the general situation modifying it to a significant and sometimes determining extent.

In *The Silent War: Imperialism and the Changing Perception of Race*, which compares the emergence of a sociology of 'race' in Britain and the USA, Furedi (1998) argues that the 'marginal man' thesis was merely another invidious strategy deployed to uphold the party line against miscegenation and the social dissolution of 'racial' boundaries. Interestingly enough, in the second and third ages of 'mixed race' studies, the 'in-between' or 'marginal' status of 'mixed race' subjects is a theme that is at once reinforced, subverted and challenged.

Contemporary genetics and the archaeology of 'mixed race'

> The principles of breeding are no longer talked about in the genetics of the 1990s. Neither is there much concern with the transmission of heritable traits. . . . The primary concern of genetics since roughly 1975 . . . has been the control of the transmission of lethal traits and disease.
>
> (Gudding 1996: 531)

This Introduction ends with an exploration of ethics and the 'racial' politics of genetic technology in order to further pave the way for the second half of Part One, in particular the section on the interface between 'old' and 'new' genetic conceptions of 'mixed race' and human origins (Young 2000). I provide some examples below which contradict Gudding's (1996) claim that genetics has retreated from an obsession with 'breeding' (Rabinow 1999). In this brave new twenty-first century, one can enlist the aid of an 'anthrogenealogist', who for a price uses the 'science of genealogy by genetics' to trace an individual's ancestry.[6] The 'evidence' generated by this new technology, can be strategically used and abused, for example, in American Indian land rights and entitlement claims (Brodwin 2002). TallBear (2003: 88) suggests that even though this suspect technology is new, the 'racial' ideology itself is old:

> If the use of DNA analysis to determine cultural affiliation is troubling because of its racial implications, the use by tribes of blood quantum to determine eligibility for citizenship cannot be ignored. It seems clear that

DNA analysis for such a purpose is not a new political concept, but simply reinforces a historical practice of both the US government and federally recognized tribes.

Furthermore, genetic 'markers' are an imprecise 'test' of Native American identity for at least two reasons.[7] First, Native American tribal membership is determined by politics and culture not biology. Second, analysis of genetic evidence is inconclusive, primarily because the 'Native American markers' identified are not exclusive to these populations.

Anthrogenealogy is not to be confused with 'anthropological genetics', which discovers/understands the past by analysing patterns/variations in human DNA. In recent times, the most notorious example of the application of anthropological genetics is the Human Genome Diversity Project. The Human Genome Diversity Project (HGDP) was developed in 1991 at Stanford University by Luca Cavalli-Sforza and colleagues (Cavalli-Sforza and Cavalli-Sforza 1995, Cook-Deegan 1994) in response to the fact that the Human Genome Project (HGP) (started in 1990 and completed in 2000) did not strive to map 'difference' but rather to produce an 'essentialist' single generic genetic map of humanity (Cooper 1994, Dennis and Gallagher 2001). The HGDP wanted to reconstruct human history and its evolution by comparing genetic variations across 'populations' (Sarkar 1998).

Critics of the HGDP included indigenous groups who accused it of 'biopiracy' and 'cultural genocide' i.e. the HGDP's findings were at odds with their own creation myths:

> The reconstruction of human prehistory and history is, I believe, a worthwhile endeavor, but it remains a contentious issue as to how best to go about it, and what exactly would be the contribution of molecular genetics. It is misguided to suggest that, given the technology we have at present, it is possible to reconstruct *the* migratory history of a specific group of people – although (Human Genome Diversity) project organisers indicate that they can do just this and claim that certain indigenous peoples in North America wish to cooperate in order that they may come to know their own past. The contested politics of boundary making looms large here, but meanwhile, local creation myths continue to serve their purpose.
>
> (Lock 1997: 285, emphasis in original)

That is, indigenous peoples believe that they have always inhabited the Americas or Australia rather than the scientific claim that Native Americans are the descendants of ancestors who migrated across the Bering Straits from Siberia 12,000 years ago, or Aborigines reached Australia 60,000 years ago (Cavalli-Sforza and Cavalli-Sforza 1995, Diamond 1998, Olson 2002). It is also believed by many indigenous groups that biological matter is sacred and not to be bought, sold or manipulated. For example, the Declaration of Indigenous Peoples of the Western Hemisphere Regarding the Human Genome Diversity Project states:

We are the original peoples of the Western Hemisphere of the continents of North, Central and South America. Our principles are based upon our profound belief in the sacredness of all Creation, both animate and inanimate. We live in a reciprocal relationship with all life in this divine and natural order . . .
. . . To negate the complexity of any life form by isolating and reducing it to its minute parts, western science and technology diminishes its identity as a precious and unique life form, and alters its relationship to the natural order.[8]

Another oppositional stance is that reinforcing 'differences' and reverting to categories strengthens 'racial' hierarchies. Moreover, the categories and terms used to distinguish 'populations' are themselves contested. For example, I have cited below the findings of a recent study by geneticists, who measured 'The Admixture of Hispanics: Distribution of Ancestral Population Contributions in the Continental United States':

Hispanics are a broad and growing community that represents 12% of the United States population. The ethnic category, Hispanics, as defined by the Office of Management and Budget (OMB) in 1978, refers to persons or descendants of people from Latin American countries or other Spanish cultures. Under this definition, Hispanics are culturally and genetically a heterogeneous group. In Latin America, each country has its own demographic and genetic structure, with its own distinct migration history between regions. All Hispanics are basically trihybrid, their ancestral populations being European, African and Native American. However, the proportion of genes Hispanics received from ancestral populations varies greatly.

(Bertoni *et al.* 2003: 1)

This is followed by Cruz-Jansen's (2001: 171–172) critique of the 'white' supremacist undertones of the term 'Hispanic':

'Hispanic' has come under intense criticism as a label that exalts and promotes whiteness by focusing on the Spanish-speaking white European Spaniard as the ideal 'Hispanic'. Hispanic connotes a homogenous race and dilutes the black, Indian and mestizo combinations that comprise this group of people. The term 'Latino' also represents European Spaniards but is more inclusive of those Latin Americans who speak Spanish and those who do not.

Juxtaposed, these two citations highlight the problematics of what Brodwin (2002) refers to as 'genetic essentialism'.
One of the most fascinating recent examples of genetic essentialism is the 'The Motherland: Genetic Journey Project'[9] commissioned by the British Broadcasting

Company (BBC), which used genetic technology to 'scientifically' confirm what scholars of slavery and descendants of slaves have always known about the racialized and gendered sexual politics of plantation slavery in the Caribbean. That is, 'white' European slave-masters had unlimited and in many instances non-consensual sexual relations with black and 'mixed race' women, whom they owned as slaves. The project had two objectives:

1   To see what genetics could reveal about the ancestry of British African Caribbeans.
2   To see whether genetics could 'reconnect' individuals to contemporary African population groups.

This three-year study involved geneticists in the UK and the US and 228 volunteers, all of whom had four African Caribbean parents. Using swab samples, they analysed DNA to trace:

1   The 'origins' of mitochondrial DNA (m-DNA) inherited exclusively from the mother.
2   The 'origins' of the Y chromosome passed on from father to son.
3   Individual 'levels' of African and European ancestry.

Project scientists discovered that only 2 per cent of British African Caribbeans have m-DNA which traces to Europe rather than Africa. However, over 25 per cent of British African Caribbean men have a Y chromosome which traces back to Europe rather than Africa. Their 'findings' were proof positive of the particular gendered, economic and erotic politics of the transatlantic slavery enterprise. The culmination of the project was the broadcast of a television documentary of the same name in February 2002. The film followed three project participants across three continents as they attempted to 'reconnect' with their lost African roots. This at once moving and at times amusing documentary also highlighted the unresolved and quite glaring tensions between *genetic' and 'cultural' inheritances* – the old 'nature/nurture' chestnut. To conclude our journey back to the past and towards the future, I hope that Part One of this Reader will shed new light on the ways in which the idea of 'mixed race' is constantly being (re)invented and contested in the present.

Reader's map

The historical conflict between whites and blacks conditioned Americans to view race in polarizing, mutually exclusive terms. But the growing presence of a racially mixed population has begun to soften the lines between 'us' and 'them.' Yet the stale debate over Proposition 54 – between those who think race is irrelevant and those who think it is paramount – only revives the divisive, binary thinking that has made racial diversity such a painful experience in the United States. California history tells us that both sides are missing the point.

(Rodriguez 2003)

'Mixed race' studies is one of the fastest growing, as well as one of the most import-ant and controversial areas in the field of 'race' and ethnic relations. A Google search using the keyword 'mixed race' generated no fewer than 973,000 entries, including countless undergraduate course syllabi. *'Mixed Race' Studies: A Reader* seeks to add a new dimension to the growing body of literature on the topic and to provide a more informative history on the origins and directions of 'mixed race' research as an intellectual movement. This multidisciplinary text brings together comprehensive but by no means either definitive or inclusive scholarship which charts the evolution of debates on 'race' and 'mixed race' from the nineteenth to the twenty-first century. The Reader covers three substantive areas:

1   It traces the origins of the problematic idea of miscegenation ('race' mixture) as social pathology as articulated and debated in biology, anthropology, sociology and history, and addresses the impact of advances in genetic technology (in particular the Human Genome Project (HP) and the Human Genome Diversity Project (HGDP) on this contested area.
2   It maps contemporary discourses, which celebrate 'mixed race' as a legitimate social category as put forward by foundational and interdisciplinary scholars of a 'new' 'mixed race' canon.
3   It defines the debates which have emerged from this reconstituted discipline as they pertain to the politics, policies, practices and paradigms of 'multiraciality' and their critiques (in particular the tangle of census terminology and the politics of identification versus categorization).

In general, *'Mixed Race' Studies: A Reader* is foundational, contextual as well as polemical. As such, the selected extracts highlight but do not resolve tensions, continuities and problematics associated with both the old 'biological' discourses of 'hybrid degeneracy' and the 'psychosociological' discourses of 'mixed race' individuals as 'maladjusted social types' as well as newer social, cultural and political applications of 'mixed race' and later 'multiraciality' as shifting, contingent, complex and multi-layered identity markers. All three interwoven and historically located perspectives rupture allegedly stable racialized faultlines and at the same time (paradoxically in the case of the latter two approaches) reinscribe 'race' – a term predicated on scientifically dubious criteria (Omi and Winant 1986).

I have selected the final list of readings with two objectives in mind. First, I wish to broaden the disciplinary and interdisciplinary scope for the burgeoning number of students and scholars of 'mixed race' and 'multiracial' experiences. Second, I hope that presenting these works in an 'evolutionary' context will extend their familiarity and application, and thereby enhance future educational and academic debates on 'mixed race'. In so doing, my intention has been to produce as comprehensive a collection of readings as is possible without compromising the integrity of individual contributions. As the interdisciplinary literature on this topic is vast and rapidly expanding, needless to say, the process of selection was extremely difficult. In the interest of space and to avoid the unnecessary repetition of themes/arguments, regretfully, some excellent works have been omitted. In the list of suggested readings which accompany each of the three sections of the Reader as well as in the Bibliography at the end of this Introduction, I have attempted to pay homage to some but obviously not all of these omitted readings.

For those of you who are new to 'mixed race' studies, I hope this text will function as a catalyst for further exploration. For 'mixed race' studies veterans, it has been my intention to provide another window into a provocative and dynamic field. It is my expectation that *'Mixed Race' Studies: A Reader* will encourage all readers to rethink taken-for-granted assumptions about the origins of ideas on 'mixed race' and to assess the ways in which earlier science fictional beliefs about 'mixed race' are reconstructed, represented and contested in the present. This is a comparative text in the sense that it will challenge readers to investigate the cross-cutting ways in which the previously mentioned *four global pillars of 'racial' mixing* created similar shifts in the local making, management and regulation of status and power as articulated through the everyday discourses and practices of 'race', 'mixed race' and social hierarchies in both African diasporas in North America and the United Kingdom as well as among other interconnected communities of colour in the USA: Asian American, Native American and Latino/Chicano. Purposely interdisciplinary, this collection of readings will demonstrate the ways in which classic and contemporary scholarship on 'mixed race' spans the social sciences, the humanities as well as the biological sciences. This is also a crucial text in the sense that it should encourage readers to think critically about the origins of the concept of 'mixed race', its re-invention in more recent times and ongoing debates concerning its conceptual limitations and political potential.

Most of the selected readings are abbreviated to extract form as appropriate to the overall theme and purpose of the collection. Where the entire article or text has been included, I have reproduced the original format. With certain extracts, during the editorial process I have deleted bibliographical references or endnotes. This is in response to contractual restrictions imposed by different publishers as well as in order to produce a format which is as consistent as possible without compromising the integrity of the individual pieces. With the exception of the nineteenth-century extracts (Darwin exempted), all of these sources are still in print. It is my hope and expectation that the compiled extracts in *'Mixed Race' Studies: A Reader* will function as a mere stepping stone on the road to further exploration of these and other suggested readings in their holistic and original contexts. To facilitate this process, at the end of each Part, or subsection within a Part, I have included a list of suggestions for further reading. After each individual extract, I have also included a set of specific study 'probes' (questions), which will encourage cross-extract comparison and further analysis. Each of the three Parts is preceded by introductory remarks, which pull together specific and contrasting themes.

Notes

1   'Although the combination of ingredients sometimes varies in different parts of India, *Garam Masala* (hot spice mixture) is usually a mixture of cloves, cinnamon and cardamon seeds ground together in equal amounts' (Sacharoff, Shanta Nimbark (1972) *Flavors of India: Recipes from the Vegetarian Hindu Cuisine*, San Francisco: 101 Productions, p.13). In the interest of coherence and word length, I have restricted my selection of extracts for this Reader to the geographical regions of North America and the United Kingdom. I have entitled this section Global *Masala* for two reasons. First, I wish to inform students that scholarship on 'mixed race' is global, and both includes and transcends conventional 'black'/'white' and British/North American boundaries, i.e. Australia, South Africa, India, Southeast Asia, the Caribbean, Latin America including Mexico and Brazil. Second, borrowing the notion that *Garam Masala's* composition varies across regions, I want to remind readers that interdisciplinary academic debates on the historical and social processes of 'racial' mixing are themselves also local.

2   A potent dynamic social and cultural imaginary, the naturalization of which attaches symbolic meanings to real or manufactured physical differences. These create, explain, justify and maintain social inequalities and injustices; and perpetuate differential access to privilege, prestige and power.

3   According to Maria Root, a leading scholar and one of the major proponents of the 'multiracial' movement, someone who is 'multiracial' is 'of two or more racial heritages. It is the most inclusive term to refer to people across all racial mixes. Thus it also includes biracial people' (Root, Maria (1996) 'The Multiracial Experience: Racial Border as a Significant Frontier in Racial Relations' in M. Root (ed.) *The Multiracial Experience*, Thousand Oaks, CA: Sage, p.xi).

4   A sub-structure of racialization in that it speaks to the specific structural, symbolic and oppositional relationship forged between people socially designated as 'black' and those deemed 'white'. That is, one is either 'black' *not/and* 'white' and never the twain shall meet.

5   The four global pillars of 'racial' mixing were developed over a number of years during my teaching of AN234: Rules of *Métissage* ('Racial' Mixing): Anthropological Perspectives on 'Race', Status and Colour'. Taught in the Anthropology Subject Area, School of Social Sciences, at the University of East London. To date, this is the only course on comparative 'mixed race' studies in the United Kingdom.

6   See http://www.familytreedna.com/tcam.html.

7   See Indigenous Peoples Council on Biocolonialism: http://www.ipcb.org.

8   The Declaration of Indigenous Peoples of the Western Hemisphere: http://nativenet.uthscsa.edu/archive/nc/9502/0137.html.

9   See http://takeawaymedia.com/motherlandscience.htm.

BIBLIOGRAPHY

Alcoff, Linda (1995) 'Mestizo Identity' in N.Zack (ed.) *American Mixed Race*, London: Rowman and Littlefield, pp.257–278.

Alexander, Claire (1996) *The Art of Being Black*, Oxford: Oxford University Press.

Ali, Suki (2003) *Mixed-Race, Post-Race: Gender, New Ethnicities and Cultural Practices*, Oxford: Berg.

Alibhai-Brown, Yasmin (2001) *Mixed Feelings: The Complex Lives of Mixed Race Britons*, London: Women's Press.

Anzaldúa, Gloria (1987) *Borderlands/La Frontera: The New Mestiza*, San Francisco, CA: aunt lute books.

Aspinall, Peter (1997) 'The Conceptual Basis of Ethnic Group Terminology and Classifications', *Social Science and Medicine*, 45 (5): 689–698.

Azoulay, Katya Gibel (1997) *Black, Jewish and Interracial*, London: Duke University Press.

Bachman, John (1850) *The Doctrine of the Unity of the Human Race Examined on the Principle of Science*, Charleston, SC: Canning.

Bertoni, Bernardo *et al.* (2003) 'Admixture in Hispanics: Distribution of Ancestral Population Contributions in the Continental United States', *Human Biology*, 75 (11): 1–11.

Bodenhorn, Howard (2002) 'The Mulatto Advantage: The Biological Consequences of Complexion in Rural Antebellum Virginia', *Journal of Interdisciplinary History*, 33 (1): 21–46.

Bonnett, Alastair (2002) 'The Metropolis and White Modernity', *Ethnicities*, 2 (3): 349–366.

Bost, Suzanne (2003) *Mulattas and Mestizas: Representing Mixed Identities in the Americas, 1850–2000*, London: University of Georgia Press.

Brennan, Teresa (1993) *History after Lacan*, London: Routledge.

Broca, Paul (1864) *Phenomena of Hybridity in the Genus Homo*, London: Anthropological Society.

Brodwin, Paul (2002) 'Genetics, identity and the Anthropology of Essentialism', *Anthropological Quarterly*, 75(2): 323–330.

Brown, Nancy and Douglas, Ramona (2003) 'Evolution of Multiracial Organizations: Where We Have Been and Where We Are Going' in L. Winters and H. DeBose (eds) *New Faces in a Changing America*, Thousand Oaks, CA: Sage, pp. 111–124.

Burroughs, W. Jeffrey and Spickard, Paul (eds) (2000) 'Ethnicity, Multiplicity, and Narrative: Problems and Possibilities' in P. Spickard and W.J. Burroughs (eds) *We Are a People: Narrative and Multiplicity in Constructing Ethnic Identity*, Philadelphia, PA: Temple University Press, pp.244–254.

Camper, Carol (ed.) (1994) *Miscegenation Blues: Voices of Mixed Race Women*, Toronto: Sister Vision Press.

Cavalli-Sforza, Luca and Cavalli-Sforza, Francesco (1995) *The Great Human Diasporas: The History of Diversity and Evolution*, Reading, MA.: Perseus Books.

Christian, Mark (2000) *Multiracial Identity: An International Perspective*, Basingstoke: Macmillan.

Colker, Ruth (1996) *Hybrid: Bisexuals,Multiracials, and other Misfits under American Law*, London: New York University Press.

Cook-Deegan, Robert (1994) *The Gene Wars*, New York: W. W. Norton.

Coombes, Annie and Brah, Avtar (2000) 'Introduction: The Conundrum of "Mixing" ' in A. Brah and A. Coombes (eds) *Hybridity and its Discontents: Politics, Science and Culture*, London: Routledge, pp.1–16.

Cooper, Grant (1994) *The Human Genome Project*, Mill Valley: University Science Books.

Cose, Ellis (1997) 'Census and the Complex Issue of Race', *Society*, 34 (6) : 9–13.

Cruz-Jansen, Marta (2001) 'Latinegras: Desired Women–Undesirable Mothers, Daughters, Sisters and Wives', *Frontiers*, 22 (3): 168–183.

D'Cruz, Glenn (1999) 'Representing Anglo-Indians: A Genealogical Study', unpublished Ph.D. Dissertation, Department of English with Cultural Studies, University of Melbourne, Australia.

dos Santos, Ivanir (1999) 'Blacks and Political Power' in M. Hanchard (ed.) *Racial Politics in Contemporary Brazil*, London; Duke University Press, pp.200–214.

da Silva, Benedita (1999) 'The Black Movement and Political Parties: A Challenging Alliance' in M. Hanchard (ed.) *Racial Politics in Contemporary Brazil*, London; Duke University Press, pp. 179–187.

Daniel, G. Reginald (2000) 'Multiracial Identity in Brazil and the United States' in P.Spickard and W.J.Burroughs (eds) *We Are a People: Narrative and Multiplicity in Constructing Ethnic Identity*, Philadelphia, PA: Temple University Press, pp.153–178.

Darwin, Charles (1859) *The Origin of Species*, London: John Murray.

Davis, James F. (1991) *Who is Black?*, University Park, Pennsylvania, PA: Pennsylvania State University Press.

Dawkins, Richard (1976) *The Selfish Gene*, Oxford: Oxford University Press.

Degler, Carl (1971) *Neither Black nor White: Slavery and Relations in Brazil and the United States*, New York: Macmillan.

Dennis, Carina and Gallagher, Richard (eds) (2001) *The Human Genome*, Basingstoke: Palgrave.

Diamond, Jared (1998) *Guns, Germs and Steel: A Short History of Everybody for the Last 13,000 Years*, London: Vintage.

Diop, Cheik Anta (1991) *Civilization or Barbarism: An Authentic Anthropology*, New York: Lawrence Hill.

Erasmus, Zimitri (2000) 'Some Kind of White, Some Kind of Black: Living Moments of Entanglement in South Africa and its Academy' in B.Hesse (ed.) *Un/settled Multiculturalisms: Diasporas, Entanglements, Disruptions*, London: Zed Books, pp.185–208.

Erasmus, Zimitri (ed.) (2001) *Coloured by History, Shaped by Place: New Perspectives on Coloured Identities in Cape Town*, Cape Town, South Africa: Kwela Books.

Ferber, Abby (1998) *White Man Falling: Race, Gender and White Supremacy*, Oxford: Rowman and Littlefield.

Fernández, Carlos (1992) 'La Raza and the Melting Pot: A Comparative Look at Multiethnicity', in M.P.P. Root (ed.) *Racially Mixed People in America*, Thousand Oaks, CA: Sage, pp.126–143.

Fisher, Jean (1995) 'Some Thoughts on "Contaminations"', *Third Text*, 38:3–7.

Frederickson, George (2001) 'Race and Racism in Historical Perspective: Comparing the United States, South Africa, and Brazil' in C. Hamilton *et al.* (eds) *Beyond Racism: Race and Inequality in Brazil, South Africa, and the United States*, Boulder, CO: Lynne Rienner, pp.1–26.

Füredi, Frank (1998) *The Silent War: Imperialism and the Changing Perception of Race*, London: Pluto Press.

Gaines, James (1993) 'From the Managing Editor', *Time*, Special Issue on 'The New Face of America: How Immigrants are Shaping the World's First Multicultural Society', 142 (21): 2.

Gerzina, Gretchen (1995) *Black England: Life Before Emancipation*, London: John Murray.

Gilroy, Paul (1987) *There Ain't No Black in the Union Jack*, London: Hutchinson.

Gilroy, Paul (2000) *Between Camps: Nations, Cultures and the Allure of Race*, London: Allen Lane.

Gist, Noel and Dworkin, Anthony (eds) (1972) *The Blending of the Races: Marginality and Identity in a World Perspective*, New York: Wiley.

Goldberg, David (1995) 'Made in the USA: Racial Mixing n Matching' in N. Zack (ed.) *American Mixed Race*, London: Rowman and Littlefield, pp.237–256.

Gordon, Lewis R. (1995) *Bad Faith and Antiblack Racism*, Atlantic Highlands, NJ: Humanities Press.

Gudding, Gabriel (1996) 'The Phenotype/Genotype Distinction and the Disappearance of the Body', *Journal of the History of Ideas*, 57(3); 525–545.

Günther, Hans (1927) *Racial Elements of European History*, translated by G.C. Wheeler, London: Kennikat Press.

Hall, Stuart (2000) 'Conclusion: The Multicultural Question' in B.Hesse (ed.) *Un/settled Multiculturalisms: Diasporas, Entanglements, Disruptions*, London: Zed Books, pp. 209–241.

Hanchard, Michael (ed.) (1999) *Racial Politics in Contemporary Brazil*, London: Duke University Press.

Hannaford, Ivan (1996) *Race: The History of an Idea in the West*, Baltimore: Johns Hopkins University Press

Haraway, Donna (1991) 'A Cyborg Manifesto: Science, Technology and Socialist Feminism in the Late Twentieth Century' in *Simians, Cyborgs and Women in the Reinvention of Nature*, New York: Routledge.

Harris, Marvin (1980) *Patterns of Race in the Americas*, Westport, CT: Greenwood Press.

Hawes, Christopher (1996) *Poor Relations: The Making of a Eurasian Community in British India, 1773–1833*, Richmond, Surrey: Curzon Books.

Hendricks, Cheryl (2001) ' "Ominous Liaisons": Tracing the Interface between "Race" and Sex at the Cape' in Z. Erasmus (ed.) *Coloured by History, Shaped by Place: New Perspectives on Coloured Identities in Cape Town*, Cape Town, South Africa: Kwela Books, pp.29–44.

Hernton, Calvin (1988) *Sex and Racism in America*, New York: Grove Press.

Hesse, Barnor (2000) 'Diasporicity: Black Britain's Post-colonial Formations' in B. Hesse (ed.) *Un/settled Multiculturalisms: Diasporas, Entanglements, Disruptions*, London: Zed Books, pp.128–165.

Hitler, Adolf (1925/1992) *Mein Kampf*, translated by Ralph Mannheim, London: Pimlico.

Hodes, Martha (1999) 'Introduction: Interconnecting and Diverging Narratives' in M. Hodes (ed.) *Sex, Love, Race: Crossing Boundaries in North American History*, New York: New York University Press, pp.1–9.

Hoffman, Paul (1994) 'The Science of Race', *Discover*, 15 (2): 4.

Hudson, Nicholas (1996) 'From "Nation" to "Race": The Origin of Racial Classification in Eighteenth-Century Thought', *Eighteenth-Century Studies*, 29 (3): 247–264.

Huhndorf, Shari (1997) 'From the Turn of the Century to the New Age: Playing Indian Past and Present' in W.Penn (ed.) *As We Are Now: MixBlood Essays on Race and Identity*, Berkeley: University of California Press, pp.181–198.

Huntington, Samuel (1996) *The Clash of Civilizations and the Remaking of the World Order*, New York: Simon and Schuster.

Hyam, Ronald (1990) *Empire and Sexuality: The British Experience*, Manchester: Manchester University Press, pp. 200–217.

Ifekwunigwe, Jayne O. (1999) *Scattered Belongings: Cultural Paradoxes of 'Race', Nation and Gender*, London: Routledge.

Ifekwunigwe, Jayne O. (2001) 'Re-Membering "Race": On Gender, "Mixed Race" and Family in the English-African Diaspora' in D. Parker and M. Song (eds) *Rethinking 'Mixed Race'*, London: Pluto Press, pp. 42–64.

Ifekwunigwe, Jayne O. (2002) '(An)Other English City: Multiethnicities, (Post)modern Moments, and Strategic Identifications', *Ethnicities*, 2 (3): 321–348.

Ignatiev, Noel (1995) *How the Irish Became White*, London: Routledge.

Jacobson, Matthew (1998) *Whiteness of a Different Color: European Immigrants and the Alchemy of Race*, Cambridge, MA: Harvard University Press.

Jaimes, M. Annette (1995) 'Some Kind of Indian: On Race, Eugenics and Mixed Blood' in N. Zack (ed.) *American Mixed Race*, London: Rowman and Littlefield, pp.133–153.

Johnson, Keith (ed.) (2003) *Mixed Race America and the Law*, New York: New York University Press.

Jones, Steve (1996) *In the Blood: God, Genes and Destiny*, London: HarperCollins.

Katz, William Loren (1986) *Black Indians: A Hidden Heritage*, New York: Atheneum.

Katz, William Loren (1993) *Proudly Red and Black: Stories of Africans and Native Americans*, New York: Atheneum.

Kelves, Daniel Jo (1995) *In the Name of Eugenics: Genetics and the Uses of Human Heredity*, London: Harvard University Press.

Kempadoo, Kamala (1999) 'Continuities and Change: Five Centuries of Prostitution in the Caribbean' in K. Kempadoo (ed.) *Sun, Sex and Gold: Tourism and Sex Work in the Caribbean*, Lanham, MD: Rowman and Littlefield, pp. 3–33.

Knight, Chris (1991) *Blood Relations: Menstruation and the Origins of Culture*, New Haven, CT: Yale University Press.

Knight, Chris, Power, Camilla and Watts, Ian (1995) 'The Human Symbolic Revolution: A Darwinian Account', *Cambridge Archaeological Journal*, 5: 75–114.

Kohn, Marek (1996) *The Race Gallery: The Return of Racial Science*, London: Vintage.

Krupat, Arnold (1999) 'From "Half-blood" to "Mixedblood": *Cogewea* and the "Discourse of Indian Blood" ', *Modern Fiction Studies*, 45 (1): 120–145.

Lock, Margaret (1997) 'Decentering the Natural Body: Making Difference Matter', *Configurations*, 5 (2): 267–292.

Lusane, Clarence (2003) *Hitler's Black Victims: The Historical Experiences of Afro-Germans, European Blacks, African and African Americans in the Nazi Era*, New York: Routledge.

Mahtani, Minelle and Moreno, April (2001) 'Same Difference: Towards a More Unified Discourse in "Mixed Race" Theory' in R. Parker and M. Song (eds) *Rethinking 'Mixed Race'*, pp. 65–75.

Malik, Kenan (1996) *The Meaning of Race*, London: Macmillan.

Marx, Anthony (1998) *Making Race and Nation: A Comparison of South Africa, the United States and Brazil*, Cambridge: Cambridge University Press.

Mengel, Laurie (2001) 'Triples – The Social Evolution of a Multiracial Panethnicity: An Asian American Perspective' in D. Parker and M. Song (eds) *Rethinking 'Mixed Race'*, London: Pluto Press, pp. 99–116.

Mirza, Heidi (ed.) (1997) *Black British Feminism*, London: Routledge.

Modood, Tariq (1988) 'Black Racial Equality and Asian Identity', *New Community*, 14 (3): 397–404.

Morning, Ann (2003) 'New Faces, Old Faces: Counting the Multiracial Population Past and Present' in L. Winters and H. DeBose (eds) *New Faces in a Changing America*, Thousand Oaks, CA: Sage, pp.41–67.

Morton, Samuel (1850) 'Additional Observations on Hybridity in Animals and on Some Collateral Subjects, Being a Reply to the Objections of the Rev. John Bachman', *Charleston Medical Review*, 5: November.

Nagel, Joane (2003) *Race, Ethnicity and Sexuality: Intimate Intersections, Forbidden Frontiers*, Oxford: Oxford University Press.

Nakashima, Cynthia (1992) 'An Invisible Monster: The Creation and Denial of Mixed-Race People in America' in M.P.P. Root (ed.) *Racially Mixed People in America*, Thousand Oaks, CA: Sage, pp. 162–178.

Nakashima, Cynthia (1996) 'Voices from the Movement: Approaches to Multi-raciality' in M.P.P. Root (ed.) *The Multiracial Experience*, Thousand Oaks, CA: Sage, pp.79–100.

Nash, Gary (1999) 'The Hidden History of Mestizo America' in M. Hodes (ed.) *Sex, Love, Race: Crossing Boundaries in North American History*, New York: New York University Press, pp. 10–32.

Nobles, Melissa (2002) 'Racial Categorization and Censuses' in D. Kertzer and D. Arel *Census and Identity: The Politics of Race, Ethnicity, and Language in National Censuses*, Cambridge: Cambridge University Press, pp.43–70.

Nott, Josiah and Gliddon, George (1854) *Types of Mankind*, Philadelphia, PA: J.B. Lippincott.

O'Hearn, Claudine Chiawei (ed.) (1998) *Half and Half: Writers Growing up Biracial and Bicultural*, New York: Pantheon Books.

Olson, Steve (2002) *Mapping Human History: Discovering the Past Through Our Genes*, London: Bloomsbury Press.

Olumide, Jill (2002) *Raiding the Gene Pool: The Social Construction of Mixed Race*, London: Pluto Press.

Omi, Michael and Winant, Howard (1986) *Racial Formation in the United States*, New York: Routledge.

Opitz, May *et al.* (eds) (1986) *Showing Our Colors: Afro-German Women Speak Out*, Amherst: University of Massachusetts.

Park, Edward and Park, John (1999) 'A New American Dilemma?: Asian Americans and Latinos in Race Theorizing', *Journal of Asian American Studies*, 2(3): 289–309.

Parker, Richard and Song, Miri (eds) (2001) 'Introduction: Rethinking "Mixed Race" ' in D. Parker and M. Song (eds) *Rethinking 'Mixed Race'*, London: Pluto Press, pp.1–22.

Phoenix, Ann and Owen, Charlie (2000) 'From Miscegenation to Hybridity: Mixed Relationships and Mixed Parentage in Profile' in A. Brah and A. Coombes (eds) *Hybridity and its Discontents: Politics, Science and Culture*, London: Routledge, pp.72–95.

Rabinow, Paul (1999) *French DNA: Trouble in Purgatory*, Chicago, IL: University of Chicago Press.

Rich, Paul (1990) *Race and Empire in British Politics* (2nd edn), Cambridge; Cambridge University Press.

Rodney, Walter (1972) *How Europe Underdeveloped Africa*, London: Bogle-L'Overture.

Rodriguez, Gregory (2003) 'Prop. 54 Could Undermine Racial Gains', *Los Angeles Times*, 31 August.

Rogers, J.A. (1944/1972) *Sex and Race, Vol.3, Why White and Black Mix in Spite of Opposition*, St Petersburg, FL: Helga Rogers.

Rogers, J.A. (1952/1980) *Nature Knows No Color-Line: Research Into the Negro Ancestry in the White Race, Leads*, St Petersburg, FL: Helga Rogers.

Root, Maria P.P. (ed.) (1992) *Racially Mixed People in America*, Thousand Oaks, CA: Sage.

Root, Maria P.P. (ed.) (1996) *The Multiracial Experience: Racial Borders as the New Frontier*, Thousand Oaks, CA: Sage.

Root, Maria P. P. (2003) 'Five Mixed Race Identities: From Relic to Revolution' in L. Winters and H. DeBose (eds) *New Faces in a Changing America*, Thousand Oaks, CA: Sage, pp. 3–20.

Rose, Steven *et al.* (1984) *Not in Our Genes*, Harmondsworth: Penguin.

Sanchez, George (2002) 'Y tú ¿qué? (Y2K): Latino History in the New Millennium' in M.M. Suárez-Orozco and M.M Páez (eds) *Latinos: Remaking America*, Berkeley: University of California Press, pp.45–58.

Sarkar, Sahotra (1998) *Genetics and Reductionism*, Cambridge: Cambridge University Press.

Shell, Robert (1994) *Children of Bondage: A Social History of the Slave Society at the Cape of Good Hope, 1652–1838*, Johannesburg, South Africa: Wits University.

Shepherd, Verene (2000) 'Gender and Representation in European Accounts of Pre-emancipation Jamaica' in V. Shepherd and H. Beckles (eds) *Caribbean Slavery in the Atlantic World*, Oxford: James Currey, pp.702–712.

Shepherd, Verene and Beckles, Hilary (eds) (2000) *Caribbean Slavery in the Atlantic World*, Oxford: James Currey.

Small, Stephen (2001) 'Colour, Culture and Class: Interrogating Interracial Marriage and People of Mixed Racial Descent in the USA' in D. Parker and M. Song (eds) *Rethinking 'Mixed Race'*, London: Pluto Press, pp. 117–132.

Spencer, Jon Michael (1997) *The New Colored People: The Mixed Race Movement in America*, London: New York University Press.

Spencer, Rainier (1999) *Spurious Issues: Race and Multiracial Identity Politics in the United States*, Boulder, CO: Westview Press.

Spickard, Paul (1989) *Mixed Blood: Intermarriage and Ethnic Identity in Twentieth-century America*, Madison: University of Wisconsin Press.

Spickard, Paul (2001) 'The Subject is Mixed Race: The Boom in Biracial Biography' in R. Parker and M. Song (eds) *Rethinking 'Mixed Race'*, pp.76–98.

Stocking, George (1982) *Race, Culture and Evolution*, London: University of Chicago Press.

Stocking, George (1987) *Victorian Anthropology*, London: Collier Macmillan.

Stoler, Ann (2000) 'Sexual Affronts and Racial Frontiers: European Identities and the Cultural Politics of Exclusion in Colonial Southeast Asia' in A. Brah and A. Coombes (eds) *Hybridity and its Discontents: Politics Science, and Culture*, London: Routledge, pp. 19–55.

Stonequist, Everett (1937) *The Marginal Man: A Study in Personality and Cultures*, New York: Russell and Russell.

Stringer, Christopher and McKie, Robin (1996) *African Exodus: The Origins of Modern Humanity*, New York: Henry Holt and Company.

Stringer, Christopher and Andrews, Peter (1988) 'Genetic and Fossil Evidence in the Origin of Modern Humans', *Science*, 239: 1263–1268.

TallBear, Kimberly (2003) 'DNA, Blood and Racialising the Tribe', *Wicazo Sa Review*, 18 (1): 81–107.

Talty, Stephan (2003) *Mulatto America*, New York: HarperCollins.

Texeira, Mary Thierry (2003) 'The New Multiracialism: An Affirmation of or an End to Race as We Know It?' in L. Winters and H. DeBose (eds) *New Faces in a Changing America*, Thousand Oaks, CA: Sage, pp.21–37.

Tizard, Barbara and Phoenix, Ann (1993) *Black, White or Mixed Race?: Race and Racism in the Lives of Young People of Mixed Parentage*, London: Routledge.

Torres, Arlene and Whitten, Norman (eds) (1998) *Blackness in Latin America and the Caribbean*, Vol. 2, Bloomington: Indiana University Press.

Twine, France Winddance (1997) 'Brown-Skinned White Girls; Class, Culture and the Construction of White Identity in Suburban Communities' in R. Frankenberg (ed.) *Displacing Whiteness*, Durham, NC: Duke University Press, pp.214–243.

Twine, France Winddance (1998) *Racism in a Racial Democracy: The Maintenance of White Supremacy in Brazil*, New Brunswick, NJ: Rutgers University Press.

Wade, Peter (1997) *Race and Ethnicity in Latin America*, London: Pluto Press.

Ware, Vron and Back, Les (2002) *Out of Whiteness: Color, Politics and Culture*, Chicago, IL: University of Chicago Press.

Waters, Mary (2000) 'Multiple Ethnicities and Identity in the United States' in P. Spickard and W.J. Burroughs (eds) *We Are a People: Narrative and Multiplicity in Constructing Ethnic Identity*, Philadelphia, PA: Temple University Press, pp.23–40.

Williams, Eric (1944) *Capitalism and Slavery*, Chapel Hill: University of North Carolina Press.

Williams-León, Teresa and Nakashima, Cynthia (eds) (2001) *The Sum of Our Parts: Mixed Heritage Asian Americans*, Philadelphia, PA: Temple University Press.

Williamson, Joel (1995) *New People: Miscegenation and Mulattos in the United States*, London: Lousiana University Press.

Wilson, Terry (1992) 'Blood Quantum: Native American Mixed Bloods' in M.P.P. Root (ed.) *Racially Mixed People in America*, Thousand Oaks, CA: Sage, pp.108–125.

Winant, Howard (1999) 'Racial Democracy and Racial Identity: Comparing the United States and Brazil' in M. Hanchard (ed.) *Racial Politics in Contemporary Brazil*, London: Duke University Press, pp. 98–115.

Winters, Loretta and DeBose, Herman (eds) (2003) *New Faces in a Changing America: Multiracial Identity in the Twenty-first Century*, Thousand Oaks, CA: Sage.

Wolfe, Patrick (1999) *Settler Colonialism and the Transformation of Anthropology: The Politics and Poetics of an Ethnographic Event*, London: Cassell.

Wolpoff, Milford and Caspari, Rachel (1997) *Race and Human Evolution: A Fatal Attraction*, Boulder, CO: Westview Press.

Young, Lola (2000) 'Hybridity's Discontents: Rereading Science and 'Race' in A. Brah and A. Coombes (eds) *Hybridity and its Discontents: Politics, Science and Culture*, London: Routledge, pp.154–170.

Young, Robert (1995) *Colonial Desire: Hybridity in Theory, Culture and Race*, London: Routledge.

Yu, Henry (1999) 'Mixing Bodies and Cultures: The Meaning of America's Fascination with Sex Between "Orientals" and "Whites" ' in M. Hodes (ed.) *Sex, Love, Race: Crossing Boundaries in North American History*, New York: New York University Press, pp. 444–463.

Zack, Naomi (ed.) (1995) *American Mixed Race*, London: Rowman and Littlefield.

Zack, Naomi (2001) 'Philosophical Aspects of the "AAA Statement on "Race" ', *Anthropological Theory*, 1(4): 445–465.

Tracing the origins

Miscegenation, moral degeneracy and genetics

INTRODUCTION

IN A CHRONOLOGICAL FASHION, the extracts in Part One trace the origins of thinking about 'mixed race' back to their problematic beginnings in nineteenth-century 'race' science in general and evolutionary anthropology in particular. The readings in the first section on miscegenation and moral degeneracy pinpoint a 'biological' discourse on 'mixed race', which invokes metaphors of contagion and pollution to describe the dangers and consequences of 'racial' mixing. The writings by Knox, Gobineau, Nott and Gliddon, Darwin and Delany highlight the popularity of 'hybrid degeneracy' theory, which promoted 'white' mental, moral, genetic and 'racial' supremacy, and mobilized 'science' to support the claim that 'pure' 'white' 'races' should not mix with 'non-white' 'races', who were deemed socially, culturally and biologically inferior. Circulating at the same time were debates over whether so-called different 'races' were of the same species, *monogenesis*, or distinct and separate species, *polygenesis*. As these excerpts reveal, at the centre of this scientific, religious, political and moral disagreement were two interwoven questions: What happened when 'races' did mix? and Were 'mixed race' offspring capable of reproducing across generations?

By the early twentieth century, the discourse had shifted from the 'biological' to the 'sociological', 'anthropological' and 'psychological'. This does not mean that pathological perspectives on 'mixed race' disappeared. Herskovits and Dover are both critical of Victorian 'racial' ideologies, while Reuter reinforces that pathological standpoint. At the same time, though, Reuter does acknowledge that 'racial' mixing is both a very old and an inevitable social process. The theory of 'hybrid degeneracy' was replaced but not stamped out by social maladjustment theory. Its most popular proponent was Stonequist, architect of the 'marginal man' thesis, published in 1937 as *The Marginal Man*. I have coupled an extract from his book with a more contemporary writing by Furedi, who not only provides an important critique of Stonequist's argument, but also locates his views on 'race', 'mixed race' and margin-ality within the broader context of an emergent 1930s Anglo-American sociological tradition. The 1930s also gave birth to 'eugenics', coined by Francis Galton, Darwin's cousin. As mentioned in the Introduction to the Reader, this was a 'science' which attempted to 'maintain' the genetic superiority of 'fit' populations by 'controlling' the inheritance of 'unfit' genes. In inter-war Britain and Nazi Germany respectively, the extracts by Rich and Lusane remind us of the dangerous consequences of (mis)applied science as a form of social engineering.

Finally, in the section on genetics, the American Anthropological Association Statement on 'Race' provides a succinct social scientific explanation of what 'race' is not. Provine's article covers the time period from the 1930s to post Second World War and explores shifts in geneticists' attitudes towards 'racial' mixing. On the other hand, the readings by Brodwin and TallBear each address the ways in which the advances of late twentieth/early twenty-first-century genetic technology have shed new light on old debates about 'race', differences and social hierarchies. At the same time, both authors illustrate how these scientific innovations have raised a different set of moral, ethical and political questions about differences and belongings.

Miscegenation and moral degeneracy

Chapter 1

Robert Knox

DO RACES EVER AMALGAMATE?

Extract from *The Races of Men* (1850), pp. 64–67.

Section I. — *Do races ever amalgamate? What are the obstacles to a race changing its original locality?*

I HAVE HEARD PERSONS ASSERT, a few years ago, men of education too, and of observation, that the amalgamation of races into a third or new product, partaking of the qualities of the two primitive ones from which they sprung, was not only possible, but that it was the best mode of improving the breed. The whole of this theory has turned out to be false: – 1st. As regards the lower animals; 2nd. As regards man. Of the first I shall say but little: man is the great object of human research; the philosophy of Zoology is not indeed wrapt up in him; he is not the end, neither was he the beginning: still, as he is, a knowledge of man is to him all-important.

The theories put forth from time to time, of the production of a new variety, permanent and self-supporting, independent of any draughts or supplies from the pure breeds, have been distinctly disproved. It holds neither in sheep nor cattle: and an author, whose name I cannot recollect, has refuted the whole theory as to the pheasant and to the domestic fowl. He has shown that the artificial breeds so produced are never self-supporting. Man can create nothing: no new species have appeared, apparently, for some thousand years; but this is another question I mean not to discuss here, although it is obvious that if a hybrid could be produced, self-supporting, the elaborate works of Cuvier would fall to the ground. The theory of Aristotle, who explained the variety and strangeness of the animal forms in Africa, on the grounds that a scarcity of water brought to the wells and springs animals of various kinds from whose intercourse sprung the singularly varied African Zoology, has been long known to be a mere fable.

Figure 1.1 Bosjeman, or Yellow African Race

Nature produces no mules; no hybrids, neither in man nor animals. When they accidentally appear they soon cease to be, for they are either non-productive, or one or other of the pure breeds speedily predominates, and the weaker disappears. This weakness may either be numerical or innate.

That this law applies strictly to man himself, all history proves: I once said to a gentleman born in Mexico, – Who are the Mexicans? I put the same question to a gentleman from Peru, as I had done before, to persons calling themselves Germans – neither could give a distinct reply to the question. The fact turns out to be, that there really are no such persons; no such *race*.

When the best blood of Spain migrated to America, they killed as many of the natives, that is, the copper-coloured Indians, indigenous to the soil, as they could. But this could not go on, labourers to till the soil being required. The old Spaniard was found unequal to this; *he could not colonize the conquered country*; he required other aid, native or imported. Then came the admixture with the Indian blood and the Celt-Iberian blood; the produce being the mulatto. But now that the supplies of Spanish blood have ceased, the mulatto must cease, too, for as a hybrid he becomes non-productive after a time, if he intermarries only with the mulatto: he can no longer go back to the Spanish blood: that stock has ceased; of necessity then he is forced upon the Indian breed. Thus, year by year, the Spanish blood disappears, and with it the mulatto, and the population retrograding towards the indigenous inhabitants, returns to that Indian population, the hereditary descendants of those whom Cortes found there; whom nature seemingly placed there; not aliens, nor foreigners, but aboriginal. As it is with Mexico, so it is with Peru.

Study probes

1   What does Knox mean when he says 'racial' hybrids ('mulattos) are 'non-productive'?
2   Which geographical example does the author put forward to support his claim?
3   What was the political and economic reason for diversifying 'the old Spanish' population?

Chapter 2

Joseph Arthur de Count Gobineau

RECAPITULATION: THE RESPECTIVE CHARACTERISTICS OF THE THREE GREAT RACES; THE SUPERIORITY OF THE WHITE TYPE, AND, WITHIN THIS TYPE, OF THE ARYAN FAMILY

Extract from *The Inequality of Human Races (Essai sur l'inégalité des races humaines)* (1853), translated by Adrian Collins (1915), pp. 208–211.

IT WOULD BE UNJUST to assert that every mixture is bad and harmful. If the three great types had remained strictly separate, the supremacy would no doubt have always been in the hands of the finest of the white races, and the yellow and black varieties would have crawled for ever at the feet of the lowest of the whites. Such a state is so far ideal, since it has never been beheld in history; and we can imagine it only by recognizing the undisputed superiority of those groups of the white races which have remained the purest.

It would not have been all gain. The superiority of the white race would have been clearly shown, but it would have been bought at the price of certain advantages which have followed the mixture of blood. Although these are far from counterbalancing the defects they have brought in their train, yet they are sometimes to be commended. Artistic genius, which is equally foreign to each of the three great types, arose only after the intermarriage of white and black. Again, in the Malayan variety, a human family was produced from the yellow and black races that had more intelligence than either of its ancestors. Finally, from the union of white and yellow, certain intermediary peoples have sprung, who are superior to the purely Finnish tribes as well as to the negroes.

I do not deny that these are good results. The world of art and great literature that comes from the mixture of blood, the improvement and ennoblement of inferior races – all these are wonders for which we must needs be thankful. The small have been raised. Unfortunately, the great have been lowered by the same process; and this is an evil that nothing can balance or repair. Since I am putting together the advantages of racial mixtures, I will also add that to them is due the refinement of manners and beliefs, and especially the tempering of passion and desire. But these are merely transitory benefits, and if I recognize that the mulatto, who may become a lawyer, a doctor, or a business man, is worth more than his negro grandfather, who was absolutely savage, and fit for nothing, I must also confess that the Brahmans of primitive India, the heroes of the Iliad and the Shahnameh, the warriors of Scandinavia – the glorious shades of noble races that have disappeared – give us a higher and more brilliant idea of humanity, and were more active, intelligent, and trusty instruments of civiliza- tion and grandeur than the peoples, hybrid a hundred times over, of the present day. And the blood even of these was no longer pure.

However it has come about, the human races, as we find them in history, are complex; and one of the chief consequences has been to throw into disorder most of the primitive characteristics of each type. The good as well as the bad qualities are seen to diminish in intensity with repeated intermixture of blood; but they also scatter and separate off from each other, and are often mutually opposed. The white race originally possessed the monopoly of beauty, intelli- gence, and strength. By its union with other varieties, hybrids were created, which were beautiful without strength, strong without intelligence, or, if intelli- gent, both weak and ugly. Further, when the quantity of white blood was increased to an indefinite amount by successive infusions, and not by a single admixture, it no longer carried with it its natural advantages, and often merely increased the confusion already existing in the racial elements. Its strength, in fact, seemed to be its only remaining quality, and even its strength served only to promote disorder. The apparent anomaly is easily explained. Each stage of a perfect mixture produces a new type from diverse elements, and develops special faculties. As soon as further elements are added, the vast difficulty of harmonizing the whole creates a state of anarchy. The more this increases, the more do even the best and richest of the new contributions diminish in value, and by their mere presence add fuel to an evil which they cannot abate. If mixtures of blood are, to a certain extent, beneficial to the mass of mankind, if they raise and ennoble it, this is merely at the expense of mankind itself, which is stunted, abased, enervated, and humiliated in the persons of its noblest sons: Even if we admit that it is better to turn a myriad of degraded beings into mediocre men than to preserve the race of princes whose blood is adulterated and impoverished by being made to suffer this dishonourable change, yet there is still the unfortunate fact that the change does not stop here; for when the mediocre men are once created at the expense of the greater, they combine with other mediocrities, and from such unions, which grow ever more and more degraded, is born a confusion which, like that of Babel, ends in utter impo- tence, and leads societies down to the abyss of nothingness whence no power on earth can rescue them.

Such is the lesson of history. It shows us that all civilizations derive from the white race, that none can exist without its help, and that a society is great and brilliant only so far as it preserves the blood of the noble group that created it, provided that this group itself belongs to the most illustrious branch of our species.

Of the multitude of peoples which live or have lived on the earth, ten alone have risen to the position of complete societies. The remainder have gravitated round these more or less independently, like planets round their suns. If there is any element of life in these ten civilizations that is not due to the impulse of the white races, any seed of death that does not come from the inferior stocks that mingled with them, then the whole theory on which this book rests is false. On the other hand, if the facts are as I say, then we have an irrefragable proof of the nobility of our own species. Only the actual details can set the final seal of truth on my system, and they alone can show with sufficient exactness the full implications of my main thesis, that peoples degenerate only in consequence of the various admixtures of blood which they undergo; that their degeneration corresponds exactly to the quantity and quality of the new blood, and that the rudest possible shock to the vitality of a civilization is given when the ruling elements in a society and those developed by racial change have become so numerous that they are clearly moving away from the homogeneity necessary to their life, and it therefore becomes impossible for them to be brought into harmony and so acquire the common instincts and interests, the common logic of existence, which is the sole justification for any social bond whatever. There is no greater curse than such disorder, for however bad it may have made the present state of things, it promises still worse for the future.

Study probes

1   According to Gobineau, what are the 'three great types of mankind', and how are they ranked?
2   In what ways does he argue for and against 'racial mixing'?
3   What is his main thesis?
4   Regarding 'race' mixing, what future predictions does he make?
5   How were Gobineau's arguments in keeping with the prevailing views of the time?

Chapter 3

Josiah Clark Nott and George Robins Gliddon

HYBRIDITY OF ANIMALS, VIEWED IN CONNECTION WITH THE NATURAL HISTORY OF MANKIND

Extract from *Types of Mankind of Ethnogical Researches* (1854), pp. 373–374 and 396–398.

IN 1842 I PUBLISHED a short essay on *Hybridity*, the object of which was, to show that the White Man and the Negro were distinct "species;" illustrating my position by numerous facts from the Natural History of Man and that of the lower animals. The question, at that time, had not attracted the attention of Dr. Morton. Many of my facts and arguments were new, even to him; and drew from the great anatomist a private letter, leading to the commencement of a friendly correspondence, to me, at least, most agreeable and instructive, and which endured to the close of his useful career.

In the essay alluded to, and several which followed it at short intervals, I maintained these propositions: –

1 That *mulattoes* are the shortest-lived of any class of the human race.
2 That *mulattoes* are intermediate in intelligence between the blacks and the whites.
3 That they are less capable of undergoing fatigue and hardship than either the blacks or whites.
4 That the *mulatto-women* are peculiarly delicate, and subject to a variety of chronic diseases. That they are bad breeders, bad nurses, liable to abortions, and that their children generally die young.
5 That, when *mulattoes* intermarry, they are less prolific than when crossed on the parent stocks.
6 That, when a *Negro* man married a *white* woman, the offspring partook more largely of the Negro type than when the reverse connection had effect.

7   That *mulattoes*, like Negroes, although unacclimated, enjoy extraordinary
       exemption from yellow-fever when brought to Charleston, Savannah,
       Mobile, or New Orleans.

Almost fifty years of residence among the white and black races, spread in
nearly equal proportions through South Carolina and Alabama, and twenty-five
years' incessant professional intercourse with both, have satisfied me of the
absolute truth of the preceding deductions. My observations, however, during
the last few years, in Mobile and at New Orleans, where the population differs
essentially from that of the Northern Atlantic States, have induced some modification of my former opinions; although still holding to their accuracy so far as
they apply to the intermixture of the strictly *white* race (*i.e.* the Anglo-Saxon, or
Teuton,) with the true *Negro*. I stated in an article printed in "De Bow's Com-
mercial Review," that I had latterly seen reason to credit the existence of certain
"*affinities* and *repulsions*" among various races of men, which caused their blood to
mingle more or less perfectly; and that, in Mobile, New Orleans and Pensacola, I
had witnessed many examples of great longevity among *mulattoes*; and sundry
instances where their intermarriages (contrary to my antecedent experiences in
South Carolina) were attended with manifest prolificacy. Seeking for the reason
of this positive, and, at first thought, unaccountable difference between *mulattoes*
of the Atlantic and those of the Gulf States, observation led me to a *rationale*;
viz., that it arose from the diversity of *type* in the "Caucasian" races of the two
sections. In the Atlantic States the population is Teutonic and Celtic: whereas, in
our Gulf cities, there exists a preponderance of the blood of French, Italian,
Spanish, Portuguese, and other *dark*-skinned races. The reason is simple to the
historian. Our States along the Gulf of Mexico were chiefly colonized by emi-
grants from Southern Europe. Such European colonists belonged to types genea-
logically distinct from those white-skinned "Pilgrim Fathers" who landed north
of Florida. Thus Spain, when her traditions begin, was populated principally by
Iberians. France received a considerable infusion of the same blood, now almost
pure in her Basque provinces. Italy's origins are questions in dispute; but the
Italians are a dark-skinned race. Such races, blended in America with the
imported Negro, generally give birth to a hardier, and, therefore, more prolific
stock than white races, such as Anglo-Saxons, produce by intercourse with
Negresses. Herein, it occurred to me, might be found a key to solve the enigma.
To comprehend the present, we must understand the past; because, in ethnology,
there is no truer saying than, "*Cœlum, non animam, mutant qui trans mare currunt.*"
This sketch indicates my conceptions. I proceed to their development.

Bodichon, in his curious work on Algeria, maintains that this Iberian, or
Basque population, although, of course, not Negro, is really an African, and
probably a *Berber*, family, which migrated across the Straits of Gibraltar some
2000 years before the Christian era; and we might, therefore, regard them as
what Dr. Morton calls a proximate race.

The Basques are a dark-skinned, black-eyed, black-haired people, such as are
often encountered in Southern Europe; and M. Bodichon, himself a Frenchman,
and attached as Surgeon to the French army during fifteen years in Algeria,
holds, that not only is the physical resemblance between the Berbers and Basques

most striking, but that they assimilate in moral traits quite as much; moreover, that their intonations of voice are so similar that one's ear cannot appreciate any difference. Singularly enough, too, the Basque tongue, while radically distinct from all European and Asiatic languages, is said to present certain affinities with the Berber dialects. The latter opinion, however, requires confirmation.

> *In the Human Species.* – There are equally distinct breeds of the human family as of any of the lower animals; and it is affirmed that the human female, when twice married, bears occasionally to the second husband children resembling the first both in bodily structure and mental powers. Where all the parties are *of the same color*, this statement is not so easy of verification; but, where a woman has had children by two men of different colors, such as a black and a white man, it would be comparatively easy to observe whether the offspring of the latter connexion bore any resemblance to the former parent. Count Strzelecki, in his *Physical History of Van Diemen's Land*, asserts that, when a native woman has had a child by a European male, "*she loses the power of conception, on a renewal of intercourse, with a male of her own race, retaining only that of procreating with the white men.*" "Hundreds of instances (says the Count) of this extraordinary fact are recorded in the writer's memoranda, *all occurring invariably under the same circumstances*, amongst the Hurous, Seminoles, Red Indians, Yakies (Sinaloa), Mendosa Indians, Auracos, South Sea Islanders, and natives of New Zealand, New South Wales, and Van Diemen's Land; and all tending to prove that the sterility of the female, which is relative only to one and not to another male, is not accidental, but follows laws as cogent, though as mysterious, as the rest of those connected with generation." In this sweeping assertion the Count may have been mistaken: a traveller could hardly have had opportunities for ascertaining a fact, which it must require years of careful observation to confirm. It is certain that no such thing exists between the whites and Negroes, the two races with which we are the most familiar; because examples are of frequent occurrence, where a Negress, after having had a child by a white man, has had a family by a husband of her own color.

Instances are cited, where a Negro woman bore mulatto children to a white man, and afterwards had by a black man other children, who bore a strong resemblance to the white father, both in features and complexion. It is supposed by some, that the influence, exerted on the generative system of a female of one race by sexual intercourse with the male of another, may be increased by repeated connexions; and Dr. Laing informs us of the case of an English gentleman in the West Indies, who had a large family by a Negro woman, and where the children exhibited successively, more and more, the European features and complexion. I have living with me a black woman, whose first child was by a white man: she has had six children since, by a black husband, who are perfectly black, and unlike the first father;

yet, it is a singular fact that these children, though strongly-marked Negroes, bear no family likeness to either father or mother – their physiognomy is as distinct as that of any two families of the same race. The children of a second husband may resemble the first sufficiently to attract attention, even where there is no striking contrast of color; thus Dr. Harvey cites a case where a lady was twice married, and had issue by both husbands. One of the children by the second marriage bears an unmistakeable resemblance to her mother's first husband; and what makes the likeness more discernible is, that there was a marked difference in features and general appearance between the two husbands.

The chain of facts herein by this time linked together, aside from many more of identical force that might easily be added, proves conclusively that prolificacy between two races of animals is no test of specific affiliation; and it therefore follows, as a corollary, that prolificacy among the different races of men carries with it no evidence of common origin. On the other hand, if it can be shown that the law of hybridity prevails between any two human races, the argument in favor of plurality of species would thereby be greatly strengthened.

I think that the genus *homo* includes many primitive species; and that these species are amenable to the same laws which govern species in many other genera. The species of men are all *proximate*, according to the definition already given; nevertheless, some are perfectly prolific; while others are imperfectly so – possessing a tendency to become extinct when their hybrids are bred together. At the beginning of this chapter I referred to my own observations, made some years ago, on the crossing of white and black races: and my investigations since that time, as well as those of many other anatomists, confirm the views before enunciated. So far as the races of men can be traced through osteography, history and monuments, the present volume establishes that they have always been distinct. No example is recorded, where one race has been transformed into another by external causes. *Permanence of type* must therefore be regarded as an infallible test of specific character. M. Jacquinot very dexterously remarks that, according to the theory of unity of races, a mulatto belongs to a "species" as much as any other human being, and that the white and black races would be but "varieties."

When two *proximate* species of mankind, two races bearing a general resemblance to each other in type, are bred together – *e.g.*, Teutons, Celts, Pelasgians, Iberians, or Jews – they produce offspring perfectly prolific: although, even here, their peculiarities cannot become so entirely fused into a homogeneous mass as to obliterate the original types of either. One or the other of these types will "crop-out," from time to time, more or less apparently in their progeny. When, on the other hand, species the most widely separated, such as the Anglo-Saxon with the Negro, are crossed, a different result has course. Their mulatto offspring, if still prolific, are but partially so; and acquire an inherent tendency to run out, and become eventually extinct when kept apart from the parent stocks. This opinion is now becoming general among observers in our slave States; and it is very strongly insisted upon by M. Jacquinot. This skilful naturalist (unread in cis-Atlantic literature) claims the discovery as original with himself; although erroneously, because it had long previously been advocated by Estwick and Long, the historians of Jamaica; by Dr. Caldwell; by Professors Dickson and Holbrook, of Charleston, S. C.; and by numerous other leading medical men of our Southern States. There are some 4,000,000 of Negroes in the United States; about whom circumstances, personal and professional, have afforded me ample opportunities for observation. I have found it impossible, nevertheless, to collect such statistics as would be satisfactory to others on this point; and the difficulty arises solely from the want of chastity among mulatto women, which is so notorious as to be proverbial. Although often married to hybrid males of their own color, their children are begotten as frequently by white or other men, as by their husbands. For many years, in my daily professional visits, I have been in the habit of meeting with mulatto women, either free or slaves; and, never omitting an opportunity of inquiry with regard to their prolificacy, longevity of offspring, color of parents, age, etc., the conviction has become indelibly fixed in my mind that the positions laid down in the beginning of this chapter are true.

Study probes

1   What are Nott's main propositions about 'mulattos'?
2   How do his assertions either support or challenge those of Knox and Gobineau?
3   In what ways does he differentiate between Northern and Southern Europeans? How does this distinction impact upon his hybridity ('race' mixing) thesis?
4   Does the author suggest that there are particular 'racial' laws governing infertility?

Chapter 4

Charles Darwin

ON THE RACES OF MEN: ... THE EFFECTS OF CROSSING

Extract from *The Descent of Man* (1871), pp. 170–175.

O**UR SUPPOSED NATURALIST** having proceeded thus far in his investigation, would next enquire whether the races of men, when crossed, were in any degree sterile. He might consult the work of Professor Broca,[1] a cautious and philosophical observer, and in this he would find good evidence that some races were quite fertile together, but evidence of an opposite nature in regard to other races. Thus it has been asserted that the native women of Australia and Tasmania rarely produce children to European men; the evidence, however, on this head has now been shown to be almost valueless. The half-castes are killed by the pure blacks: and an account has lately been published of eleven half-caste youths murdered and burnt at the same time, whose remains were found by the police.[2] Again, it has often been said that when mulattoes intermarry, they produce few children; on the other hand, Dr. Bachman, of Charleston,[3] positively asserts that he has known mulatto families which have intermarried for several generations, and have continued on an average as fertile as either pure whites or pure blacks. Enquiries formerly made by Sir C. Lyell on this subject led him, as he informs me, to the same conclusion.[4] In the United States the census for the year 1854 included, according to Dr. Bachman, 405,751 mulattoes; and this number, considering all the circumstances of the case, seems small; but it may partly be accounted for by the degraded and anomalous position of the class, and by the profligacy of the women. A certain amount of absorption of mulattoes into negroes must always be in progress; and this would lead to an apparent diminution of the former. The inferior vitality of mulattoes is spoken of in a trustworthy work as a well-known phenomenon,[5] and this, although a different consideration from their lessened fertility, may perhaps be advanced as a proof of the specific distinctness of the parent races. No doubt both animal and vegetable hybrids, when produced from extremely distinct species, are liable to premature death; but the parents of mulattoes cannot be put under the category of extremely distinct species. The common Mule, so notorious for long life and vigour, and yet so sterile, shows how little necessary connection there is in hybrids between lessened fertility and vitality; other analogous cases could be cited.

Even if it should hereafter be proved that all the races of men were perfectly fertile together, he who was inclined from other reasons to rank them as distinct species, might with justice argue that fertility and sterility are not safe criterions of specific distinctness. We know that these qualities are easily affected by changed conditions of life, or by close inter-breeding, and that they are governed by highly complex laws, for instance, that of the unequal fertility of converse crosses between the same two species. With forms which must be ranked as undoubted species, a perfect series exists from those which are absolutely sterile when crossed, to those which are almost or completely fertile. The degrees of sterility do not coincide strictly with the degrees of difference between the parents in external structure or habits of life. Man in many respects may be compared with those animals which have long been domesticated, and a large body of evidence can be advanced in favour of the Pallasian doctrine,[6] that domestication tends to eliminate the sterility which is so general a result of the crossing of species in a state of nature. From these several considerations, it may be justly urged that the perfect fertility of the intercrossed races of man, if established, would not absolutely preclude us from ranking them as distinct species.

Independently of fertility, the characters presented by the offspring from a cross have been thought to indicate whether or not the parent-forms ought to be ranked as species or varieties; but after carefully studying the evidence, I have come to the conclusion that no general rules of this kind can be trusted. The ordinary result of a cross is the production of a blended or intermediate form; but in certain cases some of the offspring take closely after one parent-form, and some after the other. This is especially apt to occur when the parents differ in characters which first appeared as sudden variations or monstrosities.[7] I refer to this point, because Dr. Rohlfs informs me that he has frequently seen in Africa the offspring of negroes crossed with members of other races, either completely black or completely white, or rarely piebald. On the other hand, it is notorious that in America mulattoes commonly present an intermediate appearance.

We have now seen that a naturalist might feel himself fully justified in ranking the races of man as distinct species; for he has found that they are distinguished by many differences in structure and constitution, some being of importance. These differences have, also, remained nearly constant for very long periods of time. Our naturalist will have been in some degree influenced by the enormous range of man, which is a great anomaly in the class of mammals, if mankind be viewed as a single species. He will have been struck with the distribution of the several so-called races, which accords with that of other undoubtedly distinct species of mammals. Finally, he might urge that the mutual fertility of all the races has not as yet been fully proved, and even if proved would not be an absolute proof of their specific identity.

On the other side of the question, if our supposed naturalist were to enquire whether the forms of man keep distinct like ordinary species, when mingled together in large numbers in the same country, he would immediately discover that this was by no means the case. In Brazil he would behold an immense mongrel population of Negroes and Portuguese; in Chiloe, and other parts of South America, he would behold the whole population consisting of Indians and Spaniards blended in various degrees.[8] In many parts of the same continent he would meet with the most complex crosses between Negroes, Indians, and Europeans; and judging from the vegetable kingdom, such triple crosses afford the severest test of the mutual fertility of the parent forms. In one island of the Pacific he would find a small population of mingled Polynesian and English blood; and in the Fiji Archipelago a population of Polynesian and Negritos crossed in all degrees. Many analogous cases could be added; for instance, in Africa. Hence the races of man are not sufficiently distinct to inhabit the same country without fusion; and the absence of fusion affords the usual and best test of specific distinctness.

Our naturalist would likewise be much disturbed as soon as he perceived that the distinctive characters of all the races were highly variable. This fact strikes every one on first beholding the negro slaves in Brazil, who have been imported from all parts of Africa. The same remark holds good with the Polynesians, and with many other races. It may be doubted whether any character can be named which is distinctive of a race and is constant. Savages, even within the limits of the same tribe, are not nearly so uniform in character, as has been often asserted. Hottentot women offer certain peculiarities, more strongly marked than those occurring in any other race, but these are known not to be of constant occurrence. In the several American tribes, colour and hairiness differ considerably; as does colour to a certain degree, and the shape of the features greatly, in the Negroes of Africa. The shape of the skull varies much in some races,[9] and so it is with every other character. Now all naturalists have learnt by dearly bought experience, how rash it is to attempt to define species by the aid of inconstant characters.

But the most weighty of all the arguments against treating the races of man as distinct species, is that they graduate into each other, independently in many cases, as far as we can judge, of their having intercrossed. Man has been studied more carefully than any other animal, and yet there is the greatest possible diversity amongst capable judges whether he should be classed as a single species or race, or as two (Virey), as three (Jacquinot), as four (Kant), five (Blumenbach), six (Buffon), seven (Hunter), eight (Agassiz), eleven (Pickering), fifteen (Bory St. Vincent), sixteen (Desmoulins), twenty-two (Morton), sixty (Crawfurd), or as sixty-three, according to Burke.[10] This diversity of judgment does not prove that the races ought not to be ranked as species, but it shows that they graduate into each other, and that it is hardly possible to discover clear distinctive characters between them.

Study probes

1   What conclusions, if any, does Darwin reach about whether or not 'mixed race' offspring are sterile?
2   Darwin challenges the claim, known as *polygenesis*, which argues that so-called different 'races' are in fact distinct and separate species. What is the basis of his argument, known as *monogenesis*, which asserts that so-called different 'races' are members of a single species?
3   Does Darwin rank so-called different 'races' on a hierarchical ladder as did so many of his contemporaries?

Notes

1   *On the Phenomena of Hybridity in the Genus Homo, Eng. translation*, 1864
2   *See the interesting letter by Mr. T.A. Murray, in the 'Anthropological Review*, April 1868, p. liii. In this letter Count Strzelecki's statement that Australian women who have borne children to a white man, are afterwards sterile with their own race, is disproved. M. A. de Quatrefages has also collected (Revue des Cours Scientifiques, March, 1869, p. 239), much evidence that Australians and Europeans are not sterile when crossed.
3   *An Examination of Prof. Agassiz's Sketch of the Nat. Provinces of the Animal World*, Charleston, 1855, p. 44.
4   Dr. Rohlfs writes to me that he found the mixed races in the Great Sahara, derived from Arabs, Berbers, and Negroes of three tribes, extraordinarily fertile. On the other hand, Mr. Winwood Reade informs me that the Negroes on the Gold Coast, though admiring white men and mulattoes, have a maxim that mulattoes should not intermarry, as the children are few and sickly. This belief, as Mr. Reade remarks, deserves attention, as white men have visited and resided on the Gold Coast for four hundred years, so that the natives have had ample time to gain knowledge through experience.
5   *Military and Anthropological Statistics of American Soldiers*, by B.A. Gould, 1869, p. 319.
6   *The Variation of Animals and Plants under Domestication*, vol. ii. p. 109. I may here remind the reader that the sterility of species when crossed is not a specially acquired quality, but, like the incapacity of certain trees to be grafted together, is incidental on other acquired differences. The nature of these differences is unknown, but they relate more especially to the reproductive system, and much less so to external structure or to ordinary differences in constitution. One important element in the sterility of crossed species apparently lies in one or both having been long habituated to fixed conditions; for we know that changed conditions have a special influence on the reproductive system, and we have good reason to believe (as before remarked) that the fluctuating conditions of domestication lend to eliminate that sterility which is so general with species, in a natural state, when crossed. It has elsewhere been shown by me (ibid. vol. ii. p. 185, and *Origin of Species*, 5th edn, p. 317), that the sterility of crossed species has not been acquired through natural selection: we can see that when two forms have already been rendered very sterile, it is scarcely possible that their sterility should be augmented by the preservation or survival of the more and more sterile individuals; for, as the sterility increases, fewer and fewer offspring will be produced from which to breed, and at last only single individuals will be produced at the rarest intervals. But there is even a higher grade of sterility than this. Both Gartner and Kolreuter have proved that in genera of plants, including many species, a series can be formed from species which, when crossed, yield fewer and fewer seeds, to species which never produce a single seed, but yet are affected by the pollen of the other species, as shown by the swelling of the germen. It is here manifestly impossible to select the more sterile individuals, which have already ceased to yield seeds; so that the acme of sterility, when the germen alone is affected, cannot have been gained through selection. This acme, and no doubt the other grades of sterility, are the incidental results of certain

unknown differences in the constitution of the reproductive system of the species which are crossed.

7   '*The Variation of Animals*', vol. ii. p. 92.

8   M. de Quatrefages has given (*Anthropological Review*, Jan. 1869, p. 22), an interesting account of the success and energy of the Paulistas in Brazil, who are a much crossed race of Portuguese and Indians, with a mixture of the blood of other races.

9   For instance, with the aborigines of America and Australia, Prof. Huxley says (*Transact. Internat. Congress of Prehist. Arch.* 1868, p. 105), that the skulls of many South Germans and Swiss are "as short and as broad as those of the Tarlars," etc.

10   See a good discussion on this subject in Waitz, *Introduction to Anthropology*, Eng. translat., 1863, pp. 198–208, 227. I have taken some of the above statements from H. Tuttle's *Origin and Antiquity of Physical Man*, Boston, 1866, p. 35.

Chapter 5

Martin R. Delany

COMPARATIVE ELEMENTS OF CIVILIZATION

Extract from *Principia of Ethnology: The Origins of Races and Color* (1879), pp. 91–93.

IT HAS BEEN SHOWN in a chapter on color that the white and black the pure European and pure African races, the most distinct and unlike each other in general external physical characteristics, are of equal vitality and equally enduring; absorbing and reproducing themselves as races, with all of their native external physical properties of complexion and hair.

That it may be indelibly fixed on every mind, we place on record the fact, that the races as such, especially white and black, are indestructible; that *miscegenation* as popularly understood – the running out of two races, or several, into a *new race* – cannot take place. A cross only produces one of a mixed race, and a continual cross from a half blood on either side will run into the pure original race, either white or black; the fourth cross on one side from the half-blood perfecting a whole blood. A general intermarriage of any two distinct races would eventually result simply in the destruction, the extinction of the less numerous of the two; that race which preponderates entirely absorbing the other.

The three original races in complexion and texture of hair are sterling; pure white, pure yellow, and pure black, with straight hair, and woolly hair; the two first being straight, and the other woolly. But it will be observed in the classes of mixed races, there is every variety of complexion and texture of hair. We have thus endeavored to be precise on a subject of such grave import to social science.

If indeed it were true, that what is implied by miscegenation could take place – the destruction of all or any of the three original rules by the formation of a new race to take the place of either or all – then, indeed, would the works of God be set at naught, his designs and purposes thwarted, and his wisdom confounded by the crafty schemes of poor, mortal, feeble man. Nay, verily, as long as earth endures, so long shall the original races in their purity, as designed by God, the Creator of all things, continue the three sterling races – yellow, black and white – naming them in the order given in Genesis of Shem, Ham and Japheth.

The sterling races, when crossed, can reproduce themselves into their original purity, as before stated. The offspring of any two of the sterling races becomes a mixed race. That mixed race is an abnormal race. Either of the two sterling races which produced the abnormal race may become the resolvent race. That is, when the offspring of a mixed or abnormal race marries to a person of sterling race, black or white, their offspring is a quadroon; and if that quadroon intermarries on the same side, and the intermarriage so continue to the fourth cross on the same side, the offspring of this fourth intermarriage, is an octaroon (whether black or white), and therefore becomes a pure blood. The race continuing the cross to its purity is the resolvent race, and each offspring of the cross till the fourth, is an abnormal race, when the fourth becomes sterling or pure blooded. Hence, to speak of a mixed race as being changed by a resolvent process, simply means that the change is being made by one race alone, which must result in normal purity of either black or white, as the case may be.

Study probes

1   Compare Delany's position on 'race' mixing to that of Knox.
2   How similar are his 'three original "races" ' to Gobineau's 'three great types of mankind'?
3   According to Delany, why is 'the mixed race' the 'abnormal' 'race'?
4   How does the author define the 'resolvent process' and how is this achieved?

Chapter 6

Melville Herskovits

THE AMALGAM HE REPRESENTS AND HIS SIGNIFICANCE FOR THE STUDY OF RACE

Extract from *The American Negro: A Study in Racial Crossing* (1928). New York: Alfred A. Knopf, pp. 3–4 and 74–76.

THE PHENOMENON OF RACE CROSSING seems to hold endless fascination for students of population, of race, of genetics – indeed, for students of all phases of human development. A maxim which is never challenged in fact – since the fact is self-evident – is that two human groups never meet but they mingle their blood. It is this fact that makes the position of the American Negro peculiarly valuable for biology. Because the Negroes were slaves, the law of the masters was paramount; and the masters, as in all slave lands, took the slave women for themselves. But the offspring of a slave was also a slave, and so the mixed-bloods were regarded as "Negroes," while the White stock remained largely free from the introduction of Negro blood.

Furthermore, there were American Indian peoples throughout the Southeast in the early days, and with these the Negroes mingled to a degree that Whites usually fail to recognize, though to a Negro knowledge of Indian ancestry is a matter of pride. This mingling also took place in the West Indian Islands, whence came many of those who later formed part of the American Negro community. Thus to the Negro-White mixture a third element was added, so that in the American Negro of today we find represented the three principal racial stocks of the world: Negro ancestry from Africa, Caucasian from northern and western Europe, and Mongoloid (American Indian) from southeastern North America and the Caribbean Islands.

Obviously we have here an approximation to laboratory conditions for studying the results of human mixture, for we are dealing not only with a crossing of two races, but with a mingling of the three principal racial stocks! How has this crossing affected the bodily form of the Negroes? Are they Africans? Have the Negroid traits predominated? Or have the component ancestral traits mingled in the physical form of these people? To what extent, indeed, are these ancestral elements present in the contemporary American Negro population? For this is the first problem we must attack. In stating that this African population has undergone extensive crossing with other racial groups during its residence in the United States I should make clear that I am advancing a postulate which is far from universally accepted. . . . Certainly the data represented in this study do not seem to justify its utilization as an index of racial purity. And yet has variability no significance for the study of race? The answer, I take it, must be sought in a consideration of the populations in which low variability is found. The American Negroes show low variability. So do the Tennessee mountaineers. So do the Bastaards, and the old White Americans measured by Dr. Hrdlička. Yet a chance sample of White Americans, such as was measured in the army, or by Professor Todd in his dissecting-room population, does not show it. The answer to be gained from a consideration of these populations appeals to me as fundamental for our concept of the term "race." We are forced to conclude, I believe, that the problem which presents itself is not to be thought of in terms of the races to which a given population may or may not belong; nor is the fundamental point the extent to which this population is mixed or pure, with regard to a particular race or races. On the contrary, we should determine the extent to which the population being studied may be considered as homogeneous or heterogeneous in type (type here meaning a large number of physical characteristics); we should discover the historical connections that have made it what it is; and we should analyze the manner in which it has developed, if we can do so by study of the parental types from which it has sprung. In the past, it seems to me, anthropologists have been too prone to place a population more or less arbitrarily according to its average in one or two or three traits (usually one, and that one the form of the head, or cephalic index) and, on the basis of the result, to say that it belongs to such and such a race, unless outstandingly obvious characteristics which could not be disregarded stood in the way. So arbitrary a method of placing populations in racial categories seems to me to be obviously unsound when one considers the amount of mixture which all contemporary peoples represent. Of course, one may broadly catalog a population as belonging to one of the major human groups – as White, as Negroid, or as Mongoloid. But this is usually a more or less self-evident classification.

The American Negroes are, after all, a homogeneous population. They are also a greatly mixed group. How may one reconcile these two statements? It is not so difficult when one really considers the proposition from all angles. For is it not true that all human groups represent large amounts of mixture? This brings us back to the theory of race. Students have wondered at the number of varieties of human types, and have been unable to account for them. They have also been at a loss to account for the degree to which all the so-called "races" of man seem to shade from one type into another; with never the sharp lines of demarcation that are found when we divide one biological species from another.

Study probes

1   According to Herskovits, what are the three principal 'racial' stocks 'represented' in the American Negro?
2   On the basis of the data gathered for his study, what conclusions does he draw about the concept of 'race'?
3   Why is he critical of conventional 'racial' classification modes?
4   How do his views support or challenge those of his Victorian counterparts, which are included in this Reader?

Chapter 7

Edward Byron Reuter

THE HYBRID AS A SOCIOLOGICAL TYPE

Extract from *Race Mixture: Studies in Intermarriage and Miscegenation* (1931). New York: McGraw-Hill Education, pp. 183–185.

THERE ARE FEW QUESTIONS OF BEHAVIOR more heavily freighted with emotional content than that of racial amalgamation. It touches the two points at which Western peoples most frequently run amuck: the violation of womanhood and the integrity of the social group. The attitudes at each point are so completely inbedded in the underlying *mores* as all but to preclude discussion of related topics. Also, there are many persons who harbor an uneasy fear that candid discussion of racial intermixture would bring into the light facts not wholly flattering to a revered ancestry. There are others who regard any objective treatment as an attempt to challenge the validity of beliefs essential to the stability of the existing racial order. To certain persons of delicate sensibilities the idea is personally distasteful; they are physically nauseated by the imagery of the intimacy involved.

By simple rationalization of these emotional attitudes, men derive opinions concerning the phenomenon that stirs their tribal fears. They see in the amalgamation of races a violation of the divine purpose manifest in the fact of racial dissimilarity; they see the decline of civilization and the recrudescence of barbarism through the contamination of the Nordic stock; they see the downfall of nations as a result of the dilution of the political genius of peoples; or they foretell some other type of major disaster according as the individual run of attention determines the specific form of the rationalization. To forestall a train of anticipated evils, men resort to external control in its varied forms: the state denies to mixed marriages the protection of organized society; the Church withholds her divine sanction; public sentiment ostracizes the participants; and unregulated mobs discipline persons violating the racial tabus of the group.

Yet, regardless of the moral indignation aroused and of its expression in ill-considered legislation and in acts of personal violence, the process of racial fusion goes on wherever individuals of divergent racial ancestry come into personal contact. The revulsion of feeling incident to abstract consideration of an aesthetically offensive relationship disappears when personal contacts and association develop an appreciation of personality.

While we may not assert that the fusion of races has always aroused the disapproval of the group, we may assert the universality of the process itself. The skeletal remains of fossil man leave no doubt that the blending of divergent stocks was in process some millennia before the historic era. Examination of the various existent backward culture peoples shows an endless mixing of stocks and blending of cultures. Knowledge of historic peoples of both the ancient and the modern world reveals invasion and conquest, the fusion of cultures, and the amalgamation of the conquered with their conquerors as characteristic elements in the formation of states. So long continued has been this crossing and recrossing and so diverse have been the ethnic elements fusing to form the present day European peoples, that the continent can show scarcely a trace of racial purity remaining. Every modern marriage continues the process of hybridization of nearly or remotely related racial types: virtually every child is the hybrid offspring of a hybrid ancestry.

The hybridization of stocks, continuous in the phenomena of marriage in the ethnic mosaic of modern nationalities, gives rise to offspring not differing in any outstanding way that would interfere with mobility and social contacts in a cosmopolitan society: each hybridized individual is a unit with a unique combination of physical and probably of mental traits but sufficiently within the group range of variation to live an individual and unmolested life. This intermixture has no sociological consequences and interests the social theorist only to the extent that it facilitates cultural contacts and contributes to the spread, acceptance, and fusion of culture heritages.

Study probes

1   At the time he was writing, what explanations does Reuter provide for the perceived controversial nature of 'mixed race' debates?
2   To what extent is this early twentieth-century opposition to 'mixed race' rooted in earlier Victorian 'racial' ideologies?
3   What is the basis of his claim that 'every child is the hybrid offspring of a hybrid offspring'?

Chapter 8

Cedric Dover

GOD'S OWN CHILLUN

Extract from *Half-Caste* (1937). London: Secker and Warburg, pp. 203–211.

FOR OUR PURPOSE, it will suffice if we visualise the American popula-tion as a rather warm ice-cream brick, varying white in colour, but with a broad band of melting chocolate, a diluted strip of 'red', a streak of yellow, all beginning to run together.

The red layer was at one time considerable, for it is estimated that in the sixteenth century there were more than a million Indians in North America. To-day there are 110,000 much hybridised Indians in Canada and 332,000 pure and mixed breeds, isolated in some two hundred concentration camps politely known as 'reservations', in the United States.

School readers and spectacular films suggest that this decrease is due to extermination, to pogroms and the acquisition of white vices, but they are only partly true. For the Indians have also been assimilated and lost in the white population. The process began with the Jamestown Colony sent out by the Virginia Company, which established itself largely through the romantic marriage in 1613 of John Rolfe with 'Princess' Pocahontas, daughter of the 'Emperor' Powhatan, who ruthlessly ruled the Atlantic seaboard. Certain Virginian families still proudly claim descent from this alliance.

In fact, the hybrids of those early days became the old aristocracy of Amer-ica. For this reason pride in early or noble Indian inheritance continues, and finds familiar expression in the sayings of two great Americans: Charles Curtis, the half-Indian who became Vice-President of the United States, and Will Rogers, the lovable cowboy comedian who never forgot his origins. But, with the subju-gation and decline of the Indian tribes, America has discovered that fresh Indian 'blood' is a eugenic menace. Six states expressly legislate against it, and even in

Virginia an individual who is more than one-sixteenth Indian (the fraction has its humour) is not allowed to marry a white. Evidently coloured genes, like wine, acquire value with age.

The marital traditions established by the early colonists reached their zenith in the old days of the fur trade, when amicable relations between the traders and the aboriginals were cemented by countless intermarriages. Every trader had a squaw or two, and few were content with the disciplines of regular concubinage. As G.F.G. Stanley (7.1) writes:

> When Henry Kelsey returned to Fort York in 1692, accompanied by an Indian woman, he only began among the Hudson's Bay Company's employees the practice which had been customary among the French traders and *coureurs de bois* since the early days of Canadian history. The Hudson's Bay Company at first viewed these unions with displeasure, but eventually favoured them as having a steadying effect upon the men and establishing useful trading connexions with the Indians. Accordingly, during the next century and a half, there were few employees of either fur company who did not contract alliances with the Indian women in the neighbourhood of the Companies' forts.

So large families, and many occasional bastards, were raised, who extended native contacts and the economic hold of their Scotch or French fathers. The process has so disintegrated the indigenous stocks that few pure Indians remain in Canada and the vicinity of the Great Lakes.

The remaining Ojibways of Minnesota, for example, are almost completely mongrelised, and have acquired a sort of hybrid aristocracy, among whom are such related families as the Warrens and the Cadottes. William W. Warren, a direct descendant of a *May flower* pilgrim, wrote a profound history of the Ojibways and was a member of the Minnesota Legislature at the age of twenty-six, while many other Warrens have distinguished themselves in professional work. Some of them are 'quite white', according to A.E. Jenks (6.2), and have found a successful place for themselves in white society, how successful the popularity of a renowned film star partly indicates. A few have bred into the Bongas, an extensive Indian family with Negro connexions.

Similarly, thousands of other Amerindians have jumped the white fence to help in giving 'one hundred per cent' Americans the Mongoloid aspect so frequently observed amongst them. For even 'a dash of Indian blood' appears to go a long way, as pedigree studies show. O.A. Merritt-Hawkes (6.1) has studied five generations of the Danish Leunbach family sprung from a Dane and a French-Carib woman in the late eighteenth century. She found them superior mentally and physically, Indian characteristics being persistent in spite of the small amount of Indian admixture. Six out of twenty-one persons in the pedigree are dominantly Carib in appearance and five are partly so. Cautiously, she therefore concludes that 'the American type may have been influenced by Indian blood much more than has, so far, been recognised.'

The Amerindian crosses that remain unassimilated are also a potent force in the extension of civilisation and adjustment to new culture patterns. An example is furnished by the Ojibway and Cree hybrids studied by R. Ruggles Gates (6.1) in Northern Ontario. They are, according to him,

> a hardy race of hunters and trappers and woodsmen, well adapted to the wild pioneering conditions under which they live; they appear to have the hardiness of the native Indians combined with greater initiative and enterprise than the pure Indian would ever show. Many of those with whom I came into contact led one to a feeling of respect for their personal qualities. They push the fringe of civilisation farther north than it would otherwise extend, and help to people a territory which would otherwise be nearly empty. They have adapted some of the Indian's productions and devices, such as moccasins, snowshoes and papoose cradles; but they at the same time attain a condition of living which the Indian alone could not reach, so they may be said to justify themselves abundantly by their works. The fact that families of every intergrade between pure Indians and pure whites occur together in the same district, although the great majority are clearly intermediate between the two races, does not vitiate the arguments I have used. Rather, it serves to show that an intermediate race may be more progressively adapted to particular conditions than either of the races from which it sprang.

To this tribute G.F.G. Stanley (7.1) adds independent testimony. 'To the half-breeds', he writes, 'the Dominion owes much. They were indispensable at the negotiation of every treaty, and to their influence was due in a large part the peaceful relations which existed between the Indians and the whites in the North-West.' Even the demonstrations which began under the half-breed Captain-General Grant in 1816, and ended with the Second Riel Rebellion at Saskatchewan in 1885, had a vitalising effect on Canadian history, though the execution of Louis Riel led to many years of acute 'racial' feeling between English and French Canadians.

The history of these rebellions, which arose out of the feeling that the whites had come 'pour piller notre pays', is of considerable interest. It emphasises the physical vigour, organising ability, and communal consciousness of the half-breeds, the bonds of unity between those of French and British origin being greater than their differences. They regarded themselves, in fact, as 'The New Nation', and periodically expressed their pride in their mixed heritage. 'It is true', said Louis Riel in his native French, 'that our savage origin is humble, but it is proper that we should honour our mothers as well as our fathers. Why do we concern ourselves so much with the degree of mixture which we possess of European and Indian blood? However little we may have of the one or the other, gratitude and filial love command us to say: "We are Half-Breeds." ' But, as Dr. Stanley writes, 'neither their racial consciousness, nor their primitive economy was strong enough to maintain the separate identity of the half-breed "nation" in the midst of an overwhelming white immigration and a competitive nineteenth century civilisation.' It is an instructive comment.

The other aboriginals of North America, the Esquimaux, scarcely concern us here, as they have made little or no contribution to the supposedly white population of America. Yet it is of interest to note that, contrary to popular opinion, pure Esquimaux are now rare. Around the Behring Sea, for example, they have been thoroughly mixed with the Athabaskan-speaking Indians and also with immigrants from Siberia. In West Greenland, where 94 per cent of the island's population is concentrated, the natives have been heavily impregnated with European genes from the days of the old Norsemen, recent admixture being mostly Danish. K. Birket-Smith (7.1) states that around Disko Bay it is hardly possible to find a pure Esquimau. This extensive hybridisation he regards as valuable, since the mixed breeds are superior to the pure type by reason of their improved physique, greater energy, wider outlook and increased power of adaptation.

The remaining Mongoloids in the United States, the Chinese and the Japanese, only form a thin streak in our ice-cream brick, but have doubtless made a weighty contribution to American physiognomy on the Pacific Coast. In 1852, there were 107,000 Chinese in this area but, following restrictive measures towards the close of the century, the strength of this population declined in 1900 to 89,863 and by 1920 to 61,639, as the result of emigration and assimilation. In 1930, however, it had risen to 74,954, the gain being evidently a natural increase, as is shown by the fact that the American-born Chinese steadily increased from 9,010 to 30,868 between 1900 and 1930.

Japanese immigration is of more recent origin. In 1890, there were only 2,039 Japanese in the United States but, in spite of the 'Gentleman's Agreement' between America and Japan and rigid exclusion since 1924, the Japanese population rose to 138,834 in 1930, the majority being concentrated in California, where it owns more than 12 per cent of the arable land and monopolises the crops in certain districts. This increase is also largely natural, the number of American-born rising, as the result of a less discrepant sex ratio than the Chinese, from 269 in 1900 to 68,357 in 1930.

The trend of these two groups is remarkable, when it is considered that in 1910 there were fourteen males to one female among the Chinese, and seven males to one female among the Japanese. Even in 1930, the sex ratio showed a male excess of 4:1 and almost 2:1 among the Chinese and Japanese respectively, there being a definite tendency, too, among American-born Chinese girls to remain unmarried because of disapproval of their Western ways and their inability to adjust themselves to the status of a Chinese wife. These ratios gain emphasis from the fact that up to 1900 the Chinese and Japanese groups were 90 per cent male – and it is difficult to imagine any appreciable proportion of these men living in states of prolonged celibacy or homosexuality. The inevitable result is not only apparent in the Mongoloid aspect of many whites from the Coastal Range, but also in differences in the appearance and physique of native and American-born Orientals.

There is, of course, legislation against white and Asiatic mixture, for Americans have a touching faith in the efficacy of the law. But in many ways it provokes unsanctioned mixture. The Chinaman finds it difficult to obtain a

Chinese wife in America, he may not bring one from China, and he cannot marry a white woman. It is an attempt at mass castration which succeeds only in making the Chinese find 'love' where they may. Moreover, many Chinese-Americans have alien wives in China whom they periodically visit and fertilise. And the fruits of these reunions have the right to enter America as American citizens, though their mothers may not.

In this way, a small but constant stream of recent immigrants from China is maintained, and it is predominantly male. The Japanese also have ways of circumventing the immigration laws, and a particular advantage in being able to come from Hawaii as American citizens. Restrictive measures therefore favour the growth of Oriental populations as such, and the more they grow the more they will eventually dilute the general population. Cultural Americanisation, which has proceeded rapidly in recent years, ensures the process. The situation is full of subtle irony, but Senators and patriots are apparently unable to appreciate it.

And there are one and a half million Mexicans, and more than fifty thousand Hawaiians and Filipinos and East Indians and Eurasians and 'Other Coloured' too, besides the prospect of further seepage from a colonial empire with a total population of at least thirty millions.

Above all there are the so-called Negroes, the chocolate band in our ice-cream brick. They came before the *Mayflower*, almost while the Jamestown colonists were still intriguing with Powhatan and indulging themselves with the amiable Werowocomoco maidens. 'About the last of August', wrote John Rolfe when he was back among his tobacco crops in 1619, 'came in a Dutch man of warre that sold us twenty Negars.' And there was already a coloured woman, Angela, in the colony at that time (J.T. Adams, 7.1). These 'Negars' were the first drops of a black inflow that has run like a dominant river through the whole course of American history, diluting whites and reds, getting diluted itself.

Within two hundred years of that first black cargo, the Negroes represented not less than 25 per cent of the total American population, but the ratio dropped, though a steady growth rate was maintained, after the wave of immigration which started in 1820. To-day there are twelve million acknowledged Negroes in the United States, of whom 78 per cent have white or Indian 'blood' in them, according to M.J. Herskovits (6.1) and others, and this estimate is generally believed to be understated. This Afroamerican mass constitutes almost 12 per cent of the total white population, and is still largely concentrated in the South, where it forms about a third of the general population, more in some individual States, such as South Carolina. But it is moving northwards. Nearly two millions went in response to industrial needs created since 1910. In New York alone there is the best part of half a million Negroes, and Harlem has become the greatest Negro city in the world.

And these Afroamericans represent a virile, fertile, growing population, with stupendous achievements to its credit in less than a century of emancipation. Almost entirely illiterate seventy years ago, they are now almost entirely literate.

Study probes

1   In historical detail, describe Dover's depiction of the American population as 'a rather warm ice-cream brick'.
2   Which geographical examples does he provide to explain the 'dilution' of 'the red strip'?
3   In his discussion of the 'streak of yellow' and the transformation of the Chinese and Japanese population on the Pacific Coast, what role does gender play?
4   Regarding the so-called inferiority or superiority of 'mixed race' populations, which argument does Dover endorse?

Chapter 9

Everett V. Stonequist

THE RACIAL HYBRID

Extract from *The Marginal Man: A Study in Personality and Culture Conflict* (1937). New York: Russell and Russell, pp. 10–11 and 49–53.

THE MOST OBVIOUS TYPE of marginal man is the person of mixed racial ancestry. His very biological origin places him between the two races. Generally he has distinctive physical traits which mark him off from both parent races. He also frequently possesses some characteristics of manner, thought and speech which are derived from both lines of his ancestry. Because of these peculiarities the mixed blood presents a special problem for the community: what is to be his place in the social organization? As he matures he too will become aware of his problematic and anomalous social position. He will become the target of whatever hostile sentiments exist between the parent races. Thus his problem of adjustment will be made more acute. Since the contact of races in the modern age has rarely been smooth and harmonious, there is something universal in the problem of racial hybrids. While emphasizing this fact it would be misleading, nevertheless, not to recognize the important differences which occur between one situation and another.

It should be pointed out in this connection that race mixture is not a new phenomenon. Indeed, from a strictly scientific point of view pure races do not exist, for the whole history of man has been characterized by the crossing and recrossing of races. In the early phases of intermixture the mixed-blood children are conspicuous merely because they differ from the parents. Theirs is a problem of incomplete social assimilation as well as of incomplete biological amalgamation. As the processes of assimilation and amalgamation continue the status of the mixed bloods changes. They gradually become the preponderant or "normal" type and then are no longer considered hybrids but a new "race." In this way complete racial intermixture in any given region solves the problem which arises from partial intermixture.

It is apparent, therefore, that the social and psychological traits of mixed bloods depend upon many factors. Among these should be mentioned the manner in which the hybrids have arisen, whether as the result of sanctioned marriages or irregular unions; the extent to which they are a numerical and social minority; their cultural role; and the general social attitudes which they have encountered from one or both of the parent races. During the course of Western expansion Southern European nations have developed relatively mild race prejudices and have intermarried freely with coloured peoples, whereas Anglo-Saxon and Teutonic nations have been noteworthy for their racial aloofness. Probably this contrast is not rooted in biological nature but is a product of divergent historical conditions. In any case it greatly influences the social position and character of racial hybrids.

To bring out what is typical and what is variable in the social psychology of the mixed blood, we shall now consider some concrete examples. In view of the limitations of space such an analysis must be confined to a relatively few cases. These cases have been selected because they illustrate a very wide range of condition, location, history and race. They consist of the following mixed-blood groups: the Eurasians or Anglo-Indians of India, the Cape Coloured of South Africa, the Mulattoes of the United States, the Coloured people of Jamaica, the Indo-Europeans of Java, the Part Hawaiians, and the *Métis* of Brazil.

[. . .]

Concluding summary and analysis

Each of the seven mixed-blood situations discussed in this chapter has its distinctive characteristics. The Anglo-Indians (Eurasians) are virtually in an outcast position, being ostracized by both English and Indians. The Cape Coloured are socially almost as isolated but receive legal equality and political recognition from the whites. The mulattoes of the United States are rejected by the whites but accepted as leaders by the blacks. The Jamaican coloured have a relatively independent position as a middle-class group and are accommodated but not assimilated to both whites and blacks. The Indo-Europeans of Java, more nearly assimilated by the Dutch in the past, are now becoming increasingly restive, group conscious and uncertain of their future. The part Hawaiians, although identified with a dual system of racial equality and racial inequality, are becoming the nucleus of a new and mixed race of "Hawaiians" whose culture will be largely American. The *métis* of Brazil are so far assimilated that they with the whites constitute the controlling class.

Each of these situations has its special influence upon the character and personality of the mixed bloods. Some of these effects have been indicated above. Here it may be sufficient to add that in those situations where race feeling is most intense (such as India, South Africa and the United States) one is likely to hear that the mixed blood is an undesirable type, having (usually thought to "inherit") the weaknesses of both parent races. In the other four situations, more favourable, even laudatory, statements are common, the mixed blood occasionally being viewed as superior to both parent races. Is it possible that the theories about the character of mixed bloods are merely "rationalizations" of the existing practices and prejudices of the particular situation?

There are important resemblances among the various mixed bloods. All of these cases represent some cultural mixture as well as racial mixture. The tendency, however, is powerfully in the direction of the dominant culture, and away from the subordinate culture. The mixed blood's first impulse is to identify himself with the race which is considered superior. Failing this he may develop a negative or ambivalent attitude, perhaps a desire for differentiation in some form. This is evident in the case of the United States, and a beginning is visible in Java. Because of his anomalous position – not fully belonging to either parent race – he becomes more than ordinarily conscious of himself and conscious of his ancestry. There is an increase in sensitiveness. This may be an advantage or a disadvantage, depending upon the existing social definitions and opportunities. His uncertain social position intensifies his concern about status. His anxiety to solve his personal problem forces him to take an interest in the racial problem as a whole. Consequently he has an important part in defining and eventually changing the general pattern of race relations. As his numbers increase he may become allied with one of the parent races, or form a new racial type. Whatever fusion of culture occurs is likely to centre about the mixed-blood group, especially in the early stages of racial contact. Thus the status and role of a particular mixed-blood group can be taken as an index of the larger race problem; and in turn the development of the mixed-blood class reacts back upon the general racial situation modifying it to a significant, sometimes determining, extent.

In general, mixed bloods are considered to be intermediate in physical and cultural traits and to have intermediary roles. This generalization requires some qualification. As regards physical and cultural traits there is a tendency to move toward the dominant group. If not too strongly opposed this tendency may in time and under certain conditions create a gulf between the mixed bloods and the subordinate race. This is evident in India, South Africa, and to a degree in Brazil. Pertinent in this respect is the fact that as regards India and the Cape Coloured, intermixture with the darker race has greatly decreased. In these as well as in other cases the culture of the dominant race continues to spread without the necessity of blood intermixture. Where slavery and enforced migration occur, the culture of the dominant group is imposed upon the subject group. This may go so far as to destroy the culture of the enslaved group.

The role of intermediary is not uniform or consistent. The Anglo-Indian once had this role but has lost it. It is not now greatly in evidence in the case of the Cape Coloured, but this may change in the future. Furthermore, the intermediary role varies: it may be by one which favours complete assimilation to the dominant culture, or it may result in a process of differentiation and the cultural revival of the subordinate race. In the latter case there is only limited assimilation. The phenomenon of nascent nationalism must be reckoned with in extensive areas of the world.

The processes of racial amalgamation and cultural assimilation are favoured or hindered by the following important conditions: (1) a deficiency of women in the dominant race encourages intermixture. The mixed bloods are then apt to be included in the paternal group. (2) Economic relations which imply reciprocity and equality – *i.e.*, trade relations -- are conducive to intermarriage. Where there is severe economic competition between divergent races, however, intense hatreds occur. Such antagonisms may lead to the segregation, the expulsion, or even the extermination of the weaker group. They reduce racial fusion. Sometimes conditions of extreme racial inequality favour interbreeding. This is true of plantations that employ slave labour. When in addition there is an excess of men in the slave-holding group, the hybrids are also assimilated more rapidly. (3) Religious organizations may encourage conversion and assimilation. This is true of the Catholic and Mohammedan religions. Hinduism, on the other hand, forbids intermarriage. (4) The relative size of each race in contact influences the rate of intermixture and assimilation. If the subordinate group is small it may be viewed with equanimity or even with pathos. On the other hand, if it is relatively large, as in Jamaica, expediency may compel a policy of tolerance and good will on the part of the dominant but smaller group. (5) Political relations which have been based upon conflict and conquest are apt to leave a heritage of hate and fear, thus slowing down the process of fusion; while peaceful co-operation, alliances, etc., work in the contrary direction. (6) The degree of racial and cultural difference is important. Other things being equal, large differences retard the growth of sympathy and understanding. (7) Relatively free sex and marriage *mores* speed up the process of assimilation. Thus it is easier for continental Europeans than for Anglo-Saxons to adopt the practice of open concubinage with native women. (8) Attitudes conditioned in one situation are carried over into another situation. The Portuguese illustrate favourable conditioning; the English and Americans unfavourable conditioning. (9) Where several races are involved, codes of segregation are difficult to establish so that assimilation is facilitated (Brazil, Hawaii). (10) The stage of race contact is important. The first contacts, especially of the frontier and slave type, speed up the process of mixture. If this does not end the problem, the process may slow down as a more settled and stable society is organized. At this point acculturation may proceed rapidly without racial amalgamation. Ultimately it is to be expected that cultural assimilation will result in racial amalgamation, unless persistent conflict reorganizes the racial groups upon another basis. However, the modern period of race mixture has hardly proceeded far enough for conclusions to be drawn about this latest stage in the interaction of races.

Study probes

1   How does Stonequist define a 'person of mixed racial ancestry'?
2   What particular 'problems' does 'the mixed blood' face?
3   According to the author, why do 'pure races not exist'?
4   What conclusions has the author reached about the similar and different 'characteristics of the seven 'mixed-blood situations' he discusses?
5   Outline the ten 'conditions' which either limit or facilitate 'racial amalgamation and cultural assimilation'.

Chapter 10

Frank Füredi

CROSSING THE BOUNDARY: THE MARGINAL MAN

Extract from *The Silent War: Imperialism and the Changing Perception of Race* (1998). London: Pluto Press and New Brunswick: Rutgers University Press, pp. 138–139, 144–145 and 149–152.

THE AMERICAN SOCIOLOGIST Everett Stonequist, author of *The Marginal Man: A Study in Personality and Culture Conflict*, was clearly influenced by these traditions. Stonequist was a student of R.E. Park, the leading representative of the Chicago School of Sociology. It was Park, drawing on the preoccupation of the European sociological tradition with the problem of order, who prevailed on Stonequist to embark on his thesis. Park was strongly influenced by the German sociologist George Simmel's ideas about the stranger, the early prototype for the Marginal Man.

There were other influences on Stonequist. In the Preface to *The Marginal Man*, he acknowledged the influence of the Oxford academic and leading imperial publicist Sir Alfred Zimmern on his writing. But more pertinent for this discussion was Stonequist's debt to Lord Lugard. Stonequist wrote in his Preface that his interest in his subject matter 'began with a lecture given by Lord Lugard at the Geneva School of International Studies in 1925 describing the effect of European ideas and practices upon native life in Africa'. He noted in passing that he was particularly interested in Lugard's comments 'upon the detribalised'. This should come as no surprise: *The Marginal Man* can be read as sophisticated sociological defence of indirect rule. Like Lugard, Stonequist considered the detribalised as a race apart. The Marginal Man suffered from 'personal maladjustment' and possessed a victim mentality.

[. . .]

Sociological contributions

It is worth noting in passing, that despite its conservative implications, many liberal social scientists felt at home with Lugard's approach. American cultural anthropology and the growth of relativism in the 1930s converged on crucial points with the policy of indirect rule. The preservation of tradition was consistent with the positive promotion of cultural differences.

[. . .]

A more coherent development of this subject of maladjustment took place in the United States where sociologists were directly confronted with the problems of immigration and of race relations. The subject of assimilating immigrants from different cultures and of integrating the black population into the mainstream of American society stimulated a focus on the in-between individual. Many sociologists concentrated on the mulatto, the American deracialised equivalent of the detribalised African. Edward Byron Reuter's 1918 study *The Mulatto in the United States*, expressed concern that this group was tending towards agitation. . . . During the interwar period the discourse cast in racial terms gradually gave way to more sociological ones.

The Chicago sociologist, Robert Park, played a major role in reorienting this discussion from its early biological emphasis on racial mixing to a more sociological focus. Park's theory of the Marginal Man was the American equivalent of the detribalised native of the British anthropological tradition. Although Park was unusually sympathetic to his subject matter, he evoked the tragic dimension of the marginal way of life. There is a kind of ambivalence, which sees the 'mulatto' as a leader of the black population as well as an individual that could never be at ease with him- or herself. . . . Park's disposition towards psychologising led him to formulate a personality type that was not the product of this or that experience but of all forms of culture conflict.

Consequently, with Park, the concept of the Marginal Man transcended the American situation. It was a generic concept that could be deployed to examine the dynamic of maladjustment in other contexts. Indeed, Park was concerned to emphasise that marginality was not reducible to racial mixing but encompassed a wider cultural and indeed moral dimension. . . . Park's sociology of race relations provided a synthesis of the hitherto fragmented accounts of culture contact, maladjustment, race consciousness and the moral disintegration of the uprooted. Park himself was careful not to condemn the Marginal Man. The 'moral turmoil' of this mind is posed in relatively neutral terms. However, the symptoms that he identified, such as 'spiritual instability', 'intensified self-consciousness' and 'restlessness' were presented by others as a moral condemnation.

[. . .]

Holding the line

The discourse on the in-between person was at once a discussion of maintaining existing social, cultural and racial boundaries. By his very existence the Marginal Man was seen to put into question the durability of these boundaries.

By questioning these boundaries, the Marginal Man or the detribalised native threatened to encroach on the status of the European. That is why there was such a clearly articulated tendency to create a moral distance between the Marginal Man and the European. The insistence on moral difference represented an attempt to uphold a line and repulse those who claimed equality. Whatever they were, the Marginal Man and the detribalised native were not European. They might be in-between, but they were not conceptualised as a bridge between races.

[. . .]

A condemnation of miscegenation was almost always implicit in the literature on the maladjusted Marginal Man. The discourse continually fluctuated between arguments that stressed the racial and those that focused on the moral. According to academic specialists, the 'hybrid' that was produced was not just a racial but also a cultural hybrid. However, most studies either implicitly or explicitly assumed that it was the effect of racial mixing that was most far-reaching.

[. . .]

Academic writers qualified their condemnation of race mixing with the caveat that the problem was not so much with the hybrid as with the circumstances which isolated such people from both the dominant and subordinate classes. Malinowski contended that the 'most dramatic, not to say tragic, configuration of racial relationships occurs' when 'whatever mixture takes place is socially degraded, and where in consequence, a rigid caste system comes into being'. But while Malinowski was sensitive to the way that society could stigmatise the hybrid, he himself had serious doubts about the wisdom of miscegenation. 'It is a questionable blessing when a lower race ousts or absorbs a higher, or when a distinctly inferior mixed race is formed', he concluded. Why? Because a 'mixed race does not rise to the level of the higher parent-stock'. . . . From this perspective, the avoidance of mixing and the strict maintenance of a racial line made the most sense.

[. . .]

In non-academic accounts the moral distancing of the Marginal Man was often strident and deliberately insulting. Hybridity was portrayed in unflattering terms and conveyed the warning: 'Do not presume to be like the white man.' Articles dealt at length on the alleged tendency of hybrids to imitate the European. Such pretensions were invariably repulsed and the reader was reminded that the products of race mixing bore the stamp of moral inferiority. The American writer Gertrude Marvin Williams observed that 'the most pathetic of India's minority groups are the mixed bloods'. . . . It was the idea that those of mixed race and the English could share the same 'home' that Williams found particularly preposterous. Such an aspiration was unacceptable to the interwar racial imagination.

During the interwar period there was little criticism of the moral repulsion of the Marginal Man. White fears regarding race mixing were treated as natural and unworthy of critical reflections. This sentiment continued well into the 1940s.

[. . .]

One of the rare attempts to engage the moral condemnation of the Marginal Man was by the American writer Lewis C. Copeland. Copeland characterised 'moral distinctions' in race relations as the 'final rationalization of racial contrasts'. His analysis stressed the importance of moral distancing and moral repulsion against mixing in American racial thinking. He took the view that racial beliefs helped create 'two social orders and moral universes'. This outlook was rooted in white racial fears: 'There is a widespread fear of the invasion of the white social order by the black man.' Fear of social invasion was illustrated by the tendency of white people to react most to those black people who stood closest to them. . . . Copeland's concept of the 'defamation of the mulatto' clearly expresses the manner in which apparently neutral descriptions of the state of mind of the Marginal Man helped masquerade moral condemnation.

Copeland's insights help place in perspective the race relations discourse in the interwar period. Apprehensions about holding the line are not directly reducible to a desire to protect economic privilege. Such fears also expressed self-doubt and anxieties about the possible exposure of white pretensions. It was almost as if there was an expectation that nothing would be the same if other races came too close and saw the European at 'home'. The fundamental assumption was that the racial line had to be maintained otherwise white prestige would suffer. Thus the racial line existed in both a metaphorical and physical sense: even the existing world order was seen to depend on keeping everything in its place.

Study probes

1   According to Füredi, who influenced Stonequist's work which was published as *The Marginal Man*?
2   Is he critical of Stonequist's thesis?
3   When discussing the vast literature on 'racial' mixing, what does the author mean by 'holding the line'?

Paul Rich

THE 'HALF-CASTE' PATHOLOGY

Extract from *Race and Empire in British Politics*, 2nd ed (1990). Cambridge: Cambridge University Press, pp. 120–121 and 130–135.

W HEN DORIAN GRAY WENT DOWN to London east and under-world in Oscar Wilde's novel, *The Picture of Dorian Gray* (1891), he came across a 'half-caste' dressed in a 'ragged turban and shabby ulster' who 'grinned a hideous greeting'.[1] This Victorian association of mixed-race people with both immorality and a slumland underclass standing outside the main social order of Britain grew in the early twentieth century to become a fairly common stereo-type by the inter-war years, reflecting a growing consciousness of black–white race relations within the metropolitan society itself. In the nineteenth century, as has been seen, the issue of race and colour was perceived as mainly an imperial one, though from the 1880s onwards there grew up in a number of British towns and cities identifiable black communities of seamen, traders and students, together with a small group of entertainers and musicians. In the case of London, a black community had begun to emerge in the eighteenth century, though during the nineteenth century the numbers of blacks declined in the wake of the abolition of slavery and only started to rise again with the settlement of numbers of blacks and Asians in the 1880s and 1890s. Other black communities in Liverpool and Cardiff also grew up at this time.[2]

The presence of blacks in Britain raised the question of inter-racial sexual liaisons in a new and politically acute form. The black middle class, such as Henry Sylvester Williams and Harold Moody, were to some extent able to avoid extreme racial prejudice by marrying white women and attaining a degree of social respectability. The same, however, could not be said for black seamen settling in seaport towns such as Bristol, Liverpool, South Shields and London's dockland, where there were growing racial tensions with the indigenous white working-class population. These finally spilled over into anti-black riots in Liverpool and Cardiff in 1919.[3] During the First World War significant numbers of black seamen from colonial territories in West Africa, the Caribbean and the Middle East were engaged on British ships and at the war's end found themselves out of work as the shipping industry contracted and the Seamen's and Firemen's Union (later to form, with the Cooks' and Stewards' Union, the National Union of Seamen in the 1920s) campaigned to keep jobs on ships for white crewmen only.[4] Flung out into the slumland culture of the port towns, the black seamen focused upon themselves considerable racial hostility as they became linked in the public mind with growing crime rates and prostitution when they cohabited with white women and produced 'half-caste' children.

The issue came to a head during the months of April, May and June of 1919, when there were widespread inter-racial attacks in London, Cardiff, Liverpool and South Shields, resulting in several casualties and a few deaths. In Cable Street, Stepney, there was violent fighting and shots fired on 16 April, while in the latter half of May black seamen in Liverpool, of whom 500–600 were reported as unemployed and anxious to be repatriated, were subject to attacks from white gangs. On 8 June, mobs of between 2,000 and 10,000 roamed the streets of Liverpool attacking blacks at random and a house occupied by blacks was set on fire. With covert support from the local police, who perceived the blacks, in the words of one police officer, as 'only big children who when they get money like to make a show', the white crowds had all the trappings of lynch mobs and were often goaded on by demobbed servicemen. In Cardiff attacks on black houses in Bute Town, referred to by *The Times* as 'nigger town', were partly provoked by ex-soldiers without jobs and there were reports of 'colonial soldiers' at the head of the mobs. There was thus a probable element of orchestration behind the white racial attacks and the riots have been described as divisive in that they fomented a racial hostility which cut through an otherwise common working-class consciousness.[5] At a time when there was widespread industrial unrest, blacks in Britain emerged after the riots as a unique and distinct 'problem'.[6]

[. . .]

'Half-caste' children and pressure for immigration control

While the main focus in the 1920s was on the presence of black seamen in the ports and their liaisons with white women, by the 1930s this had widened to the issue of mixed-race or 'half-caste' children who were the offspring of these sexual relationships. By 1929 the *Daily Herald* was already reporting that 'hundreds of half-caste children with vicious tendencies' were 'growing up in Cardiff as the result of black men mating with white women' while 'numerous dockland cafés run by coloured men of a debased and degenerate type are rendezvous for immoral purposes'.[7] The emergence of 'half-caste' children as a social problem resulted in social workers being brought into the debate and this led to a growing interest by the Liverpool University Settlement. This body had opened in 1908 in Nile Street, Liverpool, as part of the philanthropic concern of university social reformers in the tradition of Toynbee Hall in London's East End.[8] The Liverpool settlement served as an important centre for different interests in the city to come together to discuss current social issues. In December 1927, a meeting was organised by the University School of Social Science to discuss the question of the welfare of 'half-caste' children in the city and representatives of both the university, the settlement and the police were present.[9] Significantly, the main address came from the assistant to Professor H.J. Fleure at Aberystwyth, Miss R.M. Fleming, who had conducted research on 'half-castes' in Britain following pressure by the Eugenics Education Society on the Colonial Office for a survey of 'half-castes', in the early 1920s. Fleming had been schooled in an atmosphere where 'racial' and cultural traits tended to be confused and there was an implication within her research that separate races inherited certain cultural characteristics, though not necessarily within any rigid racial hierarchy.[10] At the meeting she spoke of the 'adverse factors' in 'half-caste' children's heredity 'which often involve not only disharmony of physical traits but disharmony of mental characteristics'. This resulted, she claimed, in 'great strain', for the children 'had no homes and were unable to obtain employment in any decent occupation'. Moreover, she concluded, a 'very high proportion of such children suffered from tuberculosis or similar diseases'.[11]

The meeting led to an executive committee being formed, chaired by Professor Roxby of the School of Geography in Liverpool, which launched an appeal for £2,000 to provide a fund both for alleviating the conditions of the children concerned and to pay the salary of a 'well-qualified social worker' to 'devote all her time to the finding of possible solutions to the problem'.[12] In the event, only £652 was collected by the following May in order to finance an investigation (despite a promise of $25,000 from the Rockefeller Memorial Fund).[13] Nevertheless, the executive committee, which was now the nucleus of the Liverpool Association for the Welfare of Half-Caste Children, decided to appoint a probation officer at Stoke-on-Trent (and former student of the Liverpool University School of Social Science), Miss M.E. Fletcher, to conduct the survey from October of 1928.

The inadequate resources and amateur approach of the investigator led to a controversial report being produced in 1930 entitled *Report on an Investigation into the Colour Problem in Liverpool and Other Ports*. Though praised by Professor Roxby as 'the most thorough investigation of this particular problem that has so far been made',[14] the report reinforced the initial approach of R.M. Fleming in 1927 when it perceived the presence of 'half-caste' children in Liverpool and other ports as an intrinsic moral problem conducive to the perpetuation of prostitution and a slumland culture. It also strengthened the campaign by the police and the National Union of Seamen against the presence of black 'alien seamen' in British ports since the early 1920s. The claims of many seamen to British nationality could in many cases, the report concluded, 'hardly be substantiated', for many were in fact 'Liberians or at the most, British protected persons'. Furthermore, there were 'strong reasons' for believing that the passports which were issued were done so 'by native clerks on the West Coast of Africa to all coloured seamen who apply, without their claim being questioned'.[15] The report thus recommended the replacement of black firemen by white firemen on British ships, despite recognising the 'probable political reactions' which would result from this. It also urged that black seamen from West Africa should 'sign on' there so that they would have to make a 'round trip' since they would not be paid in Britain, while 'greater discrimination' should be exercised in the issuing of British passports'.[16] Not surprisingly, the report received strong support from the National Union of Seamen.[17]

Another important feature of the report was its portrayal of the social and economic conditions of mixed-race children within hereditarian and eugenical terms. M.E. Fletcher reported an estimated total of some 450 families in Liverpool with such children; with an average number of 3.3 per family she estimated a total of 1,350 coloured children.[18] The health and welfare of these children was judged within a framework heavily influenced by the research of R.M. Fleming, who in 1929 visited Cape Town with the British Association and wrote up her research on mixed-race children in British seaport towns under some influence from the South African model. In an article, 'Human Hybrids', in the *Eugenics Review* she noted the 'higher cultural level' of those Cape Coloureds 'with a larger admixture of white blood' and condoned the Coloured practice of 'passing for white'. In general, though, Fleming opposed any discrimination against mixed-race children:

> They are British citizens, and as such need protection. Whatever action may be taken to prevent such intermixture in the future, if it can be proved to be undesirable, it certainly seems a bad policy of citizenship to penalize half-castes for a fault of birth for which they are in no way responsible.[19]

For the period, this was in some respects a 'liberal' perspective on the issue, despite the fact that it engrained both a middle-class paternalism and a view of 'miscegenation' as a 'fault of birth'. The same perspective lay behind the Fletcher Report, though the evidence collected from schools also indicated little support for a hereditarian pathology behind 'miscegenation':

> Opinions have been expressed from time to time that in the question of health the half caste children suffer in comparison with the white. In so far as school children are concerned, however, no evidence has been found to confirm these statements. Out of eighty teachers replying, sixty three stated that the half caste children were not more prone to infectious disease. In the matter of attendance at school, the half caste children appear to be quite up to standard and are quite as well clothed as the white children in the district, in some cases even better. With regard to intelligence and social aptitude, the majority of the replies received indicated that the half caste children were below average. Opinions had been stated that the Coloured children had marked ability in various branches of handwork, forty nine teachers replied, however, that the half caste children under their care exhibited no particular aptitude for handwork. In the matter of reliability, forty one teachers were of the opinion that the half caste

children were up to the average of the white children, while thirty eight replied that they were below standard. Nothing startling emerges from this enquiry. The half caste children on the whole appear to be below the average, but only slightly so.[20]

The chief influence of the report, nevertheless, lay in its reinforcement of the view that the presence of 'half-castes' in British cities contributed to a process of moral decline. When reporting on the labour prospects of the children, the Fletcher Report indicated a marked unwillingness of employers to engage 'coloured' labour. Of 119 firms written to in Liverpool, only 56 replied and 45 of these gave a negative response.[21] Furthermore, the Committee of the Liverpool Association for the Welfare of Half-Caste Children itself initiated a training scheme for coloured girls, concentrating on five girls attending a class of one hour twice a week. The scheme was eventually abandoned after the girls exhibited little motivation to complete the course and Fletcher concluded that the girls 'easily tire and lack the power of application'.[22] The failure of the scheme was probably one reason behind her conclusion that the presence of coloured families in Britain 'presents a special problem both from a moral and an economic point of view' and that the employment of 'half-caste juveniles', especially girls, should be the subject of an official inquiry.[23]

The report's findings led to an angry response from some of the missions involved with the black population in Liverpool and the League of Coloured Peoples in London also took up the issue. Ernest Adkin of the African and West Indian Mission in Parliament Street, Liverpool, claimed that it would take 'months, or even years to repair the damage the publicity of the report has carried'. Miss Fletcher, he claimed, had 'posed as an interested worker with deep sympathy for these unfortunate people, and their half-caste children, and . . . they trusted her implicitly, many thinking more of her sympathy than of mine. . . . Some of them said that they could never trust a white person again; no matter what his pretensions. I have lost several whose help and sympathy I valued, and many more who came occasionally.[24]

The furore shook both the University Settlement and the Association for the Welfare of Half-Caste Children, which failed in 1931 to secure any government interest in the issue.[25] M.E. Fletcher left Liverpool as a result of the report and the fact that no funds were available in the depression for her appointment as a permanent welfare officer for the Association.[26] The report represented a brief instrusion of eugenics into the 'half-caste' issue in Liverpool, and by the end of 1931 a different approach began with the publication of the first of the social surveys of Merseyside from the University of Liverpool by D. Caradog Jones, which perceived the issue within a much wider framework of immigration generally into the region, including Irish and Jewish immigration as well as that of black and Chinese immigrants. When seen in this wider context, the issue of black immigration into Merseyside was comparatively small, for the communities of Chinese and blacks was estimated at about 500 each. The Jewish population on Merseyside, on the other hand, was estimated at 9,000 while the total net immigration from Ireland between 1927 and 1929 was estimated at about 6,000 a year.[27] Taken as a whole, the immigration into Merseyside was estimated by Caradog Jones to have had strongly beneficial economic effects, for a higher percentage of the immigrant population was in regular work than the indigenous population while there was less overcrowding and poverty amongst them.[28] The survey noted, though, the general problem of 'Anglo-negroid' children in obtaining employment compared to the more successful Anglo-Chinese children.[29] This was not an issue that got taken up in any systematic way on Merseyside itself in the early 1930s after the Fletcher Report, though similar unpublished reports by F.S. Livie-Noble of the London Group on African Affairs on Cardiff and a survey of London and Cardiff in 1932 by Nancy Sharpe, using funds from the Methodist Church, emphasised both the environmental context in which such mixed-race children grew up and defended the right of black seamen to work on British ships and come to live in Britain if they had the necessary national documentation.[30]

Study probes

1   According to Rich, when and how did the British preoccupation with 'race' and colour shift from an imperial to a domestic concern?
2   In earlier twentieth-century Cardiff and Liverpool, why were 'half-caste' children perceived as a social problem?
3   Define eugenics and describe how Fleming and Fletcher used it to explain the alleged moral and social inferiority of 'mixed race' children.

Notes

1   Oscar Wilde, *The Picture of Dorian Gray*, 1st edn 1891 (Harmondsworth, Penguin, 1949), p. 208.
2   James Walvin, *Black and White: the Negro and English Society, 1555–1945* (London, Allen Lane, 1973), pp. 46–73; Peter Fryer, *Staying Power* (London and Sydney, Pluto Press, 1984), pp. 66–88, 191–5, 227–36.
3   In the case of the riots at Cardiff and Barry in 1919, see the *Daily Herald*, 13, 14, 16 and 17 June 1919.
4   For a short discussion on the emergence of the NUS as an effective 'company union' of the British Shipping Federation, see David Byrne. 'The 1930 "Arab riot" in South Shields: a race riot that never was', *Race and Class*, 18, 3 (1977), pp. 263–6 and *passim*.
5   Fryer, *op. cit.*, pp. 298–313, on which much of the above is based.
6   James Walvin, *Passage to Britain* (Harmondsworth, Penguin, 1984), p. 80.
7   *Daily Herald*, 11 January 1929.
8   For a study of charitable effort in Liverpool in which the University Settlement developed, see Margaret Simey, *Charitable Effort in Liverpool in the Nineteenth Century* (Liverpool, Liverpool University Press, 1951); and Lord Woolton, *Memoirs* (London, Cassell, 1952), pp. 17–37.
9   Constance and Harold King. '*The Two Nations*': *the Life and Work of Liverpool University Settlement and its Associated Institutions, 1906–1937* (London, Hodder and Stoughton with the University of Liverpool Press, 1938), pp. 127–8.
10 See pp. 110–112.
11 King and King, *op. cit.*, p. 128.
12 Ibid., p. 129. Roxby still had a strong belief in different racial 'types' at this time. See Percy Roxby, 'Geography and nationalism', *New Era* (July 1931), pp. 224–6.

13   King and King, p. 129; Minutes of the Council of the University Settlement, 22 October 1928.

14   Percy Roxby, 'Foreword' to M.E. Fletcher, *Report on an Investigation into the Colour Problem in Liverpool and Other Ports* (Liverpool, Association for the Welfare of Half-Caste Children 1930), p. 6.

15   Fletcher, *Report*, p. 9.

16   Ibid., p. 39.

17   *Seaman*, 2 July 1930.

18   Fletcher, *Report*, pp. 10–11.

19   M. Fleming, 'Human hybrids', *Eugenics Review*, 21, 4 (1930), p. 260. See also R.M. Fleming, 'Physical heredity in human hybrids', *Annals of Eugenics*, 9, 1 (1939), pp. 55–81. Cedric Dover considered by 1937 that the view of 'biological disharmony' being produced by 'inter breeding' had become somewhat undermined, though he noted the lingering belief in 'Hybrid infertility' (*Half-Caste* (London, Secker and Warburg, 1937), pp. 30–1).

20   Fletcher, *Report*, p. 28. See also M.E. Fletcher, 'The colour problem in Liverpool', *Liverpool Review* (October 1930), pp. 421–4.

21   Ibid., p. 33.

22   Ibid., p. 37.

23   Ibid., p. 39.

24   MSS Brit. Emp. S23 H1/15, Ernest Adkin to J. Harris, 7 August 1930.

25   King and King, *op. cit.*, p. 130; St Clair Drake, 'Value Systems, Social Structure and Race Relations in the British Isles', Ph.D. thesis, University of Chicago, 1954, pp. 80–1.

26   Interview with Lady M. Simey; King and King, *op. cit.*, p. 130.

27   *University of Liverpool Social Survey of Merseyside, No. 2: A Study of Migration to Merseyside, with Special Reference to Irish Immigration* (Liverpool, University of Liverpool Press, 1931), p. 2.

28   Ibid., p. 7.

29   Ibid., pp. 5–6.

30   MSS Brit. Emp. S1427 4/3, F.S. Livie-Noble, Memorandum on 'Distressed coloured seamen at Cardiff and elsewhere'. Livie-Noble asserted that repatriation was not acceptable to the black seamen, whose unemployment should be seen as part of the wide issue of unemployment within Britain generally (p. 2). For the Nancy Sharpe report, see St Clair Drake, *op. cit.*, p. 83.

Chapter 12

Clarence Lusane

NAZI-STERILIZATION OF AFRO-GERMANS

Extract from *Hitler's Black Victims: The Historical Experiences of Afro-Germans, European Blacks, Africans, and African Americans in the Nazi Era* (2003). New York: Routledge, pp. 134–143.

Nazi Sterilization of Afro-Germans

> We want to prevent . . . poisoning the entire bloodstream of the race.
> (Counselor of the Reich Ministry of the Interior)

HITLER SUBSCRIBED TO THE so-called *Entmischung* thesis, which rejected those eugenicist supporters who argued that eugenics led to a betterment of the superior race. *Entmischung* proponents believed that after many generations something akin to pure racial types would re-emerge out of mixed-race people. However, these people would still be inferior, disproving the "betterment" goal of so-called positive eugenics. Only in the most exceptional of cases, it was argued, would betterment occur. The most direct implication for Blacks in Germany (as well as other racial groups) was another rationalization for stopping their reproduction, if not their existence altogether. Race mixture, in other words, left a permanent contamination that could only be arrested, short of genocide, by sterilization. Although the Nuremberg laws and other statutes forbade the sexual liaison between Aryans and other races, the Nazis wanted to guarantee that the generation of mixed African and German children living under National Socialism would be the last. The racial science attack on the Rhineland children and the use of discourse on race driven by biology did not begin with the Nazi period in Germany. In the three decades leading up to the time of Hitler, a thriving eugenics movement existed that produced a number of the key race doctors who would emerge in the 1930s. It is telling that the largest figure in Germany's pantheon of eugenicists was trained in the United States.

Alfred Ploetz, the acknowledged founder of German eugenics, spent time in the United States where undoubtedly he solidified his admiration for the South's segregation laws and popular practice. In Germany, he would also be credited with coining the term *Rassenhygiene* (racial hygiene), whose deadly meaning would leave its bloodstain on the Nazi era. He founded the first German eugenics journal in 1904, *Archiv für Rassen- und Gesellschaftsbiologic* (*Journal of Racial and Social Biology*), and, a year later, organized the *Gesellschaft für Rassenhygiene* (Society for Racial Hygiene). In 1907, the influence of the Society for Racial Hygiene would lead to a major debate within the Reichstag regarding a proposed sterilization bill that would eventually be rejected. The issue and its advocates would not die, however. Increasingly, eugenicists found support from the Weimar government. Many proponents of eugenics were employed at state-funded *Rassenhygiene* institutes and clinics. A decade before Hitler came to power, eugenics had migrated from a theoretical discourse to an applied science and effort at social engineering.

Some have argued that anti-Semitism did not play a strong role in the pre-Hitler eugenics movement or that at least it was contested by a number of leading proponents who even considered the Jews to be Aryan. In fact, German eugenicists were race conscious in their actions throughout. The Society for Racial Hygiene began performing sterilizations for "eugenic reasons," that is, eliminating "racial diseases," as early as 1919. German eugenicists did not necessarily want initially to jump into the political fray, that is, take responsibility for the policy implications (and implementation) of their ideas. At first, they rejected the policy of mandatory government intervention. In October 1921, the Society for Race Hygiene adopted a twenty-one-point eugenics program that, inter alia, strongly opposed compulsory sterilization. Within a very short time, however, this attitude would change.

The German eugenics movement was strongly influenced by the work of the American eugenicists Ezra Gosney and Paul Popenoe. Gosney was a wealthy philanthropist who became obsessed with eugenics, and Popenoe was the editor of the *Journal of Heredity*. In 1929, Gosney and Popenoe published *Sterilization for Human Betterment*, a study of work and efficacy under the 1922 California sterilization law. A number of German eugenicists would claim that this book was the singular inspiration for the 1933 law enacted by the Nazis. As Dorothy Roberts notes, "the Nazis modeled their compulsory sterilization law after the one enacted in California." That California statute and the Model Eugenic Sterilization Law developed by Harry Laughlin in 1922 had global impact. Notably, the Nazi law was more moderate than the one proposed by their American counterparts. The Laughlin model, which influenced the California and other state laws, called for sterilizing the mentally retarded, insane, criminal, people who were habitually drunk, blind, deaf, deformed, and economically dependent. In the United States, between 1929 and 1941, more than 70,000 people had been involuntarily sterilized. Under the California law twice as many Blacks as Whites were sterilized. The law allowed for sterilization based on "hereditary diseases" including weakmindedness, schizophrenia, insanity, epilepsy, blindness, deafness, bodily deformities, and alcoholism. Even with all of these stipulations, there were, from the beginning, complaints that the law was not broad enough because it did not address hidden "defects" such as race or other traits that were not visible to the naked eye, a complaint that would be echoed in Nazi Germany.

The link between Nazism and the pre-1933 eugenics movement was strong. The anti-Semitic rantings of Ploetz and others informed the theoretical basis of Nazi thinking. Tucker contends that "while Hitler was still imprisoned in Landsberg am Lech fortress and just beginning *Mein Kampf*, renowned university scholars like [Fritz] Lenz and [Eugen] Fischer and cruder race theorists like [Hans] Gunther had already provided the intellectual and scientific foundation for much of what would become the Nazi program." In 1931, at the conference of the National Socialist Pharmacists and Physicians, it was proposed that the Aryan or Nordic part of the German population be nurtured, a middle group that was near Aryan be tolerated, and the lowest, most unfit, and non-Aryan sector be sterilized.

As this brief history demonstrates, eugenics was well established in Germany long before Hitler came to power, and before the fascist state turned its attention to the Afro-German young people and other Blacks. Although in 1927, addressing the issue of the mixed-race Rhineland children, an "official of the Bavarian Ministry of the Interior recommended sterilization, but the suggestion was turned down at Reich level because of the demoralizing effects upon the children's German mothers." Six years later, on 14 July 1933, the Law for the Prevention of Genetically Defective Progeny passed and became the legal justification for the Nazis' euthanasia and sterilization programs. The German law passed, in part, due to the appropriation of legal and medical arguments that had been used to pass similar laws in the United States. The objective of the law was to prevent or stop the spreading of so-called negative and impure hereditary diseases and illnesses.

The Nazi sterilization law went into effect on 1 January 1934. (See accompanying Table 1.) According to Kevles, about 225,000 were sterilized in the first three years of the program. Beginning on the effective date, medical professionals had to report all "unfit" individuals to the Hereditary Health Courts that had been created by the hundreds across Germany. According to the law, each court had a jurist and two physicians. This body would make a determination whether an individual was to be sterilized or not. There are no official or trustworthy figures on how many sterilizations were done overall after that time. Campt gives a figure of 300,000–400,000 individuals between 1934 and 1945. She goes on to note, however, that those figures "exclude countless *illegal* sterilizations carried out in secret on the basis of racial/racist, rather than 'hereditary' or 'biological' grounds" (emphasis in the original). These included, of course, Afro-Germans and others of African descent in addition to Gypsies and Jews. Finally, Muller-Hill estimates that 350,000–400,000 sterilizations were performed between 1934 and 1939, and then were effectively ended after the passage of new laws.

Other relevant laws included the 26 June 1935 Law for the Alteration of the Law for the Prevention of Hereditarily Disease Progeny and the 18 October

Table 12.1 Law for the protection of Hereditary Health: The attempt to improve the German Aryan Breed (July 14, 1933)

Article I

(1) Anyone who suffers from an inheritable disease may be surgically sterilized if, in the judgment of medical science, it could be expected that his descendants will suffer from serious inherited mental or physical defects.
(2) Anyone who suffers from one of the following is to be regarded as inheritably diseased within the meaning of this law:

   1 congenital feeble-mindedness
   2 schizophrenia
   3 manic-depression
   4 congenital epilepsy
   5 inheritable St. Vitus dance (Huntington's Chorea)
   6 hereditary blindness
   7 hereditary deafness
   8 serious inheritable malformations

(3) In addition anyone suffering from chronic alcoholism may also be sterilized.

Article II

(1) Anyone who requests sterilization is entitled to it. If he be incapacitated or under a guardian because of low state of mental health or not yet 18 years of age, his legal guardian is empowered to make the request. In other cases of limited capacity the request must receive the approval of the legal representative. If a person be of age and has a nurse, the latter's consent is required.
(2) The request must be accompanied by a certificate from a citizen who is accredited by the German Reich stating that the person to be sterilized has been informed about the nature and consequence of sterilization.
(3) The request for sterilization can be recalled.

Article III

Sterilization may also be recommended by:

(1) the official physician
(2) the official in charge of a hospital, sanitarium, or prison.

Article IV

The request for sterilization must be presented in writing to, or placed in writing by, the office of the Health Inheritance Court. The statement concerning the request must be certified by a medical document or authenticated in some other way. The business office of the court must notify the official physician.

Article VII

The proceedings of the Health Inheritance Court are secret.

Article X

The Supreme Health Insurance Court retains final jurisdiction.

Source: *The Holocaust/Shoah Page*.

1935 Law for the Protection of Hereditary Health of the German People. The former sanctioned compulsory abortion (for up to six months!), while the latter required that all those who sought to get married carry a "certificate of fitness to marry." Also, the Nazi eugenics racial program was one of "weed" and "breed." The SS chief, Heinrich Himmler, instituted the *Lebensborn* (The Well of Life) program that consisted of encouraging SS members to impregnate as many racially suitable women as they could who would then be given the best prenatal care possible in spalike resorts set up across Germany. Moral issues notwithstanding, these women were both married and unmarried.

On 13 April 1933, three months after Hitler came to power, Hermann Göring, the Prussian minister of the interior and one of Hitler's most loyal henchman, ordered data to be collected on the Rhineland children from the local authorities in Dusseldorf, Cologne, Koblenz, and Aachen. Dr. William Abel of the Kaiser Wilhelm Institute for Anthropology, Heredity, and Eugenics used the information collected from 145 children to conclude that these children were racially inferior and something should be done to "prevent their reproducing." Around the same time, Dr. Hans Macco, who produced a pamphlet, *Racial Problems in the Third Reich*, that also called for the sterilization of mixed-raced children as well as Gypsies, echoed these conclusions. And in that same year, Hitler's minister of agriculture Richard-Walther Darre, made the case that for the future of the German nation, the Rhineland children had to be taken care of. In the harshest terms possible, he wrote.

> It is essential to exterminate the leftovers from the black Shame on the Rhine. These mulatto children were created either through rape or by white mothers who were whores. In any case, there exists not the slightest moral obligation toward these racially foreign offspring. . . . Thus, as a Rhinelander I demand: sterilization of all mulattoes with whom we were saddled by the black Shame at the Rhine. This measure has to be carried out within the next two years. Otherwise it is too late, with the results that hundreds of years later this racial deterioration will still be felt.

Since the 1933 sterilization law did not allow for sterilization based solely on race, the Nazis were aware that they had to rewrite or amend the law, create a new law, or operate outside their own regulations. In the end, the Nazis simply chose to carry on in secret and in violation of the ordinance, usually employing the mask of "parental" consent. Applying a formal reading of the statute, as Friedlander noted, "The sterilization law did not, however, permit sterilization of children whose only hereditary disease was their race. The ministry decided to sterilize them secretly." The counselor of the Reich Ministry of the Interior, responsible for the enforcement of the sterilization law, made it clear what the Nazi objectives were with the law when he stated, "We want to prevent . . . poisoning the entire bloodstream of the race." Perhaps few outside the Nazi leadership saw this as the first step in a diabolical plan eventually to physically eliminate the "racially" unsuitable. The complete dominance of the Nazi state over the political and social life of the nation ensured that legal recourse was closed and popular resistance, to the degree it existed, was muted and brutally repressed. Although initially, about half of those sterilized were labeled as "feebleminded," this charade would soon be dropped. It is also evident that feeblemindedness itself was a cover that could be used to target any group, especially given the racial hierarchy that informed Nazi and, more generally, German thinking.

The decision to sterilize the Rhineland children was explicit. On 11 March 1935, a group that was part of the Committee of Experts for Population and Racial Policy met to address "ways to solve the question of [the Rhineland] Bastards." The children who had been born during the occupation were about to reach childbearing age, an unacceptable danger to the Nazis. It was suggested by one attendee, Dr. Walter Gross, and agreed upon by the group that the way to handle the situation was by sterilization of the children. First doing an anthropological investigation was mere window dressing for a policy of slow genocide. For unknown reasons, it took another two years to decide that there would be no pretense of a legal cover – such as extending or amending the 1933 law – and that the parent(s) or guardian(s) would be forced to sign consent statements initiating sterilization procedures.

Rather than have the process go through the Hereditary Health Courts that had been created by the 1933 law, the Gestapo created Special Commission No. 3, whose task was to locate, identify, and implement "the discrete sterilization of the Rhineland bastards." The members of Special Commission No. 3 included Eugen Fischer, Wilhelm Abel, and Heinrich Schade. Abel was in charge of the Department on Race at the Wilhelm Institute run by Fischer. Among the characteristics that were attributed to the *Mischlings* by the Nazi leadership and Reich scientists were "biological inferiority," "disharmonies in the phenotypic appearance," "preponderantly negative character traits," and "torn by inner conflicts." The medical attacks on the young Afro-Germans and other Blacks, as were all national racial policies, were sanctioned by Hitler himself.

Between 1935 and 1937, at least 385 Rhineland children were sterilized, according to available documents. These were mostly done in open secret. Hitler's race experts collected data on 385 of the Rhineland children in the Bonn and Cologne areas with the collaboration of churches, schools, and other institutions. Once identified, the youths were taken from their schools or homes, usually with the coerced signature of their parent or legal guardian, and brought before a special commission and tried. In nearly every instance, it was determined that the person on trial should be sterilized; the person was then taken away and the procedure performed. The Bonn University Women's Clinic and the Evangelical Hospital in Cologne-Sulz were among the sites used for the sterilizations. Besides the young people, black men who had been sterilized had to carry certificates showing that they had had a vasectomy.

While information concerning black sterilization exists about Afro-German and African men, there were also a significant number of sterilizations of black women athough exactly how many were done is unknown. Nazi romanticizing of German womanhood did not extend to women of African descent. This is an open arena of research and likely to demonstrate some important differences in rationale and argument. It is known that in at least one instance, a young black girl was saved at the last minute. Doris Reiprich, whose Cameroonian father bought German citizenship for fifty gold marks in 1896 and eventually married a white German woman, was taken to the clinic to be sterilized in 1943. Extremely distraught, she cried and apparently aroused the sympathy of a man at the clinic who let her go. She eventually married and had two children, including one daughter with blue eyes and blonde hair.

The ritual of an examination generated a report that served as the legal document authorizing sterilization. A typical report or finding noted the undesirable racial traits possessed by Blacks. The 2 June 1937 report from Frankfurt on Marianne Braun, who was born 16 May 1925, describes how she was driven to the hospital and questioned, with the inevitable conclusion:

> According to statements by the mother and the anthropological opinion it was established that Marianne Braun is a German citizen who, as the descendent of colored occupation forces, has characteristics alien to her race. The father of the child was then informed about the results of the examination, and it was pointed out to him that the descendants of the child would retain the colored blood alien to the race, and that for this reason propagation by the child is undesirable. He was thoroughly informed about the character and the consequences of sterilization.

A similar report was issued regarding Cacilie Borinski, who was born on 7 April 1922. The 17 June 1937 report from Bonn notes that her father was an American soldier. As with Marianne Braun, it is noted that Borinski is a German citizen. The document states:

> The Commission has reached the following conclusion: The German citizen Cacilie Borinski . . . is the descendent of a member of the former colored occupation troops and distinctly has the corresponding characteristics. Therefore she is to be sterilized.

A third example is the report done on Josef Feck. His report was issued on 19 June 1937 in Frankfurt. Again, the language is chillingly clinical and strikingly similar to those already noted:

> The German citizen Josef Feck, born 26 September 1920, and residing in Mainz is a descendent of the former colonial occupation troops (North Africa) and distinctly displays the corresponding anthropological characteristics. For that reason he is to be sterilized. His mother consents to the sterilization.

More than fifty years later, victims of these torturous operations would speak in cold bitterness of the psychological, let alone physical, destruction they felt. The Afro-German Hans Hauck, who was featured in the film *Black Survivors of the Holocaust*, tells sourly of how the Gestapo came and got him and his grandmother into a car and took them to the Health Office, where he was examined and measured. A decision was made to sterilize him without the benefit of anesthesia. After it was over, Hauck was given a vasectomy certificate and warned not to have sexual relations with white German women. He also had to sign papers stating that he would commit to that agreement and that his sterilization was not forced. Another Afro-German shown in *Black Survivors*, Thomas Holzhauzer, is also resentful about being operated on by the Nazis. He was picked up along with his sister and taken to the Elizabeth Hospital in Darmstadt. He remembers distinctly that the doctor, who was wearing a Nazi uniform, "made two cuts around my testicles" during the procedure. There is more than a little anger when he tells the filmmakers, "Sometimes I'm glad I could not have any children."

The deleterious impact of these sterilizations on Black Germans cannot be overstated. This slow holocaust terrorized an entire generation of Blacks. While there is no evidence that any of the US eugenicists were aware of the secret sterilizations that had been carried out against Afro-Germans, the threat of sterilization had been addressed fairly early in the Nazi era and was even discussed in US black newspapers of the time.

Although a number of American eugenicists would begin to break with and criticize the fascist tendencies of the movement as early as the early 1930s, it was not until the early 1940s that the discrediting was full and that nearly all involved in the US-based movement would denounce the policies of the Nazis, policies that they had championed only a short time before. Without rejecting eugenics as a "science," many contended that the violent and unrelenting execution of the Jews of Europe was not what they had been advocating. Instead, they argued, they wanted to pursue a course of "positive" and noncoercive encouragement to breed a better racial stock for the nation. There were others, of course, who continued to embrace the Nazis long after they had been exposed for the medical terrors that were being unleashed against German citizens. In 1936, upon receiving a University of Heidelberg honorary doctorate award, the Eugenics Record Office's Laughlin stated that the award was "evidence of a common understanding of German and American scientists of the nature of eugenics."

African Americans, Afro-Germans, and the response to sterilization

As early as 1934, a year before the Nazis officially met and decided to carry out their program of slow extermination of German Blacks, the issue of the sterilization of Afro-Germans and other Blacks in Germany was being raised in the US black press. On 17 February 1934, the *Washington Afro-American*, in a page-one story, warned about a "new Nazi plan is to sterilize all children born as a result of affairs between French African troops and German women during the after-war occupation." The report of the plan came from a black Republican representative, Oscar Stanton DePriest, who was the first African American elected to Congress in the twentieth century and the only Black in the US Congress at the time. Although elected from a black enclave of Chicago, DePriest (as would others to follow) saw himself and was seen as a voice of black interests nationally and internationally. Though powerless to affect the status of black America and the broader black world, DePriest used his congressional platform to articulate a politics of resistance. He was far from being a radical, but in Jim Crow America, he had little choice but to become a "race" man, if only by default, and articulate the real, perceived, and threatened grievances of black people.

The black movement against sterilization was addressed at the intersection of race, class, and gender. Roberts points out the contradictory relationship that many African Americans, including a number of leading intellectuals and civil rights leaders, had with the eugenics movement. Criticism of the so-called immoral behavior of lower-class African Americans by Du Bois, parts of the black press, and other black leaders led them to support the birth control movement that overlapped substantially with the eugenics movement. Their arguments reflected many of the same claims of "betterment" spoken by more racist elements. This debate was also a gendered discourse in a number of ways. Black women, held responsible for the socialization of their children, were principally held accountable for the "irresponsible" behavior that was manifest in the black community. As a class, they were also chastised for having children out of wedlock, promiscuity, and attempts at gaining equal footing with men, black men in particular. The responsibility of black men in these instances was elided and simply not a part of the debate. Neither was a contextualized framework that recognized the socially driven forces that determined under what circumstances poor blacks, women, and, especially, poor black women could exercise the agency necessary to control any of these factors. A (black–white) matrix of power from any number of vantage points always resulted with white men at the top, followed by white women, trailed by black men and, last, black women.

While white men could freely exercise sexual power over white and black women, and racial power over black men, white women were circumscribed to exhibit only racial power, still a very significant force nevertheless. Black men, trumped by the racial power of white women and the totalizing power of white men, were then left with only a limited gender power whose boundaries were thrown over the political and social spaces of black women. Thus, black women were doubly vulnerable due not only to the direct assault upon their physical and psychological being by white men, black men, and white women, but also to the explanatory race-sex discourse that then justified their exclusion, marginalization, and oppresion in the first instance.

Though real and expressive of the diasporic solidarity tendencies always present in black political life, the alarm sounded by some black newspapers about the sterilization threat to Afro-Germans and Africans was compromised by the political frame and behavior of black male leaders and intellectuals of the period regarding eugenics-driven birth control in the black community. Beyond the fact that there was precious little that African Americans could do to prevent the attacks on Afro-Germans, little had been concretely done to stop the profoundly racialized eugenics and sterilization campaigns that operated in the United States. It is not known if Blacks who were sterilized by the Nazis ever knew that their kinfolk of sorts had raised the issue, but no direct action of prevention was possible and none was forthcoming.

Conclusion

Sterilization was perhaps the worst action that could be taken by the Nazis against Blacks in Germany short of mass execution. It not only destroyed the future of individual Blacks but also sought to erase any future blackness on German soil. At the same time, the sterilization option reflected the complicated relationship that the Nazis had toward its black population. Unable to win consensus on extermination, yet compelled to address the "otherness" of Blacks, they used sterilization as a gradual, but inexorable death, long-term erasure that, in part, solved some of Germany's black dilemma. Hitler and other Nazi leaders made it clear that Blacks were not desired in the Third Reich, but a number of factors out of their control such as the international situation forced them to compromise.

Yet sterilization was not the end of the story. While the efforts at sterilization were an initial means by which the Nazis attempted to address one of their black dilemmas, at least as it concerned young Afro-Germans, a more evil and fatal destiny awaited many more. In the period leading up to the war and during the war, the Nazis would initiate a hurricane of brutality and death that swept all in its path. One of the most tragic legacies of Nazism was the construction, peopling, and administration of those earthbound abysses of hell known as concentration camps. For millions of those who did not die on the spot at the hands of the Nazi onslaught from the East and the West, as well as their enemies within Germany, the last stop in this life was in the thousands of death, concentration, labor, transition, and prisoner of war camps. Many of the black victims of sterilization would end up in the camps as well as other Blacks who were unlucky enough to be caught.

Study probes

1   In Nazi Germany, who were the key players in the development of eugenics as both 'an applied science' and a form of 'social engineering'?
2   In what ways was the German eugenics movement modelled on its American equivalent?
3   What were the objectives of Special Commission No.3 and how did the members carry out these tasks?
4   Compare and contrast Lusane's analysis of the plight of 'mixed race' people in Nazi Germany and Rich's discussion of the negative treatment of 'mixed race' communities in inter-war Britain.

SUGGESTIONS FOR FURTHER READING

Bodenhorn, Howard (2002) 'The Mulatto Advantage: The Biological Consequences of Complexion in Rural Antebellum Virginia', *Journal of Interdisciplinary History*, 33(1): 21–46.

Brodkin, Karen (1998) *How the Jews Became White and What That Says About Race in America*, New Brunswick, NJ: Rutgers University Press.

Butler-Evans, Elliot (1989) *Race, Gender and Desire*, Philadelphia, PA: Temple University Press.

Davis, James F. (1991) *Who is Black?*, University Park: Pennsylvania State University Press.

Degler, Carl (1971) *Neither Black nor White: Slavery and Relations in Brazil and the United States*, New York: Macmillan.

Evans, Emrys (ed.) (1992) *Reading Against Racism*, Bloomington: Indiana University.

Fernández, Carlos (1992) 'La Raza and the Melting Pot: A Comparative Look at Multiethnicity', in M.P.P. Root (ed.) *Racially Mixed People in America*, Thousand Oaks, CA: Sage, pp.126–143.

Fisher, Jean (1995) 'Some Thoughts on "Contaminations",' *Third Text*, 38:3–7.

Gerzina, Gretchen (1995) *Black England: Life Before Emancipation*, London: John Murray.

Gilman, Sander (1985) *Difference and Pathology: Stereotypes of Sexuality, Race and Madness*, London: Cornell University Press.

Gilroy, Paul (2000) *Between Camps: Nations, Cultures and the Allure of Race*, London: Allen Lane.

Gossett, Thomas (1965) *Race: The History of an Idea in America*, New York: Schocken Books.

Hamilton, Charles *et al.* (eds) (2001) *Beyond Racism: Race and Inequality in Brazil, South Africa and the United States*, Boulder, CO: Lynne Rienner.

Hannaford, Ivan Race (1996) *The History of an Idea in the West*, Baltimore, MD: Johns Hopkins University Press.

Haraway, Donna (1989) *Primate Visions: Gender, Race and Nature in the World of Modern Science*, London: Routledge.

Harding, Sandra (ed.) (1993) *The 'Racial' Economy of Science*, Bloomington: Indiana University Press.

Harris, Marvin (1980) *Patterns of Race in the Americas*, Westport, CT: Greenwood Press.

Hernton, Calvin (1988) *Sex and Racism in America*, New York: Grove Press.

Hitler, Adolf (1992) *Mein Kamp*, translated by Ralph Mannheim, London: Pimlico.

Hodes, Martha (ed.) (1999) *Sex, Race, Love: Crossing Boundaries in North American History*, New York: New York University Press.

Hyam, Ronald (1990) *Empire and Sexuality: The British Experience*, Manchester: Manchester University Press, pp. 200–217.

Ignatiev, Noel (1995) *How the Irish Became White*, London: Routledge.

Jacobson, Matthew (1998) *Whiteness of a Different Color: European Immigrants and the Alchemy of Race*, Cambridge, MA: Harvard University Press.

Jaimes, M. Annette (1995) 'Some Kind of Indian: On Race, Eugenics and Mixed-Bloods', in N.Zack (ed.) *American Mixed Race*, London: Rowman and Littlefield, pp. 133–153.

Jones, Steve *et al.* (eds.) (1992) *Cambridge Encyclopedia of Human Evolution*, Cambridge: Cambridge University Press.

Katz, William Loren (1986) *Black Indians: A Hidden Heritage*, New York: Atheneum.

Katz, William Loren (1993) *Proudly Red and Black: Stories of Africans and Native Americans*, New York: Atheneum.

Kohn, Marek (1996) *The Race Gallery: The Return of Racial Science*, London: Vintage.

Lorimer, Douglas (1978) *Colour, Class and the Victorians*, Leicester: Leicester University Press.

McGrane, Bernard (1989) *Beyond Anthropology: Society and the Other*, New York: Columbia University Press.

Malik, Kenan (1996) *The Meaning of Race*, London: Macmillan.

Nakashima, Cynthia (1992) 'An Invisible Monster: The Creation and Denial of Mixed-Race People in America', in M.P.P. Root (ed.) *Racially Mixed People in America*, Thousand Oaks, CA: Sage, pp. 162–178

Omi, Michael and Winant, Howard (1986) *Racial Formation in the United States*, New York: Routledge.

Rashidi, Runoko (1985) 'Ancient and Modern Britons', in I. Van Sertima (ed.) *African Presence in Early Europe*, London: Transaction Press, pp. 251–260.

Richards, David (1994) *Masks of Difference*, Cambridge: Cambridge University Press.

Rogers, J.A. (1941) *Sex and Race, Vol.1, Negro-Caucasian Mixing in All Ages and Lands*, New York: Helga Rogers.

Rogers, J.A. (1942) *Sex and Race, Vol.2, A History of White, Negro and Indian Miscegenation*, New York: Helga Rogers.

Rogers, J.A. (1944) *Sex and Race, Vol.3, Why White and Black Mix in Spite of Opposition*, St. Petersburg, FL: Helga Rogers.

Rogers, J.A. (1987) *As Nature Leads*, Baltimore, MD: Black Classic Press.

Rushton, Phillipe (1997) *Race, Evolution and Behavior*, London: Transaction.

Shanklin, Eugenia (1994) *Anthropology and Race*, Belmont, CA: Wadsworth.

Shuffleton, Frank (1993) *A Mixed Race: Ethnicity in Early America*, Oxford: Oxford University Press.

Smith, Paul (1992) *Representing the Other*, Oxford: Clarendon Press.

Snowden, Frank (1983) *Before Color Prejudice: The Ancient View of Blacks*, Cambridge, MA: Harvard University Press.

Sollors, Werner (1997) *Neither Black nor White Yet Both*, Oxford: Oxford University Press.

Stocking, George (1982) *Race, Culture and Evolution*, London: University of Chicago Press.

Stocking, George (1987) *Victorian Anthropology*, London: Collier Macmillan.

Stoler, Ann (2000) 'Sexual Affronts and Racial Frontiers: European Identities and the Cultural Politics of Exclusion in Southeast Asia', in A. Brah and A. Coombes (eds) *Hybridity and its Discontents: Politics, Science and Culture*, London: Routledge, pp. 19–56.

Talty, Stephan (2003) *Mulatto America*, New York: HarperCollins.

Walvin, James (1973) *Black and White: The Negro and English Society*, London: Allen Lane.

Walvin, James (2000) *Making the Black Atlantic*, London: Cassell.

Williamson, Joel (1995) *New People: Miscegenation and Mulattoes in the United States*, London: Lousiana University Press.

Wilson, Terry (1992) 'Blood Quantum: Native American Mixed Bloods', in M.P.P. Root (ed.) *Racially Mixed People in America*, Thousand Oaks, CA: Sage, pp. 108–125.

Wolfe, Patrick (1999) *Settler Colonialism and the Transformation of Anthropology: The Politics and Poetics of an Ethnographic Event*, London; Cassell.

Wolpoff, Milford and Caspari, Rachel (1997) *Race and Human Evolution: A Fatal Attraction*, Boulder, CO: Westview Press.

Young, Robert (1995) *Colonial Desire: Hybridity in Theory, Culture and Race*, London: Routledge.

Young, Lola (1996) *Fear of the Dark: Race, Gender and Sexuality in the Cinema*, London: Routledge.

Genetics

Chapter 13

American Anthropological Association

AMERICAN ANTHROPOLOGICAL ASSOCIATION STATEMENT ON 'RACE'

http://www.aaanet.org/stmts/racepp.htm (17 May 1998).

THE FOLLOWING STATEMENT was adopted by the Executive Board of the American Anthropological Association, acting on a draft prepared by a committee of representative American anthropologists. It does not reflect a consensus of all members of the AAA, as individuals vary in their approaches to the study of "race." We believe that it represents generally the contemporary thinking and scholarly positions of a majority of anthropologists.

In the United States both scholars and the general public have been conditioned to viewing human races as natural and separate divisions within the human species based on visible physical differences. With the vast expansion of scientific knowledge in this century, however, it has become clear that human populations are not unambiguous, clearly demarcated, biologically distinct groups. Evidence from the analysis of genetics (e.g., DNA) indicates that most physical variation, about 94 percent, lies *within* so-called racial groups. Conventional geographic "racial" groupings differ from one another only in about 6 percent of their genes. This means that there is greater variation within "racial" groups than between them. In neighboring populations there is much overlapping of genes and their phenotypic (physical) expressions. Throughout history whenever different groups have come into contact, they have interbred. The continued sharing of genetic materials has maintained all of humankind as a single species.

Physical variations in any given trait tend to occur gradually rather than abruptly over geographic areas. And because physical traits are inherited independently of one another, knowing the range of one trait does not predict the presence of others. For example, skin color varies largely from light in the temperate areas in the north to dark in the tropical areas in the south; its intensity is not related to nose shape or hair texture. Dark skin may be associated with frizzy or kinky hair or curly or wavy or straight hair, all of which are found among different indigenous peoples in tropical regions. These facts render any attempt to establish lines of division among biological populations both arbitrary and subjective.

Historical research has shown that the idea of "race" has always carried more meanings than mere physical differences; indeed, physical variations in the human species have no meaning except the social ones that humans put on them. Today scholars in many fields argue that "race" as it is understood in the United States of America was a social mechanism invented during the eighteenth century to refer to those populations brought together in colonial America: the English and other European settlers, the conquered Indian peoples, and those peoples of Africa brought in to provide slave labor.

From its inception, this modern concept of "race" was modeled after an ancient theorem of the Great Chain of Being, which posited natural categories on a hierarchy established by God or nature. Thus "race" was a mode of classification linked specifically to peoples in the colonial situation. It subsumed a growing ideology of inequality devised to rationalize European attitudes and treatment of the conquered and enslaved peoples. Proponents of slavery in particular during the nineteenth century used "race" to justify the retention of slavery. The ideology magnified the differences among Europeans, Africans, and Indians, established a rigid hierarchy of socially exclusive categories underscored and bolstered unequal rank and status differences, and provided the rationalization that the inequality was natural or God-given. The different physical traits of African Americans and Indians became markers or symbols of their status differences.

As they were constructing US society, leaders among European Americans fabricated the cultural/behavioral characteristics associated with each "race," linking superior traits with Europeans and negative and inferior ones to blacks and Indians. Numerous arbitrary and fictitious beliefs about the different peoples were institutionalized and deeply embedded in American thought.

Early in the nineteenth century the growing fields of science began to reflect the public consciousness about human differences. Differences among the "racial" categories were projected to their greatest extreme when the argument was posed that Africans, Indians, and Europeans were separate species, with Africans the least human and closer taxonomically to apes.

Ultimately "race" as an ideology about human differences was subsequently spread to other areas of the world. It became a strategy for dividing, ranking, and controlling colonized people used by colonial powers everywhere. But it was not limited to the colonial situation. In the latter part of the nineteenth century it was employed by Europeans to rank one another and to justify social, economic, and political inequalities among their peoples. During World War II, the Nazis under Adolf Hitler enjoined the expanded ideology of "race" and "racial" differences and took them to a logical end: the extermination of 11 million people of "inferior races" (e.g., Jews, Gypsies, Africans, homosexuals, and so forth) and other unspeakable brutalities of the Holocaust.

"Race" thus evolved as a worldview, a body of prejudgments that distorts our ideas about human differences and group behavior. Racial beliefs constitute myths about the diversity in the human species and about the abilities and behavior of people homogenized into "racial" categories. The myths fused behavior and physical features together in the public mind, impeding our comprehension of both biological variations and cultural behavior, implying that both are genetically determined. Racial myths bear no relationship to the reality of human capabilities or behavior. Scientists today find that reliance on such folk beliefs about human differences in research has led to countless errors.

At the end of the twentieth century, we now understand that human cultural behavior is learned, conditioned into infants beginning at birth, and always subject to modification. No human is born with a built-in culture or language. Our temperaments, dispositions, and personalities, regardless of genetic propensities, are developed within sets of meanings and values that we call "culture." Studies of infant and early childhood learning and behavior attest to the reality of our cultures in forming who we are.

It is a basic tenet of anthropological knowledge that all normal human beings have the capacity to learn any cultural behavior. The American experience with immigrants from hundreds of different language and cultural backgrounds who have acquired some version of American culture traits and behavior is the clearest evidence of this fact. Moreover, people of all physical variations have learned different cultural behaviors and continue to do so as modern transportation moves millions of immigrants around the world.

How people have been accepted and treated within the context of a given society or culture has a direct impact on how they perform in that society. The "racial" worldview was invented to assign some groups to perpetual low status, while others were permitted access to privilege, power, and wealth. The tragedy in the United States has been that the policies and practices stemming from this worldview succeeded all too well in constructing unequal populations among Europeans, Native Americans, and peoples of African descent. Given what we know about the capacity of normal humans to achieve and function within any culture, we conclude that present-day inequalities between so-called "racial" groups are not consequences of their biological inheritance but products of historical and contemporary social, economic, educational, and political circumstances.

Study probes

1   What genetic evidence is provided to support the claim that there are no 'pure' biologically distinct 'races'?
2   Trace the development of the concept of 'race' as it is outlined in the statement.
3   In the development and perpetuation of social inequalities, what has been the role of a 'racial' worldview?

Chapter 14

William B. Provine

GENETICS AND THE BIOLOGY OF RACE CROSSING

From *Science*, 182 (4114) (1973), pp. 790–796.

Geneticists changed their minds about the biological effects of race crossing.
(William B. Provine)

"EDUCATION IS TO MAN what manure is to the pea,"[1] wrote the young geneticist Reginald C. Punnett in 1907. He was obviously keenly aware of the social significance of his work on peas for human affairs. Like many other geneticists then and now, he believed that he should publicize the social implications of his research. In this paper I examine historically only one aspect of the social significance of genetics: the attitude of United States and British geneticists on the topic of race crossing.

Between 1860 and 1900 Europeans and Americans felt a new urgency about race problems. The Civil War and the freeing of slaves in the United States stimulated a huge outpouring of books and pamphlets about race, in Europe as well as America. Europeans divided up the entire continent of Africa and carved out spheres of imperialistic activity throughout the world, dramatically increasing their contacts with other races. Race-related social problems grew accordingly.

Most whites from Europe and the United States believed these problems resulted from the mental inferiority of nonwhite races. Nineteenth-century biologists concurred. They believed that races of man differed in hereditary physical and mental characteristics, and viewed crossing between distant races with suspicion or outright antagonism.[2] Specifically, they argued that Negroes were, on an average, mentally inferior to European whites. In 1869 Francis Galton provided a simple quantitative model for the distribution of intelligence within and between populations.[3] He theorized that the intelligence of Negroes was, on an average, two grades below that of Englishmen, while the intelligence of the "Athenian race" of the Fifth Century BC was two grades above that of Englishmen. One of Galton's grades corresponds to approximately ten points on current IQ distributions. Galton based his quantitative analysis of hereditary mental differences between races upon faulty assumptions and scanty evidence. But in the late nineteenth century his analysis convinced almost all biologists. Galton merely made quantitative what biologists already assumed: that races differed hereditarily in mental traits.

Galton's analysis of racial differences indicated that an intellectually superior race should not breed with an inferior race because a small reduction in average intelligence caused a much greater reduction in the proportion of individuals in the highest grades of intelligence. And, he said, "We know how intimately the course of events is dependent upon the thoughts of a few illustrious men"[3] (p. 343). Other biologists condemned wide race crosses because some evidence indicated that racial hybrids had weak constitutions, especially if bred among themselves. But the evidence was meager and conflicting. Some anthropologists and political thinkers advocated race amalgamation as the best solution to rising race-related problems. A greater understanding of human heredity seemed necessary to resolve the biological merits or demerits of race crossing Mendelism offered hope.

Early influence of Mendelism on ideas of race crossing

With the rediscovery of Mendelian heredity in 1900 and the consequent rapid rise of genetics in the early twentieth century came a surge of interest in the human implications of the new science. The eugenics movement, defined by Galton as "giving the more suitable races or strains of blood a better chance of prevailing speedily over the less suitable",[4] was the most visible manifestation of this interest. By 1910, when the eugenics movement was beginning in earnest, Mendelians were crossing many related varieties of plants and animals, elucidating such previously inscrutable phenomena as dominance, sterility, reversion to ancestral characters, and recombination of traits. Since they believed that humans followed the same laws of inheritance, most Mendelians naturally thought their experimental work was crucial for an objective appraisal of race mixture in humans.

Charles Benedict Davenport was the first geneticist to devote considerable attention to problems of human heredity. His 1911 book, *Heredity in Relation to Eugenics*,[5] contained almost all that was then known of human genetics. Davenport was also the leading advocate of eugenics in the United States. He was among the first to identify Mendelian characters in man, an obvious preliminary to a rational program of eugenic selection. He believed that such traits as nomadism and criminality were simple Mendelian units. But he admitted that the evidence for these traits was weak, and by 1913 he had published more careful Mendelian analyses of the inheritance of eye color, hair color, and skin pigment in man. American geneticists recognized him as the leading student of human heredity, even if some of his conclusions were questionable.

By 1917 Davenport was convinced that Mendelians could speak intelligently about the genetics of human race crosses. He first published a long article on the inheritance of stature in man,[6] concluding that many genes controlled stature and that the components of stature could be inherited separately. For instance, he thought that an individual could inherit long arms from one parent and short legs from another. These ideas formed the basis for a second 1917 paper, entitled "The effects of race intermingling".[7] Although Davenport realized that accurate scientific data on human race mixture were meager, he believed that certain conclusions could be made by inference from studies on lower organisms. He used the example of hens. Leghorns had been bred to lay eggs, but not to brood. Brahmas, on the other hand, were bred to lay a clutch of eggs and to brood and hatch them before laying more. Leghorns were obviously well suited to chicken farmers who had artificial incubators, and Brahmas to those who did not. When the two breeds were crossed, the hybrid offspring were failures both as egg layers and as brooders. Thus the good qualities of each parent variety were lost in the cross.

Davenport believed that the moral for human races was clear. Each race had, through a long process of natural selection, developed genetic traits that were harmoniously adjusted both with each other and the environment. When two races differing by a number of characters interbred, some new combinations of characters were formed in the hybrids. Mendelian segregation would produce many more new combinations in subsequent offspring of the hybrids. Davenport thought many of these new combinations would be disharmonious, although some would be beneficial. For example, he said that a large, tall race might breed with a small, short one to yield, in the second generation, some offspring with "large frames and inadequate viscera" or "children of short stature with too large circulatory apparatus." Another example was the overcrowding or wide spacing of teeth probably caused by the "union of a large-jawed, large-toothed race and a small-jawed, small-toothed race." Nor were disharmonious combinations confined to physical characters. "One often sees in mulattos an ambition and push combined with intellectual inadequacy which makes the unhappy hybrid dissatisfied with his lot and a nuisance to others." In short, "miscegenation commonly spells disharmony – disharmony of physical, mental and temperamental qualities and this means also disharmony with environment. A hybridized people are a badly put together people and a dissatisfied, restless, ineffective people"[7] (pp. 366–367). Davenport did not argue in this paper that all race crossing should be stopped in the United States, but that a stringent program of eugenic selection should be instituted. Only people with good new combinations should be allowed to breed. The resulting strains might equal or surpass any other the world had seen.

Davenport carefully avoided condemnation of entire races as inferior. Others had no such hesitancy. In 1918 two young geneticists, Paul Popenoe and Roswell H. Johnson, wrote *Applied Eugenics*,[8] the most widely used textbook on this subject for more than 15 years. In a chapter entitled "The color line," they suggested that racial antipathy was a biological mechanism to protect races from miscegenation. They also argued that Negroes were inferior to whites. Their evidence was that Negroes had made no original contributions to world civilization; they had never risen much above barbarism in Africa; they did no better when transplanted to Haiti; and they failed to achieve white standards in America. Negroes scored significantly worse than whites on the new IQ tests. Furthermore, the disease resistance of the Negro was inferior to that of the white in North America, although, of course, this relative fitness of the two races was reversed in Africa. Popenoe and Johnson concluded that "the Negro race differs greatly from the white race, mentally as well as physically, and that in many respects it may be said to be inferior, when tested by the requirements of modern civilization and progress, with particular reference to North America." Regarding race crossing between Negroes and whites, they concluded that "in general the white race loses and the Negro gains from miscegenation." Consequently, they felt that they "must unhesitatingly condemn miscegenation"[8] (pp. 291–292). They recommended legislation to prohibit intermarriage and all sexual intercourse between the two races. *Applied Eugenics* sold well. I can find no evidence that geneticists disapproved of the chapter on race.

Edward Murray East of Harvard's Bussey Institution elaborated the arguments on race mixture advanced by Davenport and Popenoe and Johnson. One of the most highly regarded research geneticists in America, East was among the first to clarify multifactorial Mendelian inheritance. He also was a pioneer in hybrid corn research and an expert on inbreeding and crossbreeding in general. During World War I the government asked his assistance in agricultural planning; this spurred his interest in the social significance of genetics. When East and his former student Donald F. Jones published *Inbreeding and Outbreeding* in 1919, they subtitled it *Their Genetic and Sociological Significance.*[9] The book was a basic contribution to the Mendelian interpretation of breeding, and its significance was recognized by all experimental geneticists.

The last two chapters of *Inbreeding and Outbreeding*, written by East alone, dealt with the sociological significance of genetics, particularly the problems of race mixture. East divided race mixture into two kinds, those between closely related races and those between distantly related races. The former, as between various white races of Europe, had produced the most civilized humans. But East cited two genetic objections to wide human race crosses, as between Negroes and whites. First, Mendelian segregation would "break apart those compatible physical and mental qualities which have established a smoothly operating whole in each race by hundreds of generations of natural selection." Second, it was "an unnecessary accompaniment to humane treatment, an illogical extension of altruism . . . to seek to elevate the black race at the cost of lowering the white" because "in reality the negro is inferior to the white. This is not hypothesis or supposition; it is a crude statement of actual fact"[9] (pp. 253–254).

Geneticists reacted favorably, at least in print, to this double-barreled view of race crossing. Raymond Pearl reviewed *Inbreeding and Outbreeding* for *Science*.[10] Pearl, who later boasted of his opposition to "Nordic enthusiasts," wrote that the last two chapters might "fairly be regarded as among the sanest and most cogent arguments for the integral incorporation of eugenic ideas and ideals into the conduct of social and political affairs of life. . . . There is a refreshing absence of blind and blatant propaganda".[10] Many geneticists simply stuck to their work on lower organisms and did not generalize to humans. But those who did express an opinion agreed with one or more of the reasons advanced by East and Davenport against wide race crossing. Published opposition from geneticists and other biologists to these arguments on race crossing was nonexistent before 1924.

Harmonic and disharmonic race crossings

In 1921 most of the well known geneticists in Europe and America attended the second international congress of eugenics in New York City. There were many papers on race mixture. The one that attracted most attention was entitled "Harmonic and disharmonic race-crossings", by Jon Alfred Mjoen, a Norwegian biologist.[11]

Mjoen argued, as had Davenport, that "single qualities" dominated in the crossings of races of animals, and that these separate units were inherited undiluted. Thus, "disharmonic" combinations of these single qualities were possible through Mendelian recombination. Mjoen presented data indicating that crosses between Lapps and Nordics in Norway produced disharmonic offspring. The hybrids exhibited mental imbalance, including criminality, feebleminded-ness, and unwillingness to work. They suffered higher rates of tuberculosis and other diseases, which indicated physical disharmony. Mjoen also presented evidence from his experiments on crossing varieties of rabbits. Individuals from later generations of the hybrids showed lack of physical vigor and, in some cases, one upright and one pendant ear, a "symptom of disharmony in general"[11] (p. 57). Mjoen believed the rabbit crosses indicated the problems to be encountered in human crosses. He denied any race prejudice, but closed his paper with an impassioned plea for restraint in mingling disparate races. The papers from the congress were published in 1923. Soon other authors began to cite Mjoen's paper with approval.[12]

Now for the first time a geneticist spoke out clearly against the theory of disharmonious race crosses advanced by Davenport, East, and Mjoen. William Ernest Castle, a colleague of East's at the Bussey Institution, prepared a reply to Mjoen. Castle had a knack for getting into heated public controversies and then having to back down from his position. In 1906 he had advocated the mutation theory of Hugo de Vries, only to change to a selection theory of evolution by 1911. At that time he believed that selection could change Mendelian factors themselves. This belief was a heresy in the thinking of most Mendelians. Castle vigorously waged this battle in the journals until 1919, when he published a retraction. Castle's criticisms certainly stimulated important research, but his colleagues did not forget his record of controversy and retraction. In 1924 Castle was advocating another heresy. He was arguing that the factors that determine size, at least in mammals, were general factors affecting all parts of the skeleton simultaneously. Davenport, Mjoen, and most other Mendelians supported the conflicting view that special factors that could be separately inherited controlled the size of individual bones.

In his reply to Mjoen, Castle challenged the basic thesis that skeletal parts and organs were controlled by specific size factors.[13] Because of general size factors. Castle argued, disharmonies in race crossing were not to be expected. His own numerous experiments on crosses of rabbits had revealed no disharmonies. Mjoen's "disharmonies" in rabbits and humans were simply his value judgments and not biologically detrimental. In humans, "most inherited characters are blending," so the observed consequences of race crossing should not be deterioration, "but rather an intermediate degree of the characters involved." Examining data on crosses between African black races and European whites, American Indians and whites, and Lapps and Nordics, Castle concluded that the data supported his theory, not Mjoen's. Castle freely admitted, however, that African blacks had less native intelligence than whites, that mulattos were intermediate in intelligence, and that race crossing might legitimately be opposed for social reasons. But "so far as biological considerations are concerned, there is no race problem in the United States"[13] (p. 366).

So Castle, like East, believed that Negroes had on an average less intelligence than whites, and that mulattos had intermediate intelligence. East, following Galton's reasoning, used these supposed facts to argue that whites would lose a sizable percentage of their most intelligent people by crossing with blacks, too great a price to pay. Castle used the same facts to argue that in crossing, blacks were raised as much as whites were lowered, so biologically the crosses were neutral.

The amount of genetic evidence about human race crossing was minimal during the mid-1920s. In 1924 Samuel J. Holmes, professor of biology at the University of California, published an extensive bibliography of eugenics, one section of which was entitled "Race mixture and the intermarriage of different stocks."[14] Although he placed 209 entries in this section, he commented, I think accurately (p. 465):

> A much fuller list than I have compiled might have been made on the subject of race mixture, but it would probably be of little value. Even most of the references I have cited contain little of really substantial merit in relation to this subject. . . . The problem of race mixture is one we have scarcely begun to attack in the careful, systematic, and scientific manner which alone can produce results of value.[14]

In 1929 Davenport and his assistant, Morris Steggerda, published a substantial study entitled *Race Crossing in Jamaica*, which they hoped would relieve this dearth of hard data.[15] The bulk of the study concerned the physical characteristics of blacks, browns (mulattos), and whites in Jamaica. The authors found that, with respect to a particular character, if blacks and whites differed considerably, the browns tended to be more variable than either parent race. They attributed this extra variability to Mendelian segregation. In only one case, however, did they point to a disharmonious physical result of the crosses. Some browns had "the long legs of the Negro and the short arms of the white, which would put them at a disadvantage in picking up things off the ground." Davenport and Steggerda did not emphasize this slight physical disharmony; they concluded that "physically there is little to choose between the three groups"[16] (pp. 237–238). They thought the greatest disharmonies were in the mental traits of the hybrids. This was expected on Mendelian grounds because Jamaican blacks and whites differed considerably on tests of these traits. The performance of the browns was, on an average, better than that of the blacks, but some browns performed excellently while others performed miserably. Davenport and Steggerda concluded that if society could select the best half of the hybrids, as breeders did with cows or chickens, the cross of blacks and whites would be beneficial. But this was unfeasible, so they opposed race mixture because of the large percentage of intellectually incompetent persons produced.

Herbert Spencer Jennings was among the first to use the results of the widely read study of Davenport and Steggerda. Jennings had achieved prominence in the early 1900s through his work on the behavior of lower organisms, and he was a highly respected geneticist. A political liberal, he had vigorously attacked the eugenics movement for its hereditarian bias. But Jennings took Davenport's conclusions seriously as he showed in his 1930 book, *The Biological Basis of Human Nature*.[17] He began his chapter on race mixture with a careful Mendelian analysis, which included a drawing of a large dog with short legs, its sternum nearly touching the ground. The dog's parents were a Saint Bernard and a dachshund. If such disharmonious combinations could be obtained from crossing dogs, Jennings suggested, similar results could be expected in human crosses. In support of his theory Jennings repeated Davenport's conclusions about the physical and mental disharmonies of the hybrid Jamaicans.

William Castle was thoroughly annoyed with this rejuvenation of the spectre of disharmonious race crossings. He prepared a rebuttal for *Science*.[18] The hybrid dog, he said, was no more ridiculous-looking than the dachshund itself. Castle accurately asserted that there was a "complete vacuum of evidence" for disharmonies of body organs and body size, hypothetically predicted by Jennings and Davenport. As for the disharmonious Jamaican browns with the long legs of the Negro and the short arms of the whites, Castle calculated from the data that the disadvantage was I centimeter of reach at most. Davenport had not been specific about the size of this disharmony in his conclusions. Castle concluded with a remark often quoted by opponents of "scientific racism"[18] (p. 605):

> We like to think of the Negro as an inferior. We like to think of Negro-white crosses as a degradation of the white race. We look for evidence in support of the idea and try to persuade ourselves that we have found it even when the resemblance is very slight. The honestly made records of Davenport and Steggerda tell a very different story about hybrid Jamaicans from that which Davenport and Jennings tell about them in broad sweeping statements. The former will never reach the ears of eugenics propagandists and Congressional committees; the latter will be with us as the bogey men of pure-race enthusiasts for the next hundred years.

Davenport immediately wrote to Jennings to ask whether they should reply to Castle. Jennings answered:

My inclination is rather to ignore Castle's outbreak, so far as my book is concerned. As you indicate, he is very much given to sudden outbursts of this sort, and at such times he has a genius for missing the point. I don't know of anyone that approaches him in the number of embittered controversies he has had, in which he ultimately admits that he was wrong. . . . What could one say, without seeming unfriendly, about his assumption and assertion that the reason you and I take the position we do on this matter is because we hold the negro to be inferior and want to prevent intercrossing? How shall we ever have any knowledge on such a matter if it not be made the object of investigation?[19]

Davenport did reply to Castle in *Science*.[20] He argued that Castle's belief in general size factors determined his reaction to *Race Crossing in Jamaica*, and Davenport challenged that belief. He further declared that he and Steggerda never claimed that browns were a degradation of the white race. He could not, however, reply to Castle's damaging observation about the 1-cm disharmony in the reach of some browns.

Castle was again playing the role of a maverick. In 1924 he had been the first geneticist to speak out against the race theories of Mjoen and Davenport; in 1930 he was continuing the argument with minimal published support from other geneticists. Many of them doubted Castle's faith in the general size factors that were the basis of his genetic argument against the possibility of disharmonious combinations in disparate human race crosses. Jennings, Davenport, and East clearly expected that Castle would eventually have to recant on this issue as he had in earlier episodes.

Jennings, Davenport, and East believed they were being purely objective scientists in their concern about race mixture in humans. All three were staunch supporters of civil liberties for every individual. East was thoroughly indignant about discrimination against Negroes on trains and in theaters, and restaurants. He exclaimed that such discriminatory actions were "the gaucheries of a provincial people, on a par with the guffaws of a troop of yokels who see a well-dressed man for the first time".[21] Davenport and Jennings would have agreed. But all three believed that objective science must be heeded, and, in their view, the biological facts were that wide race crosses in human were probably harmful.

Race Crossing in Jamaica by Davenport and Steggerda marked the end of geneticists' attempts to emphasize obvious physical disharmonies in race cross-ing. The book was thoroughly discredited in a review by Karl Pearson.[22] He pointed out that the sample sizes used by Davenport and Steggerda were too small to bear the weight of their conclusions, and that their selection of subjects was suspect. Pearson made clear the magnitude of the difficulty of conducting experiments necessary to reveal disharmonies in race crossings. Furthermore, other studies of race crossings published by geneticists and anthropologists in the late 1920s revealed no significant physical disharmonies. The most important of these studies were by Leslie C. Dunn and A.M. Tozzer on race crossing in Hawaii,[23] by R, Ruggles Gates on Amerindian crosses in Canada,[24] by

H.L. Shapiro on the descendants from the *Bounty* on Pitcairn Island,[25] and by Melville Herskovits on Negro-white crosses in the United States.[26]

As the question of obvious physical disharmonies in race mixture disappeared in the early 1930s, some geneticists began to emphasize the more subtle problems of mental and physical disharmonies in race crossing. In 1931 Jon Alfred Mjoen published an article in *Eugenics Review* entitled "Race-crossing and glands".[27] He repeated his earlier arguments, buttressed by the following new one: The physical and psychic well-being of the human body is dependent upon the functioning of the endocrine glands; these glands are in turn "dependent upon different genes"; therefore, race crossing may lead to disharmoniously correlated endocrine systems that could cause physical disturbance. Mjoen cited evidence indicating higher rates of diabetes, cretinism, and absence of disease resistance in crosses between Nordics and Lapps in Norway.

The most significant experimental support for Mjoen's glandular theory came from Charles R. Stockard's work on crossing breeds of dogs.[28] All 78 of his first-generation hybrids between Saint Bernards and Great Danes developed a strange paralysis of the hind legs. In second-generation hybrids physical and mental traits were combined in new ways, some of which Stockard believed were disharmonious. He studied especially the recombination of structures affected by achondroplasia, acromegaly, and microcephaly; all were known to be under glandular control. Thus, Stockard's experiments appeared to support Mjoen's hypothesis. Further support for Mjoen's general hypothesis appeared in 1931 with the English translation of the third edition of the human genetics textbook by Eugen Fischer, Erwin Baur, and Fritz Lenz.[29] Raymond Pearl, reviewing the 1928 German edition, had lamented: "It is a pity that we have in English no such sound, comprehensive, and stimulating work as this on human heredity".[30] The book immediately became the standard work on human heredity in England and America, as well as in Germany. The authors pointed out clearly the dangers of mental disharmony in disparate race crosses. In his section Lenz, for example, commented that "the crossing of Teutons and Jew is likely, as a rule, to have an unfavourable effect, for it will impair the peculiar excellences of both types"[29] (p. 639).

Thus, in 1931, although the issue of gross physical disharmonies was disappearing, fear of glandular and mental disharmonies still caused some geneticists to believe that race mixture was detrimental.

From condemnation to agnosticism

In the mid-1930s, geneticists' published statements about the effects of race crossing changed from condemnation to agnosticism. In part this change came from biological evidence. In the late 1920s and early 1930s geneticists experienced a growing realization that human heredity was more complex than they had previously thought. Thus they became more hesitant to make positive statements about hereditary race differences and the effects of race crossing. Also, some evidence collected or compiled by physical anthropologists Melville Herskovits[31] in the United States and J.C. Trevor[32] in England indicated that hybrid populations had no more variability than did the pure parent races. The evidence for this conclusion was suggestive, but hardly convincing, because accurate measurements of the parent races were generally unavailable and because the "hybrids" exhibited all degrees of race mixture. Herskovits claimed his findings were incompatible with Mendelian heredity because one should expect more, not less, variability in the hybrids. Geneticist H.J. Muller[33] responded by arguing that even if Herskovits' dubious data were reliable, at least two Mendelian hypotheses could account for the apparently anomalous result. On both hypotheses, Muller said, few disharmonies should be expected from race crossing. But Muller's paper was basically no more than a very theoretical exercise.

More important than new biological evidence as a factor prompting geneticists to publicly reevaluate their theories of race mixture was the application of Nazi race doctrines before World War II. The Nazi doctrines resembled those of Madison Grant, who had declared that "the cross between any of the three European races and a Jew is a Jew".[34] Recognizing the German threat to personal liberty and to the world, some geneticists and anthropologists published popular books and articles debunking Nazi propaganda. *We Europeans*, published in 1936 by Julian Huxley and A.C. Haddon,[35] and *Heredity and Politics*, published in 1938 by J.B.S. Haldane,[36] were perhaps the two most significant examples. Both Huxley and Haldane attacked Nazi race doctrines with vigor, but they stopped short of denying hereditary mental differences or condoning all racial intermingling. The genetic evidence about race mixture was simply nonexistent, they said, and that situation should be remedied. Haldane wrote (pp. 184–185):

> I would urge the extraordinary importance of a scientific study of the effects of racial crossing for the future of the British Commonwealth. Until such a study has been accomplished, and it is a study that will take generations to complete, we are not, I think, justified in any dogmatism as to the effect of racial crossing. . . . I am sure that the fact of our ignorance is a deplorable one which we ought to remedy.[36]

Huxley's view was similar. In a letter to the editor of *Eugenics Review* he stated:

> In human genetics, the most important immediate problem is to my mind that of "race crossing." . . . The question whether certain race crosses produce "disharmonious" results needs more adequate exploration. Social implications must also be borne in mind in considering this subject.[37]

Haldane and Huxley concluded accurately that the evidence was inadequate to assess the biological results of race mixture. Geneticists had previously found their greatest successes by applying Mendel's method of careful pedigree analysis, but they had no statistically significant data from similar analyses of wide human race crosses. Without this data no one could accurately assess disharmonies or disruption of smoothly working gene complexes in race crosses. Recognizing this, both Haldane and Huxley advocated immediate further study of race mixture. Their views indicate a significant shift in genetics literature since the publication of *Inbreeding and Outbreeding* in 1919. At that time East had argued without opposition that genetics showed wide race crosses in humans to be bad. By 1939 most geneticists, like Haldane and Huxley, were taking an agnostic position.

From agnosticism to certitude

During and shortly after World War II, biologists and anthropologists published many books attacking Nazi race theories and racism in general. Most of these books exhibited a further change in attitude. They declared that race crossing was sometimes biologically favorable, but never detrimental. The new orthodoxy was well represented in 1946 by Leslie C. Dunn and Theodosius Dobzhansky in their little book *Heredity, Race, and Society*.[38] They intended the book to give the layperson a precise description of human genetics. Their opinion on race mixture was clearly stated and at the time widely accepted (p. 114):

> Contrary to opinion vociferously expressed by some sincere but misguided people, . . . a trend [toward race fusion] is not biologically dangerous. Mixing of closely related races may even lead to increased vigor. As for the most distantly separated races, there is no basis in fact to think that either biological stimulation or deterioration follows crossing. The widespread belief that human race hybrids are inferior to both of their parents and somehow constitutionally unbalanced must be counted among the superstitions.[38]

To the public this statement by Dunn and Dobzhansky represented a significant change of view from that expressed by Haldane and Huxley in 1938. Race crossing now appeared to involve no biological danger. But the scientific evidence on race crossing had not changed significantly between 1938 and 1946. There simply was not a decisive study on race crossing during that time.

Another important book on human genetics appeared in 1946. *Human Genetics*, by R. Ruggles Gates,[39] was 1518 pages long and contained a summary of almost all the work in the field. Gates believed that wide race crosses could produce disharmonious results, he gave a few examples from the work of others and commented that "the existence of such conditions in crosses has frequently been denied"[39] (p. 1358). Although *Human Genetics* became a standard reference, it was published too late for most human geneticists in the United States or England to take its views on race crossing seriously. Three years later, Curt Stern published the first substantial classroom textbook on human genetics.[40] He considered it at least "conceivable that different parts of the body may sometimes be genetically determined in a sufficiently independent manner so that actual incongruities may arise"[40] (p. 569) in race crosses. Even this agnostic view would almost disappear during the early 1950s.

The Unesco statement on race

An examination of the 1951 Statement on Race by the United Nations Educational, Scientific, and Cultural Organization (Unesco) indicates clearly that the view of Dunn and Dobzhansky on race crossing was widespread among geneticists by that time. But before turning to the Unesco statement, I should emphasize that many geneticists were reluctant to formulate or sign such a statement before the war. For example, Franz Boas wrote to Raymond Pearl in October 1935, requesting him to formulate a statement on race. It was hoped that the statement, to be signed by prominent anthropologists and biologists and then circulated around the world, would counteract Nazi propaganda on race. Pearl responded by agreeing with Boas that the philosophy of the Nordic enthusiasts was "wholly absurd, unscientific, and in the highest degree mischievous." But he went on to say:

> Holding these views I think fully as strongly as you do, I nevertheless venture to question the wisdom and strategy of taking the action you suggest in your letter. . . . I have a strong aversion to round-robins by scientific men, and most particularly where the pronouncement is really, however camouflaged, about political questions or angles of political questions which have more or less relation to purely scientific matters. In my observation such round-robins never do any good in correcting an evil they are supposed or intended to correct, and, furthermore, in my observation they always do harm to the scientific men who sign them and through these men to science itself. . . . I am unalterably opposed now and all times towards any attitude of pontifical authoritarianism under the aegis of science.[41]

By 1939 some geneticists had become more concerned, and at the Seventh International Genetics Congress they formulated the "geneticist's manifesto" on the future improvement of human populations.[42] The manifesto, nine paragraphs long, rejected Nazi-like race theories in only two sentences, and no attempt was made to formalize or widely publicize this document as a statement on race. After the war, of course, geneticists were more willing to formulate and sign a formal statement on race.

In 1949 Unesco resolved to collect scientific materials on race and to publicize a statement concerning them, with the stated object of combating racism. A committee of anthropologists and sociologists, chaired by Ashley Montagu, drew up the first statement on race, and it was issued to the world on 18 July 1950.[43] Many geneticists and physical anthropologists, however, believed the statement was unscientific because it contained assertions such as (p. 93): "Biological studies lend support to the ethic of universal brotherhood; for man is born with drives toward co-operation, and unless those drives are satisfied, men and nations alike fall ill."[43]

Because many scientists were dissatisfied with the statement, Unesco officials arranged to issue a second statement on race by geneticists and physical anthropologists. Haldane and Huxley, both of whom had been firm agnostics on

the biological consequences of race crossing in the late 1930s, were members
of the committee which issued the second statement in 1951. This statement
conflicted directly with the two arguments against race crossing which Edward
Murray East raised in 1919. East argued that Mendelian segregation following
wide race crosses would produce disharmonious results. The statement read
(p. 15):

> As there is no reliable evidence that disadvantageous effects are pro-
> duced thereby, no biological justification exists for prohibiting inter-
> marriage between persons of different races.[43]

East also had argued that the Negro was mentally inferior to the white. The
statement said (p. 15–16):

> Available scientific knowledge provides no basis for believing that the
> groups of mankind differ in their innate capacity for intellectual and
> emotional development.[43]

These sentences were judiciously worded. Although stated in the negative, they
conveyed the impression that biological science showed (1) that race crossing
was at worst biologically neutral, and (2) that races were alike in hereditary
mental traits.

The Unesco statement was sent to 106 prominent physical anthropologists
and geneticists. Of the 80 who responded, 23 accepted the statement in
its published form, and 26 agreed with its tenor but disagreed on particulars.
The others had substantial criticisms. Many geneticists objected most to
point (2) above. Muller's comments represented the thrust of the objections
(p. 49):

> In view of the admitted existence of some physically expressed her-
> editary differences of a conspicuous nature, between the averages or
> the medians of the races, it would be strange if there were not also
> some hereditary differences affecting the mental characteristics which
> develop in a given environment, between these averages or medians.[43]

Muller added that he was convinced most geneticists agreed with him, even
those who signed the statement outright.

The statement's assertion that race mixture was harmless received very little
criticism, however. Only A.H. Sturtevant questioned the validity of the assertion. Joseph Needham wanted to know why the statement had failed to tell the
world that "race mixture is positively advantageous, rather than not disadvanta-
geous"[43] (p. 65). It is true that in the next 2 years Gates and C.D. Darlington
publicly criticized the statement's position on race crossing; both were dismissed
as radical hereditarians by most human geneticists in the United States and
England. Thus the 1951 Unesco statement marks a clear point at which the
public attitude of geneticists on the issue of race crossing had reached the current
dominant view: that race crossing is at worst harmless.

Summary and conclusions

Geneticists in England and the United States clearly reversed their published remarks on the effects of race crossing between 1930 and 1950. The reversal occurred in two steps. First came the change in the 1930s from a condemnation of wide race crosses to an agnostic view. The second change, from the agnostic view to the belief that wide race crosses were at worst biologically harmless, took place during and shortly after World War II.

The entire reversal occurred in the light of little new compelling data from studies of actual human race crosses. The lack of new data is unsurprising. Few geneticists wished to initiate experiments that took three human generations to complete. And controlled race crosses are hard to arrange, even with government grants. What might be more surprising was the willingness of geneticists to make such positive statements about race crossing when they had so little reliable genetic evidence.

I interviewed or wrote to ten prominent geneticists who worked on human genetics between 1930 and 1950. Not one believed that new evidence on race crossing was the primary reason why geneticists changed their minds about the effects of race crossing. One plausible explanation, that the rise of "population thinking" caused geneticists to change their minds, does not fit the evidence.[44] Castle was no more of a "population" thinker than East, yet they differed radically in their conclusions about race crossing. What, then, did cause geneticists to change their minds?

Most important was the revulsion of educated people in the United States and England to Nazi race doctrines and their use in justifying extermination of Jews. Few geneticists wanted to argue, as had the Nazis, that biology showed race crossing was harmful. Instead, having witnessed the horrible toll, geneticists naturally wanted to argue that biology showed race crossing was at worst harmless. No racist nation could misuse that conclusion. And geneticists did revise their biology to fit their feelings of revulsion.

Geneticists' ideas about the related question of hereditary mental differences between races is perhaps undergoing a similar development to that seen earlier in their ideas about race crossing. In 1951, judging from the response to the Unesco second statement on race and comments in genetics literature, most geneticists agreed with Muller that races probably differed in significant average mental traits. By 1969, when Arthur Jensen advocated this view in his controversial article,[45] most geneticists who spoke publicly on the issue had adopted an agnostic position. Knowledge of hereditary racial differences in IQ had scarcely changed since 1951, but society had changed considerably in racial attitudes. It will be interesting to see if during the next several decades geneticists will argue, on the basis of little additional evidence, that hereditary mental differences between races do not exist.

I am not condemning geneticists because social and political factors have influenced their scientific conclusions about race crossing and race differences. It is necessary and natural that changing social attitudes will influence areas of biology where little is known and the conclusions are possibly socially explosive. The real danger is not that biology changes with society, but that the public expects biology to provide the objective truth apart from social influences. Geneticists and the public should realize that the science of genetics is often closely intertwined with social attitudes and political considerations.

Study probes

1   How does Galton define the eugenics movement?
2   In what ways did both eugenics and Mendelian genetics influence early twentieth-century geneticists' views on 'race crossing'?
3   Outline the 1951 Unesco first and second statements on 'race', which represented a shift in 'scientific' attitudes towards 'race crossing'.
4   According to Provine, why did this change occur?
5   How are science and politics linked?

References and notes

1   R.C. Punnett, *Mendelism* (Bowes & Bowes, Cambridge, England, ed. 2, 1907), p. 80.
2   J.S. Hatler, Jt., *Outcasts from Evolution* (University of Illinois Press, Urbana, 1971).
3   F. Galton, *Hereditary Gentius* (Appleton, New York, 1870), chaps. 3 and 20.
4   F. Galton, *Inquiries into Human Faculty* (Macmillan, London, 1883), p. 24.
5   C.B. Davenport, *Heredity in Relation to Eugenics* (Holt, New York, 1911).
6   C.B. Davenport, *Genetics* **2**, 313 (1917).
7   C.B. Davenport, *Proc. Amer. Phil. Soc.* **56**, 364 (1917).
8   P. Popenoe and R.H. Johnson, *Applied Eugenics* (Macmillan, New York, 1918).
9   E.M. East and D.F. Jones, *Inbreeding and Outbreeding* (Lippincott, Philadelphia, 1919).
10   R. Pearl, *Science*, **51**, 415 (1920).
11   J.A. Mjoen, in *Eugenics in Race and State* (Williams & Wilkins, Baltimore, 1923), pp. 41–61.
12   See, for example, S.A. Rice, *J. Hered.* **15**, 183 (1924).
13   W.E. Castle, *J. Hered.* **15**, 363 (1924).
14   S.J. Holmes, *A. Bibliography of Eugenics* (University of California Press, Berkeley, 1924).
15   C.B. Davenport and M. Steggerda, *Race Crossing in Jamaica* (Publication No. 395, Carnegie Institution of Washington, Washington, D.C., 1929).
16   C.B. Davenport, *Sci. Mon.* **27**, 225 (1928). This article was taken from a draft of the book by Davenport and Steggerda (*15*).
17   H.S. Jennings, *The Biological Basis of Human Nature* (Norton, New York, 1930).
18   W.E. Castle, *Science* **71**, 603 (1930).
19   Letter from H.S. Jennings to C.B. Davenport, 20 June 1930 (Herbert Spencer Jennings Papers, American Philosophical Society, Philadelphia).
20   C.B. Davenport, *Science* **72**, 501 (1930).

21   E.M. East, *Heredity and Human Affairs* (Scribners, New York, 1927), p. 181.

22   K. Pearson, *Nature* **126**, 427 (1930).

23   L.C. Dunn and A.M. Tozzer, *Pap. Peabody Mus. Amer. Archaeol. Etchol. Harvard Univ.* **11**, 90 (1928).

24   R.R. Gates, *J. Roy. Anthropol. Inst. Gt. Brit. Ireland* **53**, 511 (1928).

25   H.L. Shapiro, *Mem. Bernic P. Bishop Mus. Honolulu* **11**, 1 (1929).

26   M.J. Herskovitz, *The American Negro: A Study in Racial Crossing* (Knopf, New York, 1928).

27   J.A. Mjoen, *Eugen. Rev.* **23**, 31 (1931).

28   C.R. Stockard, *The Physical Basis of Personality* (Norton, New York, 1931), chaps. 13 to 15.

29   E. Fischer, E. Baur, F. Lenz, *Human Heredity* (Macmillan, New York, 1931).

30   R. Pearl, *Quart. Rev. Biol.* **3**, 136 (1928).

31   M.J. Herskovits, *Amer, Natur.* **61**, 68 (1927).

32   J.C. Trevor, *Eugen. Rev.* **30**, 21 (1938).

33   H.J. Muller, *Amer: Natur.* **70**, 409 (1936).

34   M. Grant, *Passing of the Great Race* (Scribners, New York, 1916), p. 16.

35   J. Huxley and A.C. Haddon, *We Europeans* (Harper, New York, 1936).

36   J.B.S. Haldane, *Heredity and Politics* (Norton, New York, 1938).

37   J. Huxley, *Eugen. Rev.* **29**, 294 (1938).

38   L.C. Dunn and Th. Dobzhansky, *Heredity, Race, and Society* (Pelican, New York, 1946).

39   R.R. Gates, *Human Genetics* (Macmillan, New York, 1946).

40   C. Stern, *Human Genetics* (Freeman, San Francisco, 1949).

41   Letter from R. Pearl to F. Boas, 3 October 1935 (Franz Boas Papers, American Philosophical Society, Philadelphia).

42   *J. Hered.* **30**, 371 (1939).

43   Both statements on race and excerpts from scientists' responses are found in *The Race Concept* (Unesco, Paris, 1951).

44   A view expressed by E. Mayr and B. Wallace.

45   A. Jensen, *Harvard Educ. Rev.* **39**, 1 (1969).

Chapter 15

Paul Brodwin

GENETICS, IDENTITY AND THE ANTHROPOLOGY OF ESSENTIALISM

From *Anthropological Quarterly*, 75 (2) (2002), pp. 323–330.

F OR SEVERAL DECADES, anthropology has participated in the general deconstruction of "identity" as a stable object of scholarly inquiry. The notion that individuals craft their identity through social performances, and hence that their identity is not a fixed essence, fundamentally drives current research into gender and sexuality. The notion that collective identity emerges out of political struggle and compromise underlies contemporary studies of race, ethnicity and nationalism. The anti-essentialist mood of today's anthropology fits with wider currents in philosophy (e.g., critiques of the autonomous, self-sustaining subject within Western metaphysics) as well as feminism and cultural studies (e.g., examination of the unconscious aspects of identity formation and the political resistance enabled by multiple and hybrid identities) (see Hall and Du Gay 1996, McRobbie 1994).

Outside the academy, however, and to the dismay of anthropologists who fancy themselves as the cultural avant-garde, essentialist identities grow ever more powerful and seductive. New genetic knowledge, for example, adds the cachet of objective science to the notion that one's identity is an inborn, natural, and unalterable quality. Rapid advances in sequencing and analyzing the human genome have strengthened essentialist thinking about identity in American society and elsewhere, and anthropologists can help elucidate what is at stake.

Emerging genetic knowledge thus has the potential to transform contemporary notions of social coherence and group identity. I am the co-principal investigator of an interdisciplinary group pursuing this topic, funded by a multiyear grant from the National Human Genome Research Institute through its program on Ethical, Legal and Social Implications (ELSI). Our research team, comprising leading bioethicists, geneticists, and ethnic studies specialists, is building a common vocabulary and conceptual framework for the effects of current-day genetics on notions of individual and collective identity, and hence the fundamental basis for social connection.

Why is this a compelling question for anthropology? As genetic technologies move out of research laboratories and into public life, there arise enormous debates about their proper use and interpretation (see Brodwin 2000). The ramifying debates about genetic technologies (which appear in court cases, internet sites, articles and books) are driven by large questions about inclusion and diversity in American society, as Rayna Rapp (1999) and Kaja Finkler (2000) have demonstrated for genetic testing and predictive diagnosis. Not surprisingly, contemporary debates over claims of identity (who I am, fundamentally) and of social connection (who I belong with, fundamentally) have very high stakes. Moreover, the meaning of the "fundamental," in that last sentence, changes in the presence of genetic evidence.

For example, tracing your ancestry – via a pattern of particular alleles, or mutations on the Y chromosome or in mitochondrial DNA – has become not just a laboratory technique, but a political act. Who in our society requests this sort of DNA analysis, and who provides it? Once people learn the results, who controls what those results mean? It is no longer just geneticists and population biologists, but also political activists, individuals claiming inclusion in a particular ethnic, racial, or national group, and those who must decide to accept or reject their claims. To interpret the results of research with genetic markers means not just judging whether the laboratory used the right population-specific allele or had a large enough sample size. It also involves judging the worth of genetic knowledge against other kinds of claims to authentic identity and group membership (oral history, written documentation, cultural practices, inner convictions). What is at stake in genetically-based claims of identity or rightful belonging is not just good or bad science. What is at stake is also personal esteem and self-worth, group cohesion, access to resources, and the redressing of historical injustice.

It turns out that setting the record straight about who is related to whom is contested right from the start, and for good reason. Adding genetic evidence does not make things any easier; it might even make things harder. In any case, it adds an entirely new set of experts to the debates (not just the archivist, historian, the professor of ethnic studies or anthropology, but also the bioethicist and geneticist). At the end of my essay, I will raise some questions about the place of expert authority in this arena. But let me begin with some axioms for thinking about identity claims in the wake of contemporary genetics.

The techniques I mentioned above – use of genetic markers, especially Y chromosome and mitochondrial DNA mutations – generate knowledge of ancestry, the links between people in the present and their biological forbears. They announce a long-term generational connection. But people always use knowledge of ancestry to illuminate social connections in the present. Knowledge of ancestry ratifies or even creates a social connection in the present. For example, geneticists in England have used Y-chromosome markers to demonstrate that at least one of the clans of Lemba, a tribe in South Africa and

Zimbabwe, may be descended from Semitic peoples. Lemba interpreted the genetic finding as confirming their oral tradition of Jewish descent. It also confirmed their conviction that they are Jews, which they already believed because of such practices as keeping one day of the week holy, circumcising newborn males, and not eating pork. However, what does it mean to say that this evidence "confirms" the Jewish identity of Lemba? After all, Jews themselves have their own complex and historically rooted rules for judging membership (which govern the efficacy of conversion, specify the matrilineal inheritance of Jewish identity, etc.). Genetic evidence will probably not fit perfectly into these long-standing and canonically-based rules of ethnic inclusion and exclusion.

For the Lemba, finding out that they were "genetically Jewish" (a loaded term) confirmed their oral tradition, but it did not lead to mass immigration to Israel and demand for citizenship papers. But what if it had? (Remember that Israel offers the "right of return" to all Jews.) It's an important thought experiment, and it illustrates my major point. To claim a certain social identity always implies certain rights and obligations. To specify what counts as legitimate belonging will affect how people respect such rights or enforce these obligations. For example, specifying what counts as a mother-child relationship (in a world of sophisticated surrogacy technologies where children can have two or even three mothers) is prior to deciding what mothers and children owe to each other. Specifying who counts as a citizen precedes conventional judgments of what a nation and its citizens owe each other and what sort of moral claim they have on each other.

We must therefore ask, how does new genetic knowledge change the ways people claim connection to each other and to larger collectivities? How, in turn, does this process change the resulting webs of obligation and responsibility: personal, legal, moral, and financial? Knowledge of genetic connection alters how we imagine our "significant same": those people who are significantly like me, connected to me, and hence the same as me in some categorical sense. Genetic knowledge has the power to change the group with whom we share a "deep, horizontal comradeship" (Anderson 1991). The changes could unfold in two ways: (1) such knowledge may undermine received wisdom about family, ethnic, and racial identity or (2) it may shore up conventional understandings of identity. Of course, knowledge itself doesn't change anything. Particular people use such knowledge either to undermine or buttress conventional understandings. Even more, they use the knowledge as historical actors, aware of their group's unique tragedies and longed-for future, and also as political actors seeking out compromise and short-term gains.

The possibility of tracing genetic links between African-Americans and populations in West and Central Africa illuminates similar issues, and it also paves the way for my final point about the ambiguities of professional expertise. Is it possible to use DNA markers to trace a genealogical link between individuals or families in the USA and ethnic or tribal communities in Africa? Is it feasible to do so (in terms of time and money, access to individuals in African countries willing to donate their genetic material, etc.) How should genetic evidence be integrated with oral history and archival evidence (manifests of slave ships, plantation records, contemporary chronicles, etc.)? The turn to genetics obviously demands careful methodological thinking.

But it also raises overarching and quite sensitive political and ethical questions. To begin with, we should interrogate the very way we discuss this use of genetic technologies. Who is posing the questions, and before what audience? At what point, in the long history of American racism, have Americans begun to raise these questions about genetic and cultural connections? How do the questions arise from popular self-consciousness about multi-culturalism? We should also recognize the emotional stakes in the discussion. Culture loss, as experienced in the Middle Passage, is something to be mourned. To refer to this use of population genetics as the "restoration of African-American genealogy" or a "vital step in helping . . . heal the historical wounds of slavery" (in the words of supporters of such tests quoted in the national media) already raises expectations and sets in motion a powerful narrative of loss and redemption.

Again we must ask, how does the addition of genetic evidence change the way people figure their membership in a certain group? Think of the experience of Jews who visit the Western Wall in Jerusalem. Many American Jews who visit it report an unexpected experience: their collective history has suddenly become material, rendered tangible and visible. Visiting it, seeing it, and touching it creates the sense that their group's myth has just been authorized as non-fiction. A mere notion or shared recollection of the past has become certified as object-ive history. (This is a crucial change, since notions of objective history typically function as charters for political mobilization in the present.) Establishing genetic connections is thus enormously compelling for people who mourn the passage from homeland to diaspora, and whose collective identity involves the sense of unjust dislocation and culture-loss.

However, there are also potential dangers to this use of genetic evidence. In the case of African-American ancestry projects, it may provide a competing basis for ethnic identification (e.g., Yoruba, Fulani, Wolof) which can undercut the sense of shared interests (and hence unity) among African-American communities in the USA. Giving people an alternative basis of ethnic identification may well run into the same opposition as the use of "mixed race" as an American census category, and for the same reasons. Moreover, what new collective identity terms should people use? Would it make sense to use ethnic terms (such as Yoruba)? Wouldn't regional terms (e.g., the Casamance region, the Niger delta) be more appropriate, given the scientific frameworks of population genetics? What about terms such as Senegalese or Malian which refer simultaneously to a geographic region and a political entity (albeit one created in part by European colonialism). In general, such questions demonstrate how genetic evidence can de-stabilize long-standing patterns of community membership. Additionally, genetic knowledge might also provoke "ethnogenesis" or the emergence of novel ethnic formations.

Mitochondrial DNA and Y-chromosome tracing concerns genealogical descent in exclusively the female or male line, respectively. But precisely because of the nature of New World slavery, many people have complex mixed genealogies, created by sexual exploitation and the deliberate mixing of enslaved Africans during the Middle Passage and on American or Caribbean plantations.

Basing an account of one's "cultural past" on genetic evidence may thus substi-tute a fictively pure genealogy for a more historically accurate, but mixed, one. We need to ask, therefore, what people wish to accomplish through the use of genetic tracing of African ancestries. Arguably, people here are turning to genetic evidence in order to stabilize a particular historical consciousness: the conviction of connectedness to a certain cultural group over vast distance and centuries-long separation. Such evidence becomes compelling for two reasons. First, it acquires the general cachet of science as the ultimate guarantor of truth. But second, people regard genes as "more stable over time than more putatively accidental aspects of identity" (such as nationality, citizenship, religion, etc.).

To be blunt: are people being seduced by the promise of a pure, but fictive genealogy? Consider the following example. Y chromosomes are passed only through the male line, and an individual has 16 male ancestors in the 5th preceding generation. If you had 1 European ancestor in that generation, and the rest of your male (and female) ancestors were African, then you would be 1/32 European, but phenotypically black, and of course culturally black in the USA. But if that European man happened to be your father's father's father's father's father, then Y-chromosome typing would place your ancestry entirely in Europe (for example, in some Scottish village). Finding that you are genetically descended from a Scottish highlander will certainly de-stabilize your ethnic identity! Such knowledge ruptures the backward-looking narrative that you had hoped to confirm.

Do the experts in relevant fields (biological and cultural anthropologists, geneticists, ethicists, etc.) have a professional responsibility to ensure that the users of African-American genetic genealogies don't make mistakes – that is, that they don't succumb to a population-based genetic essentialism? To begin with, no responsible geneticist would say that there exists a single gene for a complex behavioral trait, let alone the marker for an ethnic-racial group. A gene is simply a long string of base nucleotides, and the passage from nucleotide to protein to anatomical structure to behavior to collective behavior to self-conscious, historically emergent notion of ethnic distinction is very long indeed. So, the scholarly (and left-liberal) opposition to "genetic essentialism" is not really a reaction to contemporary genetics, but rather to its reception. The essentializing occurs at the level of popular reconstructions of genetic science, and professional anti-essentialist interventions should be directed there as well.

What is the place of expert knowledge (of the geneticist, the philosopher, the anthropologist) in the scenario about Y-chromosomal tracing and African-American genealogies (or similar genetic identity projects)? Is it to replace a misunderstanding of genetics with a true understanding? Is it to warn the "users" of genetic knowledge not to make mistakes? Is it to become "culture broker" between lay and scientific views? If so, should we carry out the brokerage in only one direction (make sure the lay views conform to the scientific views?) Why not the other way around? What if the misunderstanding of genetics, in a particular case, actually has politically advantageous (and progressive) effects (such as increased pride in one's heritage)? Should expert voices still attempt to demolish genetic essentialism? One alternative use of expert knowledge is to support what one scholar calls strategic essentialism. From this standpoint, the ratification, via genetic knowledge, of one's collective memory ("my group's story/memory just becomes scientific history; its 'fiction' just became non-fiction") should not be corrected. Redemptive memory carries its own justification; it has strategic uses given certain oppressive political realities. Therefore, the re-possession of a dis-possessed past should not be blocked by an otherwise salutary warning against genetic essentialism (cf. Williams and Chrisman 1994: 11).

Such questions about expert authority – expert for whom, and to whose benefit? – must be asked anew for each case: Lemba identity as Jews, African-American ancestry projects, and the use (or non-use) of genetic evidence for various identity claims among Native Americans. In the contests over recognition, expert authorities do not stand outside or above the fray. Their opinions affect who controls recognition and how claims of connection are evaluated. In the long run, they also affect how resources get allocated and how people imagine their "deep comradeship" and authentic selves. Entering this field demands humility as well as attention to who is participating (and not participating) in the debate and among the circle of experts.

Nonetheless, certain questions do cry out for anthropological expertise. Why does genetic evidence prove so compelling in some cases (e.g., among diasporic Jews and certain voices in the African-American community) and not in others (notably Native Americans)? Why is it easily accepted by some groups, but the target of extreme suspicion in others? The availability of genetic tracing surely alters the playing field of identity claims, but it does so differently in each case, and anthropologists can help pinpoint the historical and political factors at work. Current debates over genetically based identity claims thus challenge the reflexive anti-essentialism of contemporary anthropology. Yet they also reanimate the historic mission of our discipline; to conceptualize difference in precise ways and with full awareness of the political stakes of expert knowledge.

Acknowledgements

Research has been funded by a grant from the National Human Genome Research Institute, Program on Ethical, Legal, and Social Implications (ELSI): "Ethnicity, Race, Citizenship: Identity After the Human Genome Project" (Grant No. 5R01–02196). Thanks to Carl Elliott (PI), Laurie Zoloth (co. Pl). Mark Thomas, Francoise Bayliss, and other grant participants. Please direct comments to the author [brodwin@uwm.edu].

Study probes

1   How do new genetic technologies enter the realms of ethics and politics?
2   Why is the author critical of what he describes as 'genetic essentialism' as it impacts upon 'genetic identity projects'?
3   What example does he provide for the selective nature of genetic identity projects?

References

Anderson, Benedict, 1991. *Imagined Communities: Reflections and the Origins and Spread of Nationalism*, London: Verso Press.

Brodwin, Paul (ed.), 2000, *Biotechnology and Culture: Bodies, Anxieties, Ethics*, Bloomington, IN: Indiana University Press

Finkler, Kaja 2000, *Experiencing the New Genetics: Family and Kinship on the Medical Frontier*, Philadelphia: University of Pennsylvania Press.

Hall, Stuart and Paul du Gay (eds) 1996. *Questions of Cultural Identity*, London: Sage Publications.

McRobbie, Angela, 1994. *Postmodernism and Popular Culture*, London: Routledge.

Rapp, Rayna, 1999. *Testing Women, Testing the Fetus: The Social Impact of Amniocentesis in America*, New York: Routledge Press.

Williams, Patrick and Laura Chrisman, 1994. *Colonial Discourse and Post-Colonial Theory: A Reader*, New York: Columbia University Press.

Chapter 16

Kimberly TallBear

DNA, BLOOD AND RACIALIZING THE TRIBE

From *Wicazo Sa Review*, 18 (1) (2003), pp. 88–93 and 98–99.

The politics of blood quantum

IF THE USE OF DNA ANALYSIS to determine cultural affiliation is troubling because of its racial implications, the use by tribes of blood quantum to determine eligibility for citizenship cannot be ignored. It seems clear that DNA analysis for such a purpose is not a new political concept, but simply reinforces a historical practice of both the US government and federally recognized tribes.

Since the late 1800s, blood quantum has been used by the US Department of the Interior, the BIA, and many tribal governments to determine eligibility (although not always as a sole criterion) for tribal membership and benefits.[1] It has been reported that the inception of federal identification policies for American Indians based on racialized notions of blood were first instituted in treaties and subsequently reinforced or reaffirmed by the General Allotment Act of 1887 (the Dawes Act). Others have disputed how clearly such a practice was mandated and suggest that the Dawes Act did not explicitly require the measure of blood quantum. Rather, the Dawes Act required that tribal group members be defined for the purpose of allotting Indian tribal property to individuals. And this requirement was interpreted by the Department of the Interior (home of the BIA) to support its existing ideology of using blood quantum as a determinant of tribal affiliation:[2]

> [This] exposition of the law [the Dawes Act] went beyond the cryptic words of the act, which specified no implementing procedures and articulated no qualifications for allotted land other than "belonging"

or "tribal relations." . . . Federal supremacy was the most fundamental of [the legal principles that the Indian Office felt entitled to
apply whenever there was Indian tribal property to allocate] . . .
[T]he year before, the Supreme Court had asserted the federal
government's sweeping power in a dispute about eligibility for land
on another reservation. Construing an allotment plan for Wichita
Indians, which did not stipulate a way to identify Wichitas, the
court declared that the interior secretary had authority to make such
identifications . . . because general statutes gave him responsibility for
managing all Indian affairs.[3]

Although US courts, since the 1905 precedent set by *Waldron v. United
States*, have upheld tribal authority to determine their own enrollment policies,
most federally recognized tribes retain a requirement that a certain level of
blood quantum (ranging from full Indian blood to ½₃₂ Indian blood) must be
demonstrated by potential members. The federal government does not force
tribes to implement blood quantum criteria and clearly states tribal authority in
enrollment. However, the BIA provides patronizing step-by-step process guidance on tribal enrollment, emphasizes federal review of tribal law, and even
provides charts on how tribes should determine blood quantum. The BIA also
acknowledges that it generated most of the records used in enrollment.[4] Finally,
tribal powers to determine enrollment are limited by the federal requirement
that the BIA certify due process of the enrollment ordinance.[5] In theory at least,
tribes have control over substantive enrollment criteria. Nonetheless, it is understandable how critics familiar with BIA language and policy view their involvement in tribal enrollment as a heavy-handed and colonial intervention.

Many critics characterize blood quantum policies as solely representing
Euro-American definitions of race imposed on native peoples by the US government.[6] Ward Churchill, a vocal critic of blood quantum policies, has asserted
that

> virtually every indigenous nation within the United States had, by
> way of an unrelenting substitution of federal definitions for their
> own, been stripped of the ability to determine for themselves in any
> meaningful way the internal composition of their polities.[7]

Churchill argues that tribes were forced to adopt racial codes that linked identity
to quantities of Indian blood and that such ideology was "psychologically
and intellectually internalized by Native America," a self-imposed "sort of
autogenocide by definitional and statistical extermination."[8]

On the other hand, a handful of scholars have argued that the historical
politics of blood quantum are more complex than is usually reported. Alexandra
Harmon provides an insightful analysis that reveals the complexity of the politics
involved in the Colville Reservation Indian's symbolic, strategic, and contradictory use of blood quantum historically to help determine eligibility of individuals
for tribal affiliation and allotment of lands:

Government agents apparently saw a need to teach Indians the basic qualifications for membership in a US-supervised tribe. They announced ground rules for enrollment and overrode some Indian council decisions for failing to comport with those rules. They insisted that ancestry – metaphorically termed "Indian blood" – be one of those qualifications, and they argued on several occasions that excluding people with a low Indian "blood quantum" would protect the economic interests of Indians already on the roll. Some council members adopted this line.

However, the Coleville documents tell a more complex, ambiguous story than [some blood quantum critics and advocates] do. In the enrollment councils, federal agents did not brainwash or impose their will on Indians; neither did Indians resolve to draw an economically strategic, racially defined boundary around themselves. Rather, officials and Indians participated in a prolonged discourse that I would characterize as incomplete mutual education and accommodation.[9]

This scholar argues that "to provide a sounder foundation for conclusions about the influence of US law and racial ideology on the composition of tribes, more historical studies [grounded in specific tribal membership histories] are essential."[10] Without such historically grounded studies, she suggests that claims that tribes are ubiquitously forced or duped into acceptance of Euro-American racial ideology are conjecture. Harmon concludes that tribal enrollment efforts in the early 1900s prompted "an unprecedented conversation – one that would take place in many tribal communities and continue for decades – about what it meant to be Indian in the twentieth-century United States":

All tribal enrollment efforts obliged the descendants of Native people to think about where they fit in a white-dominated, racialized world. The government offered them a vocabulary to use in their analysis, but as they tried to employ that vocabulary, they influenced its practical connotation. Anyone who accepted an unsolicited plot of reservation land, applied for enrollment, provided information about an applicant, or attended an enrollment council learned something about the government's concept of tribal membership. In response, such people had to rethink their relationships, taking into account the momentous consequences of US domination. Whether or not the government accepted their views on a particular individual's status, enrollment gave them occasion to articulate, debate, and revise their definitions of "Indian" and "tribe."[11]

Pauline Turner Strong and Barrik Van Winkle have similarly discussed the interplay in the works of certain tribal writers between literal and metaphorical interpretations of blood and "positive" uses of blood imagery, such as using it as "a vehicle of connection and integration . . . rather than one of calculation and differentiation":[12]

Dismantling the intricate edifice of racism embodied in "Indian blood" is not simply a matter of exposing its essentialism and discarding its associated policies, but a more delicate and complicated task: that is, acknowledging "Indian blood" as a discourse of conquest with manifold and contradictory effects, but without invalidating rights and resistances that have been couched in terms of that very discourse. . . . "Indian blood," dangerous and essentialist as it may be, is at present a tragically necessary condition for the continued survival and vitality of many individuals and communities.[13]

I disagree with the final statement that "Indian blood" is "tragically necessary." Perhaps "tragically strategic" would be a more appropriate characterization. Still, the above summary of the complex politics of Indian blood is eloquent and very helpful for our purposes.

Yet another scholar, Melissa L. Meyer, traces and summarizes the meaning of "blood" in the English language since the Middle Ages in an attempt to convey the varying symbolic and physiological meanings of the term. The author argues that it is "incorrect to assume that the term 'blood' is and always has been simply a metaphoric reference to genetic composition." She argues that it is more likely that "the metaphorical connection of blood with lineage, descent, and ancestry preceded its literal physiological use" and that indigenous peoples' "notions of family lineage come closer to the origins of the term 'blood' than current physiological meanings." Meyer therefore credits tribes with some degree of agency in their use of blood or blood quantum terminology. She suggests that tribes attempted to describe with the metaphorical use of "blood" their understandings of kinship, genealogical lines of descent, and group membership.[14]

Later, US policy makers set a precedent for measuring blood, especially for the purpose of determining which individuals were eligible for limited benefits and resources, but this precedent was not synonymous with how tribes demonstrated understandings of kinship and lineage.[15] While Meyer does not elaborate on the various means by which native peoples determined lineage, she argues that "*family* considerations, however construed, were paramount."[16]

Finally, Meyer brings attention to the interplay between idealized American longings and tangible economic benefits that prompt some individuals to seek out a tribal identity. She reveals the historical baggage that prompts some tribes to severely limit tribal enrollment through membership requirements such as blood quantum:

The Indians who populate the American popular imagination bear absolutely no relationship to real native people either in the past or in the present. The imagery allows Americans and people over the world to sustain highly romanticized notions of Indianness. It encourages people with little or no cultural affiliation to claim Indian identity. People yearn to document descent from some relative lost in the past to enhance their chances of acquiring educational funds and gaining admittance to prestigious universities. Native people know this better than anyone. Neverbefore-seen "relatives" emerge as claimants every time any tribal group receives a court settlement or royalties from economic development. Such exploitation pierces as a thorn in the side of legitimate tribal members.[17]

Meyer notes that "most tribes desire that enrollment reflect some sort of valid *cultural* affiliation." She credits tribes with understanding that blood doesn't guarantee cultural affiliation and that some people with "legitimate cultural ties will be eliminated," but they assume that higher degrees of Indian blood will increase the odds of true affiliation. Another writer also emphasizes the economic incentives for exclusive tribal enrollment criteria: "Propertied tribes have tended to be more exclusive, in part from fear of losing federal recognition and thus losing tribal property (as well as federal aid). Less propertied, and larger, tribes have tended to be more inclusive."[18]

These scholars attempt to do justice to the complexity of blood quantum politics among Indian peoples. Yet in the final analysis, Meyer zeros in on the implications for tribes of maintaining the practice of measurement and thus accepting the racial ideology (and its attendant economic benefits) implied in US federal practice:

> In their purest form, blood quantum requirements amount to a celebration of race. But turning the tables in this fashion, though it may have accorded to some degree with their own notions of "blood" and lineage, would not spare tribes or individuals from the destructive consequences of basing policies on racial criteria.[19]

[. . .]

The implications of racializing the tribe for tribal self-determination

Racialized (often romanticized and pan-Indian) images are common in the writing of some Indian activists, poets, scholars, politicians, and our advocates – perhaps more common than images that reinforce *specific* tribal cultural practices and beliefs. Such ideas are often intended to be flattering or sympathetic and helpful to the cause of tribes. But we should be gravely concerned that such images actually reinforce the role of blood in assertions of cultural and political authority. (Ironically, such romanticized images sometimes come from critics of blood quantum.) Romanticized, pan-Indian, and racialized approaches to tribal identity all de-emphasize specific tribal beliefs, histories, and place-based practices that are sometimes contradictory between tribes. This robs future generations of specifically applied cultural knowledge that can help guide tribes through the challenges they face.[20]

The Colville enrollment history has demonstrated the importance of historical research related to citizenship practices as they developed in the late 1800s and early 1900s, which might also include ideas of nation or people, kinship and community as these are reflected in tribal languages, and in both historical and contemporary cultural practices associated with specific tribes. Such research can help generate new citizenship strategies that aren't racialized as well as promote culturally informed and critical goverance more generally. This is not to say that tribes should work in isolation from each other. Each tribe or group of related tribes must reckon with their own history and cultural practice in relation to citizenship. But their process models for doing so can be shared between tribes to make better use of intellectual and financial resources.

On the other hand, continuing to use blood quantum and DNA analysis to claim individual or tribal cultural and political authority is a strategy that could be used against tribes to challenge such authorities. There are other strategies by which tribes might determine citizenship to better reflect tribal political authority, to encourage a thriving culture, economic investment, and social commitment to the tribal community. The specific historic practices of tribes may be a good source of ideas if they can be adapted, applied, and enforced within a contemporary sociopolitical context.[21]

As tribes seek to build the governing infrastructures and the educational, cultural, and economic institutions that will increase tribal capacity to govern, it seems that resistance to racial ideology is imperative. We have seen in war-torn nations all over the world the horrific results of clinging to racial and essentialist views of who is an authentic member of the nation and who, therefore, deserves political, cultural, and human rights. It will be a sad turn of events if such violations are perpetuated on a smaller scale within tribal communities.

Study probes

1   Chart the use of blood quantum to establish American Indian tribal membership.
2   Discuss the scholarly arguments for and against the measurement of blood quantum which TallBear outlines.

Notes

1   Robert Desjarlait, "Blood Quantum vs. Lineal Descent: How Much Indian Are You? The Debate over How to Define Who Is Indian," *Circle* 22, no. 11 (November 2001), William Glaberson, "Who Is a Seminole and Who Gets to Decide?" *New York Times*, January 29, 2001, Alexandra Harmon, "Tribal Enrollment Councils: Lessons on Law and Indian Identity," *Western Historical Quarterly*, 32: 175–200; Malcomson, *One Drop of Blood. The American Misadventure of Race*; Melissa Meyer, "American Indian Blood Quantum Requirements," in V. Matsumoto and B. Allmendinger (eds) *Over the Edge: Remapping the American West*, Berkeley and Los Angeles: University of California Press.

2   Joanne Barker, "Indian-Made: Sovereignty and the Work of Identification" (Ph.D. diss., University of California, Santa Cruz, 2000), Ward Churchill, "The Crucible of American Indian Identity" Harmon, "Tribal Enrollment Councils."

3   Harmon, "Tribal Enrollment Councils," 183–84.

4   US Department of the Interior, Bureau of Indian Affairs, *Tribal Enrollment Training Text* (Phoenix, BIA Phoenix Area Office, 1984).

5   US Department of the Interior, Bureau of Indian Affairs, memorandum from the Acting Deputy Area Director for the Aberdeen (South Dakota) Area Office to the Area Director

of the Aberdeen Area Office regarding "Flandreau Santee Sioux Tribe Title 11 Enrollment Ordinance under Tribal Resolution No. 98.06," May 23, 1998, Flandreau Santee Sioux Tribe (FSST) Enrollment Ordinance (Title 11 of the Tribal Code, Resolution 98.06), May 22, 1998, Jon C. Wade (former FSST Tribal Secretary), interview by author, Santa Cruz, California, December 28, 2000.

6   Ward Churchill, "The Crucible of American Indian Identity: Native Tradition versus Colonial Imposition in Postconquest North America," *North American Indian Culture and Research Journal*, 23(1): 29–67; also see R. David Edmunds, "Native Americans, New Voices," *American Historical Review* 100 (June 1995): 733–34, M. Annette Jaimes, "Federal Indian Identification Policy: A Usurpation of Indigenous Sovereignty in North America," in *The State of Native America, Genocide, Colonization, and Resistance*, ed. M. A. Jaimes (Boston: South End Press, 1992); and Sheba R. Wheeler, "Indian Lineage Rules Decried," *Denver Post*. March 25, 1999.

7   Churchill, "The Crucible of American Indian Identity," 50.

8   Ibid., 56, 52.

9   Harmon, "Tribal Enrollment Councils," 179.

10 Ibid., 177.

11 Ibid., 200.

12 Pauline Turner Strong and Barrik Van Winkle, " 'Indian Blood': Reflections on the Reckoning and Refiguring of Native North American Identity," *Cultural Anthropology* 11, no. 4 (1996) 547–76, 562. See their discussion on the use of "blood" or "mixed-blood/crossblood" metaphors in the writings of Kiowa writer N. Scott Momaday and Chippewa writer Gerald Vizenor.

13 Ibid., 565.

14 Meyer, "American Indian Blood Quantum Requirements," 234, 236, 232. My personal experience with the use of "blood" in tribal communities is anecdotal evidence of Meyer's assertion that it often reflects indigenous notions of family lineage rather than physiological meanings. While I am officially (on paper) "7/16 Indian blood" (1/4 Cheyenne and Arapaho and 3/16 Dakota), I have never been referred to as a mixed blood. I am an enrolled tribal member and have been since infancy. This is important to other enrolled Indians, although it is certainly not the only or even chief marker of my authenticity when I am asked where I am from and who my grandparents are. I grew up between reservation and urban Indian communities. While I am enrolled Cheyenne and Arapaho, my cultural identification is actually Dakota, because I was raised among my Dakota, or Sioux, relatives. I lived most of the time until I was fourteen with my maternal great-grandmother and grandparents on the Flandreau Santee Sioux Reservation. I spent occasional periods with my mother in Minneapolis where she worked to develop urban Indian housing and education programs and was heavily involved in history and cultural activities with Dakota peoples in Minnesota. My white father and his family were almost totally absent from my upbringing. Because my cultural identification, sense of history, and home place were so strongly Dakota, it did not occur to anyone to call me mixed blood. And anyway, I have nearly always understood the social construction of race. My mother taught me this by example when she reprimanded, "Don't act white!" While my mother's idea of what it meant to act white may have been a generalization, she implied that whiteness constituted behavior that reflected cultural values. She would also refer to her white colleague, husband of a fellow Dakota, as "really an Indian," thereby reflecting the fact that he generally followed Indian ways (i.e., spoke the language, held the spiritual beliefs, and was a long-time accepted member of the community). Therefore, "mixed blood" and "full blood" are not terms to which I subscribe any truth – whether they are used negatively or positively. However, while I disagree with the use of such terms, which I believe perpetuates racial ideology, I do understand there are cultural meanings in how other Indians might strategically use them.

15 Also see Harmon, "Tribal Enrollment Councils," for references to government documents and positions that went beyond metaphorical talk of Indian blood and used language of racial classification that suggested that Indian blood might be measured (i.e., whole or in part Indian blood). Also see Malcomson, *Our Drop of Blood*, for reference to how "the

language of blood was used to make sense of behavior" (67) and for how "*blood* had little to do with the red fluid universally recognized as blood." It had to do with (yes, "facial features and skin tone," but also) "dress, perhaps, language, maybe; family name . . .; and the general tenor of a community"(110)

16   Meyer, "American Indian Blood Quantum Requirements," 232.
17   Ibid., 241.
18   Malcomson, *One Drop of Blood*, 115.
19   Meyer, "American Indian Blood Quantum Requirements," 241.
20   This is not to disregard the importance of tribal peoples (and indigenous peoples internationally) working together on artistic projects and in political alliances. But this might be done better by focusing on the common politics and histories of colonization.
21   Admittedly, developing alternatives is a difficult task within a colonial system in which tribes historically traded land for survival. Along with that came government oversight memorialized in law and dependence on federal budgets. But there is room for tribes to maneuver.

SUGGESTIONS FOR FURTHER READING

Bertoni, Bernardo *et al.* (2003) 'Admixture in Hispanics: Distribution of Ancestral Population Contributions in the Continental United States', *Human Biology*, 75 (11): 1–11.

Brown, Andrew (1999) *The Darwin Wars: The Scientific Battle for the Soul of Man*, London: Simon and Schuster.

Cooper, Grant (1994) *The Human Genome Project*, Mill Valley: University Science Books.

Darwin, Charles (1859/1971) *The Origin of Species*, London: Dent.

Dawkings, Richard (1976) *The Selfish Gene*, Oxford: Oxford University Press.

Dennis, Carina and Gallagher, Richard (eds) (2001) *The Human Genome*, Basingstoke: Palgrave.

Diamond, Jared (1998) *Guns, Germs and Steel: A Short History of Everybody for the Last 13,000 Years*, London: Vintage.

Fraser, Steven (ed.) (1995) *The Bell Curve Wars: Race, Intelligence and the Future of America*, New York: Basic Books.

Gudding, Gabriel (1996) 'The Phenotype/Genotype Distinction and the Disappearance of the Body', *Journal of the History of Ideas*, 57(3): 525–545.

Jones, Steve (1996) *In the Blood: God, Genes and Destiny*, London: HarperCollins.

Jones, Steve *et al.* (1993) *Genetics for Beginners*, Cambridge: Icon Books.

Kelves, Daniel Jo (1992) *The Code of Codes: Scientific and Social Issues in the Human Genome Project*, London: Harvard University Press.

Kelves, Daniel Jo (1995) *In the Name of Eugenics: Genetics and the Uses of Human Heredity*, London: Harvard University Press.

Murphy, Timothy and Lappe, Mark (1994) *Justice and the Human Genome Project*, London: University of California.

Murray, Thomas (ed.) (1996) *The Human Genome Project and the Future of Health Care*, Bloomington: Indiana University.

Olson, Steve (2002) *Mapping Human History: Discovering the Past Through Our Genes*, London: Bloomsbury.

Rose, Steven *et al.* (1984) *Not in Our Genes*, Harmondsworth: Penguin.

Sarkar, Sahotra (1998) *Genetics and Reductionism*, Cambridge: Cambridge University.

Shennan, Stephen (2002) *Genes, Memes and Human History: Darwinian Archaeology and Cultural Evolution*, London: Thames and Hudson.

Sloan, Phillip (ed.) (1999) *Controlling Our Destinies*, Notre Dame: University of Notre Dame.

Smith, Edward and Sapp, Walter (eds) (1997) *Plain Talk About the Human Genome Project*, Alabama: Tuskegee University.

Steinberg, Deborah Lynn (2000) 'Reading Genes/Writing Nation: Reith, "Race" and the Writings of Geneticist Steven Jones', in A.Brah and A.Coombes (eds) *Hybridity and its Discontents: Politics, Science and Culture*, London: Routledge, pp. 137–153.

Stock, Gregory (2002) *Redesigning Humans: Choosing Our Children's Genes*, London: Profile.

Stringer, Christopher and McKie, Robin (1996) *African Exodus: The Origins of Modern Humanity*, New York: Henry Holt and Company.

Tudge, Colin (2002) *In Mendel's Footnotes: An Introduction to the Science of Technologies of Genes and Genetics from the Nineteenth Century to the Twenty Second*, London: Vintage.

Weiss, Kenneth (1993) *Genetic Variation and Human Disease*, Cambridge: Cambridge University.

Wilike, Tom (1993) *Perilous Knowledge*, London: Faber.

Young, Lola (2000) 'Hybridity's Discontents: Rereading Science and "Race"', in A.Brah and A.Coombes (eds) *Hybridity and its Discontents: Politics, Science and Culture*, London: Routledge, pp. 154–170.

Websites

http://www.bbc.co.uk/genes

Family Tree DNA:
http://www.familytreedna.com/tcam.html

Human Genome Project Information:
http://www.ornl.gov/TechResources/Human_Genome

American Society of Human Genetics:
http://genetics.faseb.org/genetics/ashg/ashgmenu.htm

Human Genome Organization (HUGO):
http://www.gene.ucl.ac.uk/hugo/

Blueprint of the Body:
http://edition.cnn.com/SPECIALS/2000/genome/

Stanford Human Genome Center:
http://www.shgc.stanford.edu

Rural Advancement Foundation International (RAFI):
http://www.etcgroup.org/

Institute for Agriculture and Trade Policy: Intellectual Property Rights:
http://www.rz.uni-frankfurt.de/-ecstein/gen/biofacts.html

Human Genome Diversity Project:
http://www/stanford.edu/group/morrinst/hgdp.html

Indigenous Peoples Council on Biocolonialism:
http://www.ipcb.org

'Motherland: A Genetic Journey':
http://takeawaymedia.com/motherlandscience.htm

Mapping contemporary and foundational discourses

'Mixed race', identities politics and celebration

INTRODUCTION

PART TWO COMPRISES A by no means definitive selection of contemporary and foundational readings, which illustrate the emergence of celebratory and social constructionist discourses on 'mixed race' and highlight the political and historical events that precipitated this revival. In similar and different ways, all of the trail-blazing authors featured in Part Two, many of whom themselves identify as 'mixed race', recognize the persistence of objectifying and damaging perspectives on 'mixed race' in the present. At the same time they argue in favour of 'actor-centred' conceptual approaches which presume that processes of identities formation are fluid, shifting, contingent, situational, multiple and complex.

While on the whole, I have selected readings which are neither readily available nor anthologized, I have made an exception here and to a lesser extent with Part Three. In Part Two, I have reproduced extracts from *Racially Mixed People in America* (Root 1992) and in Part Three from *Rethinking 'Mixed Race'* (Parker and Song 2001) because these authors are recognized as pioneers in this field. Their work has been significant in the development of ideas on 'mixed race' (Root and Spickard in Part Two) or they are making important interventions in the more critical domain of 'multiraciality' (Mahtani in Part Three). At this moment in time, with the proliferation of college courses, edited books, autobiographical texts, magazines, websites, conferences and support groups on 'mixed race' issues, it is now appropriate and necessary to mark this intellectual moment and historically locate its foundational scholarship as part of a broader continuum.

While I have attempted to select foundational scholarship which represents Native American, Asian American, Latino/Chicano and African American vantage points on 'mixed race', the chosen readings are not necessarily meant to be 'representative' or 'separatist'. Nor are they to be viewed as reductionist, essentialist or tokenistic. I am also mindful that there is a geographical imbalance in the number of entries from the USA as opposed to the UK (with the exception of Ifekwunigwe) and Canada (with the exception of Camper). This is not an oversight, but rather is indicative and representative of current intellectual trends. That is, despite demographic trends to the contrary in the United Kingdom, with the notable exceptions of the text I have included (and the few others I have cited in suggestions for further reading: e.g. Alibhai-Brown 2001, Benson 1981, Olumide 2002, Parker and Song 2001, Tizard and Phoenix 1993, Wilson 1987), the majority of the scholarship has been produced in the USA and to a certain extent in Canada. Regarding the latter, I am aware that I have not included any literature on the established *métissage* discourse as it pertains to the rights and identity paradigms/politics of First Nations people. As always, coherence and word-length constraints have been motivating factors. Finally, there are many more excellent writings by foundational 'mixed race' studies scholars, many of which may be found in the important collections *Racially Mixed People in America* (1992 edited by Root), *American Mixed Race* (1995 edited by Zack) and *The Multiracial Experience* (1996 edited by Root). Although I have not been able to include all of them in this Reader, in the section on suggestions for further readings which accompany each Part, I have pointed the reader in the direction of some of

Chapter 17

Gloria Anzaldúa

LA CONCIENCIA DE LA MESTIZA:
TOWARDS A NEW CONSCIOUSNESS

Extract from *Borderlands/La Frontera* (1987). San Francisco, CA: aunt lute books, pp. 77–80 and 82–83.

Por la mujer de mi raza
hablará el espiritu.

JOSE VASCOCELOS, MEXICAN PHILOSOPHER, envisaged *una raza mestiza, una mezcla de razas afines, una raza de color — la primera raza síntesis del globo*. He called it a cosmic race, *la raza cósmica*, a fifth race embracing the four major races of the world. Opposite to the theory of the pure Aryan, and to the policy of racial purity that white America practices, his theory is one of inclusivity. At the confluence of two or more genetic streams, with chromosomes constantly "crossing over," this mixture of races, rather than resulting in an inferior being, provides hybrid progeny, a mutable, more malleable species with a rich gene pool. From this racial, ideological, cultural and biological cross-pollinization, an "alien" consciousness is presently in the making – a new *mestiza* consciousness, *una conciencia de mujer*. It is a consciousness of the Borderlands.

> *Una lucha de fronteras*/A Struggle of Borders
> Because I, a *mestiza*,
> continually walk out of one culture
> and into another,
> because I am in all cultures at the same time,
> *alma entre dos mundos, tres, cuatro,*
> *me zumba la cabeza con lo contradictorio.*
> *Estoy norteada por todas las voces que me hablan*
> *simultáneamente.*

The ambivalence from the clash of voices results in mental and emotional states of perplexity. Internal strife results in insecurity and indecisiveness. The mestiza's dual or multiple personality is plagued by psychic restlessness.

In a constant state of mental nepantilism, an Aztec word meaning torn between ways, *la mestiza* is a product of the transfer of the cultural and spiritual values of one group to another. Being tricultural, monolingual, bilingual, or multilingual, speaking a patois, and in a state of perpetual transition, the *mestiza* faces the dilemma of the mixed breed: which collectivity does the daughter of a darkskinned mother listen to?

El choque de un alma atrapado entre el mundo del espíritu y el mundo de la técnica a veces la deja entullada. Cradled in one culture, sandwiched between two cultures, straddling all three cultures and their value systems, *la mestiza* undergoes a struggle of flesh, a struggle of borders, an inner war. Like all people, we perceive the version of reality that our culture communicates. Like others having or living in more than one culture, we get multiple, often opposing messages. The coming together of two self-consistent but habitually incompatible frames of reference causes *un choque*, a cultural collision.

Within us and within *la cultura chicana*, commonly held beliefs of the white culture attack commonly held beliefs of the Mexican culture, and both attack commonly held beliefs of the indigenous culture. Subconsciously, we see an attack on ourselves and our beliefs as a threat and we attempt to block with a counterstance.

But it is not enough to stand on the opposite river bank, shouting questions, challenging patriarchal, white conventions. A counterstance locks one into a duel of oppressor and oppressed; locked in mortal combat, like the cop and the criminal, both are reduced to a common denominator of violence. The counterstance refutes the dominant culture's views and beliefs, and, for this, it is proudly defiant. All reaction is limited by, and dependent on, what it is reacting against. Because the counterstance stems from a problem with authority – outer as well as inner – it's a step towards liberation from cultural domination. But it is not a way of life. At some point, on our way to a new consciousness, we will have to leave the opposite bank, the split between the two mortal combatants somehow healed so that we are on both shores at once and, at once, see through serpent and eagle eyes. Or perhaps we will decide to disengage from the dominant culture, write it off altogether as a lost cause, and cross the border into a wholly new and separate territory. Or we might go another route. The possibilities are numerous once we decide to act and not react.

A tolerance for ambiguity

These numerous possibilities leave *la mestiza* floundering in uncharted seas. In perceiving conflicting information and points of view, she is subjected to a swamping of her psychological borders. She has discovered that she can't hold concepts or ideas in rigid boundaries. The borders and walls that are supposed to keep the undesirable ideas out are entrenched habits and patterns of behavior; these habits and patterns are the enemy within. Rigidity means death. Only by remaining flexible is she able to stretch the psyche horizontally and vertically. *La mestiza* constantly has to shift out of habitual formations; from convergent thinking, analytical reasoning that tends to use rationality to move toward a single goal (a Western mode), to divergent thinking, characterized by movement away from set patterns and goals and toward a more whole perspective, one that includes rather than excludes.

The new *mestiza* copes by developing a tolerance for contradictions, a tolerance for ambiguity. She learns to be an Indian in Mexican culture, to be Mexican from an Anglo point of view. She learns to juggle cultures. She has a plural personality, she operates in a pluralistic mode – nothing is thrust out, the good the bad and the ugly, nothing rejected, nothing abandoned. Not only does she sustain contradictions, she turns the ambivalence into something else.

She can be jarred out of ambivalence by an intense, and often painful, emotional event which inverts or resolves the ambivalence. I'm not sure exactly how. The work takes place underground – subconsciously. It is work that the soul performs. That focal point or fulcrum, that juncture where the *mestiza* stands, is where phenomena tend to collide. It is where the possibility of uniting all that is separate occurs. This assembly is not one where severed or separated pieces merely come together. Nor is it a balancing of opposing powers. In attempting to work out a synthesis, the self has added a third element which is greater than the sum of its severed parts. That third element is a new consciousness – a *mestiza* consciousness – and though it is a source of intense pain, its energy comes from continual creative motion that keeps breaking down the unitary aspect of each new paradigm.

En unas pocas centurias, the future will belong to the *mestiza*. Because the future depends on the breaking down of paradigms, it depends on the straddling of two or more cultures. By creating a new mythos – that is, a change in the way we perceive reality, the way we see ourselves, and the ways we behave – *la mestiza* creates a new consciousness.

The work of *mestiza* consciousness is to break down the subject–object duality that keeps her a prisoner and to show in the flesh and through the images in her work how duality is transcended. The answer to the problem between the white race and the colored, between males and females, lies in healing the split that originates in the very foundation of our lives, our culture, our languages, our thoughts. A massive uprooting of dualistic thinking in the individual and collective consciousness is the beginning of a long struggle, but one that could, in our best hopes, bring us to the end of rape, of violence, of war.

[. . .]

El camino de la mestiza/The *mestiza* way

> Caught between the sudden contraction, the breath sucked in and the endless space, the brown woman stands still, looks at the sky. She decides to go down, digging her way along the roots of trees. Sifting through the bones, she shakes them to see if there is any marrow in

them. Then, touching the dirt to her forehead, to her tongue, she takes a few bones, leaves the rest in their burial place.

She goes through her backpack, keeps her journal and address book, throws away the muni-bart metromaps. The coins are heavy and they go next, then the greenbacks flutter through the air. She keeps her knife, can opener and eyebrow pencil. She puts bones, pieces of bark, *hierbas*, eagle feather, snakeskin, tape recorder, the rattle and drum in her pack and she sets out to become the complete *tolteca*.

Her first step is to take inventory. *Despojando, desgranando, quitando paja.* Just what did she inherit from her ancestors? This weight on her back – which is the baggage from the Indian mother, which the baggage from the Spanish father, which the baggage from the Anglo?

Pero es difícil differentiating between *lo heredado, lo adquirido, lo impuesto.* She puts history through a sieve, winnows out the lies, looks at the forces that we as a race, as women, have been a part of. *Luego bota lo que no vale, los desmientos, los desencuentos, el embrutecimiento. Aguarda el juicio, hondo y enraizado, de la gente antigua.* This step is a conscious rupture with all oppressive traditions of all cultures and religions. She communicates that rupture, documents the struggle. She reinterprets history and, using new symbols, she shapes new myths. She adopts new perspectives toward the darkskinned, women and queers. She strengthens her tolerance (and intolerance) for ambiguity. She is willing to share, to make herself vulnerable to foreign ways of seeing and thinking. She surrenders all notions of safety, of the familiar. Deconstruct, construct. She becomes a *nahual*, able to transform herself into a tree, a coyote, into another person. She learns to transform the small "I" into the total Self. *Se hace moldeadora de su alma. Según la concepción que tiene de sí misma, así será.*

Study probes

1   What did Vascocelos mean by 'a cosmic race'?
2   In her charting of a '*mestiza* consciousness', how does Anzaldúa develop this concept?
3   What are the contours of 'the *mestiza* way', which the author traces?

Chapter 18

Maria P.P. Root

WITHIN, BETWEEN, AND BEYOND RACE

From M.P.P. Root (ed.) *Racially Mixed People of America* (1992). Thousand Oaks, CA: Sage, pp. 3–11.

T HE "BIRACIAL BABY BOOM" in the United States started about 25 years ago, around the time the last laws against miscegenation (race mixing) were repealed in 1967. The presence of racially mixed persons defies the social order predicated upon race, blurs racial and ethnic group boundaries, and challenges generally accepted proscriptions and prescriptions regarding inter-group relations. Furthermore, and perhaps most threatening, the existence of racially mixed persons challenges long-held notions about the biological, moral, and social meaning of race.

The emergence of a racially mixed population is transforming the "face" of the United States. The increasing presence of multiracial[1] people necessitates that we as a nation ask ourselves questions about our identity: Who are we? How do we see ourselves? Who are we in relation to one another? These questions arise in the context of a country that has held particular views of race – a country that has subscribed to race as an immutable construct, perceived itself as White, and been dedicated to preserving racial lines. Thus such questions of race and identity can only precipitate a full-scale "identity crisis" that this country is ill equipped to resolve. Resolving the identity crisis may force us to re-examine our construction of race and the hierarchical social order it supports.

The "racial ecology" is complex in a phenotypically heterogeneous society that has imbued physical differences with significant meaning in a convention that benefits selective segments of the society. At a personal level, race is very much in the eye of the beholder; at a political level, race is in the service of economic and social privilege. Similarly, ethnic identity is relevant only in an ethnically heterogeneous environment. Whereas race can contribute to ethnicity, it is neither a sufficient nor necessary condition for assuming one's ethnicity, particularly with multiracial populations. Our confusion of race and ethnicity indicates that it will be difficult to abandon the smoke screen that hides our "caste system" surrounding theory, politics, health care, education, and other resources.

Our tendency to think simplistically about complex relationships has resulted in dichotomous, hierarchical classification systems that have become vehicles of oppression. The way in which we have utilized the construction of race has placed the multiracial person "betwixt and between" (G.R. Daniel, personal communication, 1991) in the racial ecology since colonial times. The publication of this volume suggests that the emerging critical mass of multiracial persons, catalyzing a national identity crisis, might enable us to disassemble the vehicle of oppression.

Although oppression takes different forms, it is consistently characterized by the hierarchical interpretation of differences. . . . Extending this model, racially mixed men and women would occupy the fifth and sixth tiers in this model, respectively, because of the rigidity of the dichotomy between White and non-White. Subsequently, multiracial people experience a "squeeze" of oppression *as* people of color and *by* people of color. People of color who have internalized the vehicle of oppression in turn apply rigid rules of belonging or establishing "legitimate" membership. The internalization of either/or systems of thinking operates even between communities of color, such as Asian American and African American communities.

[. . .]

The mechanisms that have historically evolved to suppress multiple heritage identification have largely benefited White society. The rules of hypodescent enlist simplistic, dichotomous rules of classification (e.g., White versus non-White) and have been obviously employed in our historical amnesia. These strategies have fueled the oppression of America's people of color and definitely that of the multiracial people of our country. In fact, attempts by racially mixed persons to move back and forth between color lines have been viewed pejoratively rather than as creative strategies in a multiracial reality. Furthermore, persons of color mixing with other persons of color – such as American Indians and Blacks, Filipinos and Native Americans, Latinos and Blacks – has been given little attention in the literature. This mixing does not conventionally threaten the border between White and non-White. The racial mixes over which there has been the most concern are those between groups that are most distant culturally and socially – Blacks and Whites, Japanese and Blacks, and Japanese and Whites. Furthermore, this concern has involved groups that are most convinced of the immutability of race and most wedded to preserving "purity" of race: Whites and Asians.

The simplicity and irrationality of our basis for conceptualizing race affects how we subsequently think about social identity. Linear models of social relations have provided the basis for many social psychological theories about racially mixed persons. The monoracial and monocultural bias of these theories is evident in constructions of assimilation and acculturation models and many early theories addressing identity issues for persons with mixed heritages. The theories, like our racial classification system, are characterized by dichotomous or bipolar schemes and as such can only marginalize the status of racially or ethnically mixed persons.

The recent consideration of multidimensional models has allowed the possibility that an individual can have simultaneous membership and multiple, fluid identities with different groups. These models abolish either/or classifications systems that create marginality. Multidimensional models of identity will not be perplexed that phenotype, "genotype," and ethnicity do not necessarily coincide with or reliably predict identity. Several studies illustrate this phenomenon. A person of Black-Japanese heritage may look Filipino and may identify as both African American and Asian American. Similarly, a person of White-Asian background may phenotypically appear more similar to someone of European than Asian descent but may identify as a first-generation Japanese American. It is confusing to our linear models of identity to consider that a multiracial Black-Indian-European person who looks African American self-identifies as multiracial, when someone of a similar heritage identifies as a monoracial African American. Moreover, the difference is more likely to be pathologized in a linear model. Many persons will be challenged to consider that the multiracially identified person is liberated from oppressive rules of classification rather than confined by them if they do not fit his or her experience.

Why has the United States suppressed the historical reality that a significant proportion of its citizenry has multigenerational multiracial roots? On one hand, it might be suggested that we have manufactured a media image. On the other hand, this tendency may be seen as simply consistent with social models of assimilation that encourage a casting off of cultural ties and roots to blend into the mythical "melting pot." It is more likely, however, that this tendency is largely tied to economic motives and class privileges and to ideas of supremacy that guide rules of hypodescent (assignment to the racial group with lower status). An ethnic past remains relevant to the extent that it is physically visible, such as with people of color and multiracial people.

The silence on the topic of multiraciality must be understood in context. In the not-so-distant past – in the lifetimes of almost all the contributors to this volume – antimiscegenist sentiments were profound. These attitudes were supported by legislation in most states, ruling these interracial unions and marriages illegal until a US Supreme Court ruling in 1967. The history of antimiscegenist laws and attitudes combined with rules of hypodescent, a pseudoscientific literature on race mixing, and the internalized oppression still evident in communities of color have unquestionably contributed to the silence on this topic.

Whereas one of the breakthroughs of the civil rights movement was empowerment of American racial minority groups by self-naming, this process is just beginning among multiracial persons. In essence, to name oneself is to validate one's existence and declare visibility. This seemingly simple process is a significant step in the liberation of multiracial persons from the oppressive struc-ture of the racial classification system that has relegated them to the land of "in between." A confluence of factors has prevented this form of empowerment until now:

1   The social understanding of race has allowed only one category of racial identification (a practice supported by the US Census Bureau).
2   Recent pride in being a person of color has demanded full-fledged commitment to the racial and ethnic minority group in order to pass "legitimacy tests."
3   Epithets, which have been multiracial persons' only "universal" labels, have discouraged pride in self-identification.
4   Isolation of interracial families, in part because of antimiscegenist legislation, has kept many multiracial families and individuals from meeting and accumulating a critical mass, a catalyst for empowerment.
5   Race and ethnicity have been confused such that many multiracial people may identify monoculturally, as in the case of many Latinos, American Indians, and African Americans.

The biracial baby boom forces us to confront the meaning of race and the social order predicated upon it. *Race*, as constructed by social Darwinism and government construction by *blood quantum*, is more an artifice of the mind than a biological fact. . . . A significant number of people around the world are not classifiable by such a system, including multiracial people. Unfortunately, this problematic taxonomy has been transformed into a sociopolitical system that has been deeply imprinted in our psyches. Subsequently, race has become insidiously enmeshed with our social structure, determining the distribution of resources among social groups and even influencing the methodologies and theories of social science research.

Nowhere is the validity or reliability of race more questionable than in government policies. For example, blood quantum, used to operationalize the definition of race biologically, has been used liberally to justify the dislocation of American Indians and Native Hawaiians off their native lands, to intern Japanese Americans during World War II, to determine immigration quotas and to determine African Americans' racial identity and subsequent limits of access to resources. Generally, small blood quantum have been used to deprive people of color of their civil rights. Conversely, in more recent years conservatives have used blood quantum – that is, proportions of heritage – to determine allocations of lands to Native Americans (including Native Hawaiians) or qualification for government funding. Race cannot be a scientific construct if it has changing boundaries mitigated by laws, history, emotions, or politics.

Despite the significant number of people of all colors who have questioned the validity of race and the way it is abused in this country, taxonomies and institutions, like attitudes, are slow to change. Nowhere is this illustrated better than in how the US Census Bureau has insisted on distinct monoracial categories. When Hawaii became the fiftieth state, the US Census Bureau imposed its categories on a population that up until then had recorded its population according to categories and mixtures that reflected its multiracial reality. The Census Bureau does not acknowledge multiple heritages, despite the following facts: Currently, it is estimated that 30–70% of African Americans by multigenerational history are multiracial; virtually all Latinos and Filipinos are multiracial, as are the majority of American Indians and Native Hawaiians. Even a significant proportion of White-identified persons are of multiracial origins. The way in which the Census Bureau records data on race makes it very difficult to estimate the number of biracial people, let alone multiracial persons, in the United States. Any estimates that have been made are conservative.

Now that we have almost 25 years' distance from the 1967 Supreme Court ruling that required the last 14 states holding antimiscegenist laws to repeal them, perhaps we can reconsider the subject of racially mixed persons in a less biased and less hostile context. It is likely that in the next decade, many persons previously identified as monoracial will begin to identify as multiracial, as they experience the dynamic nature of identity. As time evolves we will have more and more difficulty "judging the book by its cover." If we are truly to attempt constructive answers to the questions offered earlier (Who are we? How do we see ourselves? Who are we as a nation in relation to one another?), we will need to perform several social, political, and psychological "surgeries" to remove the deeply embedded, insidious, pseudoscientific construct of race from our social structure.

Initially, I thought my interest in exploring this topic was too personal. However, after a decade of contemplation, reading, writing, doing therapy, teaching, and finally a year of living in Honolulu, Hawaii, I think there is much to say. The topic of racially mixed persons provides us with a vehicle for examining ideologies surrounding race, race relations, and the role of the social sciences in the deconstruction of race. To this end, a progressive group of 28 interdisciplinary scholars, teachers, mentors, activists, administrators, and psychotherapists have collaborated to publish this first collection of contemporary American descriptive, empirical, conceptual, and theoretical studies on racially mixed persons since the repeal of antimiscegenist laws. The chapters are intellectually and personally challenging. An array of methodologies and twists to conventional research are described; some of the multiracial history of the United States is summarized; conventional constructs such as identity and passing are reexamined in the light of a multiracial ecology. The authors repeatedly and independently break with the characterization of the racially mixed person as a tragic figure relegated to a marginal, anomic existence as they offer multidimensional theories as contexts within which to examine multiracial phenomenology. It is suggested that the multiracial person's understanding of her- or himself can enhance society's understanding of intra- and intergroup relations, identity, and resilience.

Study probes

1   According to Root, how is 'the biracial baby boom' transforming American 'race' relations?
2   Outline Sandoval's four-tier model and Root's fifth and six additions.
3   What observations does the author make about varying attitudes to 'racial' mixing among and between different groups?
4   Why is the author critical of linear models of 'racial' identity formation and what does she advocate as an alternative?
5   What factors inhibited the previous empowerment of 'mixed race' people?

Note

1   In this chapter the terms *biracial* and *multiracial* are sometimes used interchangeably. *Biracial* refers to someone with two socially and phenotypically distinct racial heritages – one from each parent. However, this term can also refer to a multigenerational history of prior racial blending. For example, someone may have a parent or grandparent who was biracial and may acknowledge this heritage through self-identification as biracial. In this "looser" definition, one moves away from the notion of "halves" – half Black, half White. *Multiracial* includes the case of the biracial person and persons synthesizing two or more diverse heritages, such as the person with African, Indian, and European heritages. It also is a term that acknowledges that the suppression of multiracial heritage in this country may limit people's knowledge about their "racial" roots; subsequently, *multiracial* may be a more accurate term than *biracial*. This term is inclusive of all racially mixed persons.

Chapter 19

Paul R. Spickard

THE ILLOGIC OF AMERICAN RACIAL CATEGORIES

From M.P.P. Root (ed.) *Racially Mixed People of America* (1992). Thousand Oaks, CA: Sage, pp. 18–23.

Race as a social category

RACE, THEN, IS PRIMARILY A SOCIAL CONSTRUCT. It has been constructed in different ways in different times and places. In 1870, the US Bureau of the Census divided up the American population into races: White, Colored (Blacks), Colored (Mulattoes), Chinese, and Indian. In 1950, the census categories reflected a different social understanding: White, Black, and Other. By 1980, the census categories reflected the ethnic blossoming of the previous two decades: White, Black, Hispanic, Japanese, Chinese, Filipino, Korean, Vietnamese, American Indian, Asian Indian, Hawaiian, Guamanian, Samoan, Eskimo, Aleut, and Other. In England in 1981, the categories were quite different: White, West Indian, African, Arab, Turkish, Chinese, Indian, Pakistani, Bangladeshi, Sri Lankan, and Other – because the sociopolitical land-scape in England demanded different divisions. (The fact that some of these are also nationality labels should not obscure the fact that many in the United States and Great Britain treat them as domestic racial units.) In South Africa, there are four racial categories: White, African, Coloured, and Asian. In Brazil, the gradations between Black and White are many: *preto*, *cabra*, *escuro*, *mulato escuro*, *mulato claro*, *pardo*, *sarará*, *moreno*, and *branco de terra*. Each of these systems of racial classification reflects a different social, economic, and political reality. Such social situations change, and so do racial categories.

Social distinctions such as race and class come about when two or more groups of people come together in a situation of economic or status competition. Frequently such competition results in stratification – in the domination of some groups by others. People in Africa did not experience their lives as Africans or as Blacks; they were Hausa or Ibo or Fon, or members of any of several other groups. But when they were brought to America they were defined as a single group by the Europeans who held power over their lives. They were lumped together as Africans or Negroes or Blacks, partly because they shared certain physical similarities, especially when contrasted with Europeans, and partly because they shared a common status as slaves.

From the point of view of the dominant group, racial distinctions are a necessary tool of dominance. They serve to separate the subordinate people as Other. Putting simple, neat racial labels on dominated peoples – and creating negative myths about the moral qualities of those peoples – makes it easier for the dominators to ignore the individual humanity of their victims. It eases the guilt of oppression. Calling various African peoples all one racial group, and associating that group with evil, sin, laziness, bestiality, sexuality, and irresponsibility, made it easier for White slave owners to rationalize holding their fellow humans in bondage, whipping them, selling them, separating their families, and working them to death. The function of the one-drop rule was to solidify the barrier between Black and White, to make sure that no one who might possibly be identified as Black also became identified as White. For a mixed person, then, acceptance of the one-drop rule means internalizing the oppression of the dominant group, buying into the system of racial domination.

Race is by no means only negative, however. From the point of view of subordinate peoples, race can be a positive tool, a source of belonging, mutual help, and self-esteem. Racial categories (and ethnic categories, for they function in the same way)[1] identify a set of people with whom to share a sense of identity and common experience. To be a Chinese American is to share with other Chinese Americans at least the possibility of free communication and a degree of trust that may not be shared with non-Chinese. It is to share access to common institutions – Chinese churches, Chinatowns, and Chinese civic associations. It is to share a sense of common history – immigration, work on the railroads and in the mines of the West, discrimination, exclusion, and a decades-long fight for respectability and equal rights. It is to share a sense of peoplehood that helps locate individuals psychologically, and also provides the basis for common political action. Race, this socially constructed identity, can be a powerful tool, either for oppression or for group self-actualization.

At the margins: race as self-definition

Where does this leave the person of mixed parentage? Such people have long suffered from a negative public image. . . . What is a person of mixed race? Biologically speaking, we are all mixed. That is, we all have genetic material from a variety of populations, and we all exhibit physical characteristics that testify to mixed ancestry. Biologically speaking, there never have been any pure races – all populations are mixed.

More to the point is the question of to which socially defined category people of mixed ancestry belong. The most illogical part of all this racial categorizing is not that we imagine it is about biology. After all, there *is* a biological component to race, or at least we identify biological referents – physical markers – as a kind of shorthand to stand for what are essentially socially defined groups. What is most illogical is that we imagine these racial categories to be exclusive. The US Census form says, "Check one box." If a person checks "Other," his or her identity and connection with any particular group is immediately erased. Yet what is a multiracial person to do?

Once, a person of mixed ancestry had little choice. Until fairly recently, for example, most Americans of part Japanese or part Chinese ancestry had to present themselves to the world as non-Asians, for the Asian ethnic communities to which they might have aspired to be connected would not have them.[2] For example, in the 1920s, 7-year-old Peter fended for himself on the streets of Los Angeles. He had been thrown out of the house shortly after his Mexican American mother died, when his Japanese American father married a Japanese woman, because the stepmother could not stand the thought of a half-Mexican boy living under her roof. No Japanese American individual or community institution was willing to take him in because he was not pure Japanese.

On the other hand, the one-drop rule meant that part-Black people were forced to reckon themselves Black. Some might pass for White, but by far the majority of children of African American intermarriages chose or were forced to be Black. . . . The salient point here is that once, before the last third of the twentieth century, multiracial individuals did not generally have the opportunity to choose identities for themselves.[3] In the 1970s and particularly the 1980s, however, individuals began to assert their right to choose their own identities – to claim belonging to more than one group, or to create new identities

[. . .]

Some even dared to refuse to choose. In 1985 I observed a wise Caucasian-Chinese 5-year-old. Dining with her family in Boston's Chinatown during Chinese New Year, she was asked insistently by an adult Chinese friend of the family, "Which are you really – Chinese or American?" It was clear the woman wanted her to say she was really Chinese. But the girl replied simply, "I don't have to choose. I'm both." And so she was.

This child probably could not have articulated it, but she was arguing that races are not types. One ought not be thrust into a category: Chinese or American, White or Black. Her answer calls on us to move our focus from the boundaries between groups – where we carefully assign this person to the White category and that person to the Black category – to the centers. That is, we ought to pay attention to the things that characterize groups and hold them together, to the content of group identity and activity, to patterns and means of inclusiveness and belonging. A mixed person should not be regarded as Black *or* White, but as Black *and* White, with access to both parts of his or her identity. In the poem presented at the outset of this essay, Joseph Cotter's mulatto felt the pull of the various parts of his heritage, but felt constrained to choose only one. In the 1990s, that choice is still available to mixed people, but it is no longer *necessary*. Today a person of mixed ancestry can choose to embrace all the parts of his or her background. Many of the essays in this volume are about the issues attendant upon such a choice of a multiethnic identity. As the essays attest, the one-drop rule no longer applies.

Study probes

1   According to Spickard, how are 'racial distinctions a necessary tool of dominance'?
2   Why can 'racial' distinctions also be 'a positive tool'?
3   How does the author illustrate 'the illogic of racial categories'?

Notes

1   Since both are defined on the basis of social and not biological criteria, a race and an ethnic group are in essence the same type of group. They reckon (real or imagined) descent from a common set of ancestors. They have a sense of identity that tells them they are one people. They share culture, from clothing to music to food to language to child-rearing practices. They build institutions such as churches and fraternal organizations. They perceive and pursue common political and economic interests.
2   This was true for people of mixed Jewish and Gentile background as well: They were shunned by Jewish people and institutions and typically had to adopt Gentile identities.
3   Sometimes the assignments were a bit arbitrary. Anthropologist Max Stanton tells of meeting three brothers in Dulac, Louisiana, in 1969. All were Houma Indians, had a French last name, and shared the same father and mother. All received their racial designations at the hands of the medical people who assisted at their births. The oldest brother, born before 1950 at home with the aid of a mid wife, was classified as a Negro, because the state of Louisiana did not recognize the Houma as Indians before 1950. The second brother, born in a local hospital after 1950, was assigned to the Indian category. The third brother, born 80 miles away in a New Orleans hospital, was designated White on the basis of the French family name (M. Stanton, personal communication, 1990).

Chapter 20

Naomi Zack

BLACK, WHITE, AND GRAY: WORDS, WORDS, WORDS

Extract from *Race and Mixed Race* (1993). Philadelphia, PA: Temple University Press, pp. 167–172.

I HAVE BEEN ARGUING THROUGHOUT THIS WORK that in a context where a race is devalued, such as in the United States, racial designations are as racist, i.e., as cruel, as racist devaluations. Such racial designations limit individuals in their subjectivities, even when they take up the designations themselves, about themselves. The mythology about race which underlies racial devaluations and racial designations is evident in the language of race that is used in the United States. Everyone knows that racial epithets and slurs represent a breakdown of normal cooperative assumptions of communication – these derogatory *race-words* are insults and as such easily bridge gaps between words and action.[1] But people are less aware of the way in which seemingly neutral racial language is racist. Because the racism inherent in various concepts of race has already been discussed, it seems appropriate at this point to turn to the words themselves.

First, there is a general myopia about the black–white dichotomy. When Americans hear the word "race," they immediately assume it means "black" or "white." In many places, for long periods of time in American history, all people could be divided into black or white racial categories. This was before there were large numbers of Hispanic Americans, Asian Americans, and recognized Native Americans. It was before these other racial groups became large or strong enough to demand recognition or, as in the case of Native Americans, before they were permitted voices which could be heard by some of those in the society from which they had been alienated. The black–white racial dichotomy imposes a myopic linguistic convention, which holds that everyone belongs to a race but that there are only two races: Negro and Caucasian. Of course, even the most emphatic biracialists know that there are also Asians, but when the topic of race comes up they speak as if everyone were either black or white.

In Anglo-American cultural history, the words "black" and "white" are symbols with positive and negative moral connotations. Sin in the sense of sexual transgression, for example, is "black," and virginity and other traditional states of moral virtue are "white." Thus the black–white sin–virtue dichotomy was available historically as a justification for the exploitation of blacks by whites when Europeans first began to exploit Africa, the "dark" continent.[2] (The moral-religious connotations of a black–white dichotomy are so exaggerated in American culture that it can be a locution of criticism, imputing ignorance, stupidity, and possibly insanity, to say that someone "sees" such and such "in black and white.")[3] In addition to this symbolism, there are other racist aspects of the American use of the black–white dichotomy of race.

There is no parity in the derivation of the words used for the two racial categories: Caucasian and Negro. The word "Caucasian" has a geographical reference to the Caucasus area and thereby derives from a proper name. The word "Negro" comes from the French or Spanish word *negro*, meaning the color black, which derives from the Latin word *niger*, having the same meaning.[4] Until the 1920s, American blacks were referred to as "negroes," with a small *n*. The insistence on the capital *N* was based on the demand for the acceptance of American blacks as a national group, like other national groups whose names were capitalized.[5] The insistence on the word "black" to refer to black Americans in the 1960s was, in this context, a change to an English translation of *negro*. When "black" is used to refer to black Americans as an ethnic group, it is capitalized. But when "black" is simply a racial designation in contrast to the racial designation "white," it is not capitalized. It is ironic that when American blacks insisted on racial respect, "Negro" became capitalized; and when Black Culture was revalued, "black" became the preferred racial designation. The word "white" as a racial designation is almost never capitalized these days, outside of white supremacist literature.

When American blacks are referred to as "African Americans," this appears to establish a parity of terminology with "Caucasian" because the word "African," like the word "Caucasian," is an adjective deriving from the proper name of a place. But people were first designated as Caucasian because of their resemblance to the physical appearance of people who inhabited the Caucasus geographical areas. By contrast, most American blacks are designated as African Americans on the basis of an assumption that they have forebears whose physical appearance resembled people who inhabit the geographical area of Africa. So again there is no parity.

The words "black" and "white" purport to categorize people racially on the basis of their skin color. There are some, but very few, Americans who have skin the actual colors of objects that are accurately described as having black and white surfaces. As colors, black and white are anomalous: In quasi-scientific language, black is the perceptual experience of the absence of all colors from the visible spectrum, and white is the perceptual experience of the presence of all colors from the visible spectrum.[6] (These optical facts make a joke out of the use of the sobriquet "of color" for all non-white people.) Still, it is possible to manufacture black and white pigments, and like all other colors that can be applied to the surfaces of objects, black and white can be mixed.

When the colors black and white are mixed, they produce various shades of gray. When people who are black and white "mix" genetically, it is commonly acknowledged that the skin colors of their offspring fall on a continuum of colors that are in the ranges of brown and tan. On one end of this continuum are those whose skin color would be called "white," in the absence of knowledge of their black forebears. On the other end of the continuum are those whose skin color would cause them to be racially designated black. Thus, as racial words, "black" and "white" purport to refer to skin color, but in fact they are only loosely related to the actual skin colors of human beings. In the case of individuals who are called "white" racially, the word "white" is not expected to refer either to their actual skin color or to the actual skin color of their ancestors. In the case of individuals who are called "black" racially, the word "black" may be believed to be a more accurate description of the skin color of their ancestors than of the individuals themselves.

By contrast, as Carl N. Degler describes the racial system in Brazil, there race is not determined by the race of a person's ancestors but by money. Thus a poor Brazilian mulatto is a Negro, whereas a rich Negro who is not visibly of mixed race is white. This has been called the "lightening" effect of money – and social class. American slave owners bred their slaves as a way of increasing their capital. This was less so in Brazil.[7] It may be that the strong hereditary aspect of American race derives from the strong property interest in the hereditary aspects of American slavery.[8] If this is so, it would suggest that Americans have stronger property traditions than Brazilians do. Even though Brazilians are now more "materialistic" about race, historically, Americans have been more materialistic about people, a form of materialism that lives on in all biracial American racial designations to this day.

There is every reason to believe that Americans are just as sentient of colors as people who live in other countries. That is, only a small percentage of Americans are color blind, or perceive only black, white, and gray. So it is fairly clear that the racial words "black" and "white" are not the color words that they purport to be but labels that refer to nineteenth-century concepts of race, which associated nonphysical characteristics with racial designations.

The current scientific view of a race is that a race is a group of people who have more of some physical traits than do other groups of people. Skin color is not a particularly accurate standard for determining races, nor is skin color in combination with body types, facial features, hair textures, or any of the other physical characteristics associated with races. Henry Louis Gates, Jr., makes the point of how inadequate those physical criteria are that purport to be racial criteria, in a quote from a contemporary American work on "Left" political theory:

> The division of the human species into races is biologically – though
> not socially – arbitrary. We could differentiate humans along count-
> less axes, such as height, weight and other physical features. If we
> assigned racial categories to groups of humans with different heights

– for example, every foot of height from four feet up determines a new race – we would be more biologically precise than the usual racial designation by skin color. For no fixed biological boundary exists between Asian and Caucasian, black and Indian, whereas a fixed boundary does exist between those who are shorter than five feet and those who are between five and six feet.[9]

However, it is not racial-group membership that determines race in the United States but lines of descent – genealogy. As groups, races are not stable entities. In Melville J. Herskovits's often-quoted words, "Two human groups never meet but they mingle their blood." And of course, this has always been the case in the United States. But due to the alchemy of American racism, no new race ever results. Black and white do not make gray here, but black.

It is important to note that when the acknowledgment of a mixed-race individual does not go beyond a reference to the racial diversity of that individual's forebears, the individual is called "of mixed race." But if the individual is acknowledged to be a racial mixture *in himself*, then he would be called "mixed race," without the "of." The use of the word "of" in the designation "of mixed race" leaves open the question of what the mixed-race individual *is* racially, and this "of" is compatible with the American one-drop rule. But if "of" is left out and an individual is called simply "mixed race," it becomes more difficult conceptually to designate that individual black (or white, for that matter).

It is interesting, however, that wherever there is some recognition that mixed-race people exist, as there was in the old lower South and as there still is in Brazil, the metaphors "black" and "white" are abandoned in favor of color words which come closer to describing what it is that people see when they look at skin colors.[10] The skin colors of people of acknowledged mixed race are called words such as "coffee," "almond," "almond shell," "piney," "honey," "ivory," "mahogany," "tan," and so on.[11] It is almost as if, in the presence of those individuals who are perceived to be mixed black and white race, the reality of human perception reasserts itself, and an attempt is made to speak the truth about visual experience. As offensive as such mixed-race color words may be against the backdrop of a biracial system, they nevertheless have more human reality than those color words "black" and "white" (which most Americans could never approximate in appearance without being badly burned or suffering massive blood loss).

However, once an American begins to formulate a theoretical entitlement to consideration as a mixed-race person, the word "gray" might look attractive as a racial name, for the sake of parity (even though it is now used to describe an appearance of illness in practically everyone, without prejudice). Of course, it would be a more liberal society if all people could be described physically as other natural objects are described (without anachronistic metaphors that, if taken literally, refer to death and disease). It would be a far more liberal society if racial designations were *allowed* to go the inevitable way of all historically vestigial categories. And if there is an intention that this be so, in the interim between the world of today, when people are categorized like so many breeds of domestic animals, and tomorrow, when the dog show will be over, what should "black," "non-white," "gray," and perhaps "red" and "yellow" people be called? Call us what we are, plain and simple: "racially designated."

Study probes

1   How does Zack illustrate the ways in which 'the mythology about race . . . is evident in the language of race that is used in the United States'?
2   Why is she critical of the terms 'black' and 'white'?
3   What does the author mean by the statement: 'it is not racial-group membership that determines race in the United States but lines of descent-genealogy'?
4   What 'term' does she advocate and why?

Notes

1   According to H.P. Grice, normal communication presupposes cooperation. On the assumption of cooperation, if certain obvious rules of discourse are broken, the listener has reason to infer a logical implication behind what the speaker has literally said. For example, if we are cooperating and I ask you how X's performance was last night and you tell me that X knew all her lines, I can infer, according to the Rule of Relevance, that X's performance was not very good, because you have flouted the Rule of Relevance. See H.P. Grice, "Logic and Conversation," in Donald Davidson and Gilbert Harman, eds., *The Logic of Grammar* (Encino, Calif.: Dickinson, 1975), pp. 64–153. Insults, especially racial insults and implied racial insults, do not merely flout the normal rules but signal that cooperation in communication is not present. This may be why insults lead so easily to acts of violence, i.e., they signal that verbal communication is no longer possible.
2   See John L. Hodge, "Equality: Beyond Dualism and Oppression," in David Theo Goldberg, ed., *Anatomy of Racism* (Minneapolis: University of Minnesota Press, 1990), pp. 89–108.
3   See Carl N. Degler, *Neither Black nor White* (Madison, University of Wisconsin Press, 1986), p. xviii.
4   See *Webster's New Collegiate Dictionary*, 2d edn (1960), s.v. "Caucasian," "Negro."
5   See Degler, *Neither Black nor White*, p. 277.
6   William Cecil Dampier, *A History of Science* (Cambridge: Cambridge University Press, 1943), p. 176.
7   See Degler, *Neither Black nor White*, pp. 105–107.
8   Not only was there, in Brazil, a lack of interest in breeding slaves, as compared to the United States, but manumission was easier and more frequent in Brazil, especially in the case of slaves of mixed race. See ibid., pp. 19–20, 39–47, 61–67.
9   Henry Louis Gates, Jr., "Critical Remarks," in Goldberg, ed., *Anatomy of Racism*, p. 332.
10   Degler, *Neither Black nor White*, pp. 102–103, John C. Mencke, *Mulattoes and Race Mixture* (Ann Arbor: University of Michigan Institute of Research Press, 1979), pp. ix, 2–3, Joel Williamson, *New People* (New York: Free Press, 1980), pp. 23–24. It should be noted that the old racial words for mixed black and white race, e.g., "quadroon," "octaroon," etc., are no more naturalistically descriptive than the words for people who are racially pure.
11   The nineteenth-century fiction sympathetic to mulattoes was replete with such descriptions. Many writers claim that among contemporary American blacks, close attention is paid to gradations in skin color. See, e.g., Beth Day, *Sexual Life between Blacks and Whites* (New York: World, 1972), pp. 185–187. Also, there is a tradition in black letters of aesthetic racial pride, based on the variation in appearance among people who are designated as black in the United States. See W.E.B. Du Bois, *The Dusk of Dawn*, in idem, *Du Bois Writings*, comp. Nathan Huggins (New York: Literary Classics of the US, 1986), pp. 657–658.

Chapter 21

Lewis R. Gordon

RACE, BIRACIALITY, AND MIXED RACE

Extract from *Her Majesty's Other Children* (1997). Lanham, MD: Rowman and Littlefield, pp. 55–57 and 62–67.

WE CAN NOW EXPLORE THE QUESTION of how both mixed race and biraciality can be understood in this context. In the United States, the significant factor of differentiation is premised on whites in an epicenter of swirling colors. In effect, then, to be "mixed" is a function of colored realities, not white ones, on the level of "race." Although whites may speak of being "mixed" with various European ethnicities and religions, racial mixture and white identity are antipathetic to each other. Whiteness, in other words, usually signifies purity. The "child," if you will, of white-nonwhite liaisons exists as an onto-biological point of difference from at least one parent. One finds, in such circumstances, a rigid order of hierarchies according to social subordination. Thus, in all matrices, it is the white parent who loses onto-racial connection to her or his offspring. But in other matrices – for example, Northeast Asians ("mongoloids") with blacks – it is the Asian parent who loses the connection.[1] In terms of membership, then, the black parent finds a permanent racial connection with the child. (Of course, there are children who reject the racial designation and, in effect, reject, although not intentionally, their parents. But our concern here is the social reality of the hierarchies.)

One finds, then, that offsprings who are biracial mixtures with blacks are pretty much excluded from most racial categories except for black. Although it can be shown that among Native Americans the story differs – for Native American and African American offsprings are often both (Native American and black) – there is still the social reality of the different quality of life available for a child who is a result of Native American unions with whites or Asians versus blacks. I recall speaking at a state university in Tennessee. A member of the audience introduced himself as a redneck with a Confederate flag on his truck. He also identified himself as part Cherokee by virtue of his grandmother, and he added that that has posed no problem at efforts to recruit him at Ku Klux Klan and right-wing militia rallies. I asked him to consider what his affiliations may have been if his grandmother were black or Asian. I also asked him to think about the significance of his Confederate flag as a sign of willingness to join right-wing and racist organizations. And finally, I asked him why he was so proud of being taken by such people as someone who is ideologically in their camp. Before he could respond, a woman in the audience, who announced herself as part Cherokee as well, voiced her objection. "Indians aren't white," she said. "There are whites with some Indian in them. But to be Indian, that's another story. Go to the reservations. You'll see."

Later that year, I found myself having lunch with a prominent couple from Toronto, Canada, one of whom regarded herself as being a biracial mixture of European and Chinese parentage. Her husband was white. As we discussed matters of race and theory, I eventually asked her and her husband to consider this: Most racially mixed marriages in North America occur between white men and Asian women. I recall a Chinese male associate in San Francisco lamenting that, in order to marry an Asian woman in California, he would have to find a way to become white. If the possibility of having children is still a central concern in most marriages, and if people also consider the possibility of desirable children in their choice of matrimonial partners, why don't white men seem to worry about having children with Asian women? Why is the least mixture between blacks and every other group, and the highest mixture between whites and every other group except blacks?[2] And finally, why is there such a qualitatively different life in racial terms for Asians who are mixed with blacks versus Asians mixed with whites? Do we find Asians (and Latin Americans) rushing to wed blacks to uplift their gene pool, as seems to be the case with their marrying whites? Blackness, in the end, functions as a constant, underlying mark of racialization as does no other racial designation. Its persistence suggests that the fluidity of racial identities points upward in continuing spirals of potential whiteness.

But blackness also points to a history of mixed racialization that, although always acknowledged among blacks, is rarely understood or seen among other groups. I have argued elsewhere, for instance, that to add the claim of "mixture" to blacks in both American continents would be redundant, because blacks are their primary "mixed" populations to begin with. Mixture among blacks, in particular, functions as an organizing aesthetic, as well as a tragic history. On the aesthetic level, it signifies the divide between beauty and ugliness. On the social level, the divide is between being just and unjust, virtuous and vicious; "fair skin" is no accidental, alternative term for "light skin." And on the historical level, the divide signifies concerns that often are denied. Consider the striking similarity of the subtext of the following two observations – the first by El-Haji Malik El-Shabazz and the second by Frantz Fanon.

> Out in the world later, in Boston and New York, I was among the millions of Negroes who were insane enough to feel that it was some kind of status symbol to be light-complexioned – that one was

actually fortunate to be born thus. But, still later, I learned to hate every drop of that white rapist's blood that is in me.[3]

[. . .]

The fight against racism is an existential/moral phenomenon. Proof is found in the nineteenth century when people who actually believed in the scientific validity of the concept of race simultaneously fought against slavery, genocide, and exploitation, and the myriad of ways in which *racism* is made manifest. Against Anthony Apprah's position then, where it is claimed that racism needs to be rejected because of the scientific invalidity (which for him constitutes the ontological illegitimacy) of the concept of race, the obvious conclusion here is that the scientific invalidity of races is not the relevant point.[4]

The antirace gatekeepers have had an unfortunate relationship with the evolution of one dimension of mixed-race movements and contemporary biracial politics. As we've seen, the whole point is not to be the darkest/most inferior.

So, given the existential dimensions of what we have discussed thus far, what, may we say, are the goals and possibilities available for a critical theory of mixed race?

Some claims that can be asserted in favor of a critical race theory premised on mixed-race identity are:

1   Accuracy and consistency of racial ideology demand a mixed-race stand-point, for if whites and blacks are "pure," then mixtures signify "other" forms of race. (This argument supports the reasoning behind constructing separate racial categories for mixed-race people.)

2   The question of accuracy raises questions of affiliation. Filial recognition plays an important role in our self-identities. The need to recognize fully one's ancestry calls for recognition of mixture. Saying that one's ancestry is all-black because of the "one drop rule," for instance, fails to identify relatives whose lineage is multiracial beyond their African ancestry.

3   On the biracial end, there is the fact of converging embodiments to con-sider. A biracial offspring "is" biologically and often culturally both of her or his parents.

4   If race *means* black or white, then mixture becomes an enigma. It signifies "racelessness." (This argument goes both ways. In favor of a separate cat-egory for mixed-race people, it is advanced as a way of eliminating their exclusion from racial matrices by making such a provision. Against a cat-egory of mixed-race people, it is advanced to claim that even a racial designation will be an inaccurate articulation of their reality. And there are those who argue that it provides a critique of racial categories to begin with and perhaps point to a [raceless] future.)[5]

5   On the practical end, biraciality and mixed-race designations can serve an antiracist strategy: recognition of racial mixture dilutes identities premised on conceptions of "purity" and can therefore be an important stage on the road to a raceless or more racially free future.

6   And finally, but not exhaustively, there is the existential claim: Mixed and
    biracial people have unique experiences that can be shared and cultivated
    through a recognized group identification. (This existential turn is also, of
    course, support for the political implications designated by the first claim.)

Now, recall my point about the two dominant principles of racist ideology:
(1) be white, but above all, (2) don't be black. We can call the first *the principle of
white supremacy*; and we can call the second *the principle of black inferiority*. Given
these two principles, the following responses can be made to our six afore-
mentioned claims.

First, we have already shown that to be racialized means not to be "white."
And in fact, when white is spoken of as a race, many whites experience
discomfort for good reason: it violates their place in the social order. Thus, when
all is said and done, the question of mixed-race people being an "other" race is
only significant in regard to principle (2), which signifies the importance of not
being black. Now, although this principle doesn't apply to biracial and mixed
people along Euro-Asian or Euro-Native American lines — and given the racial
hierarchies, it is rare, very rare indeed, that we find principle (2) being articulated in relation to any group other than blacks — it becomes clear that the
"other" race argument is really about not being black.[6] Since the practice is
geared toward adhering to principle (2), the political consequence will be an
institutionalization of a certain place in the racial hierarchy. There will, in short,
be an institutionally recognized group of nonblacks. One can readily see why
certain groups of blacks are very suspicious of such a move, for its consequence
is, after all, a quantitative reduction, by a legal stroke, of the population of
designated black people. A whole group of black people will, that is, legally
disappear.

Perhaps the best critical response to this move stems from our articulation of
racism as a desire for black people to disappear. The first claim about accuracy
requiring a mixed-race standpoint has the consequence of facilitating such a
process, at least in terms of legal measures that can be taken. Such a consequence
clearly violates W.E.B. Du Bois' famous admonition against problematizing
people instead of responding to the social problems that people experience.[7]
There is nothing in the first claim that can reject the conclusion that the world
will be better off if it had a lot less black folks, especially since the number of
white people in the world will in no way diminish from such a move.

The second claim about affiliation seems to me to be correct but also in need
of other considerations, for the question of filial recognition pertains primarily
to *white* affiliation. The history of ancestral denial and rejecting descendants
hasn't been a problem of colored folks. It is a white problem. There are whites
who deny black ancestry and whites who reject black descendants; the issue
pertains to the principle of white supremacy. But the principle of black inferiority also emerges through the lack of appreciation of black filial recognition. In
black communities, for instance, talk of ancestry nearly always pertains to non-
black ancestry. It was only during brief moments of African ancestral pride,
periods under attack today as "nationalist" and "Afrocentric," that a search for
specificity of African lineage emerged. There are, however, surprising sites of

such recognition. On a research visit to Cuba, for instance, my US colleagues and I were astonished by a tour guide's response to a question raised by a member of our delegation: "Are there any Cuban Indians still around?" The guide, without missing a beat, responded, "Native Caribbeans were killed off within a century of Columbus's landing. All Cubans are of African and European ancestry." Because Cubans, at least the Cubans who remain on the island, are for the most part a "colored" people, the point of colored recognition is here affirmed. But even in Cuba, there are clearly black-designated people. There, as in most of the Caribbean, Central America, and South America, such people hardly stand as racially superior. The project of the ancestral claim, then, is to affirm *mixture* itself, which is to establish the force of the principle of black inferiority.

The third claim is clearly true. Biracial offsprings are from both parents biologically and often culturally. But again, once one introduces a racial designation other than white, the principle of black inferiority becomes the dominant factor. The biracial person can embody white superiority if the current group of people who are designated white people disappear. But in that case, whoever is next on the racial hierarchical scale will become white people. This turn, then, affirms the principle of black inferiority only because of the *current* limitations of embodying the principle of superior whiteness. In countries such as Brazil and Mexico, this is exactly what occurs. I recall a colleague of mine being shocked, for instance, while staying with a family in Guatemala. The family whom he saw as not only colored but "mixed," categorically hated black people. What were they? Their answer was simple: white.

Moreover, the biracial offspring who attempts to affirm both identities faces the social reality of both identities existing on unequal terms. In short, to affirm whiteness on the level of blackness has the consequence of equalizing whiteness, which, in effect, is to "blacken" it. There is thus the catch-22 of being unable to affirm their white side *as white* without encountering two perversions of reality: Either the white side is treated as superior or it is treated as a form of nonwhite whiteness; as, in a word, colored. These considerations bring us to the fourth claim, which addresses the supposed racelessness of mixed groups.

The fourth claim is subject to all the criticisms of race-neutrality. Since whites function as normative standpoints of humanity, they normally live as raceless. Angela Y. Davis, in a public lecture, phrased the situation thus: If colored means not to be white, then white means to be colorless.[8] Thus, to declare, as Michael Jackson did in his song "Black or White." "I don't want to spend my life being a color," means, in effect, to spend one's life surreptitiously being white. The problem with using this route as a means to a raceless future, then, is that it affirms a future premised on both principles by ultimately advocating the elimination of black people.

In an essay entitled, "White Normativity and the Racial Rhetoric of Equal Protection," Robert Westley unmasks some insidious dimensions of racelessness in the present age."[9] When the search for a legal remedy to racism took the form of *equal* protection, many whites suddenly gained the consciousness of being *racialized*. In the previous world, there were only human beings and coloreds – at the bottom of which were *the blacks*. Today, the law says that blacks are equal to every other group, which for these groups means that the law considers them equal to blacks. A strange equality: blacks move up while everyone else moves "down." For many whites, the metaphor of being treated "like the blacks" became a source of deeply rooted anxiety. In effect, social policy demanded that they take, as Adam and Eve apparently did, a "fall." Needless to say, many whites couldn't take it, and a full-scale attack on affirmative action and an array of antirace and so-called reverse-discrimination constructions emerged. The goal of this attack is supposedly a raceless future, but because racism can persist without race, such a future holds the key to a special nightmare of exploitation and invisibility without reference. It problematizes race, ultimately, to preserve racism.

The fifth claim, which sees an antiracist strategy in which racelessness is the carrot at the end of the rod, is problematic for the same reasons as the fourth one: It portends a world without blacks

The sixth claim, that biracial and mixed-race people have a unique existential situation, strikes me as correct. Mixed-race and biracial people do have unique experiences that are functions of their existential situation. For the biracial child, the anonymous white man may be, in his specific instantiation, Daddy. And all the literature and cultural knowledge of victimized femininity – white, pure, rapable – may be Mommy. Similarly, the complex social forces that say that one is more one's black parent than one's white parent (or one's Asian or Native American parent) raises a complex question of who one is by virtue of one's choice and that choice's relation to one's social situation. Since black Americans and Native Americans are already mixed peoples (what is a "pure" New World black and Native American today?), the question relates, mostly, to people of color elsewhere: African Americans, for example, experience a profound anxiety when they travel to "black" countries; they seem, in those places, to be the least or lesser blacks, they carry with them, that is, the United States as a history of white domination and, for the most part, the masculine history of white "insemination."

On the existential level, biracial people at least have the unique experience of living the racial realities of more than one group in the course of their innermost private lives. That reality alone substantiates something unique, since among all other groups, "others" function anonymously. "God knows what they do in their homes!" is not a rhetorical appeal in biracial people's lived realities.

The question of the political significance of the sixth claim is undermined, however, by our critique of the other claims, especially the first. After all, having a unique situation does not mean that the principle of white superiority and the principle of black inferiority should be affirmed. For the biracial child stands below whiteness and, by virtue of biraciality, in affirmation of black inferiority. The impact of building policy on the uniqueness of biracial people, then, is that it fails to account for political realities that are already in place against people who are clear and present violators of the principle against blackness – in a word, *blacks*.

In spite of contemporary resistance to "binary" analyses, a critical discussion of mixed-race categories calls for an understanding of how binary logic functions in discourses on race and racism. Without binaries, no racism will exist. We have seen the politics of mixed-racialization come to the fore, for instance, on matters of legal recognition of multiple categories. There, principle (2), which affirms the importance of not being black, is the most significant principle. That is because there are social benefits in not being designated black. It is a waste of time to discuss the social losses of being designated white, since the distribution of resources on a global scale falls disproportionately in favor of whites. Affirming principle (2), therefore, affirms the whole racist hierarchy that we may be attempting to avoid. It solidifies the significance of the expression. "Well, at least you're not black."

The struggle against racism from a mixed-race critical position cannot work, then, through simply a rejection of principle (1). To reject the importance of being white in no way addresses the social revulsion with being black. A mixed-race racial position is compatible with the rejection of principle (1), but it is not compatible with the rejection of principle (2). That is because there is no way to reject the thesis that there is something wrong with being black beyond the willingness to "be" black – not in terms of convenient fads of playing blackness, but by paying the social costs of anti-blackness on a global scale. Against the raceless credo, then, racism cannot be rejected without a dialectic in which humanity experiences a blackened world. But therein lies the suicidal irony of a *critical* mixed-race theory.

Study probes

1   What does Gordon mean by the assertion: 'mixture among blacks, in particular, functions as an organizing aesthetic, as well as a tragic history'?
2   Outline the six main critical 'mixed race' claims as well as the author's responses.
3   Compare and contrast Gordon's arguments to those of Root, Spickard and Zack.

Notes

1   For some discussion of Afro-Asian dynamics, see Ernest Allen, Jr. "When Japan Was 'Champion of the Darker Races': Satokata Takahashui and the Flowering of Black Messianic Nationalism," *The Black Scholar* 24, no. 1 (Winter 1994), pp. 23–46, and Joy Ann James, *Resisting State Violence in US Culture* (Minneapolis: University of Minnesota Press, 1996), ch. 15. For specifically Northeast Asian encounters with racial mixture in the United States, see Stephen Satris, " 'What Are They?' " in *American Mixed Race: The Culture of Microdiversity*, ed. Naomi Zack (Lanham, MD: Rowman and Littlefield, 1995), pp. 53–60. Satris argues that children of European (Caucasian) and Northeast Asian (Mongoloid) descent tend to be regarded as Asian only when mongoloid morphology is visually apparent. Children who don't appear as such are regarded and treated by the white and Asian communities as white.
2   According to the US Census, as of 1993, only 2% of interracial marriages were between blacks and "other" races, 20% between blacks and whites, but the number of interracial marriages between whites and non-black "others" was 77%. See also Connie Leslie, Regina Elam, Allison Samuels, and Danzy Senna. "The Loving Generation: Biracial Children Seek Their Own Place." *Newsweek* (February 13, 1995), p. 72, where these figures also are cited.

3   From *The Autobiography of Malcolm X as Told to Alex Haley* (New York: Ballentine Books, 1965), p. 2.

4   For discussion, see K. Anthony Appiah's "Racisms" in *Anatomy of Racism*, ed. David Theo Goldberg (Minneapolis: University of Minnesota Press, 1990), pp. 3–17; Appiah's *In My Father's House: Africa in the Philosophy of Culture* (New York and Oxford Oxford University Press), pp. 13–15; and "Race, Culture, and Identity: Misunderstood Connections" in *Color Conscious*.

5   All of these possibilities are discussed in Naomi Zack's *Mixed Race* and *American Mixed Race*.

6   On the nonracial level, a correlative is in religious cultural affiliation, where the goal of the assimilating Jew is not to be Jewish. The closest similarity to the racial question emerges when the assimilating Jew of "mixed" Gentile-Jewish parentage experiences this question through having a Jewish mother.

7   W.E.B. Du Bois, *The Souls of Black Folks*, with introductions by Nathan Hare and Alvin F. Poussaint, revised and updated bibliography (New York and Scarborough, Ontario: New American Library, 1982 [originally published, 1903]). ch. 1.

8   Angela Y. Davis, Keynote Address, *10th Annual Empowering Women of Color Conference: Reaping Fruit, Throwing Seed* (22 April 1995). University of California at Berkeley.

9   Robert Westley, "White Normativity and the Rhetoric of Equal Protecting" in *Existence in Black*.

Chapter 22

Teresa Kay Williams

RACE-ING AND BEING RACED: THE CRITICAL INTERROGATION OF 'PASSING'

From *Amerasia Journal*, 23 (1) (1997), pp. 61–65.

Maybe because I didn't grow up with my father, even though I was born of mixed blood, I have always considered myself Japanese. That's how I was brought up; that's who I am . .

Judy Sato-Gilbertson, "1996 Nisei Week Queen"[1]

I'm Japanese. To me it seems so clear, especially when I see someone who's Japanese, I can see some features in myself. And those are the strongest features that I have, my Asian features, without a doubt.

Dean Cain, "Superman"[2]

THE ASSUMPTIONS AND LAYERS of social meanings attached to socially defined racial groups and their phenotypical, behavioral presentation have become the social barometer for how we come to understand, respond to, and interact with individuals as representatives of these groups. However, the phenotypical ambiguity and cultural fluidity of many multiracial persons have often left folks at a loss in relation to their customary practices of racial pigeonholing. As a result, Asian-descent multiracial individuals have chapters and chapters worth of "What are you?" stories they can share.[3]

In a racially ordered, racially invested society, the social phenomenon of passing has often been one of the few strategies available to, and utilized by, multiracial individuals to escape the detrimental impact of race. Multiracial individuals are often able to assume the phenotypical and cultural characteristics of various socially defined racial groups. By passing, multiracial individuals can make radical shifts in their racial positionality – for example, from "minority" to "majority" status or from one "minority" status to the "more acceptable minority" status – in order to raise their prestige, advance their chances for a qualitatively improved life, and engage in a bit of racial opportunism. It has also been argued that "the underground tactic" of racial passing, however, could be interpreted as "a form of racial alchemy that seeks to best oppression at its own game by subverting both the comportment line between dominant and subordinate."[4]

Whether or not "passing" is understood as "racial opportunism" or "radical resistance" to oppression, it is the multiracial individuals' phenotypical and cultural ambiguity that allows for them to "pass" or for the social context to place them situationally into pre-existing, socially defined racial or ethnic groups.[5] Therefore, the cultural and phenotypical ambiguity of Asian-descent multi-racials operates as the fulcrum upon which "passing" teeters back and forth as a possibility to escape their lower-status ancestry and opt for the higher-status one (via "rational choice").

Active and conscious passing (implying racial disclosure, concealment, and even dishonesty) can be argued as an instrumental choice made by multiracial individuals to maximize their benefits, life chances, and quality of life.[6] However, the cultural and phenotypical ambiguity of many multiracial individuals also facilitates the possibility of what sociologist Ari Rosner has called, "passive passing." Passers can be active, passive, or manipulative participants. Passing can occur based on physical appearance, cultural display, or both. The participants, their intentions and motivations, and the social context within which "passing" occurs must all be interactively understood because "passing" does not necessitate taking place objectively, consistently, or even rationally.

Passing manifests in many forms and in different contexts, in which the interaction and the negotiation of "self" and the environment's response to it inform and influence the process of passing. For example, is a European-descent *hapa* who is mistakenly being spoken to in Spanish or Tagolog on the streets, passing for "Latino" or "Pilipino"? If his sibling is stopped for speeding and her race marked as "white" by the highway patrol officer on the ticket, is she guilty of "passing for white?" Is a multiracial woman of Samoan and Mexicana ancestries, who is most comfortable identifying as Mexicana, "passing for Mexicana" and denying her Samoan roots? Can a multiracial individual pass for what he or she is *not*? Can a multiracial individual pass for what he or she is? Does passing for what you are count as really passing? How do we determine authentic membership into a racial group: by birth? blood-ties? kinship organization? geographic upbringing? cultural socialization? presence or absence of one parent's heritage? phenotypical resemblance? a combination of these variables? And moreover, who determines racial and ethnic authenticity? Thus, both the interaction among *hapa* individuals and the social, ecological structure must be taken into consideration when interrogating the phenomenon of passing, as well as understanding its social consequences.

Passing in and of itself is problematic for multiracial individuals because it accepts and further reifies the exclusive, oppositionalized, unequal structure of race in which either fluidity across its boundaries or multiple situationality within many boundaries is not permitted. Some European-descent *hapas* have been criticized by monoracial Asian Americans, as well as their African-descent counterparts, for their potential to pass – in particular, for the most privileged racial category for whom the entire racial stratification system exists – (i.e., "white") because of their so-called phenotypical likeness to European Americans. It goes something like, "You can leave your minority self in the racial closet because you can pass *if* you want to." This criticism illuminates the problematic structure of race in American society. If a European-descent *hapa* embraces her or his European heritage, she or he must grapple with the possibilities and accusations of internalized (and externalized) racism. If an African-descent *hapa* embraces his or her African ancestry, perhaps, he or she must struggle with the possibilities and accusations of succumbing to the "one-drop rule" of hypodescent. The monoracial identity choices made by some *hapas* – be it "passing for white, passing for black, passing for Asian, passing for Latino/a, or passing for Pacific Islander" – seem to undercore the problematic nature in which race has come to be organized and ordered. That is to say, races have been socially constructed in such a way that they have remained separate, monoracially-boundaried, exclusive, and unequal. Thus, just as the one-drop rule of racial definitions are remnants of a racist past that grips the present-day identities of multiracial people, so is the twin-concept of passing a sad legacy of racism.

Asian descent multiracials have long debated, "Is Russell Wong passing for Asian? Is Meg Tilly passing for white?" However, sociologist Michael Thornton's conceptual distinction between "personal" and "social" identity may explain why one's personal understanding of self does not necessarily coincide with his or her public articulation of "self."[7] Social, political, and cultural forces must be taken into consideration when understanding how one arrives at understanding one's self-concept and group identification. And therefore, so long as people are passing or perceived to be passing within a society which rewards and punishments are part of the racial passing package, as opposed to the same phenomenon being interpreted and understood as the expression of multiple selves or the impression management of identity,[8] old adages of scientific and cultural racism shall remain deeply and stubbornly embedded and influence their thoughts and actions.

Asian-descent multiracials, already belonging to – at least – one intermediate racial parentage (i.e., Asian, Asian American, or Asian Pacific Islander) and then simultaneously being mixed, locate themselves within, between, and across "no passing zones" – critical spaces of resistance and empowerment.[9] How each Asian-descent multiracial individual arrives at understanding who he or she is, in relationship to others, is contingent upon complex social factors.

The journey of identity formation is lifelong. Along the way, Asian-descent multiracials make, manipulate, change, and flirt with their many possible identities. Though their identities may shift and reconfigure themselves, the core of their being often remains anchored in a sense of self that is informed by their social encounters and their life experiences. Certainly, being viewed, treated, and labeled as belonging to various racial and ethnic groups all have their consequences, both positive and negative, impacting how many Asian-descent multiracials have arrived at understanding their multiple identities and various social locations.

Ultimately, Asian-descent multiracials, like many marginalized peoples, live along the *fronteras* of passing and no passing. They pass and get passed upon. Or as my colleague, Dave Lemmel, has put forth, "Multiracial people 'do race' and get 'race done to them' " as well. Some Asian-descent multiracials pass up the no passing zone because the speed limit is most often not adequate for many of them. One day, the debate on passing will become obsolete (will pass), when Asian-descent multiracials can express the full range of their humanity in which boundaries of race, ethnicity, nation, class, gender, sexuality, body, and language can be crossed and transgressed without judgement, without scorn, and without detriment.

Study probes

1   How does Williams define 'passing'?
2   What are the different strategies of 'passing' used by 'multiracial' individuals?
3   In what ways is the author's critique of 'passing' linked to a criticism of racism's enduring legacy?
4   What are 'no passing zones'?

Notes

1   Deke Babamoto, "Sho Tokyo No Musume Little Tokyo Cinderalla Story," *Nisei Week: 56th Annual Japanese Festival*, 1996, 39.
2   Brett Tam, "Inside Yolk: The Dean Cain Interview," *Yolk Magazine*, Summer 1996, 19.
3   Teresa Kay Williams, "Race as Process: Reassessing the 'What Are You?' Encounters of Biracial Individuals," in Maria P.P. Root, ed., *The Multiracial Experience: Racial Borders as the New Frontier* (Newbury Park, California: Sage Publications, 1996), 191–210.
4   Daniel G. Reginald, "Passers and Pluralists: Subverting the Racial Divide," in Maria P.P. Root, *Racially Mixed People in America* (Newbury Park, California: Sage Publications, 1996), 91–107.
5   Carla Bradshaw, "Beauty and the Beast: On Racial Ambiguity," in *Racially Mixed People in America*, 77–90; Teresa Kay Williams, "Race as Process: Reassessing the 'What Are You?' Encounters of Biracial Individuals."
6   Michael Omi and Howard Winant, *Racial Formation in the US* (New York: Routledge and Kegan Paul, 1986); Paul Spickard, *Mixed Blood* (Madison: University of Wisconsin Press, 1989); Paul Spickard, "The Illogic of American Racial Categories," in *Racially Mixed People in America*, 12–23.
7   Michael C. Thornton, "Is Multiracial Status Unique? The Personal and Social Experience," in *Racially Mixed People in America*, 321–325.
8   Rebecca Chiyoko King and Kimberbly McClain DaCosta, "Changing Face, Changing Race in the Japanese and African American Communities," in *The Multiracial Experience*, 227–244; Teresa Kay Williams, "Race as Process: Reassessing the 'What Are You?' Encounters of Biracial Individuals."
9   Christine I.I. Hall, "The Ethnic Identity of Racially Mixed People: A Study of Black-Japanese," Ph.D. dissertation, University of California, Los Angeles, 1980; George K. Kich, "Eurasians: Ethnic/Racial Identity Development of Biracial Japanese/White Adults," Ph.D. dissertation, the Wright Institute of Professional Psychology, Berkeley, 1982; Michael C.A. Thornton, "Social History of a Multiethnic Identity: The Case of Black Japanese Americans," Ph.D. dissertation, University of Michigan, 1983; Stephen L. Murphy-Shigematsu, "The Voices of Amerasians: Ethnicity, Identity, and Empowerment in

Interracial Japanese Americans," Ph.D. dissertation, Harvard University, 1986; Maria P.P. Root, *Racially Mixed People in America. The Multiracial Experience: Racial Borders as the New Frontier*; Teresa Kay Williams, "Re-conceptualizing Race: The Identity Formation of Japanese European Americans," Ph.D. dissertation, University of California, Los Angeles, 1997.

Chapter 23

William S. Penn

INTRODUCTION

From W.S. Penn (ed.) *As We Are Now: Mixblood Essays on Race and Identity* (1997). Berkeley: University of California Press, pp. 1–3 and 6–8.

CURRENTLY, THERE IS A BROAD and often romanticizing interest in and fascination with things Indian – literature, crafts and art, music, dance, and medicine. Conceiving of Indians as aboriginal also entails perceiving them as anthropological artifacts that are tragic, romantic, and vanishing or already vanished. Even the best of current ethnography tends to articulate the traditions and presence of Native Americans who live on or near reservations, failing to account for the traditions and beliefs of the three to four million Indians who have been living and working in urban or suburban settings for two or three generations. In many cases, these Indians, who make up more than half the Indian population in the United States, have grown up with mixed blood – a result of intermarriages between tribes relocated to Indian Territory as well as between Indians and African- and Latino-Americans. Only a few can remake themselves as full-blood essentialists. The rest have grown up influenced by a mixture of Native traditions as a result of their participation in urban Indian centers such as those in Los Angeles or Chicago where Hopi children learned Apache ways, or Nez Perce children learned Osage dances. *As We are Now* aims to begin correcting the perceptions that define contemporary Indians in terms of the tragic and outmoded vision of early anthropologists – in terms, in other words, of the false classifications of race. More than that, this collection aims to envision and articulate the outer limits and the complexity of Native American experience by expressing the autobiographical, historical, intellectual, cross-cultural, and artistic experiences of mixblood Americans who, in all cases but one, have grown up in cities and towns, away from reservations and tribal councils.

Umberto Eco suggests that the American imagination demands the authentic or real and that to attain it has to create the absolute fake. In relation to Native Americans, this creation of fakery is pervasive: Kachinas made in Taiwan, Sweat Lodge ceremonies at local health clubs, dream-catcher key chains, authentic reproductions of Anasazi dwellings at "The Garden of the Gods" in Colorado Springs, or crystal skulls through which Laguna women teach people to channel. In literature, there are examples such as Forrest Carter, a one-time member of the Ku Klux Klan, who fakes an Indian child's narrative (*The Education of Little Tree*), or the most famous fake of all, *Black Elk Speaks*, in which John Neihardt freely augmented, embellished, and altered the notes his niece recorded in her own invented stenographic shorthand as Black Elk's nephew translated what his uncle was saying – without regard for the multiple difficulties of translation, recording, and transmission.

In the midst of all the fakery, much of it commercially produced and propagated by Native Americans themselves, there is a steadier renaissance in the descriptions of Native America and its relation to the umbrella of American culture – race and identity – and American history. These descriptions – which cross boundaries in the fields of storytelling, ethnography, history, psychology, dance, music, and art – are often narrative and nonlinear: rooted as they must be in the overwhelming respect for the power of words and the oral tradition of "telling" or "saying," the new generation of Native American writers is appropriating the genres and modes of the Western tradition to its own purposes. Ignoring some of the "Western" demarcations, they are writing prose that sometimes incorporates poetic language and even the line lengths of poetry, as well as playlike dialogues and stage directions, mixing genres and modes as well as chronology and tense on purpose, to better bridge the gap between themselves and the dominant culture around them, as well as the gap within themselves (for example, Indian and white, Chicano and Anglo). This narrative mixture of modes is often produced by the act of reclamation, an imaginative act of identity and selfhood that must be re-enacted every time the mixblood writer sets out to write, an act that always involves recognizing the gap, entering the dialogue between disagreements (European or Native American, linear or circular, direct or indirect, historical image or historical actuality), and then finding a way to bridge that gap – or to express it. Behind *As We Are Now* is the belief that to lose that gap, to lose the tension, to lose the enhancements, transformations, and experimentations that result from the dialogue is – for urban mixbloods, at least – to lose whatever is American Indian.

Concurrently, *As We Are Now* aims to express the idea that the non-reservation or urban mixblood, besides being underrepresented in literature about Native America, is a person whose comfort with English combines with his or her desire to be, remain, or represent "Indian," to create possibilities, choices of technique as well as of relations, writer to story, writer to audience or other people, writer to world. If Karl Kroeber (quoted in *Narrative Chance*) is correct that the American idea of progress "destroys diverse modes of imagining," then a renewed diversity of imagination and thinking is something mixblood writers – whatever their backgrounds or disciplines – offer postmodern America and Western culture. *As We Are Now* intends to offer a new vision of race and identity, of Indians – at least that half of Indian America that has grown up in the need to confront "unpleasant truths about our individual and collective past."

[. . .]

Ultimately, the collection is unique because of the way in which it presents diverse modes of imagining race and identity by mixbloods who are not yet well known. The essayists come from varied backgrounds and disciplines. Some are historians, some are trained in literature, and others are storytellers, writers, or people who have been struggling with the problems of race and identity and found they had something to say for this collection. The claim to newness or novelty, of course, invites irony: the Museum of the American Indian in New York, which offers up the same old, static repetitions of an artifactual and romanticized Native America, a "New" Museum of the American Indian housed in the "Old Customs House" in an irony that is so thorough that it achieves perfection. These essays, I hope, are not subject to that kind of irony, aiming as they do at creating dialogue about some serious questions about "race" and "identity."

To those of us classified to one extent or another by it, "race" is both a curse and an invention, a problem and a celebration. Most of us might agree with Kwame Anthony Appiah's saying that "there is nothing in the world that can do all we ask race to do for us"; personally, historically, and politically race has done a lot, both negative and, more recently, positive. Even though we may agree with Rainier Spencer, who finds a delicate irony in his need to use inaccurate terms like "black" and "white" if only to discredit them as terms, whenever we say that race does not matter, we are forced in the moment of saying to admit that yes it does – if only because it matters so much to other people. Other people invent it and use it and make it matter, sometimes unintentionally like a college department chair who claims only experts can teach his field but "anyone" can teach a course titled "The Oral Tradition and Native American Literature and Ideas," especially if that "anyone" is also identifiable as "Indian." Sometimes the intention is obvious in legislative propositions like the one in California that is meant to discriminate and exclude the people on whose backs the Golden State was constructed. Its meaning continually shows in the faces of all those senators and journalists and pundits who assert that race doesn't matter, that the experience of a Native American novel or an African American novel is for the Native or the African, essentially, the same as the experience of a Finn or a Pole.

While I would never in my life deny the intensity or importance or sensitivity of the Finn or the Pole, the British or the German, there is a particular moment in which Indian or Chicano or black readers and listeners recognize the well-intentioned skewer of race. It comes when a reviewer of a grant proposal for a new collection of Indian legends and stories says that there are already enough of these around, as though there is no new work being done in the translation of stories and as though we have not heard endless collections of tales and stories from other, more dominant and dominating cultures. It comes hidden beneath the linear faces of clocks and the sour faces of those baptized in the faith called Progress and the assumption that anything other than their "progress" means regress. It comes, too, when academics assume that all Native American scholars are experts in Indian literature or Indian history (all Indian literature and history), categorizing the young Native American student as someone who has automatic interests and automatic associations. It comes back when Native people assert that only Native Americans can study, write about, or teach Native American literature and ideas, and yet once again when we notice the certain and continuous cultural assumptions at play in even very liberal-minded and sympathetic non-Native scholars. As a young black man of about my height put it, "Nobody ask *you* if you play basketball." True, but they may allow a hungry audience to equate the surprise of Sand Creek with the iconographic romance of Custer's "defensive" posture at the Battle of the Little Big Horn (a.k.a. "Custer's Last Stand").

The project that has resulted in this book was born two years ago when I was invited to participate on a university panel on "Ethnic Studies." I was asked by the associate dean to give a paper on my views of what a future "Ethnic Studies" program at Michigan State University should be. There was precious little else in the way of definition or description of what we'd be panelizing about, so I went prepared to speak or (preferably) not speak, hating, as I do, the sound of my own voice (an honest statement that my graduate and undergraduate students alike would find odd if not comic). But lately I had been finding support for some of my inclusive views in storytelling by Leslie Silko, Louis Owens, Tomás Rivera, Rolando Hinojosa, Manlio Argueta, Rosario Ferré, and Jack Forbes, or in essays like those included in Arnold Krupat and Brian Swann's anthologies. Inclusion had been with me since my early boyhood when my innocent first love affair had been with a Mexican girl whose mother fed me spicy lunches, and I had grown up with the visual and aural joy of Olvera Street, which is so nicely recalled in Patricia Hilden's "Richie Valens Is Dead: *E Pluribus Unum.*"

I found myself – the passivity is literal, like Dante's "I came to myself in the middle of the journey of my life" – up on a dais beside a local Asian and an imported Chicano "star" facing an audience of deans, directors, low-level administrators, and professors (possibly with the odd student thrown in like bell peppers for color and spice), wondering if the fever I felt (my forehead beaded with sweat) was due to being very sick or to being made sick with words. Or both.

"I am panelizing," I told myself, trying to keep old habits of truth and directness down like the flu. "You (I said, feverishly adopting yet a second person to get through the afternoon) asked for this by agreeing to be empaneled on the dais."

What was billed as a panel discussion of Ethnic Studies had turned into a skirmish over turf, a skirmish that I have turned into full-dress battle, an unpitched battle over who owns the past and present, with the "star" panelizer calling for a "domestic ethnic studies."

Domestic Ethnic Studies? I wondered. No cross-border influences? No studying Guatemalan or Quechua Indigenos? It's like a stockade fence, the US border. Used to keep people out as well as to keep people in, to keep people on their familiar turf – turf they, minority or nonminority, can defend.

Out of that moment came a new course to teach, one that would side-step the question of what Ethnic Studies was or wasn't, and would cross the old borders to celebrate the mixture.

Out of that moment came this project. The project itself has sometimes made me feel sad with a comic abrasion. In the long run, however, the comic won out, and these are the results: of reading and talking with other people who identify themselves as mixbloods . . . "Mixbloods" and not "mixed bloods" because they express the unified and inseparable strands of their heritage and experience. Mixblood instead of crossblood, though in this instance mainly because crossblood has been so long confused with "mixedblood."

Study probes

1   According to Penn, how does new scholarship on 'urban mixbloods' correct past and present misperceptions of Native Americans?
2   What examples of 'the well-intentioned skewer of race' does the author provide?
3   In what ways is his discussion part of a broader debate about 'ethnic studies'?

Chapter 24

Carol Camper

INTO THE MIX

From C. Camper (ed.) *Miscegenation Blues: Voices of Mixed Race Women* (1994). Toronto: Sister Vision Press, pp. xv–xxiv.

MISCEGENATION BLUES: VOICES OF MIXED RACE WOMEN comes at a time when more than ever, mixed race people must speak. Identity, loyalty and belonging are issues which reside at the very heart of our existence and it is up to us to define who we are and identify our needs. This book emerges out of an increasing urgency in the lives of many women to end isolation and to understand racial multiplicity within our own bodies, families and cultures.

My decision to create this anthology sprang from my awareness that more and more young mixed race women were experiencing a difficult and sometimes lonely struggle to find identity. I felt that after forty years of living, I had something to share from my own experiences. Isolation was something I had known well, having survived adoption by White people and growing up in an all-White suburb of a small city (London, Ontario). I had considered running support groups but I decided that anthologizing a book would actually mean that more mixed race women would be involved and become connected either by writing for the anthology or reading it. Connections feel very important. Some of us don't even have a sibling that looks like us let alone anyone else. No one wants to feel this alone. To be perceived as a racial oddity is isolating and confusing.

Initially, I was not confused as a child about my race. I didn't know my race at all. I was not informed by my parents that I was Black. I knew that I didn't resemble anyone else in my world. The only Black people I knew were enter-tainers on television and I didn't quite look like them either. My confusion started when I moved to London and heard those first identifying cries of

'Nigger' and the question, 'What are you?' On some level I could see why I was called 'nigger' but there was still no discussion, no explaining, only urges to ignore the nasty words. These were the firsts of many times that I would be called upon to declare my loyalties, to identify myself.

When I was ten years old I was reading books about anthropology and discovered information about racial mixing. For the first time I had an idea of how to explain myself to myself. I went to the mirror and made my own assessment of what I was and then confronted my adoptive mother 'What am I, Mum? Am I part white and part Black?' "Yes" the reply came, along with sketchy information about a Black birth mother. I thought that my Black mother may have had non-Black ancestry as well, because of my light skin. I found out many years later that she has First Nations' ancestry and that this is very common. My mother's family are descendants of American slaves (escapees via the Underground Railroad) from the Carolinas who had mixed with Native people.

Prior to this discovery, the only people I knew that resembled me were Polynesian. I eagerly watched movies that featured actual Polynesians (rather than Dorothy Lamour) like the first two versions of *Mutiny on The Bounty*. I poured over an early sixties issue of *National Geographic* which featured articles about the people of Tahiti and the filming of the 1962 version. I was so uplifted that I resembled such a beautiful people and in my lonely efforts to be treated as a worthwhile and not-ugly person, I decided to claim that I was Polynesian. I needed tangible evidence to prove that my looks were good after all and so I stole the *National Geographic* issue. Once I learned of my Black identity, and of the existence of a relative who would resemble me (my half-sister is mixed – it actually turned out that I had several siblings who are), I no longer needed to believe I was Polynesian. But I still remember fondly the Tahitian people who were not my relatives, but made me feel beautiful when I needed to.

In my attempts to understand race and mixing I began to search for faces like mine in my immediate world. I had no idea how dangerous that could be. In grade eight my discussions with apparently-White Gayle about what her full lips and broad nose could mean, led to her grandmother's instruction to slap my face the next time I dared to say such a thing. I had ventured into forbidden territory. In grade ten, when beautiful Paula walked into class the first time, I knew she must be mixed. I knew this, but because her hair was light brown, because she never said anything to me about being like me and because I might get my face slapped, I said nothing about race to her. I had learned the earlier lesson well and had been effectively silenced. For the next three years of school with her, we friends never said a thing to one another. I saw on an inner level the lovely Blackness in her face, but I had learned that we could not meet at the place of our Blackness, but only at a place where her race would not be spoken. A shade of skin and two shades of hair colour and texture meant she was passing, whether she intended to or not. I forgot Paula's Blackness for twenty years until new lessons about being unsilenced came to me. Now, I would like to reach out again and speak the truth.

In creating this anthology, I had to look at some truths about race itself. I actually had to examine how race physically or genetically exists. This is not just political. I had to do this because, the truth is, many people have passed completely into one race or the other and mixing from previous generations has had no impact on their lives. Many people have fairly recent mixed heritage deliberately hidden from them and have virtually become White, for example. They may be guessing about mixed race heritage and their guesses may be correct. Do these people's stories belong? Ultimately, I feel unable to address issues of possible mixing unsupported by any evidence. If this is the case, then the mixing has probably had no impact on the life experience that is the point of this anthology.

In my calls for submissions I asked that contributors identify their racial background either in their piece or their bio. One contributor was concerned about this request. It appeared to be a demand to authenticate herself, which for her (and many of us) recalls the troubling demands for 'proof' of race that we sometimes experience. In truth, I *was* asking for some kind of authentication. I did not want to end up publishing White women whose racial mixing was no more than a fervent, baseless desire on their part. People often come to this belief because they wish to escape oppressor status and not deal with their own racism.

This book is about the lives and experiences of mixed race women who are affected by the socio-political aspects of racism. I will not give a platform to White women who believe they must be mixed because they 'feel connected' to a non-White culture. Because of my upbringing, I am forever connected to White North American culture, but this does not mean I am White. I don't believe it is relevant to have been another race in a past life, therefore previously mixed race women 'need not apply.' This book is for racially mixed women of colour who want to say something about their lives and for anyone wishing to read about it.

Ethnicity and race are not the same thing. Racial differentiation in human evolution happened long ago, has never been static and there are racially mixed people all over the world. I chose to restrict this anthology to issues of racial and not ethnic mixing, therefore I had to decide what I thought race actually was. I am not an anthropologist who might be able to give a more scientific definition of race. But should it even be the anthropologists' role to define race? Science is not without race bias. In the end, I had to return to experience. Race is an experienced thing. We are part of a race, or races, because experience, history, genetics, physicality, family and politics evidence it. The same can be said for ethnicity but to a lesser degree. Ethnicity focuses more around cultural and national boundaries. Persons of the same race can belong to different ethnic groups. For the purposes of a book that had to have some parameters, and as a lay person, these were my guidelines in determining the existence of race as different from ethnicity.

Because of my existence as a Black woman with a White parent, I experience my races in a certain way. I identify as a Black woman. If anyone chooses to inquire, I may also say that I have other racial ancestry. I have not taken on a mixed/Native identity because this is new information for me. I am still processing its meaning. I have very little information about it and I don't feel comfortable rushing into a new culture to which my claim is questionable. I do not wish to take from Native cultures as others who do not belong there have done. If I fill out a form that asks for my race I say Black. I do this because it is my Black self that has shaped most of my experiences in life. I don't experience myself as parts but as one whole and if that is a paradox, so be it. This paradox of existence in two or more races is crystallized in Faith Adiele's poem 'Remembering Anticipating Africa' where she writes:

> crowds of children churning up the dust
> they chase me shouting
> . . .
> white lady! white lady!
> at me
> a nigger for 25 years.

I recognize that due to skin colour, I am certain to have received privilege from Whites (and later from Blacks) but having been the only Black person I knew for fourteen years, I never had a Blacker person in my life to compare experiences with. I only knew I was treated like dirt.

It was when I was a teenager, with a Black American boyfriend, that I discovered the hierarchy of skin tone. I seemed to be prized by him and his friends because of my 'Red' colouring. My light skin, freckles, green eyes and looser hair meant that I was sought after exoticized. After messages of ugliness and worthlessness, exoticization was okay by me. So this is who I became. I was the voluptuous, café au lait sister. The gypsy/Creole woman, big breasted, big afroed courtesan, welcome in any man's bed, as Camille Hernandez-Ramdwar experienced in 'Ms Edge Innate':

> In grade one I was called 'sex maniac' by gangs of six-year-old boys
> . . . and in later years, acquired the trappings of that myth – the
> over-sexed mama, the hot tamale, hot Latin blood, ball-busting black
> woman who could fuck you in half.

But then I was tired of being exoticized. This was not who I was either. It didn't get me anywhere but into bed, where I was a slightly more desirable piece of dirt. I realized that all I needed was a vagina to get into a straight man's bed. Sex was not an indicator of worth but only of gender and availability. I realized that to commodify myself as exotic meant incredible loss. Loss of self, family, community and spirit. I began working to reject the hierarchy of colourism.

Colourism is one legacy of colonization. The invasion of women's bodies is always a device of war. The creation of a mixed European and local 'class' helped ensure division and conflict among the indigenous people. This has happened all over the world. The mixed race progeny often were given access to things their unmixed sisters and brothers would never have. The lighter-skinned people were also indoctrinated into the colourism hierarchy and believed themselves to be superior, creating their own history as oppressors and justifiable mistrust which is still having impact on our lives today. Even in countries no longer under white rule, the colour hierarchy is often still intact. Many people, including those of mixed race, need to look at this history and excise any lingering colonization of ourselves. As Joanne Arnott states in 'Speak Out, For Example':

> participating in the diminishing of ourselves and of others is how we learned to survive, and it takes conscious effort, storming and weeping, and courageous collaboration to turn things around.

I chose to present mixed race women's stories in this anthology partly because my life and creativity revolve so much around women's energy and partly because women of mixed race experience a unique stereotyping that is compounded by gender bias.

Here in North America, popular culture's tiresome, racist images of racially mixed women show up in characters like Julie in Edna Ferber's *Showboat* (a recent production in Toronto, that has caused great pain in Black communities). If you look for us in these places, we are always either 'good,' self-sacrificing creatures, like Julie, who have just enough White in us to have nobility; to know when it is time to go back to our 'places': or, we are 'tragic Mulattos (or Halfbreeds or Eurasians . . .)' like Freddi Washington's character in the 1934 version of *Imitation of Life* (played in the remake by White woman Susan Kohler). Washington's character is the light-skinned child of two Black parents who is thwarted in her attempts to 'pass' each time her darker mother comes on the scene. Usually, mixed women did not survive long in movies but in this case the character loses her mother who dies of a broken heart due to her daughter's rejection. As for Freddi, she left Hollywood, bitter at the racism of the movie and of Hollywood itself. She resumed her career at the Negro Federal Theatre in Washington D.C. where her radicalism was welcomed.

The other stereotype of mixed race women is that of moral and sexual degeneracy. It is as if our basic degeneracy as women of colour is magnified by White ancestry. Our so called 'Whiteness' increases our 'beauty' along with our awareness of it, driving us to a frenzy of bitter abandon so agreeable and piquant to our White male pursuers. It is this particular stereotype that affects our understanding of the word miscegenation itself. Literally this word means simply, 'mixed marriage' and 'mixed race,' the prefix '*misc*,' meaning mixed. Post-emancipation fear, outrage and racism in Whites resulted in anti-miscegenation laws in the United States. Other countries such as South Africa, have also had such laws. Not only were miscegenates abominations, but the word miscegenate became virtually synonymous with degenerate. This negative aspect still affects understanding of the word. I had assumed that the prefix of this word was 'mis,' which would indicate 'error' or 'wrong,' relating its meaning to the idea that we should not exist.

Not only have White supremacists created race laws, they have also dictated our understanding of words such as miscegenation. I had to examine the reasons why I initially had a negative reaction to this word. For me, it came down to the fact that I had taken on the White mainstream view of this word and, therefore, had agreed with the racist interpretation of it. Since I now know the factual meaning (as well as knowing the historical misuse), I use the word without any reservations. Having this word in the title of this anthology has been a challenge to some, but this is the word I have chosen.

The way White North American culture sees the word 'blues' and the art form of the 'Blues' is also negative. This is because White culture's opinion of the creators of this art form is essentially negative. It has been comforting to White supremacists to see Blacks as lowly, powerless unfortunates coping with their lot in life by creating music to soothe themselves. I don't see the Blues this way at all. I see it as a powerful, defiant, creative expression claiming victory out of oppression. This is what I believe *Miscegenation Blues. Voices of Mixed Race Women* is. It does chronicle and analyze our lives and our experiences of difficult circumstances. It also proclaims that we lead positive, powerful lives and that we are not tragic. There have been objections to the use of the word 'blues' in the title. Again, this is the word I have chosen. As a Black Canadian descended from Black Americans, the Blues are a part of my culture and so I use the term as a metaphor that I understand. I cannot speak for other cultures, which is why this is an anthology. Mine is not the only culture represented in this book and it is not entirely about a White versus colour struggle or North American situations.

Women of mixed race have many different experiences and points of view. We live and think about our lives in ways that may not seem at all feminist or political. I am a feminist but I feel that women do not need feminist analysis to speak about their lives. The women whose writing and art work appear in this book are not all 'political' women. They do not all describe their lives through a political framework. Even those of us who do, have not necessarily escaped our own racism or gender bias. We are simply in a process of living and learning our lives. Many of the contributors have never written or been published before. Some submissions were from such a colonized point of view they were painful. I did not include these because they represented a negative and misguided place where I did not want this anthology to go. One such place is the idea that racial mixing would be the so called 'future' of race relations and the future of humanity. One or two contributors do mention it, briefly, without necessarily agreeing with it. I strongly disagree with this position. It is naive. It leaves the race work up to the mixed people and it means the annihilation of existing racial groups and our entire histories and cultures as if we are obsolete. It is essentially a racist solution.

For this reason I think it is important for mixed people who have White ancestry to not identify only as mixed but to stress identity with their coloured ancestry. This would be different for those who have no White ancestry, though there can still be oppressor/oppressed history in their lineage which may require examining.

Our existence is not meant to annihilate. We simply exist. We should not be forced into a 'closet' about White or any other parentage, but we must recognize that our location is as women of colour. Recent US census taking has helped to create a political hotbed in that country about how mixed Black and White people identify. Some mixed people loving and not wishing to erase White parentage opted to identify as 'other.' They may not have seen themselves as Black. They may have been challenged or disputed about their Blackness by White or Black people. Many Black people felt that it was internalized racism that led these folk to apparently opt out of Blackness. There was also the concern that this would lower the numbers of Blacks in America and possibly lead to a decreased power-base along with decreased attention to Black community goals in federal and state initiatives. I identify as Black for the purposes of census-taking or any other purpose, but I am not ashamed of my non-Black ancestry. I should be allowed to be who I am and so should everyone else. Just let's do it with enough awareness to know where we are really located.

My goal for *Miscegenation Blues*, over the three years of working on it, was to create a book where mixed race women can document their lives, define themselves, connect with one another and examine some of the challenges they face. Because what we look like is such an issue, I have included many photographs of us along with artwork.

Study probes

1   Why did Camper decide to focus on 'racial' rather than ethnic mixing?
2   How does the author define and critique 'the hierarchy of colourism'?
3   What are the two stereotypes of 'mixed race' women she discusses?
4   Trace the origins of the term 'miscegenation'?
5   Why is the author critical of the idea that 'racial mixing' is the hope for the future?
6   Compare and contrast this Canadian assessment of 'mixed race' politics to the previous extracts, which debate 'mixed race' in the USA.

Chapter 25

Jayne O. Ifekwunigwe

LET BLACKNESS AND WHITENESS WASH THROUGH: COMPETING DISCOURSES ON BI-RACIALIZATION AND THE COMPULSION OF GENEALOGICAL ERASURES

Extract from *Scattered Belongings: Cultural Paradoxes of 'Race', Nation and Gender* (1999). London New York: Routledge, pp. 183–187 and 190–191.

If you don't honor your ancestors in the real sense then you are committing a kind of suicide.

(Sam Shephard 'Interview,' *Bookmark*, BBC2, London, September 1997)

IN THE FIRST PART OF THIS TEXT, in their own voices and from their own emblematic experiences, six *métis(se) griottes* speak against the generalizing and subjugating tendencies of discourses on Blackness and Whiteness which contain, exclude and silence them. In this chapter, to substantiate their critiques of essential Blackness and normative/naturalized Whiteness, I have culled extracts by under-represented *métis(se)* authors from disparate literary and social science sources and varied geopolitical and historical contexts. Collectively, these *métis(se)* discourses stage debates which do not resolve but rather elucidate both the discursive and political problematics of Blackness and Whiteness. Their evocations function as agents of change, shaping and molding critiques of particular bi-racialized societies and demanding a revision of a double caste system, which binds all Black people both economically and socially.

[. . .]

In the first part of the book, aspects of six women's testimonies remind us of painful psychosocial consequences for *métisse* women, whose lived realities defy the false one drop rule. That is, at different life stages and across age, class, ethnicity and locality, at times, the six *métisse* women subject themselves to self-destructive regimens of physical and emotional torture in an attempt to position themselves in a racially polarized society, which denies them full womanhood – whether it is performing "Black" and "White" subjectivities through oppositional dress as Similola did, or attempting suicide as Yemi did – all the narratives speak to a desire for "racial" reconciliation and an integrated sense of self, which can embrace both maternal and paternal sociocultural inheritances.[1]

In the following two sections, I intend to shed light on paradoxes of identity and affiliation for *métisse* women, whose White British or White European mothers or mother-surrogates have been central socializing influences. "Racial" regulation, in the form of the one drop rule, collapses ideas about "race" and culture in general and disallows White British or European maternal and cultural influences in particular. As they mention, the six featured *métisse griottes* all have White English, German or Irish mothers. Akousa and Sarah, and Bisi and Yemi were raised by their White Irish and White English birth mothers, respectively. Ruby and Similola were raised by White English women, who were the matrons in the children's homes where they spent their formative years. However, based on locality, family circumstances, social class and ethnicity, the two sets of sisters and the two women who grew up in care all deploy different strategies to make sense of the process of becoming (Black) women.

Feminist analyses are replete with, at times, ambivalent recognition of the primacy of the mothering role in the social rather than biological reproduction of gendered identities . . . the "great unwritten story" is that which critically acknowledges the fact that, at times, young *métisse* girls first witness the complex world of womanhood through everyday interactions with White female caretakers. Through the psychosocial processes of White English mothering, the primary culture the women I spoke with inherit is White English. Societal assumptions based exclusively on their physical appearances frequently deny this reality. Furthermore, society tells them that they must deny this socializing fact and remember that they are "just Black." As Yemi remembers:

> We were at home with our mother and our father. Although my mother worked, she was the primary influence in our house – culturally. We didn't really know very much about Yoruba culture. We just didn't.

Similarly, Similola recounts:

> When I was growing up the main influence was the {White English} house mother in the children's home, who totally dominated my life up until I was 16 years old. Her views were my views.

As Bisi recalls, despite their best intentions, sometimes White mothers do not completely understand the extent to which their own White privilege separates them from the "everyday racism" which their Black daughters face:

> A lot of the modern consciousness I have of being African and being Black, which is not the same thing, is probably in spite of my mother. Being Black in the sense that I feel now, that would be in spite of her. It's not something she agrees with . . . She has very little knowledge of how racism operates and how it affects people.

Furthermore, as Ruby describes, White grandmothers of Black grand-daughters grapple even further with their own White daughters "transracial" transgressions, which "contaminate" allegedly "pure blood lines":

> That period of time with my gran brought out very much to the fore what her attitude to me was and why it was like that. It was 80 percent because of the color of my skin; the other 20 percent was the fact that I was an illegitimate child. For my grandmother and her generation, that was quite a shameful thing. But had I been a White illegitimate child, it would have been very different. So as I say, 80 percent because of the color – she didn't want to be associated in the blood line with a Black grand-daughter.

One could argue that from the cradle, *métisse* women who have been mothered by White women are potentially equipped with the social tools for understanding White feminists and building coalitions across the Black/White feminist divide. Yet, amid all the feminist academic attention paid to mothering and mother/daughter relationships, very little if any textual space attends to this strategic political possibility. Both Black and White feminists have also neglected the specific problematic of the biracialization of White mother/Black (*métisse*) daughter dyads. Perhaps, like many theoretical innovations, this critical issue must begin its life on the pages of (auto)biographies or in the creative arts before continuing its journey with textual treatment by critical/social/cultural/feminist theorists. For example, in the following excerpt from the 1990 auto-biographical film piece *The Body Beautiful*, English–Nigerian film-maker, Ngozi Onwurah, declares her allegiance to her White English mother. In this scene, she and her mother are lying naked in bed together, pink and brown skins mingle, youthful and aging bodies lie side by side:

> A child is made in its parents' image. But to a world that sees only in Black and White, I was made only in the image of my father. Yet, she has molded me, created the curves and contours of my life, colored the innermost details of my being. She has fought for me, protected me with every painful crooked bone in her body. She lives inside of me and cannot be separated. I may not be reflected in her image, but my mother is mirrored in my soul. I am my mother's daughter for the rest of my life.

At the same time, this impress of maternal circumstance can be misperceived as a weakness by those espousing a Black separatist feminist standpoint.

[. . .]

Nevertheless, unfortunately, in the long run, any solidarity which *métisse* filial loyalty may cultivate is usually over-ruled by the bi-racialized trappings of the White feminist privilege which the one drop rule perpetuates.

[. . .]

Overall, this psychosocial splitting breeds *métisse* confusion and motivates women to seek compulsory Black legitimacy when in an ideal de-racialized world, the more sensible existential project should be that of psychic and social unity.

[. . .]

> When we look into each other's eyes, our war torn souls communicate in their silences.

"Other-mothers," black cultural surrogate sisters, and male/African daughters

For the most part, all six women had other Black continental African, African Caribbean or African American safety nets into which they could fall when identifying exclusively with White English maternal culture either led to "malnourishment" or in Yemi's case resulted in a suicide attempt. For example, Akousa and Sarah fondly recollect the pivotal role played by "fictive kin" in the form of Black "other-mothers." Fictive kin are not related to individuals by "blood." However, they perform the same functions as these family relations. For example, Sarah remembers:

> All the people that I call auntie and uncle aren't really relatives – blood relatives. Like a group of people that have become relatives, they are from all parts of the world, and, well – mainly from the Caribbean. Auntie Hyacinth was from Guyana. . . . I do remember how much I loved my Aunt Hyacinth plaiting my hair. I used to sit down on the floor between her knees feeling secure. She always smelled wonderful, like cocoa butter and musk.

Similarly, Akousa pays homage to the dual role her mum and this same Aunt Hyacinth played in her successful passage from girl to woman:

> Also I didn't have a White extended family in the same way that a lot of other people did. . . . My extended family was a Black extended family rather than havin' this other White family. . . . My mum was the only White person within the family. She took on board a lot of Caribbean culture. . . . Basically there was a Caribbean upbringin' in some respects – not totally. Because at the end of the day, my mum is not a West Indian woman. So there were certain aspects to Caribbean culture that I didn't start on, because she didn't have that. My Aunt Hyacinth provided certain aspects of that instead. I had two that were there growin' up.

Akousa and Sarah point to two Black women, one African American and the other from Sierra Leone who acted as Black cultural surrogate sisters. In so doing, these two older women nurtured their younger surrogate sisters' emerging Black feminist consciousness. Akousa recalls:

> I did some voluntary work at Baobab Community Center and met a Black American woman from Chicago and another woman from Sierra Leone. They were workin' at this community center. Pamela was a very strong Black woman. The two of them gave me and my sister quite a lot. . . . They helped move me in the right direction. I started buyin' a lot more Black literature, readin' a lot more widely. They got us out to theater. I think that's where my love of culture and art now comes from. I think they started to give us a good appreciation of it.

At the age of 13, a falling out with her mother led Yemi closer to her father's Yoruba Nigerian culture and turned her into what Amadiume (1987) would refer to as a "male daughter":

> The result of this was that she had very little to do with me after that. My dad took me every evening, when he came back, to my uncle's house. . . . When he was going out, he didn't actually leave me with her ever again. . . . My dad and I became very close, which was very good. . . . Also, because of this change with my father, I got very close to my cousins. So, I am closer to my cousins than my other sisters, very, very close. They are all boys. So, I now get to know how to speak Yoruba – Yoruba morals, the life itself – better than my sisters. Ostensibly, because I was actually flung out by my mother, or I stepped away from my mother. Then, all of these things were accessible to me.

Ruby and Similola became African daughters when they travelled to Nigeria and Tanzania, respectively, to meet their African fathers and extended African families. In fact, Ruby describes her connection with her African relations as a source of strength and pride:

> After we had been to Nigeria, and lived there for a year or more, and come back. I got a great deal out of that, I did then begin to feel that I wasn't just Black in an isolated situation. There was this whole family that I had who were Black, and who supported me, and whom I could go to at anytime. If life got really heavy, I can jump on a plane and go to Nigeria and I'd have a home and a family. That made me feel a lot less lonely and get to a situation where I could begin to feel some pride about being Black.

[. . .]

Black is the totalizing term that names us and which we claim as an act of political resistance. . . . The facts of designated ethnic minority status and shared bi-racialized locality do not create consensus as to the anthropological and sociopolitical criteria, which determine the classification of *Black*. In fact, the term Black has become an essentialized political term lacking both dynamism and fluidity and frequently confused with ethnicity and nationality.

The Official Census classification system clearly embodies this rigid fixity of terminology. The first time the British government Census attempted to calculate the number of *non-White* people in Britain was 1991. Out of a total British population of 54.9 million people, just over 3 million or 5.5 percent are designated as ethnic minorities. The major "ethnic" subheadings of the 1991 Census are White, Black-Caribbean, Black-African, Black-Other (please describe), Indian, Pakistani, Bangladeshi, Chinese, and Any Other Ethnic Group (please describe). This classification system is flawed in its conflation of race, ethnicity and nationality, discriminatory in its homogenization of peoples from continental Africa and the Caribbean, and problematic in its presumption that White is the normative homogeneous category. [. . .]

As Similola recalls:

> So many things have happened to me because of what I am, and they shape the way I am today. I had a very unhappy childhood because of it. I had suddenly felt my world had fallen apart. I was Black and I was brought up in a White society.

The transgenerational psychic damage of global and historical processes of bi-racialization is meted out equally to all socially designated Black constituents of the African Diaspora(s) as well as to those living on the African continent and results in skin bleaching, cosmetic surgery and other remedies to alter Black African physical features so that they more approximate to a White European appearance. Not surprisingly, almost always *métis(se)* individuals with immediate both Black continental African, African Caribbean or African American *and* White continental European, British or North American parentage join other constituents of the African Diaspora(s) in paying far too much covert and overt lip service to what Russell *et al.* refer to as "the color complex: a psychological fixation about color and features that leads Blacks to discriminate against each other" (Russell *et al.* 1992: 2). Others refer to this preoccupation with skin color and the previleging of "paler" skin as shadeism or colorism (Mama 1995). Frequently, these unhealthy externalized obsessions with skin color and other facial features extend to White family members of *métis(se)* individuals. . . . In households with *métis(se)* children, public racial politics govern private family realities. *Métis(se)* siblings with the same biological parents but with different physical appearances will be spared or subjected to the psychological injuries of a social hierarchy that privileges individuals with paler skin, straighter hair and more "White European" facial features.

In general, in the English–African Diaspora, all psyches have been wounded by individual and collective experiences of racism and other forms of discrimination. In particular, for Black/White couples and their *métis(se)* children, the one drop rule disrupts conventional notions of kinship and stigmatizes the ordinary institution of the family. Yet, by virtue of genealogy and domestic circumstances, most *métis(se)* individuals, including the women featured in this text, can actually become whole at the precise meeting point of the same White British or White

European *and* Black continental African or Black African Caribbean social borders, which the one drop rule fights fiercely to protect.

. . . In other words, as *métis(se)* children many have been nurtured, supported, by White British or White European carers. As adults in close quarters, many recreate family with White British or White European partners.[2] Within both private spaces and in the public domain, the particular challenge for multigenerational *métis(se)* families remains recognizing and negotiating the invidious signs of bi-racialization while not falling prey to the demands of genea-logical erasure. That is, it is possible to equip *métis(se)* children with the psycho-social tools to recognize and cope with prejudice and discrimination without forcing them to deny their natal origins. In the long term, both the specificities and complexities of *métis(se)* subject positions demand a refashioning of the constricted and bi-racialized criteria for both citizenship and belonging in the English-African Diaspora. In the short term, I suggest "Additive Blackness" as a survival strategy for *métis(se)* individuals who are unwilling or unable to sever ties with their White British or White European origins.[3]

From "compulsory heterosexuality" to compulsory Blackness to Additive Blackness as a *métis(se)* survival strategy

In a classic essay entitled "Compulsory heterosexuality and lesbian existence," American feminist Adrienne Rich dares to challenge what she refers to as "the erasure of lesbian existence from so much of scholarly feminist literature" (Rich 1986: 24). The critical theoretical framework within which she worked is that of the "political institution" of "compulsory heterosexuality," where "heterosexual-ity is presumed 'the sexual preference' of 'most women' either implicitly or explicitly" (ibid.: 28). In 1980 she suggested that heterosexual and lesbian researchers bring the same critical insights gleaned from studies of motherhood to feminist studies of heterosexuality. Although groundbreaking at the time, Rich's critique homogenized the different "race," class and ethnic experiences of women in general and lesbians in particular.

[. . .]

Nevertheless, this criticism does not detract from the potential potency of Rich's concept of compulsion as an analytical tool for understanding the politics of Blackness. Hence, to extrapolate, compulsory Blackness is a political institu-tion wherein it is presumed that identification with Blackness is the implicit or explicit personal preference of most *métis(se)* women or men with one Black continental African or Black African Caribbean parent and one White British or White continental European parent. However, with just one exception, in my research project, the parental combination was exclusively, Black father and White mother.

More specifically, in the previous section, I discussed the lack of consensus in the English-African Diaspora as to "Who is Black?" and the concomitant prob-lematic official census minority "ethnic" classification scheme. At the center are minority intracthnic disagreements over what constitutes Blackness as well as who can legitimately claim an authentic Black identity. . . . Since genotype has little bearing in a society that discriminates based on phenotype, the differential push by Black and White people to encourage *métis(se)* people to identify as Black is supposed to provide what *griotte* Bisi refers to as "protective coloration." With the criteria for Black membership as limited as they are, society at large generally "sees" *métis(se)* people as "just Black."

On the other hand, what one's family and life experiences have been as well as the cultural constitution of one's household account for very little in a bi-racially confused world. . . . As a *métis(se)* person, aligning oneself with Blackness is supposed to provide a cushion against the inevitable blows of bi-racialization. In the long run, I maintain that embracing an exclusive Black identity – as a political strategy – is counterproductive. In the name of elusive solidarity, this monolithic Black identity masks the many differences that exist across cultures, nations, ethnicities, classes, religions, gender, regions, and generations. However, what this recommendation ignores is the indelible impress of individual circumstance, which makes the process of identifying with Blackness, Black people and Black culture painful, mystifying, and gradual for many *métis* men and *métisse* women. Black children who have grown up in care or in predominantly White suburbs also struggle with these issues.

For *métis(se)* individuals, many of whom have grown up in primarily White English environments, this form of 'Black-washing" also threatens to erode a substantial part of their psychosocial foundation, which at the contested time is often exclusively socially and culturally White and *métis(se)*. I refer to this moment of identification as "The Day of Reckoning" or "When the Mirror Speaks." In this chapter, mirrors are a useful motif, since *métis(se)* individuals images of themselves are frequently distorted by the bi-racializing, objectifying and exoticizing gazes of a zebra-driven society.

In part, affirmation of one's Blackness necessitates the reification of nineteenth-century bi-racialized hierarchies based on skin color, hair texture, and eye color. From Nigeria to Brazil, from New York to Bristol, barometers of Blackness – hair texture, skin tone, width of nose, fullness of lips, rise of buttocks – travel.

[. . .]

To paraphrase *griotte* Sharon, one of the members of the original group of twenty-five project participants – we can try to deprive ourselves of our realities but in the darkest hour of the night when no one else is around and we have gone to the loo to spend a penny, we must look in the mirror. Eventually, that moment comes when we look in the mirror and we see what a bi-racialized society tells us we must see – a Black woman. . . . For many this closer scrutiny is sparked by someone pointing out to them or reminding them of either their physical sameness or difference – that is, their Blackness. *Griotte* Claudia, another *métisse* voice from the original group, recounted an incident to me. She was in a club in Liverpool with a group of her White English friends and a Black man kept shouting out, "Hey, Black Sister." At age 27, she went home that night looked in the mirror and cried.

Psychologists refer to this as "negriscence" – coming to terms with one's Blackness, or becoming Black. Though their model is a cumulative one, its typology of Black traits seems to suggest that there is both an essential Blackness and an illusory Whiteness, which *métis(se)* people can strive to embody, but they can never completely attain. This paradigm also does not stress the qualitative importance of the starting point of the journey. Once a *métis(se)* person recognizes the ways in which the one drop rule designates them as "just Black" in society, I refer to the process of coming to terms with one's Blackness as both affirmative and as a source for social discrimination as "Additive Blackness." That is, an individual must start with her or his familiar social foundation and build forward without having to sever ties with her or his often White English roots. Bisi's notion of a "synthesized" Black culture corresponds with my formulation of "Additive Blackness":

> coming to terms with a Black identity in Bristol. You have a lot of things within you to cope with. One of the things you have as a coping mechanism is your identity as a member of a family as a child of a family, who has been given a name more or less by the head of the family. You have a place there. You have that, which is actually not a part of your racial identity. What the "race" of the family is is incidental. The fact that it was a Black African family has . . . Let's see, supposing I had grown up in Britain, except I had a White extended family and I knew my place in that family. I had been given a name, say, by my mother alone, which my grandmother had then changed, say, to a pet name. Then I think a Black identity would have been a lot more problematic. One gets to the point where one realizes that you cannot a hundred percent identify with a White culture. You have to go and look and find and seek that Black culture from somewhere. If you can't find it, then you have to synthesize it, which I think many people here have done.

However, many *métis(se)* people, as well as perhaps those who have grown up in care, or in predominantly suburban areas, have grown up in a social context wherein Whiteness is qualitatively and quantitatively valued at the expense of Blackness. When the forces of bi-racialization, leaving home or other transformative factors lead a person to question their predominantly White English upbringing, that individual frequently reacts by seeking out what they perceive to be an oppositional at times 'hyper Black" identity or what my colleague Peter Bond (1998, personal communication) would refer to as a "compensatory Black identity."

"Racial" reconciliation is most successfully accomplished after the individual has accepted the fact that their psychocultural starting point has been for the most part White English. Unfortunately, many *métis(se)* individuals feel they must abandon both their White English parentage as well as their White English cultural roots in order to "become Black." When in fact, most project participants' testimonies reveal that a reformulated Black identity with an acknowledged White English reference point – a "synthesis," as Bisi says, is generally in less conflict with the overall process of self-transformation than a process wherein White English parentage and White English cultural influences are denied.

When I used to walk along the streets of Thatchapee, I was aware of the fact that many people did not make eye contact. However, whenever I came face to face with [another] *métis(se)* person, there was a particular way in which they did not make eye contact. That made me wonder where they were on their journey of self-transformation:

> When I see your faces, I cannot help but remember the war.

[. . .]

It is this law of "hypodescent" that has created essential "inferior" Black African-ness and normative and naturalized "superior" White Europeanness. Being or becoming White is never presented as an option: "Lara, lovey, so long as you're of negroid stock, diluted or not, you're black". *Métis(se)* individuals are never entitled to address the ways in which they are also White. As I discussed at the beginning of this chapter, the cry for unification on the basis of compulsory Blackness also situates *métis(se)* individuals in a precarious position *vis-à-vis* their so-called White kin.

Soundings from the bloodlines frontlines: on *métis(se)* existences or the skins we are in

> When we break that silence, we find community and that is reconciliation.

Ultimately, I am interested in the rehumanization of all experiences. The answers are not to be found in discerning which are Black issues and which are White, but in attacking and eradicating institutionalized racism and discrimination. After abandoning the hegemonic qualities of bi-racialization, perhaps we can attend to the seemingly insignificant concerns of humanity. To let the Blackness and Whiteness wash through is to embrace – among others – a redefined identity that is crafted from the annals of each *métis(se)* person's particular multidimensional histories. For *métis(se)* people in particular and all people in general, one's subjectivities are multiple and not singular. Rather, we negotiate and narrate our experiential selves through disparate and hybrid mani-festations of diaspora(s), cultures, classes sexualities, religions, ethnicities, nations and gender.

. . . This sense of multiple and migratory subjectivities forms the foundation upon which *métis(se)* subjects construct their particular individual and collective narratives of self.

[. . .]

Frequently, it is a life event such as getting married, the birth of a child, or the death of a parent which hurls the *métis(se)* individual into a heightened state of bi-racialized self-consciousness. However, the face-to-face and situational encounters comprising daily life can just as easily trigger bi-racialized contempla-tion. For example, *griotte* Akousa is sitting next to a White English woman on the bus, who says something to the effect that "If we put a straight wig on you you would be White." At times as in the previous example, gendered Blackness is at the contested center; at other times, Whiteness is interrogated. On other occasions, *métis(se)* affiliations, ethnicities or nationalities are challenged. In other instances, they may all collide at once.

[. . .]

Griottes Sarah and Akousa grew up in an African Caribbean community in Liverpool with their White Irish mother and a certain degree of consistency around being *métisse*, Black but not White, and Caribbean. Yemi and Bisi grew up in Nigeria with a White English mother and a Black Nigerian father and many contradictions around "race." As Bisi says, "If you are a mixed race person in Africa you are considered White." Ruby and Similola grew up in isolated predominantly White English settings with an imposed Black consciousness. Both their experiences and their relationships with others illuminate the different and complex ways in which, over time, they have forged identities that are neither necessarily essentialized nor exclusively bi-racialized. Their perspectives challenge the homogenization of Blackness as political strategy as well as the exclusionary practices of normative Whiteness. The affirmations and celebrations of *métis(se)* cultural influences provide alternative paradigms for other constituents of the English–African Diaspora who are also exploring the political possibilities of critical multiculturalism. These selves-transformations involve the reappropriation of differences and marginalities and their reworking in a positive light. At the center is the interrogation of the taken-for-granted constructs of "race," nation, culture and family and their confluent relationships to gendered identities. The narratives of the *griottes* reveal dynamic articulations of selves. They also account for the situational ways in which bi-racialist societies attempt to situate those of us who have already been named.

Study probes

1   How does Ifekwunigwe illustrate 'the paradoxes of identity and affiliation' for 'mixed race' daughters with White mothers?
2   What are the roles of 'Black other-mothers' and how are they performed?
3   How does the author define 'compulsory Blackness'?
4   Define 'negriscence'. Why is the author critical of this model?
5   Compare and contrast Ifekwunigwe's conclusions about 'mixed race' identities politics to those of her American and Canadian counterparts, which are highlighted in the previous extracts.

Notes

1   Ruby and Similola were raised exclusively by White English mother surrogates, while Akousa and Sarah were raised by their White Irish mother and Black Guyanese 'other-mother.' Yemi and Bisi were raised by both their White English mother and their Black Nigerian father. With the exception of Yemi's adolescent bonding with her father, all of the women's testimonies speak to the important socializing influences of the women in their lives. With gender, class, ethnicity, religion, sexuality, locality and bi-racialization as important mediating variables, future research on *métis(se)* individuals and their families

should focus on the differential agency of 'majority' and 'minority' parents, i.e. White mothers and fathers or Black mothers and fathers.

2   As I will discuss later on, due to the fuzzy and slippery nature of official ethnic/racial categories, there are no demographic statistics available which track the actual relationship patterns or reproductive activities of specific multiple generations of *métis(se)* individuals in the English-African Diaspora.

3   I will discuss and define the concept of Additive Blackness later on in this chapter.

References

Amadiume, Ifi (1987) *Male Daughters, Female Husbands*, London: Zed Books.

Essed, Philomena (1991) *Understanding Everyday Racism*, London: Sage.

Evaristo, Bernandine (1997) *Lara*, Tunbridge Wells, Kent: Angela Royal Publishing.

Mama, Amina (1995) *Beyond the Masks: Race, Gender and Subjectivity*, London: Routledge.

Rich, Adrienne (1986) *Blood Bread and Poetry*, London: Virago.

Russell, Kathy *et al.* (1992) *The Color Complex: The Politics of Skin Color Among African Americans*, New York: Doubleday.

SUGGESTIONS FOR FURTHER READING

Ahmed, Sara (1997) ' "It's a Sun Tan Isn't It?": Auto-biography as an Identificatory Practice', in H. Mirza (ed.) *Black British Feminism*, London: Routledge, pp.153–167.

Alibhai-Brown, Yasmin (2001) *Mixed Feelings: The Complex Lives of Mixed Race Britons*, London: Women's Press.

Alibhai-Brown, Yasmin and Montague, Anne (1992) *The Color of Love*, London: Virago.

Alcoff, Linda (1995) 'Mestizo Identity', in N. Zack (ed.) *American Mixed Race*, London: Rowman and Littlefield, pp.257–278.

Andrews, Lori (1999) *Black Power, White Blood: The Life and Times of Johnny Spain*, Philadelphia, PA: Temple University Press.

Azoulay, Katya Gibel (1997) *Black, Jewish and Interracial*, London: Duke University Press.

Back, Les (1996) *New Ethnicities and Urban Culture*, London: University College Press.

Bailey, (1994) 'Naming and Claiming Multicultural Identity', in C. Camper (ed.) *Miscegenation Blues*, Toronto: Sister Vision Press, pp.331–339.

Benson, Sue (1981) *Ambiguous Ethnicity*, Cambridge: Cambridge University Press.

Dalmage, Heather (2000) *Tripping on the Color Line*, New Brunswick, NJ: Rutgers University Press.

Camper, Carol (ed.) (1994) *Miscegenation Blues: Voices of Mixed Race Women*, Toronto: Sister Vision Press.

Colker, Ruth (1996) *Hybrid: Bisexuals, Multiracials, and other Misfits under American Law*, London: New York University Press.

Coombes, Annie and Brah, Avtar (2000) Introduction: The Conundrum of 'Mixing', in A. Brah and A. Coombes (eds) *Hybridity and its Discontents: Politics, Science and Culture*, London: Routledge, pp.1–16.

Evaristo, Bernandine (1994) 'Letters from London', in C. Camper (ed.) *Miscegenation Blues*, Toronto: Sister Vision Press, pp.320–325.

Friedman, Jonathan (1997) 'Global Crises, The Struggle for Cultural Identity and Intellectual Porkbarrelling', in P. Werbner and T. Modood (eds) *Debating Cultural Hybridity*, London: Zed Books, pp.70–89.

Gardner, Leroy (2000) *White/Black Mixing*, St. Paul, Minnesota: Paragon House.

Funderburg, Lise (1994) *Black, White, Other: Biracial Americans Talk About Race and Identity*, New York: William and Morrow.

Gilroy, Paul (1993) *Small Acts: Thoughts on the Politics of Black Culture*, London: Serpent's Tail.

Goldberg, David (ed.) (1994) *Multiculturalism*, Oxford: Blackwell.

Goldberg, David (1995) 'Made in the USA: Racial Mixing n Matching', in N. Zack (ed.) *American Mixed Race*, London: Rowman and Littlefield, pp.237–256.

Haizlip, Shirlee Taylor (1994) *The Sweeter the Juice: A Family Memoir in Black and White*, New York: Simon and Schuster, pp.13–42.

Hernandez-Ramdwar, Camille (1994) 'Ms. Edge Innate', in C. Camper (ed.) *Miscegenation Blues*, Toronto: Sister Vision Press, pp.2–7.

Hoyles, Asher (1999) *Remember Me: Achievements of Mixed Race People Past and Present*, London: Hansib.

Johnson, Keith (1999) *How Did You Get to be Mexican?*, London: Temple University Press.

Johnson, Keith (ed.) (2003) *Mixed Race America and the Law*, New York: New York University Press.

McBride, James (1998) *The Color of Water: A Black Man's Tribute to his White Mother*, London: Bloomsbury Press.

O'Hearn, Claudine Chiawei (ed.) (1998) *Half and Half: Writers Growing up Biracial and Bicultural*, New York: Pantheon Books.

Olumide, Jill (2002) *Raiding the Gene Pool: The Social Construction of Mixed Race*, London: Pluto Press.

Papastergiadis, Nikos (1994) *The Complicities of Culture: Hybridity and 'New Internationalism'*, Manchester: Manchester University Press.

Papastergiadis, Nikos (1997) 'Tracing Hybridity in Theory', in P. Werbner and T. Modood (eds) *Debating Cultural Hybridity*, London: Zed Books, pp.257–281.

Papastergiadis, Nikos (2000) *The Turbulence of Migration: Globalization, Deterritorialization and Hybridity*, Cambridge: Polity Press.

Parker, David (1995) *Through Different Eyes: The Cultural Identities of Young Chinese People in Britain*, London: Avebury.

Parker, Richard and Song, Miri (eds) (2001) 'Introduction: Rethinking "Mixed Race"', in D. Parker and M. Song (eds) *Rethinking "Mixed Race"*, London: Pluto Press, pp.1–22.

Penn, William S. (1997) *As We Are Now: Mixblood Essays on Race and Identity*, Berkeley, CA: University of California Press.

Phoenix, Ann and Owen, Charlie (2000) 'From Miscegenation to Hybridity: Mixed Relationships and Mixed Parentage in Profile', in A. Brah and A. Coombes (eds) *Hybridity and its Discontents: Politics, Science and Culture*, London: Routledge, pp.72–95.

Rockquemore, Kerry (2002) *Beyond Black: Biracial Identity in America*, London: Sage.

Root, Maria P. P. (ed.) (1992) *Racially Mixed People of America*, Thousand Oaks, CA: Sage.

Root, Maria P. P. (ed.) (1996) *The Multiracial Experience: Racial Borders as the New Frontier*, Thousand Oaks, CA: Sage.

Root, Maria P. P. (2001) *Love's Revolution: Interracial Marriage*, London: Sage.

Russell, Kathy *et al.* (1993) *The Color Complex*, New York: Anchor Books.

Scales-Trent, Judy (1995) *Notes of a White Black Woman: Race, Color, Community*, University Park: Pennsylvania State University Press.

Small, Stephen (2001) 'Colour, Culture and Class: Interrogating Interracial Marriage and People of Mixed Racial Descent in the USA', in D. Parker and M. Song (eds) *Rethinking 'Mixed Race'*, London: Pluto Press, pp.117–132.

Spencer, Jon Michael (1997) *The New Colored People*, London: New York University Press.

Spickard, Paul (1989) *Mixed Blood: Intermarriage and Ethnic Identity in Twentieth-Century America*, Madison: University of Wisconsin Press.

Spickard, Paul (2001) 'The Subject is Mixed Race: The Boom in Biracial Biography', in R. Parker and M. Song (eds) *Rethinking 'Mixed Race'*, pp.76–98.

Talty, Stephen (2003) *Mulatto America: At the Crossroads of Black and White Culture*, New York: HarperCollins.

Tizard, Barbara and Phoenix, Ann (1993) *Black, White or Mixed Race?: Race and Racism in the Lives of Young People of Mixed Parentage*, London: Routledge.

Twine, France Winddance (1997) 'Brown-Skinned White Girls: Class, Culture and the Construction of White Identity in Suburban Communities', in R. Frankenberg (ed.) *Displacing Whiteness*, Durham, NC: Duke University Press, pp.214–243.

Weekes, Debbie (1997) 'Shades of Blackness: Young Female Constructions of Beauty', in H. Mirza (ed.) *Black British Feminism*, London: Routledge, pp.113–126.

Werbner, Pnina and Modood, Tariq (eds) (1997) *Debating Cultural Hybridity*, London: Zed Books.

Wilson, Anne (1987) *Mixed Race Children*, London: Allen and Unwin.

Wolfman, Brunetta (1995) 'Color Fades Over Time', in N. Zack (ed.) *American Mixed Race*, London: Rowman and Littlefield, pp.13–24.

Zack, Naomi (ed.) (1995) *American Mixed Race*, London: Rowman and Littlefield.

PART THREE

Debating definitions

Multiraciality, census categories and critiques

INTRODUCTION

PART THREE MARKS THE emergence of 'multiraciality' as a new canon and the subject of intense debate. More specifically, the extracts in this section highlight ongoing social, political and policy concerns (i.e. government census 'racial'/'ethnic' categorizations and monitoring as they dovetail with divergent perspectives on identity politics, community formations and new social movements). In 'The census and categories' section, readings by Senna, Jones, Nash and Spencer weigh the arguments for and against the inclusion of a 'multiracial' category on the 2000 US Census. The brief by Grieco and Cassidy summarizes the results of the 2000 US Census as they pertain to the issue of 'race' and 'Hispanic' origin.

While the 'multiracial' lobby was not completely successful in the USA, without the exertion of political pressure from 'mixed race' constituents, the UK Census 2001 did include a question on 'mixed ethnic' origin. In light of particular demographic trends, the Owen excerpt explores the potential long-term implications of this policy decision. Although, to date, the UK Census 2001 data have not been entirely analysed, I have also included an excerpt from the Office of National Statistics who administered the UK Census. When compared with the US 'data', the preliminary UK findings highlight significant differences both in the perception of 'mixed race' in these two nations as well as in their historical and political trajectories. Finally, Aspinall provides a useful cross-national comparison of the 'official' reporting of 'mixed race' in the USA, the UK and Canada.

In the section on 'Multiraciality and critiques', the chosen readings demonstrate the at times problematic ways in which theorizing on 'mixed race' and now 'multiraciality' inform academic processes, public policies, political practices and popular cultures. The excerpt by Ropp addresses the limitations of a social constructionist and celebratory standpoint on 'multiracial' identity. Both Nakashima and Sanchez provide a broader historical and critical context for the mainstreaming of 'multiracial' politics by the popularity of 'Cablinasian' Tiger Woods. Although Daniel is another 'mixed race' studies pioneer and as such should have been showcased in Part Two, in this Part I have chosen to include an extract from his most recent book. Among other objectives, he attempts to reconcile the competing and contested political projects of the 'multiracial' movement and black activisms. I have paired this with an extract by Njeri, who engages in critical dialogue with Daniel's earlier work. Given the fact that African Americans are one of the largest 'multiracial' communities in the world, in this selection, Njeri also advances a position regarding the important role African Americans can play in the 'multiracial' identities politics debate. The Christian reading offers a comparative and complex analysis, which argues for both cultural and historical specificity and the recognition of the enduring legacy and overarching impact of 'white' supremacy. Mahtani and Moreno, two of my former postgraduate students, have been given the last word, which is critical of perspectives which privilege 'whiteness/non-whiteness' as the primary and binary 'mixed race' paradigm. Their contribution is also visionary, in that it forces all of us to (re)think what the future holds for 'mixed race' studies.

The census and categories

Chapter 26

Danzy Senna

THE MULATTO MILLENNIUM

From C Chiawei O'Hearn (ed.) *Half and Half: Writings on Growing Up Biracial and Bicultural* (1998). New York: Pantheon Books, pp. 12–13 and 22–27.

STRANGE TO WAKE UP and realize you're in style. That's what happened to me just the other morning. It was the first day of the new millennium and I woke to find that mulattos had taken over. They were everywhere. Playing golf, running the airwaves, opening their own restaurants, modeling clothes, starring in musicals with names like *Show Me the Miscegenation!* The radio played a steady stream of Lenny Kravitz, Sade, and Mariah Carey. I thought I'd died and gone to Berkeley. But then I realized. According to the racial zodiac, 2000 is the official Year of the Mulatto. Pure breeds (at least the black ones) are out and hybridity is in. America loves us in all of our half-caste glory. The president announced on Friday that beige is to be the official color of the millennium. Major news magazines announce our arrival as if we were proof of extraterrestrial life. They claim we're going to bring about the end of race as we know it.

[. . .]

These days, there are M.N. folks in Congress and the White House. They've got their own category on the census. It says "Multiracial." But even that is inadequate for the more extremist wing of the Mulatto Nation. They want to take it a step further. I guess they have a point. I mean, why lump us all together as multiracial? Eskimos, they say, have forty different words for snow. In South Africa, during apartheid, they had fourteen different types of coloreds. But we've decided on this one word, "multiracial," to describe, in effect, a whole nation of diverse people who have absolutely no relation, cultural or otherwise, to one another. In light of this deficiency, I would like to propose the following coinages. Perhaps the Census Bureau should give them a try.

Variations on a theme of a mulatto

Standard mulatto: white mother, black father. Half-nappy hair, skin that is described as "pasty yellow" in the winter, but turns a caramel tan in the summer. Germanic-Afro features. Often raised in isolation from others of its kind. Does not discover his or her "black identity" till college. At this point, there is usually some physical change in hair or clothing, and often speech, so much so that the parents don't recognize their child when he or she arrives home for Christmas vacation. (E.g., "Honey, there's some black kid at the door.")

African American: The most common form of mulatto in North America, this breed is not often described as mixed, but is nevertheless a combination of African, European, and Native American. May come in any skin tone, and of any cultural background. Often believe themselves to be "pure" due to historical distance from the original mixture, which was most often achieved through rape.

Jewlatto: The second most prevalent form of mulatto in the North American continent, this breed is made in the commingling of Jews and blacks who met while registering voters down South during Freedom Summer or at a CORE meeting. Jewlattos will often, though not necessarily, have a white father and a black mother (as opposed to the more common case, a black father and a white mother). Will also be more likely to be raised in a diverse setting, around others of his or her kind, such as New York City (Greenwich Village) or Northern California (Berkeley). Have strong pride in their mixed background. Will often feel that their dual cultures are not so dual at all, considering the shared history of oppression. Jewlattos are most easily spotted amid the flora and fauna of Brown University. Famous Jewlattos: Lenny Kravitz and Lisa Bonet (and we can't forget Zoe, their love child).

Mestizo: A more complicated mixture, where either the black or white parent claims a third race in their background (e.g., Native American or Latino) and therefore confuses the child more. The mestizo is likely to be mistaken for some other, totally distinct ethnicity (Italian, Arab, Mexican, Jewish, East Indian, Native American, Puerto Rican) and in fact will be touted by strangers as a perfect representative of that totally new race. (E.g., "Your face brings me right back to Calcutta.") The mestizo mulatto is more prevalent than commonly believed, since they often "disappear" into the fabric of American society, wittingly or unwittingly passing as that third, "pure," totally distinct race. It takes an expert to spot one in a crowd.

Gelatto: A mixture of Italian American and African American, this breed often lives in either a strictly Italian neighborhood if the father is white (e.g., Bensonhurst) or in a black neighborhood if the father is black (e.g., Flatbush). Usually identifies strongly with one side of the family over the other, but sometimes with marked discomfort becomes aware of the similarities between the two sides of his cultures, and at this point, often "flies the coop" and begins to practice Asian religions.

Cultural Mulatto: Any American born post-1967. See *Wiggers*.

Blulatto: A highly rare breed of "blue-blood" mulatto who can trace their lineage back to the *Mayflower*. If female, is legally entitled to membership in the Daughters of the American Revolution. Blulattos have been spotted in Cambridge, Massachusetts, and Berkeley, California, but should not be confused with the Jewlatto. The Blulatto's mother is almost always the white one and is either a poet or a painter who disdains her Wasp heritage. The father of the Blulatto is almost always the black one, is highly educated, and disdains his black heritage. Unlike the Jewlatto, the parents of the Blulatto are most likely divorced or separated, although the black father almost always remarries another blue-blood woman much like the first. Beware: The Blulatto may seem calm and even civilized, but can be dangerous when angry. Show caution when approaching.

Negratto: May be any of the above mixtures, but is raised to identify as black. Negrattos often have a white mother who assimilated into black culture before they were born, and raised them to understand "the trouble with whitey." They will tend to be removed from the white side of their family and to suppress the cultural aspects of themselves that are considered white. Will tend to be more militant than their darker brothers and sisters and to talk in a slang most resembling ebonics circa 1974. Has great disgust for the "so-called mulatto movement" and grows acutely uncomfortable in the presence of other mulattos. Despite all of this posturing, there is a good chance that they have a white lover hidden somewhere in their past, present, or future.

Cablinasian: A rare exotic breed found mostly in California. This is the mother of all mixtures, and when caught may be displayed for large sums of money. The Cablinasian is a mixture of Asian, American Indian, Black, and Caucasian (thus the strange name). A show mulatto, with great performance skills, the Cablinasian will be whoever the crowd wants him to be, and can switch at the drop of a dime. Does not, however, answer to the name Black. A cousin to other rare exotic mixes found only in California (Filipino and Black; Samoan and Irish; Mexican and Korean). Note: If you spot a Cablinasian, please contact the Benetton Promotions Bureau.

Tomatto: A mixed or black person who behaves in an "Uncle Tom-ish" fashion. The Tomatto may be found in positions of power, being touted as a symbol of diversity in otherwise all-white settings. Even if the Tomatto has two black parents, his skin is light and his features are mixed. If we are ever to see a first black president, he will most likely be a Tomatto.

Fauxlatto: A person impersonating a mulatto. Can be of white, black, or other heritage, but for inexplicable reasons claims to be of mixed heritage. See *Jamiroqui*.

Ho-latto: A female of mixed racial heritage who exploits and is exploited sexually. See any of Prince's Girlfriends.

The categories could go on and on, and perhaps, indeed, they will. And where do I fit into them? That's the strange thing. I fit into none and all of the above. I have been each of the above, or at least mistaken for each of them, at different moments in my life. But somehow, none of them feel right. Maybe that makes me a Postlatto.

There are plans next week to paint the White House rainbow colored. And just last month, two established magazines, both bastions of liberal thought, had cover stories predicting "the end of blackness." Not too long ago, *Newsweek* officially declared it "hip" to be multiracial. Race relations have been boiled down to a game of semantics – as if all that matters is which box one checks on the census.

And me? I've learned to flaunt my mixedness at dinner parties, where the guests (most of them white) ooh and aaah about my flavorful background. I've found it's not so bad being a fetishized object, an exotic bird soaring above the racial landscape. And when they start talking about black people, pure breeds, in that way that used to make me squirm before the millennium, I let them know that I'm neutral, nothing to be afraid of. Sometimes I feel it, that remnant of my old self (the angry black girl with the big mouth) creeping out, but most of the time I don't feel anything at all. Most of the time, I just serve up the asparagus, chimichangas, and fried chicken with a bright, white smile.

Study probes

1 On what grounds does Senna object to the term 'multiracial'?
2 Compare and contrast Senna's 'variations on the theme of mulatto'.
3 What do her 'tongue-in-cheek' categories tell us about the politics of 'race', gender, colour and status in the contemporary USA?

Chapter 27

Lisa Jones

IS BIRACIAL ENOUGH (OR, WHAT'S THIS ABOUT A MULTIRACIAL CATEGORY ON THE CENSUS?: A CONVERSATION)

Extract from *Bulletproof Diva: Tales of Race, Sex and Hair* (1994). New York: Doubleday, pp. 56–62.

Give us your off-the-cuff take on this census movement.

THE IDENTITY FAIRY: I haven't been to any meetings, but I did speak at length with several organizers and foot soldiers, including, among others, Carlos Fernandez, president of AMEA, Susan Graham, executive director of Project RACE, Kendra Wallace, Project's vice-president in California, and Michelle Erickson of Chicago. Erickson pulled her five-year-old son out of the public school system rather than choose between existing racial categories. (She identifies Andrew, her son, as biracial.) Instigated by Erickson's letter-writing campaign and the lobbying of Project RACE, the state of Illinois is now considering the "multiracial" category.

Many in the census movement see the bottom line of their crusade as a fight for the self-esteem of their children. Graham of Project RACE, who is a white mother of two, as she calls them, "multiracial kids," says children are psychologically healthiest when they have accurate racial labels at their disposal. But what on earth constitutes an accurate racial label? And if the census movement is ultimately out to do away with such sacrosanct labels, will creating new ones accomplish this?

Beyond the children's self-esteem issue, the movement's larger agenda and philosophical goals registered blurry. Race is configured as choice, as a category on a school form. Race is not seen as a political/economic construct, a battleground where Americans vie for power and turf, but a question of color, a stick-on, peel-off label. If there *is* an end goal to the census movement's efforts, it appears to be assimilation. I don't mean this in the didactic sense of chiding others for wanting their piece of American pie: I mean it as finding a place to fit in, creating a space of comfort for self, away from the choke hold of race. The business as usual of discrimination, against the have-nots, who are usually shades of brown, and in favor of the have-sos, who are usually shades of pink, is left undisturbed.

When I heard that all state legislation for school forms would remain symbolic until the Congress and the Office of Management and Budget vote to add multiracial to the list of official categories, I scratched my head. And when I heard that the activists couldn't agree on whether those who checked the "multiracial" box would be considered a disadvantaged minority deserving of federal protections under the Voting Rights Act, I scratched some more. Why was this movement – potentially a vital movement for the acknowledgment of hybrid cultures/lives – being tied to a kite that no one could steer?

Do you have other concerns about the census movement?

THE IDENTITY FAIRY: Let's look at a few:
Is race (and racism) left intact? Instead of fighting for a new racial category, if the end goal is, as census activists say, to do away with the biological pseudoscience of race, why aren't they in the trenches casting stones at institutional racism? Anna Deavere Simth's *Fires in the Mirror* quotes an interview the playwright did with Angela Davis. Davis says she feels tentative about the meaning of race these days, but not tentative at all about racism. People of color, whether they call themselves biracial, Swirls (as they do in Fostorio, Ohio), or zebra Americans are disproportionately members of America's underclass. Here's a meaningful contrast: Ohio became the first state last year to adopt the multiracial category on school forms. This year, Ohio saw a bloody uprising at the Lucasville state prison. Almost 60 percent of prisoners there are black men, though African Americans make up barely one quarter of the state's population. Will the symbolic recognition of multiracial identity reverse numbers like these?

I was struck that the census movement had no alliances with progressive organizations representing other people of color. None of these organizations had staged a teach-in or protested over the miscarriage of justice in the Rodney King case. Was biraciality being constructed as a less progressive stance than identifying as a "person of color," that catchphrase invented in the eighteenth century, then popularized in the seventies, as an expression of solidarity with other p.o.e.s worldwide?

Cape Town U.S.A.? It's been asked before, and until I hear a good comeback, the question stands: Would "multiracial" be akin to South Africa's "colored" caste created under apartheid? Carlos Fernandez of AMEA believes that an "in-between" racial category isn't racist in itself, it is how such a category is used. Yet why wouldn't multiracial/colored be mythologized or positioned politically any differently in America?

Are we special? The census movement and its "interracial/biracial nationalists," as I refer to them playfully, claim biraciality as a mark of "racial" singularity, one that in America (where most racial groups are multiethnic and multicultural) has little grounding. Their insistence on biraciality's unique status borders on elitism. They marvel at the perks of biraciality: That biracials have several cultures at their disposal. (Though don't we all as Americans?) They say things like "biracial people are free of bias because they embody both black and white." Can you fight essentialism with essentialism? Are we to believe that all biracials are chosen people, free of prejudice, self-interest, and Republican Christian fundamentalism?

By proclaiming specialness aren't biracials still clinging to the niche of exotic other? "How could we not love them, they're so cute," boasted one white mother active in the census movement of her biracial children. Minus butter-pecan skin and Shirley Temple curls would they be less of an attractive proposition?

The nationalist vibe. The writer Kristal Brent-Zook calls nationalism a search for home, for family, and for sameness. Young movements of any kind are prone to nationalism, yet it's hard to forgive the biracialists for indulging. A large part of why they disassociate themselves from traditional ethnic communities is just *because* of their hybridity, their lack of purity.

Is there now to be a biracial party line to tow and a biracial lifestyle to upkeep? *Interrace*, a magazine chronicling the census movement and interracial and biracial social life, called the actress Halle Berry's choice *not* to marry interracially a "cop-out." (One guesses they made this judgment about the race of Berry's husband, baseball star David Justice, based on photographs. A few issues later, when *Interrace* found out that Justice happened to be "Afro-European," they laid out the biracial carpet.) Are those of us who marry the same, "mono-race" partners now retro, antiprogressive? Have the inter-racial/biracial police determined that the only way to change the world is to breed a "new race?" "Like it or not," read a letter to *Spectrum*, the newsletter published by Multiracial Americans of Southern California (MASC), "racially mixed people are the most beautiful people of all." The new Stepford people.

What's history got to do with it? As black/white biracials, when we distance ourselves from the African-American freedom struggle, from aging, though historically critical, ideas like "black power" and "black community," do we fail to honor a history that brought us to where we are today? Is biraciality political sedition? And if it feels that way, and it shouldn't, how can we make it feel less so? Are there ways to be responsible to a history that we are indebted to without being imprisoned by it?

I found the generalizations the census movers made about African-Americans disturbing. Resistance from some blacks to the multiracial category was translated into resistance from the entire African-American population. Aren't some of the parents involved in the census movement African-Americans? The bills to add the "multiracial" category on the state level have all been introduced by African-American legislators. The census initiative has garnered support from local chapters of the NAACP. *Essence* magazine and other black publications spread the word about AMEA and fellow interracial groups long before their white counterparts.

To say that biracials have been cold-shouldered by African-Americans throughout history, as some activists suggested, is selective ignorance. Black communities have always been shelter to multiethinc people, perhaps not an unproblematic shelter, yet a shelter nonetheless. Black folks, I'd venture, have welcomed difference in their communities more than most Americans.

Nothing but a photo-op? Watching biraciality gobbled up so eagerly on the Donahue and Oprah circuit makes me pause. If it weren't such a fashionable and marketable identity these days would so many folks be riding the bandwagon? (And like the hip-hop club, media darlings of the late eighties, the biracial lobby comes across on television as having have no agenda other than its own pride politics.)

Are biracial people being offered up as the latest market ripe for exploitation? *Interrace* magazine sells T-shirts inscribed with Webster's definition of biracial. The ads urge buyers to "Wear the Right Thing" or to "end racism . . . advertise in *Interrace.*" *New People: The Journal for the Human Race* hawks ceramic wedding figurines in your choice of complexions. Not unlike trade or hobby magazines, both publications look at the world through one prism: biracialism.

Are we family? Shouldn't we ask what makes biracial people a community? What holds us together other than a perceived sense of our own difference from the ethnic mainstream? Consider if the Mexican-Samoan kid in San Diego has the same needs as the black-Jewish kid from New York's Upper West Side? Maybe politically as people of color, but do they share a definitive mixed-race culture? And if they do, should we call it "biraciality" or should we call it "American culture"?

Does blackness remain a stigma? As my telephone travels made clear, the census camp is not minus attitudes of: "If you had a choice you'd be anything but black." Biraciality was posited by some as an escape from the "blemish of blackness." Chicago mother Michelle Erickson asked me quite innocently if I knew how degrading it was "to be attached to categories like black or Hispanic." Kendra Wallace, a biracial woman in her early twenties, pronounced rules of membership in the black community to be too stiff – based, she feels, on such criteria as "hair texture and whether one speaks proper English or not." (Is African-American diversity still that invisible to the world? One could have come away with a picture far more complex by watching a week's worth of sitcoms.)

A moment of cruel and unusual irony took place in a conversation with Project RACE's Susan Graham. During Black History Month, Graham's son returned home with some materials on Langston Hughes. Graham was disappointed that the school had failed to focus on "Langston Hughes's biraciality." I reminded Graham that African-Americans as a whole were a multiethnic and multiracial folk, and that Hughes never hid the fact that he had white family, yet he "cast his lot," as the expression went back then, with his darker kin. Hughes's writing, one can safely say, celebrates, if not romanticizes African-American culture. Graham seemed irritated. The one-drop rule was the only thing that kept him in the black community, she insisted. If Hughes were alive today, he would choose to be multiracial, he would identify first with mixed-race people and the work of her lobbying group.

People of all races and cultures should feel free to claim Hughes as an idol, but wasn't Graham aware of a rather painful history? One where black people have had their every gift confiscated and attributed to others? Would this now happen in the name of multiracialism?

Seems like you've exhausted the critical tip. Did you happen upon anything constructive in your telephone encounters with the biracial movement?

THE IDENTITY FAIRY: Carlos Fernandez said something that made sense. Official recognition of multiracial identity may not end racism, it is, however, a necessary step. If we refuse to recognize that any material reality exists between black and white, we do nothing except enshrine these social boundaries – and enshrine the political divide that upholds them.

Certainly the daguerreotype of mixed-race people as freaks of nature could use a long overdue slashing. If the biracial lobby can help in this regard, bless them. Says Kendra Wallace: "We're invisible or our identities are always problematized and sexualized." Our "bloods" are at war inside of us. If mixed race were made normal, we could look forward to the comic mulatto, the introspective, the slovenly. We might one day come to miss ye olde tragic mulatto, the world's pet mule.

As much as I found myself resisting the biracial nationalists, to deny a group the right to identify as they wish to seems equally reactionary. In October last year the San Diego Unified School District, known for its conservatism, balked at admitting a little boy to grammar school until his mother, Patricia Whitebread, who is black, assigned him an "appropriate race." (Unlike many school forms nationally, San Diego's has no "other" designation.) Whitebread refused. The school district admitted the child anyway. Later the district classified her son as black without Whitebread's permission.

The activists I spoke to framed their cause as a civil rights movement. Perhaps one not as transparently vital as a movement for equal opportunity in employment or fair access to housing, but certainly one consummate with religious freedom or freedom of expression.

Study probes

1   According to Jones, what is the main political platform of the 'multiracial' census movement?
2   Outline her criticisms of the 'multiracial' census movement.
3   How is her critique grounded in an historical analysis of complex American 'race' relations?

Chapter 28

Philip Tajitsu Nash

WILL THE CENSUS GO MULTIRACIAL?

From *Amerasia Journal* 23 (1) (1997), pp. 21–27.

The multiracial census category

IN THE 1970s, as America began to more fully acknowledge its increased diversity, some federal, state, and local officials joined with social scientists and community activists calling for a uniform racial data classification scheme that would improve statistical reporting, facilitate the oversight of governmental grants and programs, and allow the Justice Department, Equal Employment Opportunity Commission, and other agencies to monitor civil rights and equal employment compliance reports.[1]

The Office of Management and Budget (OMB), located in the Executive Office of the President, undertook a process that resulted in 1977 in OMB's Statistical Policy Directive No. 15, Race and Ethnic Standards for Federal Statistics and Administrative Reporting.[2] On the positive side, Directive No. 15 stated that the division of the universe into "white" and "nonwhite" categories had to end, and that uniform definitions and data-gathering methods were to be used by all federal agencies. Unfortunately, however, multiracials were to continue to be unrecognized, because the Directive continued the practice that persons of mixed racial and ethnic origins should use the single category which most closely reflected the individual's recognition in his or her community.

The 1980 Decennial Census, reflecting the procedures described in Directive No. 15, led some interracials to accept the "choose one" strategy, while others wrote in other answers. By 1990, fully 2 percent of those answering the census wrote in multiple responses to the question about race, and 30 percent responding to a separate question about ancestry said that they had multiple ancestries. This response reflected, in part, the ambiguity caused by the overlapping issues of race and Hispanic ethnicity, but it also reflected a growing number of individuals who refused to be forced to accept a single racial label.

With the Year 2000 Census just a few years away, OMB has embarked on another round of research, public hearings, and policy reviews. Their stated goal is to review the current racial and ethnic categories found in Directive No. 15, establish guiding principles that would govern changes to these standards, and raise specific suggestions for changing those categories. Public hearings were held in 1994 in Boston, Denver, San Francisco, and Honolulu, and a major notice about the proposed changes was published in the Federal Register.[3] What followed were a National Content Test and a Race and Ethnic Targeted Test (RAETT) conducted by the Census Bureau in the Spring of 1996, publication of the results of those tests in early 1997, one last call for comment on proposed changes to Directive No. 15 in the Spring of 1997, and then publication by mid-1997 of the final version of Directive No. 15 that will guide the Year 2000 Decennial Census. Hopefully, the result will live up to the OMB's own desire for "consistent, publicly accepted data on race and ethnicity that will meet the needs of the government and the public, while recognizing the diversity of the population and respecting the individual's dignity."[4]

Although the question about whether to include a multiracial census category has generated significant debate, other political issues could have an even bigger impact on the Asian American community. The biggest, which would lead to the abolition of the category "Asian or Pacific Islander," is the drive by some Native Hawaiians to have themselves moved to the Native American category due to similarities in concerns such as land sovereignty.[5]

The six big issues explored by the OMB during the review process were the following:

1   Should the federal government even be collecting data on race and ethnicity, and, if so, should there be any standards at all? Some feel that the government has no business collecting this type of data, while others see this data as vital to civil rights law enforcement. The public comment in 1994 was strongly in favor of having standards for the collection of race and ethnicity data.

2   Should Directive No. 15 be revised at all? And should there be different collection standards for different purposes? One alternative is to keep the data collection standards the same as they were before the post-1994 review process. Another is to collect data necessary for trend analysis and data necessary for civil rights law monitoring in separate ways.

3   Should questions about race and ethnicity be asked together, or should they be asked separately? The way the questions are asked have an effect on the outcome of the data.

4   Should self-identification or observer perceptions guide the methods for data collection? Again, the answer to this question will have an effect on the census results. For example, a blonde, blue-eyed person may look "White," but may identify closely with the fractional part of her ancestry that is Filipino.

5   Should population size and geographic distribution (such as some groups

being concentrated in certain states or regions) be factors in the final determination of federal census categories? Some groups, such as Native Hawaiians, are concentrated in one state or region, and have small numbers when compared with other groups.

6   Given all of the above, what should be the data collection and presentation categories formalized in Directive No. 15?

The initial hearings and requests for comment on Directive No. 15 have clarified the positions of those supporting and opposing a multiracial category. Briefly summarized, those who favor it say that the categories are imprecise anyway; forcing someone to choose one race denies that person of his or her full heritage, demeans that person's existence with the label "other," and forces that person to provide factually false information. On the other side are agencies and organizations concerned that reducing the count of persons in the current categories will jeopardize hard-won gains in civil rights, education, and electoral arenas, and prevent the formation of future arguments in favor of appropriate remedies.

If a multiracial category were to be allowed, options raised so far in the review process include:

- Creating a separate "Multiracial" category
- Allowing respondents to "check all that apply"
- Providing open-ended questions
- Retaining the "Other" option
- Asking about the geographic ancestry of the respondent's mother and father
- Asking respondents, in a throwback to nineteenth century pseudo science, to compare their skin color to a uniform skin-color gradient chart. If no multiracial category is allowed, options raised so far include retaining the old "choose one" system, using the father's ethnic/racial designation, using the mother's racial/ethnic designation, and using the race of the minority-designated parent if one parent is white and the other a minority.

Analysis

Directive No. 15 represented a big conceptual leap forward for 1977. Today, however, it needs revision. While it is certain that the racial and ethnic categories it describes are imprecise and unscientific, tremendous gains have been made by racial and ethnic minorities since 1977 using the data based on those categories.

Given how far these minorities still have to go to reach economic, political, and social parity with whites[6] it is not the time to move away from the present five categories. Instead of throwing out categories that provide information essential to civil rights monitoring and advocacy, a better solution might be to add a "Multiracial" category that could be marked as an *option* by any respondent. This would allow civil rights groups to continue advocating, for instance, not only for the person who is denied housing because she is African American or Asian American, but also for the multiracial person denied housing because she is assumed to be African American or Asian American.

In addition to checking "Multiracial," each person would be asked to check his or her primary group affiliation at this time, recognizing that "identification of ethnicity is fluid and self-perceptions of race and ethnicity change over time and across circumstances for many people. This is especially true among persons with heterogeneous ancestries."[7]

For multiracial people, issues of identity bring a lifetime of questioning and searching. So far, however, these identity questions have not led to a political movement like the Asian-American movement and other social identity movements that gained prominence in the late 1960s.

When it comes to filling out a census form, the issue is not one of identity, it is one of political and economic empowerment. The problem is not race.[8] It is *racism*, the inferior treatment accorded someone based on their *perceived* race or ethnicity. To combat racism, stereotypes must change, opportunities must be opened up, and governmental agencies must continue monitoring the steady but incremental progress achieved in recent decades. All of this requires the kind of data that comes from the admittedly flawed categories currently in place.

How or whether someone classifies herself, whether by culture, language, religion, region of origin, or sexual orientation, that person deserves respect as an individual. Therefore, an appropriate strategy for achieving that goal is for multiracial people to continue using the present census scheme while advocating for a "Multiracial" check-off category that would not be included in the tallying of the other five categories. This would produce a total count of people who consider themselves multiracial without adversely affecting the civil rights and equal employment monitoring that are especially necessary in the present anti-immigrant and anti-affirmative action political climate.

Conclusion

At its core, the discussion about a multiracial census category is intimately tied to the present-day discussion about multiculturalism. Each American has diverse cultural and biological backgrounds, often including ancestry that is overlooked by both the individual and the society. The difficult and often painful race and ethnicity problems that continue to plague this country will not go away by abolishing socially defined racial categories in the census. Neither will they disappear by allowing a "choose all that apply" alternative that will diminish the usefulness of the race and ethnicity data Directive No. 15 has given us since 1977.[9]

As the number of people checking off the "Multiracial" box after choosing one primary racial or ethnic identifier grows over the next few decades, we should continue to revisit the question of whether to alter or abolish the race and ethnicity criteria on the census. Until racism itself is abolished, however, any census that ignores the importance of race and ethnicity in the lives of Americans turns a blind eye to injustice.

Study probes

1   What was the Office of Management and Budget's (OMB) Statistical Policy Directive No.15?
2   What was its stance on 'multiracials'?
3   According to Nash, what were the six big reform issues confronting the OMB?
4   Were specific issues raised regarding a 'multiracial' category?
5   What recommendations does the author make, and why?

Notes

1   Margo J. Anderson, *The American Census: A Social History* (New Haven: Yale University Press, 1988), 209–212.
2   This document, published in the Federal Register in 60:166, August 28, 1995, 44692-693, can be found in the Government Documents section of most public and university libraries, or on the internet at the following World Wide Web address (URL): http://www.fedworld.gov/ftp.htm#omb
3   59 Federal Register 29831, June 9, 1994.
4   60 Federal Register 44692, August 28, 1995.
5   60 Federal Register 44683–84, August 28, 1995; Samuel Cacas, "New Census Category for Multiracial Persons?" *Asian Week*, July 15, 1994, 1; Haunani-kay Trask, "Politics in the Pacific Islands: Imperialism and Native Self-Determination," *Amerasia Journal* 16:1 (1990), 1–19.
6   By 1993, minorities held half as many management jobs as whites, while 91.5 percent of Senior Executive Service (SES) jobs in the federal government were held by whites. Loretta Guttierrez, "EEOC's Casellas Joines Affirmative Action Debate," *Minority Law Journal*, Fall 1995, 22. Meanwhile, the federal Glass Ceiling Commission found that 97 percent of senior management positions in Fortune 1000 Industrial and Fortune 500 Service Industries were held by white males. Loretta Guttierez Nestor, "Minority Bars Meet to Address Legislative Concerns," *Minority Law Journal*, Fall 1995, 3.
7   60 Federal Register 44675, August 28, 1995.
8   Even physicians are beginning to question the use of racial categories as a diagnostic or therapeutic tool. Stephen Caldwell and Rebecca Popenoe, "Perceptions and Misperceptions of Skin Color," *Annals of Internal Medicine* 122:8, April 15, 1995, 614–621.
9   Some fear that a multiracial category will become like the "colored" category in South Africa during the days of apartheid. See Lynn Norment, "Am I Black, White, or In Between?"

Chapter 29

Rainier Spencer

THINKING ABOUT TRANSCENDING
RACE

Extract from *Spurious Issues: Race and Multiracial Identity Politics in the United States* (1999). Boulder, CO: Westview Press, pp. 192–199.

ADVOCATES OF MULTIRACIAL IDEOLOGY were aided in their endeavor in no small measure by the stunning success of professional golfer Tiger Woods, who is of Thai, Chinese, European, Native American, and Afro-American descent. Indeed, Woods has seen himself appropriated from all sides — by Afro-Americans, who hail him as the first black Masters Tournament champion, as well as by multiracial advocates, who have declared him the symbol of their struggle for a federal multiracial category. This appropriation is evident in the words of Association of MultiEthnic Americans (AMEA) president Ramona Douglass: "Whether he wants to or not, he is sort of becoming the poster person for multiracial identity."[1] In the same vein, Project RACE executive director Susan Graham offered that "Tiger Woods could not have come at a better time. The public can now see a face of what it means to be multiracial."[2] Finally, if there is any doubt concerning the appropriation of Woods, one need look no farther than Representative Thomas Petri, who named his multiracial category bill (H.R. 830) the "Tiger Woods Bill."[3]

In terms of popular understandings of the multiracial category debate, it would be a mistake to underestimate Woods's influence. This is not to say that Woods ever agreed to be a spokesperson for multiracial advocacy, but by focusing on his racial identity, and by doing so with a distinct lack of critical tools, the popular media redirected the national spotlight onto simplistic conceptions of race as well as multiraciality. For instance, the cover of the May 5, 1997, issue of *Time* magazine reads "Tiger and Race," while the article itself opens with a two-page photograph of Woods seated in a golf cart with his parents.[4] An article in that same week's *Newsweek* contains a photograph of Woods and leads with the following: "Tiger Woods is the exception that rules. For his multiracial generation, hip isn't just black and white."[5]

These journalistic attempts to cover the multiracial category debate inevitably lack depth and are geared more toward presentation through color graphs and photographs than through anything approaching deep or rigorous analysis.[6] Nevertheless, many Americans have educated themselves about the multiracial category debate through this kind of shallow, popular journalism. Thus, Woods's impact at the popular level, while having no effect on scholarly interpretations of the multiracial issue or on the factors that OMB took into account when rendering its decision on revising the federal race categories, remains a phenomenon that works to present the multiracial category debate as solely an issue of self-esteem and federal validation of personal identity.

This shift of focus away from the actual purpose of the federal categories has revealed the tenuous nature of multiracial ideology as well as its inherent inconsistency. In general, the leaders of multiracial advocacy groups as well as individuals who write and speak in favor of multiracial ideology will, in the course of an extended conversation, admit that Afro-Americans do not actually constitute a monoracial biological group.[7] In the words of former AMEA president Carlos Fernández: "Yes, race as a biological concept is illogical . . . Arguing for a 'multiracial' category should not be read as an endorsement of race as a biological concept."[8] Fernández is precisely wrong here, however; for a multiracial category can neither be argued for nor even conceived of without acknowledging some notion of biological race. Indeed, and in no uncertain terms, arguing for a multiracial category can *only* be read as an endorsement of race as a biological concept. To assert otherwise, as Fernández does, is no more than logical nonsense.

Ramona Douglass as well seems very clearly to disavow the notion of biological race when she asserts:

> Race itself is simply a conversation people either align with or they don't. It is real only in our speaking of it – not in science . . . The 'one drop rule' is an irrational notion born out of economic greed exploitation and repression over 200 years old. It is time to let it die once and for all in our hearts and in our minds. To continue to speak [of] it as if it is real or has any merit only serves to limit the possibilities that human diversity has for today and for all our tomorrows.[9]

Yet multiracial ideology clearly requires the explicit acknowledgement of biological race in order to arrive at the alleged existence of multiracial individuals. This, again, is the internal contradiction of multiracial identity politics that cannot be denied. Even Douglass, after her eloquent argument against biological race, invokes race – and presumably hypodescent – when she says that "the blood running through the veins of black children cannot be distinguished from the blood running through the veins of other children no matter what color they are or what culture they eventually embrace."[10] The unanswered question, of course, is to what does she appeal in making the black children in her example black, if not biological race?

Moreover, as I have pointed out previously, even if one accepts for the sake of argument the idea of racial groups, it is a logical and biological impossibility to posit Afro-Americans as pure blacks, whatever "pure blacks" might be. The long history of Native American and European admixture in the ancestry of Afro-Americans, as well as their tremendous phenotypic diversity, militates against any conception of them as making up a monoracial group. Given the apparent acceptance of this reality by multiracial adherents, how does the ideology then account for its distinction between Afro-Americans and black/white multiracial individuals? It does so in one of two ways. First, it might follow the logic of Project RACE's California proposal by arbitrarily drawing an exclusionary line at great-grandparents. Second, it might assert that racial identity is subjective, such that multiracial Afro-Americans who identify as black are black and multiracial Afro-Americans who identify as multiracial are multiracial. These justifications illustrate the extent to which multiracial ideology – contrary to the statements its spokespeople make on behalf of the importance of accuracy, especially medically relevant accuracy – is in fact not concerned with accuracy but is instead driven by issues of self-esteem. When proper identification depends not on physical facts but on personal preference, the argument for accuracy is exposed as the red herring it is.

A brief return to the *Time* and *Newsweek* articles mentioned above will demonstrate the extent to which accuracy on the issue of race in general, and multirace in particular, is an illusion. Each piece contains a color graph illustrating the supposed rise of interracial marriages in the United States. Each article also graphs the percentage of black/white interracial marriages in America. A profound question must be asked about these graphs, a question the respective editors apparently failed to grasp. What exactly is an interracial marriage? What assumptions do people take for granted when categorizing this or that marriage as interracial? What the editors of *Time* and *Newsweek* did in their graphs was to deploy the racist apparatus of hypodescent by perpetuating the idea that the extremely diverse people of African descent in the United States, the vast majority of whom possess European and Native American ancestry as well, all constitute a single biological race. There is, after all, no way to have a black/white interracial marriage unless one of the partners is black.

Simplistic journalism is not the only party guilty of acquiescence to hypodescent on the question of interracial marriages. The Census Bureau's 1997 report on the Race and Ethnic Targeted Test (RAETT) claims:

> An increase in interracial marriages [has] led to a higher proportion of the population being of mixed race or ethnicity Census data show that there were about 1.5 million interracial couples in 1990. In all but 8 percent of these interracial couples, one spouse (or unmarried partner) was White. In 14 percent of interracial couples, the other spouse was Black . . . Census data also show that the number of children in interracial families increased from less than 500,000 in 1970 to about two million in 1990.[11]

It cannot be stated emphatically enough that the foregoing analysis is biological nonsense. It is not possible to arrive at the above numbers, or to conceptualize the relevant relationships in the 14 percent of interracial marriages in which one partner was Afro-American, without appealing to hypodescent. Consider one of the children mentioned in the last sentence of the above passage, a child having one white and one black parent, in accord with the race concept utilized by the author. Now let us consider as well an ancestor of the black parent – a white ancestor. In order for the Census Bureau statement to be valid, one would have to demonstrate that the child with one black and one white parent is multiracial in a way that the black parent, who also has black and white ancestry, is not. My argument throughout this book has been that such a demonstration is a logical and physical impossibility. The unchallenged acceptance of statements such as that of the Census Bureau, and of the *Time* and *Newsweek* graphs, regarding the rise of multiracials as a suddenly appearing, new population flies in the face of what we know to be the history of genetic mixture in the ancestries of African-descended people in the United States.

This idea of a suddenly rising multiracial population merely reinscribes the race fallacy while simultaneously upholding the racist notion of hypodescent. What does it mean, what sense does it make, when a person who possesses both European and African ancestries is categorized as black, as if the European component did not exist? What does it mean when such a person is said – because she procreated with a white partner – to have given birth to a multiracial child, when that child is no more the product of genetic mixture than she herself is? This kind of interpretation only means that a selective hypodescent has been deployed in the case of the parent, but not in the case of the child.

The assertion that multiracial births increased from fewer than 500,000 to about 2 million over several decades is a meaningless fantasy that ignores both past and present population mixture and internal miscegenation, as we know that at least 30 million Afro-Americans of mixed ancestry have been born in the United States in the past 100 years. Not only are Afro-Americans not "pure" blacks (whatever that might mean) but they are the most biologically heterogeneous population in the United States. If multiracialism were valid (which it most assuredly is not), then the 30 million Afro-Americans in the United States would already be multiracial, not black, and the idea of a suddenly rising multiracial population would therefore be moot.

People who accept the notion of a new and rising multiracial population merely reinforce hypodescent and the corrupt idea of white racial purity on which it is based. Americans will not advance from their backward belief in biological race if they validate the idea of multiracial people as being the products of differently raced parents, especially when the blackness of black parents is based on the racist fallacy of hypodescent. When a very dark-skinned person with tightly kinked hair and brown eyes and a very light-skinned person with naturally straight hair and blue eyes can each be uncritically considered the black partner in an interracial marriage, the concepts of race, interracial marriage and multiracial people are all exposed as absurd fantasies, divorced from biological reality.

The vast majority of Afro-Americans have individuals like the so-called black/white multiracial child of today in their ancestries, so the distinction between them and that child is illusory.

[. . .]

Multiracial ideology, like the monoracial ideology it depends on, is a false consciousness. The frustration its adherents feel would be better directed at criticizing the American racial paradigm itself rather than at attempting to modify the paradigm's configuration. A modified paradigm, one containing a multiracial category, would be as fallacious as one without a multiracial category. As long as the idea of race has legitimacy, and as long as the racial hierarchy remains undisturbed, nothing will really change.

Study probes

1   Why does Spencer make a distinction between 'colour blindness' and 'moving beyond race'?
2   What reasons does the author give for his opposition to the inclusion of a 'multiracial' Census category? Compare these to Nash's in the previous extract.
3   On what basis is 'multiracial' ideology a form of 'false consciousness'? How does Spencer's historically informed critique of the socially designated 'monoracial' status of multigenerational 'multiracial' African Americans support this argument?

Notes

1   Quoted in Janita Poe, "Woods Spotlights Multiracial Identity," *Chicago Tribune*, April 21, 1997, sec. 2, 2.
2   Quoted in Jeffry Scott, "Race, Labels, and Identity," *Atlanta Journal Constitution*, May 6, 1997, D1.
3   Thomas Petri, press release, April 23, 1997 ⟨http://www.house.gov/petri/press/census.htm⟩. Petri's H.R. 830 never received floor action in the House and was not passed by the 105th Congress. The identical fate had previously befallen the same bill, which Petri had introduced as H.R. 3920 in the 104th Congress.
4   Jack E. White, " 'I'm Just Who I Am,' " *Time*, May 5, 1997, 32–33.
5   John Leland and Gregory Beals, "In Living Colors," *Newsweek*, May 5, 1997, 58–59.
6   The *Time* and *Newsweek* articles each contain two color graphs as well as numerous photographs.
7   I, as well as others, have debated these very issues with Ramona Douglass, Susan Graham, and Carlos Fernández on the Interracial Individuals Discussion List, and I feel confident that no current leader of a legitimate multiracial organization would assert directly that biological race exists. This is quite separate from the fact that the multiracial ideology these leaders espouse, absolutely requires their acceptance of biological race at some level, again illustrating that multiracial advocacy is an inherently contradictory enterprise.
8   Carlos Fernández, online posting, Interracial Individuals Discussion List, January 22, 1996 [ii@gnu.ai.mit.edu].
9   House Subcommittee on Government Management, Information, and Technology, Committee on Government Reform and Oversight, *Hearings on Federal Measures of Race and Ethnicity and the Implications for the 2000 Census*, testimony by Ramona Douglass on May 22, 1997, 105th Cong., 1st Sess., April 23, May 22, and July 25, 1997, 385.

10   Ibid., 386.

11   Department of Commerce, Bureau of the Census, *Results of the 1996 Race and Ethnie Targeted Test*, Population Division Working Paper no. 18 (Washington, D.C., May 1997), 1–3.

Chapter 30

Elizabeth M. Grieco and Rachel C. Cassidy

OVERVIEW OF RACE AND HISPANIC ORIGIN: CENSUS 2000 BRIEF

http://www.census.gov/population/www/cen2000/briefs.html.

EVERY CENSUS MUST ADAPT to the decade in which it is administered. New technologies emerge and change the way the US Census Bureau collects and processes data. More importantly, changing lifestyles and emerging sensitivities among the people of the United States necessitate modifications to the questions that are asked. One of the most important changes for Census 2000 was the revision of the questions on race and Hispanic origin to better reflect the country's growing diversity.

This report, part of a series that analyzes population and housing data collected from Census 2000, provides a portrait of race and Hispanic origin in the United States and discusses their distributions at the national level. It is based on the Census 2000 Redistricting (Public Law 94–171) Summary File, which is among the first Census 2000 data products to be released and is used by each state to draw boundaries for legislative districts.[1]

Understanding race and Hispanic origin data from Census 2000

The 1990 census questions on race and Hispanic origin were changed for Census 2000

The federal government considers race and Hispanic origin to be two separate and distinct concepts. For Census 2000, the questions on race and Hispanic origin were asked of every individual living in the United States. The question on Hispanic origin asked respondents if they were Spanish, Hispanic, or Latino.[2] The question on race asked respondents to report the race or races they considered themselves to be. Both questions are based on self-identification.

The question on Hispanic origin for Census 2000 was similar to the 1990 census question, except for its placement on the questionnaire. For Census 2000, the question on Hispanic origin was asked directly before the question on race. For the 1990 census, the order was reversed – the question on race preceded questions on age and marital status, which were followed by the question on Hispanic origin.

The question on race for Census 2000 was different from the one for the 1990 census in several ways. Most significantly, respondents were given the option of selecting one or more race categories to indicate their racial identities.[3]

Because of these changes, the Census 2000 data on race are not directly comparable with data from the 1990 census or earlier censuses. Caution must be used when interpreting changes in the racial composition of the US population over time.

Census 2000 used established federal guidelines to collect and present data on race and Hispanic origin

Census 2000 adheres to the federal standards for collecting and presenting data on race and Hispanic origin as established by the Office of Management and Budget (OMB) in October 1997.

The OMB defines Hispanic or Latino as "a person of Cuban, Mexican, Puerto Rican, South or Central American, or other Spanish culture or origin regardless of race." In data collection and presentation, federal agencies are required to use a minimum of two ethnicities: "Hispanic or Latino" and "Not Hispanic or Latino."

Starting with Census 2000, the OMB requires federal agencies to use a minimum of five race categories:

- White;
- Black or African American;
- American Indian or Alaska Native;
- Asian; and
- Native Hawaiian or Other Pacific Islander

For respondents unable to identify with any of these five race categories, the OMB approved including a sixth category – "Some other race" – on the Census 2000 questionnaire. The category Some other race is used in Census 2000 and a few other federal data collection activities. As discussed later, most respondents who reported Some other race are Hispanic. For definitions of the race categories used in Census 2000, see the box opposite.

The Census 2000 question on race included 15 separate response categories and three areas where respondents could write in a more specific race group (see

---

How are the race categories used in Census 2000 defined?

- "White" refers to people having origins in any of the original peoples of Europe, the Middle East, or North Africa. It includes people who indicated their race or races as "White" or wrote in entries such as Irish, German, Italian, Lebanese, Near Easterner, Arab, or Polish.
- "Black or African American" refers to people having origins in any of the Black racial groups of Africa. It includes people who indicated their race or races as "Black, African Am., or Negro," or wrote in entries such as African American, Afro American, Nigerian, or Haitian.
- "American Indian and Alaska Native" refers to people having origins in any of the original peoples of North and South America (including Central America), and who maintain tribal affiliation or community attachment. It includes people who indicated their race or races by marking this category or writing in their principal or enrolled tribe, such as Rosebud Sioux, Chippewa, or Navajo.
- "Asian" refers to people having origins in any of the original peoples of the Far East, Southeast Asia, or the Indian subcontinent. It includes people who indicated their race or races as "Asian Indian," "Chinese," "Filipino," "Korean," "Japanese," "Vietnamese," or "Other Asian," or wrote in entries such as Burmese, Hmong, Pakistani, or Thai.
- "Native Hawaiian and Other Pacific Islander" refers to people having origins in any of the original peoples of Hawaii, Guam, Samoa, or other Pacific Islands. It includes people who indicated their race or races as "Native Hawaiian," "Guamanian or Chamorro," "Samoan," or "Other Pacific Islander," or wrote in entries such as Tahitian, Mariana Islander, or Chuukese.
- "Some other race" was included in Census 2000 for respondents who were unable to identify with the five Office of Management and Budget race categories. Respondents who provided write-in entries such as Moroccan, South African, Belizean, or a Hispanic origin (for example, Mexican, Puerto Rican, or Cuban) are included in the Some other race category.

Figure 30.1). The response categories and write-in answers can be combined to create the five minimum OMB race categories plus Some other race. In addition to White, Black or African American, American Indian and Alaska Native, and Some other race, seven of the 15 response categories are Asian and four are Native Hawaiian and Other Pacific Islander.

Hispanic origin in Census 2000

According to Census 2000, 281.4 million people resided in the United States, and 35.3 million, or about 13 percent, were Latino (see Table 30.1). The remaining 246.1 million people, or 87 percent, were not Hispanic.

→ **NOTE: Please answer BOTH Questions 5 and 6.**

5. **Is this person Spanish/Hispanic/Latino?** *Mark* ☒ *the "No" box if **not** Spanish/Hispanic/Latino.*

☐ **No**, not Spanish/Hispanic/Latino   ☐ Yes, Puerto Rican
☐ Yes, Mexican, Mexican Am., Chicano   ☐ Yes, Cuban
☐ Yes, other Spanish/Hispanic/Latino – *Print group.* ⌐

6. **What is the person's race?** *Mark* ☒ ***one or more races** to indicate what this person considers himself/herself to be.*

☐ White
☐ Black, African Am., or Negro
☐ American Indian or Alaska Native – *Print name of enrolled or principal tribe.* ⌐

☐ Asian Indian   ☐ Japanese   ☐ Native Hawaiian
☐ Chinese   ☐ Korean   ☐ Guamanian or Chamorro
☐ Filipino   ☐ Vietnamese   ☐ Samoan
☐ Other Asian – *Print race.* ⌐   ☐ Other Pacific Islander – *Print race.* ⌐

☐ Some other race – *Print race.* ⌐

Figure 30.1 Reproduction of questions on race and Hispanic origin from Census 2000
Source: US Census Bureau, Census 2000 questionnaire

Race in Census 2000

The race data collected by Census 2000 can be collapsed into seven categories

People who responded to the question on race by indicating only one race are referred to as the race *alone* population, or the group that reported[4] *only one* race category. Six categories make up this population:

- White *alone*;
- Black or African American *alone*;
- American Indian and Alaska Native *alone*;
- Asian *alone*;
- Native Hawaiian and Other Pacific Islander *alone*; and
- Some other race *alone*.

Individuals who chose more than one of the six race categories are referred to as the *Two or more races* population, or as the group that reported *more than one* race.

Table 30.1 Population by race and Hispanic origin for the USA: 2000

Race and Hispanic or Latino	Number	Percent of total population
Race		
Total population	281,421,906	100.0
One race	274,595,678	97.6
White	211,460,626	75.1
Black or African American	34,658,190	12.3
American Indian and Alaska Native	2,475,956	0.9
Asian	10,242,998	3.6
Native Hawaiian and Other Pacific Islander	398,835	0.1
Some other race	15,359,073	5.5
Two or more races	6,826,228	2.4
Hispanic or Latino		
Total population	281,421,906	100.0
Hispanic or Latino	35,305,818	12.5
Nol Hispanic or Latino	246,116,088	87.5

Source: US Census Bureau, Census 2000 Redistricting (Public Law 94.171) Summary File, Tables PL1 and PL2.

All respondents who indicated more than one race can be collapsed into the *Two or more races* category, which combined with the six *alone* categories, yields seven mutually exclusive and exhaustive categories. Thus, the six race *alone* categories and the *Two or more races* categories sum to the total population.

The overwhelming majority of the US population reported only one race

In Census 2000, nearly 98 percent of all respondents reported only one race (see Table 30.1). The largest group reported White alone, accounting for 75 percent of all people living in the United States. The Black or African American alone population represented 12 percent of the total. Just under 1 percent of all respondents indicated only American Indian and Alaska Native. Approximately 4 percent of all respondents indicated only Asian. The smallest race group was the Native Hawaiian and Other Pacific Islander alone population, representing 0.1 percent of the total population. The remainder of the "one race" respondents – 5.5 percent of all respondents – indicated only Some other race.[5]

Only 2.4 percent of all respondents reported two or more races

The Two or more races category represents all respondents who reported more than one race. The six race categories of Census 2000 can be put together in 57 possible combinations of two, three, four, five, or six races (see Table 30.2).

Table 30.2 Population of two or more races, including all combinations, for the USA: 2000

Race	Number	Percent of two or more races population
Two or more races	6,826,228	100.0
Two races	6,368,075	93.3
White; Black or African American	784,764	11.5
White; American Indian and Alaska Native	1,082,683	15.9
White; Asian	868,395	12.7
White; Native Hawaiian and Other Pacific Islander	112,964	1.7
White; Some other race	2,206,251	32.3
Black or African American; American Indian and Alaska Native	182,494	2.7
Black or African American; Asian	106,782	1.6
Black or African American; Native Hawaiian and Other Pacific Islander	29,876	0.4
Black or African American; Some other race	417,249	6.1
American Indian and Alaska Native; Asian	52,429	0.8
American Indian and Alaska Native; Native Hawaiian and Other Pacific Islander	7,328	0.1
American Indian and Alaska Native; Some other race	93,842	1.4
Asian; Native Hawaiian and Other Pacific Islander	138,802	2.0
Asian; Some other race	249,108	3.6
Native Hawaiian and Other Pacific Islander, Some other race	35,108	0.5
Three races	410,285	6.0
White; Black or African American, American Indian and Alaska Native	112,207	1.6
White; Black or African American; Asian	21,166	0.3
White; Black or African American; Native Hawaiian and Other Pacific Islander	2,938	–
White, Black or African American; Some other race	43,172	0.6
White; American Indian and Alaska Native; Asian	23,766	0.3
White; American Indian and Alaska Native; Native Hawaiian and Other Pacific Islander	4,843	0.1
White; American Indian and Alaska Native, Some other race	29,095	0.4
White; Asian, Native Hawaiian and Other Pacific Islander	89,611	1.3
White; Asian; Some other race	34,962	0.5
White; Native Hawaiian and Other Pacific Islander; Some other race	8,364	0.1

Black or African American; American Indian and Alaska Native; Asian	5,798	0.1
Black or African American; American Indian and Alaska Native; Native Hawaiian and Other Pacific Islander	998	–
Black or African American; American Indian and Alaska Native; Some other race	7,023	0.1
Black or African American; Asian; Native Hawaiian and Other Pacific Islander	5,309	0.1
Black or African American; Asian; Some other race	8,069	0.1
Black or African American; Native Hawaiian and Pacific Islander, Some other race	2,167	–
American Indian and Alaska Native; Asian; Native Hawaiian and Other Pacific Islander	3,063	–
American Indian and Alaska Native; Asian; Some other race	2,544	–
American Indian and Alaska Native; Native Hawaiian and Other Pacific Islander, Some other race	586	–
Asian; Native Hawaiian and Other Pacific Islander, Some other race	4,604	0.1
Four races	**38,408**	**0.6**
White; Black or African American; American Indian and Alaska Native; Asian	10,672	0.2
White; Black or African American; American Indian and Alaska Native; Native Hawaiian and Other Pacific Islander	988	–
White; Black or African American; American Indian and Alaska Native; Some other race	4,645	0.1
White; Black or African American; Asian; Native Hawaiian and Other Pacific Islander	2,128	–
White; Black or African American; Asian; Some other race	1,376	–
White; Black or African American; Native Hawaiian and Other Pacific Islander; Some other race	325	–
White; American Indian and Alaska Native, Asian, Native Hawaiian and Other Pacific Islander	6,450	0.1
White; American Indian and Alaska Native, Asian, Some other race	1.099	–
White; American Indian and Alaska Native, Native Hawaiian and Other Pacific Islander; Some other race	309	–

Table 30.2 Continued

White; Asian; Native Hawaiian and Other Pacific Islander; Some other race	7,932	0.1
Black or African American; American Indian and Alaska Native; Asian; Native Hawaiian and Other Pacific Islander	750	–
Black or African American; American Indian and Alaska Native, Asian; Some other race	334	–
Black or African American; American Indian and Alaska Native; Native Hawaiian and Other Pacific Islander; Some other race	111	–
Black or African American; Asian, Native Hawaiian and Other Pacific Islander; Some other race	1,082	–
American Indian and Alaska Native; Asian, Native Hawaiian and Other Pacific Islander; Some other race	207	–
Five races	**8,637**	**0.1**
White; Black or African American; American Indian and Alaska Native; Asian; Native Hawaiian and Other Pacific Islander	6,611	0.1
White; Black or African American; American Indian and Alaska Native, Asian; Some other race	724	–
White; Black or African American; American Indian and Alaska Native, Native Hawaiian and Other Pacific Islander, Some other race	68	–
White, Black or African American; Asian, Native Hawaiian and Other Pacific Islander, Some other race	379	–
White; American Indian and Alaska Native, Asian; Native Hawaiian and Other Pacific Islander; Some other race	639	–
Black or African American; American Indian and Alaska Native; Asian, Native Hawaiian and Other Pacific Islander, Some other race	216	–
Six races	**823**	**–**
White; Black or African American; American Indian and Alaska Native; Asian; Native Hawaiian and Other Pacific Islander; Some other race	823	–

Source: US Census Bureau, Census 2000 Redistricting (Public Law 94–171) Summary File. Table PL1.
Note: Percentage rounds to 0.0.

Less than 3 percent of the total population reported more than one race. Of the 6.8 million respondents who reported two or more races, 93 percent reported exactly two. The most common combination was "White *and* Some other race," representing 32 percent of the Two or more races population.[6] This was followed by "White *and* American Indian and Alaska Native," representing 16 percent. "White *and* Asian," representing 13 percent, and "White *and* Black or African American," representing 11 percent. Of all respondents reporting exactly two races, 47 percent included Some other race as one of the two. Of all respondents who reported more than one race, 7 percent indicated three or more. Most of these (90 percent) reported three races.

The office of management and budget identified four combinations of two races for civil rights monitoring and enforcement

In March 2000, the OMB established guidelines for the aggregation and allocation of race responses from Census 2000 for use in civil rights monitoring and enforcement. These guidelines included the five OMB race categories and identified four specific combinations of two races.[7] These four OMB race combinations, which were the largest combinations reported in recent research, are:

- "White *and* American Indian and Alaska Native"
- "White *and* Asian"
- "White *and* Black or African American"
- "Black or African American *and* American Indian and Alaska Native."

In fact, these four combinations are the largest categories, when combinations that include Some other race are excluded. Combined, these four combinations accounted for 43 percent of the population reporting Two or more races (see Figure 30.2) and 1 percent of the total population.

The maximum number of people reporting a particular race is reflected in the race alone or in combination category

Respondents who reported only one race together with those who reported that same race plus one or more other races are combined to create the race *alone or in combination* categories. For example, the White *alone or in combination* group consists of those respondents who reported White alone plus those who reported White combined with one or more other race groups, such as "White *and* Black or African American," or "White *and* Asian *and* American Indian and Alaska Native." Another way to think of the group who reported White alone or in combination is as the total number of people who identified entirely or partially as White. This group is also described as people who reported White, whether or not they reported any other races.

Just as there are six race alone categories, there are six race alone or in combination categories:

- White *alone or in combination*;
- Black or African American *alone or in combination*;
- American Indian and Alaska Native *alone or in combination*;
- Asian *alone or in combination*;
- Native Hawaiian and Other Pacific Islander *alone or in combination*; and
- Some other race *alone or in combination*.

The *alone or in combination* categories are tallies of *responses* rather than *respondents*. That is, the alone or in combination categories are not mutually exclusive. Individuals who reported two races were counted in two separate and distinct alone or in combination race categories, while those who reported three races were counted in three categories, and so on. For example, a respondent who indicated "White **and** Black or African American" was counted in the White alone or in combination category as well as in the Black or African American alone or in combination category. Consequently, the sum of all alone or in combination categories equals the number of races reported (i.e., responses), which exceeds the total population (see Table 30.3).

In Census 2000, the population indicating their race as White, either alone or with at least one other race, was the largest of all the alone or in combination categories and represented over three-fourths (77 percent) of the total population. The next two largest response categories were the Black or African American alone or in combination group, which represented 13 percent of the total population, and the Some other race alone or in combination category, which represented 7 percent of the population.

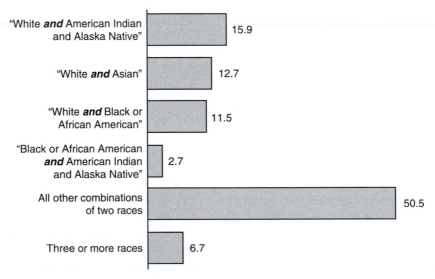

Figure 30.2 Percent distribution of population of two or more races, showing the four two race combinations identified by the Office of Management and Budget: 2000
Source: US Census Bureau, Census 2000 Redistricting (Public Law 94.17 1) Summary File, Table PL1.
Note: Population reporting two or more races was 2.4 percent of the total population

Table 30.3 Responses to the question on race by the alone or in combination categories for the USA: 2000

Race	Number of responses	Responses as percent of total population	Responses as percent of total responses
All race categories alone or in combination with one or more other races	288,764,438	102.6	100.0
White alone or in combination	216,930,975	77.1	75.1
Black or African American alone or in combination	36,419,434	12.9	12.6
American Indian and Alaska Native alone or in combination	4,119,301	1.5	1.4
Asian alone or in combination	11,898,828	4.2	4.1
Native Hawaiian and Other Pacific Islander alone or in combination	874,414	0.3	0.3
Some other race alone or in combination	18,521,486	6.6	6.4

Source: US Census Bureau, Census 2000 Redistricting (Public Law 94–171) Summary File, Table PL1.
Note: The total population is equal to the number of respondents. In Census 2000, there were 281,421,906 respondents. The total of all race categories alone or in combination with one or more other races is equal to the number of responses, therefore, it adds to more than the total population.

The Asian alone or in combination group represented 4.2 percent. The American Indian and Alaska Native alone or in combination group represented 1.5 percent. The Native Hawaiian alone or in combination group was the smallest and represented 0.3 percent of the total population.

Discussion of specific race groups in Census 2000

The next six sections discuss the results of Census 2000 for the White, Black or African American, American Indian and Alaska Native, Asian, Native Hawaiian and Pacific Islander, and Some other race populations. Numbers and percentages are presented in three ways: (1) for the race alone category, (2) for the race in combination category, and (3) for the race alone or in combination category.

With the exception of the section on the Some other race population, each of the following discussions is restricted to the five race categories defined by the Office of Management and Budget. Within the tables presented in these five sections, combinations of the OMB race categories with the Some other race category are not shown separately but are included in the "All other combin-ations" category. Because the Some other race category is not a standard OMB race, the data for the Some other race category, including combinations with the five standard OMB groups, are presented and discussed in a separate section.

The white population

Table 30.4 shows the number and percentage of respondents to Census 2000 who reported only White, as well as those who reported White and at least one other race.

Approximately 211.5 million people, or 75 percent of the total population, reported only White. An additional 5.5 million people reported White and at least one other race. Within this group, the most common OMB combinations were "White *and* American Indian and Alaska Native" (20 percent of the popula-tion reporting White and one or more other races), followed by "White *and* Asian" (16 percent), and "White *and* Black or African American" (14 percent). Approximately 216.9 million people, or 77 percent of the population, reported White alone or in combination with one or more other races.

The Black or African-American population

Table 30.5 shows the number and percentage of respondents to Census 2000 who reported only Black or African American, as well as those who reported Black or African American and at least one other race.

Table **30.4** White population for the USA: 2000

Race	Number	Percent of total population
Total population	281,421,906	100.0
White alone	211,460,626	75.1
White in combination with one or more other races	5,470,349	1.9
White, American Indian and Alaska Native	1,082,683	0.4
White, Asian	868,395	0.3
White, Black or African American	784,764	0.3
White, Native Hawaiian and Other Pacific Islander	112,964	–
All other combinations including White	2,621,543	0.9
White alone or in combination with one or more other races	216,930,975	77.1

Source: US Census Bureau, Census 2000 Redistricting (Public Law 94–171) Summary File, Table PL1.
Note: Percentage rounds to 0.0.

Table 30.5 Black or African American population for the USA: 2000

Race	Number	Percent of total population
Total population	281,421,906	100.0
Black or African American alone	34,658,190	12.3
Black or African American in combination with one or more other races	1,761,244	0.6
Black or African American; White	784,764	0.3
Black or African American; American Indian and Alaska Native	182,494	0.1
Black or African American, White, American Indian and Alaska Native	112,207	–
Black or African American, Asian	106,782	–
All other combinations including Black or African American	574,997	0.2
Black or African American alone or in combination with one or more other races	36,419,434	12.9

Source: US Census Bureau, Census 2000 Redistricting (Public Law 94–171) Summary File, Table PL1.
Note: Percentage rounds to 0.0.

Approximately 34.7 million people, or 12 percent of the total population, reported only Black or African American. An additional 1.8 million people reported Black or African American and at least one other race. Within this group, the most common OMB combinations were "Black or African American *and* White" (45 percent of the population reporting Black or African American and one or more other races), followed by "Black or African American *and* American Indian and Alaska Native" (10 percent), and "Black or African American *and* White *and* American Indian and Alaska Native" (6 percent). Approximately 36.4 million people, or 13 percent of the population, reported Black or African American alone or in combination with one or more other races.

The American Indian and Alaska Native population

Table 30.6 shows the number and percentage of respondents to Census 2000 who reported only American Indian and Alaska Native, as well as those who reported American Indian and Alaska Native and at least one other race.

Approximately 2.5 million people, or 0.9 percent of the total population, reported only American Indian and Alaska Native. An additional 1.6 million people reported American Indian and Alaska Native and at least one other race. Within this group, the most common OMB combinations were "American Indian and Alaska Native *and* White" (66 percent of the population reporting American Indian and Alaska Native and one or more other races), followed by

Table 30.6 American Indian and Alaska Native population for the USA: 2000

Race	Number	Percent of total population
Total population	281,421,906	100.0
American Indian and Alaska Native alone	2,475,956	0.9
American Indian and Alaska Native in combination with one or more other races	1,643,345	0.6
American Indian and Alaska Native, White	1,082,683	0.4
American Indian and Alaska Native, Black or African American	182,494	0.1
American Indian and Alaska Native, White; Black or African American	112,207	–
American Indian and Alaska Native, Asian	52,429	–
All other combinations including American Indian and Alaska Native	213,532	0.1
American Indian and Alaska Native alone or in combination with one or more other races	4,119,301	1.5

Source: US Census Bureau, Census 2000 Redistricting (Public Law 94–171) Summary File, Table PL1.
Note: Percentage rounds to 0.0.

"American Indian and Alaska Native *and* Black or African American" (11 percent), and "American Indian and Alaska Native *and* White *and* Black or African American" (7 percent). Approximately 4.1 million people, or 1.5 percent of the population, reported American Indian and Alaska Native alone or in combination with one or more other races.[8]

The Asian population

Table 30.7 shows the number and percentage of respondents to Census 2000 who reported only Asian, as well as those who reported Asian and at least one other race.

Approximately 10.2 million people, or 3.6 percent of the total population, reported only Asian. An additional 1.7 million people reported Asian and at least one other race. Within this group, the most common OMB combinations were "Asian *and* White" (52 percent of the population reporting Asian and one or more other races), followed by "Asian *and* Native Hawaiian and Other Pacific Islander" (8 percent), and "Asian *and* Black or African American" (6 percent). Approximately 11.9 million people, or 4.2 percent of the population, reported Asian alone or in combination with one or more other races.[9]

Table 30.7 Asian Population for the USA: 2000

Race	Number	Percent of total population
Total population	281,421,906	100.0
Asian alone	10,242,998	3.6
Asian in combination with one or more other races	1,655,830	0.6
Asian, White	868,395	0.3
Asian Native Hawaiian and Other Pacific Islander	138,802	–
Asian Black or African American	106,782	–
Asian, Native Hawaiian and Other Pacific Islander, White	89,611	–
All other combinations including Asian	452,240	0.2
Asian alone or in combination with one or more other races	11,898,828	4.2

Source: US Census Bureau. Census 2000 Redistricting (Public Law 94–171) Summary File, Table PL1.
Note: Percentage rounds to 0.0.

The native Hawaiian and other Pacific Islander population

Table 30.8 shows the number and percentage of respondents to Census 2000 who reported only Native Hawaiian and Other Pacific Islander as well as those who reported Native Hawaiian and Other Pacific Islander and at least one other race.

Approximately 399,000 people, or 0.1 percent of the total population, reported only Native Hawaiian and Other Pacific Islander. An additional 476,000 people reported Native Hawaiian and Other Pacific Islander and at least one other race.[10] Within this group, the most common combinations were "Native Hawaiian and Other Pacific Islander *and* Asian" (29 percent of the population reporting Native Hawaiian and Other Pacific Islander and one or more other races), followed by "Native Hawaiian and Other Pacific Islander *and* White" (24 percent), and "Native Hawaiian and Other Pacific Islander *and* Asian *and* White" (19 percent). Approximately 874,000 people, or 0.3 percent of the population, reported Native Hawaiian and Other Pacific Islander alone or in combination with one or more other races.

The Some other race population

Table 30.9 shows the number and percentage of respondents to Census 2000 who reported only Some other race as well as those who reported Some other race and at least one other race.

Approximately 15.4 million people, or about 5 percent of the total population, reported only Some other race. An additional 3.2 million people reported

Table 30.8 Native Hawaiian and other Pacific Islander population for the USA: 2000

Race	Number	Percent of total population
Total population	281,421,906	100.0
Native Hawaiian and Other Pacific Islander alone	398,835	0.1
Native Hawaiian and Other Pacific Islander in combination with one or more other races	475,579	0.2
Native Hawaiian and Other Pacific Islander; Asian	138,802	–
Native Hawaiian and Other Pacific Islander; White	112,964	–
Native Hawaiian and Other Pacific Islander, Asian, White	89,611	–
Native Hawaiian and Other Pacific Islander, Black or African American	29,876	–
All other combinations including Native Hawaiian and Other Pacific Islander	104,326	–
Native Hawaiian and Other Pacific Islander alone or in combination with one or more other races	874,414	0.3

Source: US Census Bureau, Census 2000 Redistricting (Public Law 94–171) Summary File, Table PL1.
Note: Percentage rounds to 0.0.

Table 30.9 Some other race population for the USA: 2000

Race	Number	Percent of total population
Total population	281,421,906	100.0
Some other race alone	15,359,073	5.5
Some other race in combination with one or more other races	3,162,413	1.1
Some other race, White	2,206,251	0.8
Some other race. Black or African American	417,249	0.1
Some other race, Asian	249,108	0.1
Some other race, American Indian and Alaska Native	93,842	–
All other combinations including Some other race	195,963	0.1
Some other race alone or in combination with one or more other races	18,521,486	6.6

Source: US Census Bureau, Census 2000 Redistricting (Public Law 94–171) Summary File, Table PL1.
Note: Percentage rounds to 0.0.

Some other race and at least one other race. Within this group, the most common combinations were "Some other race *and* White" (70 percent of the population reporting Some other race and one or more other races), followed by "Some other race *and* Black or African American" (13 percent), and "Some other race *and* Asian" (8 percent). Approximately 18.5 million people, or 7 percent of the total population, reported Some other race alone or in combination with one or more other races.

Hispanic origin by race in Census 2000

Nine out of ten Hispanics reported white alone or some other race alone

Nearly half (48 percent) of Hispanics reported only White, while approximately 42 percent reported only Some other race, when responding to the question on race (see Table 30.10). Less than 4 percent of Latinos reported Black or African American alone, American Indian and Alaska Native alone, Asian alone, or Native Hawaiian and Other Pacific Islander alone. In contrast, 79 percent of the non-Hispanic population reported only White and 0.2 percent reported only Some other race.

About 19 percent of all non-Hispanics reported only one of the remaining race categories. Of all race and Hispanic origin combinations,

Table **30.10** Hispanic and not Hispanic population by race for the USA: 2000

Race	Number	Hispanic or Latino		Number	Not Hispanic or Latino	
		Percent of Hispanic population	Percent of total population		Percent of Non-Hispanic population	Percent of total population
Total	35,305,816	100.0	12.5	246,116,088	100.0	87.5
One race	33,081,736	93.7	11.8	241,513,942	98.1	85.8
White	16,907,852	47.9	6.0	194,552,774	79.1	69.1
Black or African American	710,353	2.0	0.3	33,947,837	13.8	12.1
American Indian and Alaska Native	407,073	1.2	0.1	2,068,883	0.8	0.7
Asian	119,829	0.3	–	10,123,169	4.1	3.6
Native Hawaiian and Other Pacific Islander	45,326	0.1	–	353,509	0.1	0.1
Some other race	14,891,303	42.2	5.3	467,770	0.2	0.2
Two or more races	2,224,082	6.3	0.8	4,602,146	1.9	1.6

Source: US Census Bureau, Census 2000 Redistricting (Public Law 94–171) Summary File, Tables PL1 and PL2.
Note: Percentage rounds to 0.0.

Table 30.11 Some other race population by Hispanic origin for the USA: 2000

Hispanic or Latino	Some other race alone		Some other race alone or in combination with one or more other races		Some other race alone or in combination with one or more other races	
	Number	%	Number	%	Number	%
Total	15,359,073	100.0	3,162,413	100.0	18,521,486	100.00
Hispanic or Latino	14,891,303	97.0	1,859,538	58.8	16,750,841	90.4
Not Hispanic or Latino	467,770	3.0	1,302,875	41.2	1,770,645	9.6

Source: US Census Bureau, Census 2000 Redistricting (Public Law 94–171) Summary File, Tables PL1 and PL2.

the group reporting as only White and non-Hispanic was the largest, representing 69 percent of the total population.

Approximately 6 percent of all Hispanics reported two or more races, compared with just under 2 percent of non-Hispanics. Among the 2.2 million Latinos who reported more than one race, 1.8 million (81 percent) reported only two races, one of which was Some other race. Of the 6.8 million respondents reporting two or more races, nearly one third (2.2 million or 33 percent) were Hispanic.

Study probes

1   What are the five main Office of Management and Budget (OMB) 'racial' categories used in the United States Census 2000 and how are they defined?
2   Summarize the data on 'race' collected by Census 2000.
3   Why was an additional sixth category added? In the analysed data, why is a distinction made between 'race alone' responses and 'two or more races' responses? Compare the findings of these two sets of responses.
4   Of the 'two or more races' responses, which four combinations were selected for civil rights monitoring and enforcement?
5   Go back to the extracts by Senna, Jones, Nash and Spencer. How do the actual findings of the Census 2000 either support or challenge their arguments?

Notes

1   This report includes data for 50 states and the District of Columbia but not Puerto Rico. The Census 2000 Redistricting (Public Law 94–171) Summary File will be released on a state-by-state basis in March 2001. It does not contain data for specific Hispanic origin groups (for example Mexican or Puerto Rican) or specific race groups or tribes (for example, Chinese. Samoan or Cherokee), and therefore these specific groups are not discussed in this report.

2   Hispanics may be of any race. The terms 'Hispanic' and 'Latino' are used interchangeably in this report.

3   Other changes included terminology and formatting changes, such as spelling out 'American' instead of 'Amer' for the American Indian and Alaska Native category and adding 'Native' to the Hawaiian response category. In the layout of the Census 2000 questionnaire the Asian response categories were alphabetized and grouped together, as were the Pacific Islander categories after the Native Hawaiian category. The three separate American Indian and Alaska Native identifiers in the 1990 census (i.e., Indian (Amer) Eskimo, and Aleut) were combined into a single identifier in Census 2000. Also American Indians and Alaska Natives could report more than one tribe.

4   In this report the term 'reported' is used to refer to the response provided by respondents as well as responses assigned during the editing and imputation processes.

5   The Some other race alone category consists predominantly (97.0 percent) of people of Hispanic origin, and is not a standard OMB race category.

6   The Two or more races categories are denoted by quotations around the combinations with the conjunction *and* in bold and italicized print to indicate the separate race groups that comprise the particular combination.

7   *Guidance on Aggregation and Allocation of Data on Race for Use in Civil Rights Monitoring and Enforcement.* Office of Management and Budget Bulletin Number 00.02, March 9, 2000. Also included in the guidelines was the inclusion of any multiple race combinations [excluding Some other race] that comprise more than 1 percent of the population of interest. For more information, see www.whitehouse gov/omb/bulletins/ 1:00.02.html

8   The size of the American Indian and Alaska Native population – alone or in combination – is just one dimension of this population covered by Census 2000. The wide diversity of the specific American Indian and Alaska Native populations delineated by Census 2000 will be discussed in a future report.

9   The size of the Asian population – alone or in combination – is just one dimension of this population covered by Census 2000. The wide diversity of the specific Asian populations delineated by Census 2000 will be discussed in a future report.

10   The size of the Native Hawaiian and Other Pacific Islander population – alone or in combination – is just one dimension of this population covered by Census 2000. The wide diversity of the specific Native Hawaiian and Other Pacific Islander populations delineated by Census 2000 will be discussed in a future report.

Chapter 31

Charlie Owen

'MIXED RACE' IN OFFICIAL STATISTICS

From D. Parker and M. Song *Rethinking 'Mixed Race'* (2001). London: Pluto Press, pp. 146–151.

The 2001 Census question

THE QUESTION ON ETHNICITY for the 2001 census was published in the 1999 census White Paper and is shown in Figure 31.1. (This is the question for England and Wales: different questions are to be asked in Scotland and Northern Ireland.) The 'Mixed' category is one of five possible boxes respondents can tick (along with 'White', 'Asian or Asian British', 'Black or Black British', and 'Chinese or Other ethnic group').

Interestingly, for the question, 'What is your ethnic group?', Figure 31.1 shows that the box for 'White' is at the top, immediately followed by the 'Mixed' category, then by 'Asian or Asian British', then 'Black or Black British', and finally, 'Chinese or Other ethnic group'. Given the relatively small numbers of the mixed population in Britain, it seems significant, somehow, that the 'Mixed' category is the one that follows the category at the top – 'White'. The 'Mixed' category itself contains four subheadings ('White and Black Caribbean', 'White and Black African', 'White and Asian', and 'Any other mixed background – please describe'). Note that 'White and Chinese' is not an option – unlike the case for Black and Asian groups.

The introduction of the 'Mixed' category is bound to give more accurate information on the mixed race populations than did the 1991 census. The British census will, therefore, officially validate the notion of mixed race and the existence of mixed race people in British society. However, such orderings and omissions are not explained by the Office of National Statistics, and they raise questions about the rationale behind the design of the question on ethnic origin.

What is your ethnic group?

Choose one section from (a) to (e) then tick the appropriate box to indicate your cultural background.

(a)   **White**

☐   British

☐   Irish

☐   Any other White background. Please describe:

....

(b)   **Mixed**

☐   White and Black Caribbean

☐   White and Black African

☐   White and Asian

☐   Any other mixed background. Please describe:

....

(c)   **Asian or Asian British**

☐   Indian

☐   Pakistani

☐   Bangladeshi

☐   Any other Asian background. Please describe:

....

(d)   **Black or Black British**

☐   Caribbean

☐   African

☐   Any other Black background. Please describe:

....

(e)   **Chinese or Other ethnic group**

☐   Chinese

☐   Any other. Please describe:

....

Figure 31.1 Ethnic question for 2001 census for England and Wales
Source: The 2001 Census of Population (1999), Cmnd 4253

The preparations for the 1991 census explicitly rejected a Mixed category, yet just 10 years later such a category appears on the census form. How did this reversal come about? As can be seen from the discussion above, very little information on the mixed parentage population could be obtained from the 1991 census. Furthermore, what data could be obtained were only arrived at by the ONS second-guessing what people had meant when they gave a written description. This was clearly unsatisfactory. Given the significance of this group – sociologically, psychologically and demographically – it was concluded that better information was needed from the 2001 census.

In an ONS report of a consultation on the ethnic group question, a number of factors were identified as indicating the need for an explicit 'Mixed' category. These included demand from the mixed race population, the growing size of the group, and users' needs. According to this report:

> The 'mixed group', known from the full census classification and the Labour Force Survey to be one of the largest ethnic groups, is regarded as a strong candidate for inclusion, based on the group's happiness to describe themselves as such and the increasing numbers in this group are not currently met by identification through free-text responses.[1]

The consultation found that people of mixed parentage wanted to be able to identify themselves as such. This positive identification with being mixed had already been found in a study of (black and white) mixed race adolescents in London schools,[2] and had contrasted with earlier studies, particularly from the USA, which had suggested that people of mixed parentage would necessarily experience problematic and painful identities.

An issue discussed in the ONS consultation report was how many categories to include. Would it be sufficient to have a single category of 'Mixed', or was more detail required?:

> Discussion took place on the issue of whether the needs of the population of Mixed Black and Mixed Asian parentage were significantly different from other groups to justify identification. In addition to differences in age structure, the different geographical distribution of the group was commented on (mainly outside metropolitan areas in contrast to the Black and South Asian groups).[4]

As has been noted above, the mixed race groups form over 10 per cent of the ethnic minority population in Britain. In addition, their very young age profile and the growth in mixed relationships mean that the group will form an increasingly large part of the population in the future, making them demographically even more significant.

One problem identified by users of the data involved the elaborate processing applied to the written answers in the census. This was not feasible for other agencies using the census categories, such as local authorities. Consequently it was difficult to compare local data with census figures. Among those supporting an explicit 'Mixed' category was the Commission for Racial Equality (CRE). In their submission to the ONS consultation, the CRE highlighted two issues: one was that, in their view, ethnic monitoring must be based on self-identification, so that official categories need, as far as possible, to reflect the way people see themselves. In the CRE's view, a significant number of people want to identify themselves as mixed race. Their second argument was that particular problems experienced by children of mixed parentage (such as their over representation in the care system)[5] indicated the possibility of failures in social services, which was an important issue for the CRE.[6]

Other organisations, such as People in Harmony, a British organisation which supports mixed couples and people of mixed race, also supported a mixed option on the census. Some voices, though, were raised against. Perhaps the best known was that of the late Bernie Grant, the black Labour MP, who argued that people of mixed race are subject to racism in the same ways as other minority ethnic groups. For that reason, Grant claimed, mixed race people (with black heritage) should be counted together with other black people. Furthermore, in the *Guardian* newspaper, Grant argued, 'Society sees mixed-race people as black, and they are treated as black. They are never accepted as white, so they have no choice'.[7]

Unfortunately the ONS has no plans to publish the reasons for its final question choice before the 2001 census. This contrasts with the very full publication of details of field trials prior to the 1981 and 1991 censuses. The US 2000 census has decided not to include a 'Mixed' category, but to allow people to tick more than one category, even though this was fiercely opposed by some mixed race groups and organisations such as Interracial Voice (the Internet journal), who advocated a 'mixed race' box. It is not known whether this option was considered by the ONS, and, if it was, why it was rejected.

Conclusions

We know very little from official statistics about the mixed race populations of Britain. This is partly due to the fact that the 1991 census ethnic question had no explicit 'Mixed' category. The census question on ethnic group is very important because it was adopted as the standard ethnic classification in all official statistics and was widely adopted by other organisations conducting research or monitoring. In this way the question and its classification came to be seen as an objective description of British society. Yet the question itself was a compromise, arrived at by trying to steer between competing priorities. Importantly, by not including a 'Mixed' category, either in the question or in the outputs from the census (except for one table), the census has not only hidden information about the mixed parentage populations, but it may even have reduced the information we have, by displacing questions from other surveys which had previously included a 'Mixed' category, such as the Labour Force Survey.

The 2001 census question, which includes a 'Mixed' category (with four sub-groups), will, in turn, become the new mode of standardised classification. This means that far more data on mixed race people in Britain will become available following the 2001 census, not just from the census itself, but from other sources which will use the census question.

The statistical information we have can be summarised as follows:

- The 1991 census estimated that there were 230,000 people of mixed race in Britain. According to the Labour Force Survey, this is almost certainly an underestimate, with the correct figure being at least 290,000.
- The mixed populations constitute 0.6 per cent of the total population of Britain, but 11 per cent of the minority ethnic population.

- The mixed population is younger than the population in general, with 54 per cent being children under 15 (compared to 20 per cent of the total population). Two per cent of children under 5 are of mixed race.
- In the 1991 census, of ethnic minority respondents living with a partner, 16 per cent of the men and 13 per cent of the women were living with a white partner. Mixed relationships were more common among the black and Chinese populations than among South Asian groups; they were also more common for younger people (aged under 35) and for those born in the UK.
- Reported attitudes towards mixed relationships are generally accepting, and have become more so over time, although South Asian groups generally report themselves to be more opposed to such relationships than do other ethnic minority groups.

These statistics, however, cannot be taken to imply that Britain is moving inexorably towards a society where everyone is so mixed that ethnicity or the recognition of racial distinctions cease to be an issue. There is still opposition to mixed relationships by some white Britons, and this opposition can take violent forms. Furthermore, the racial and ethnic terms in usage at any one time in society (and which are acceptable to ethnic minority groups) are not neutral but carry social and political distinctions and values. If the terms which people use are constantly in flux, this can pose some major problems for demographic analysis.

This is why some analysts such as Richard Berthoud have argued that the British census needs to obtain a more accurate picture about people's ethnic origins. Berthoud suggests that the census question should ask for the ethnic origin of each parent, with separate columns for 'your mother' and 'your father'.[8] By phrasing the question on ethnic origin in this way, we can, according to Berthoud, avoid the real possibility that people conflate their ethnic origins with their ethnic identities. We must remember that people's ethnic identities may differ from their actual ethnic origins; there is no automatic correspondence between the two, and avoiding such confusion between the two is crucial in getting an accurate picture of multiethnic societies such as Britain today.

Although the introduction of a 'Mixed' category has not conclusively resolved these thorny issues, by revising the question to include a 'Mixed' category, the census has adapted to an important social trend in Britain's racialised demography. The significance of the change goes far beyond the census itself: the change signifies that mixed race is – officially – part of social reality.

Acknowledgements

Material from the Labour Force Survey is Crown Copyright: has been made available by the Office for National Statistics through the Data Archive and has been used with permission. The census data analysed in this chapter were made available by ONS, also Crown Copyright and used with permission. Neither the

ONS nor the Data Archive bear any responsibility for the analysis or interpretation of the data reported here.

Study probes

1   What were the arguments put forward in support of a 'mixed' category? Why did the late Labour MP (Member of Parliament) Bernie Grant oppose the inclusion of a 'mixed' category?
2   Why does Owen make an important distinction between 'ethnic origin' and 'ethnic identity'?
3   Overall, why does Owen support the inclusion of a 'mixed' category on the 2001 ONS Census?

Notes

1   P.I. Aspinall, 'The Development of an Ethnic Question for the 2001 Census. The findings of a consultation exercise of the 2001 Census Working Subgroup on the Ethnic Group Question' (Office for National Statistics, 1996), p. 50.
2   B. Tizard and A. Phoenix, *Black, White or Mixed Race?* (London: Routledge, 1993).
3   See, for example, E.V. Stonequist, *The Marginal Man: A Study in Personality and Culture Conflict* (New York: Russell & Russell, 1937).
4   P.I. Aspinall, 'The Development of an Ethnic Question for the 2001 Census: The findings of a consultation exercise of the 2001. Census Working Subgroup on the Ethnic Group Question' (Office for National Statistics, 1996), p. 60.
5   R. Barn, *Black Children in the Public Care System* (London: Batsford, 1993); M. Boushel, 'Vulnerable Multiracial Families and Early Years Services'. *Children & Society*, 10 (1996), pp. 305–16.
6   D. Owen, *Towards 2001: Ethnic Minorities and the Census* (Coventry: University of Warwick, 1996).
7   G. Younge, 'Beige Britain', G2 section, p.2, *Guardian*, 22 May 1997.
8   R. Berthoud, 'Delining Ethnic Groups: Origin or Identity:', *Patterns of Prejudice*, 32, 2 (1998).

Chapter 32

Office for National Statistics

CENSUS 2001 – ETHNICITY AND RELIGION IN ENGLAND AND WALES (2002)

http://www.statistics.gov.uk/census2001/profiles/commentaries/ethnicity.asp.

THIS RELEASE gives information on answers to three Census questions: ethnic group; country of birth and religion. For more detail on the questions, see Background Notes.

First detailed results on ethnicity and religion from the 2001 Census reveal that 87.5 per cent of the population of England and Wales (seven out of eight people) gave their ethnic group as White British.

The highest proportions describing themselves as White British are in the North East, Wales and the South West (all over 95 per cent).

Ethnic group

- Eighty-seven per cent of the population of England and 96 per cent of the population of Wales gave their ethnic origin as White British.
- White Irish people make up 1.2 per cent of the population of England and Wales as a whole, with the highest proportion in the London borough of Brent (6.9 per cent of the population). The largest proportions of White Other (that is, not White British or White Irish) people are in central London, particularly the borough of Kensington and Chelsea (25.3 per cent).
- London has the highest proportion of people from minority ethnic groups apart from more who identified themselves as of Pakistani origin, of whom there is a higher proportion in Yorkshire and the Humber (2.9 per cent) and the West Midlands (2.9 per cent).

- Two per cent of the population of England and Wales are Indian, with Leicester having the highest proportion (25.7 per cent).
- Bangladeshis formed 0.5 per cent of the population of England and Wales, with the highest proportion in the London borough of Tower Hamlets (33.4 per cent).
- In England and Wales, 1.1 per cent of people are Black Caribbean, 0.9 per cent are Black African and a further 0.2 per cent are from Other Black groups.
- Black Caribbeans form more than ten per cent of the population of the London boroughs of Lewisham, Lambeth, Brent and Hackney. Over ten per cent of Southwark, Newham, Lambeth and Hackney are Black African. More than 2 per cent of people describe themselves as Other Black in Hackney, Lambeth and Lewisham.
- Chinese people form more than 2 per cent of the population in Westminster, Cambridge, City of London and Barnet.
- The largest proportions of people of Mixed origin are in London, with the exception of Nottingham, where 2 per cent of people are Mixed White and Black Caribbean.

Comparisons with the 1991 census show:

- The proportion of minority ethnic groups in England rose from 6 per cent to 9 per cent – partly as a result of the addition of Mixed ethnic groups in 2001.
- There were increases in each of the Asian ethnic groups in England and increases in the proportion of Black Caribbean and Black African people. However, the proportion in the Black Other Category fell. Some of these people in 2001 may have ticked Mixed White and Black Caribbean or Mixed White and Black African.
- The proportion of Chinese rose from 0.3 per cent in 1991 to 0.4 per cent in 2001.
- The numbers of people in Other ethnic groups fell – some people may have classified themselves as Mixed in 2001.
- In Wales, there were increases in the proportion of Indian, Pakistani, Bangladeshi and Chinese people, and 0.6 per cent classified themselves in 2001 as mixed ethnicity.

Country of birth

- Of people living in England, 87.4 per cent gave their country of birth as England and a further 3.2 per cent of the population came from other parts of the UK. London has the lowest proportion of people born in the UK (72.9 per cent) while the North East has the highest proportion (97.1 per cent).

- The highest proportion of people born in the UK are found in Easington and Derwentside, both in County Durham (nearly 99 per cent).
- Nearly 97 per cent of the population of Wales were born in the UK, including 75 per cent born in Wales and 20 per cent born in England.
- The Welsh authority with the highest proportion born in the UK is Blaenau Gwent (98.9 per cent) which also has the highest proportion born in Wales (92.1 per cent). Flintshire had the highest proportion of people born in England (44.7 per cent). One in 20 (5.5 per cent) of the population of Cardiff were born outside the EU – almost twice as many as any other part of Wales.
- In general, the largest proportion of people migrating into England from Scotland and Wales live in the border countries; Welsh-born in Shropshire, Gloucestershire and Cheshire, and Scottish-born in Northumberland and Cumbria.
- An exception is Corby in Northamptonshire, where 19 per cent were born in Scotland (and 1 per cent in Northern Ireland).

Comparisons with the 1991 Census show:

- The proportion of English-born people living in England has dropped from 89 per cent to 87 per cent, while the proportion born outside the EU has risen from 5.3 per cent to 6.9 per cent.
- In Wales, there was a drop from 77 per cent to 75 per cent in the proportion of Welsh-born people and an increase in people born in England from 19 per cent to 20 per cent.
- In Brent, the proportion of people born outside the EU has increased from 31 per cent in 1991 to 38 per cent in 2001. Two other London boroughs have seen large rises in the proportion of people born outside the EU: Newham from 25 per cent in 1991 to 36 per cent and Harrow from 20 per cent to 28 per cent.
- In Corby, Northamptonshire, the proportion of people born in Scotland has declined from 22 per cent to 19 per cent.

Religion

- There are 37.3 million people in England and Wales who state their religion as Christian. The percentage of Christians is similar between the two countries but the proportion of people who follow other religions is 6.0 per cent in England compared with 1.5 per cent in Wales.
- In England, 3.1 per cent of the population state their religion as Muslim (0.7 per cent in Wales), making this the most common religion after Christianity.

- For other religions, 1.1 per cent in England and 0.2 per cent in Wales are Hindu, 0.7 per cent in England and 0.1 per cent in Wales are Sikh, 0.5 per cent in England and 0.1 per cent in Wales are Jewish and 0.3 per cent in England and 0.2 per cent in Wales are Buddhist.
- In England and Wales, 7.7 million people state they have no religion (14.6 per cent in England and 18.5 per cent in Wales).
- The English region with the highest proportion of Christians is the North East (80.1 per cent). London has the highest proportion of Muslims (8.5 per cent), Hindus (4.1 per cent) Jews (2.1 per cent) Buddhists (0.8 per cent) and people of other religions (0.5 per cent).
- Fifty-eight per cent of people in London gave their religion as Christian, with the highest proportion in the borough of Havering (76 per cent). Thirty-six per cent of the population of Tower Hamlets and 24 per cent in Newham are Muslim. Over one per cent of the population of Westminster are Buddhist, while Harrow has the highest proportion of Hindus (19.6 per cent) and Barnet the highest proportion of Jewish people (14.8 per cent). Over 8 per cent of the populations of Hounslow and Ealing are Sikh.
- Sixteen per cent of the population of London say they have no religion, including 25 per cent in the City of London.
- Outside London, the counties with the highest proportion of Christians are Durham, Merseyside and Cumbria, each with 82 per cent or more. The districts with the highest proportions of Christians are all in the North West: St Helens, Wigan and Copeland (Cumbria) each have 86 per cent or more.
- The district with the highest proportion of Sikhs is Slough. One person in seven of the population of Leicester is Hindu. One person in nine of the population of Hertsmere in Hertfordshire, is Jewish. Over 1 per cent of the population of Cambridge are Buddhist. Brighton and Hove has most people stating other religions (0.8 per cent).
- The districts with the highest proportions of people with no religion are Norwich, Brighton and Hove and Cambridge, all with over one quarter.
- In Wales, the highest proportion of Christians is found on the Isle of Anglesey (79 per cent) and the fewest in Blaenau Gwent (64 per cent). Rhonnda, Cynon, Taff has the highest proportion with no religion (25 per cent). Cardiff has the highest proportion of Muslims, Hindus, Sikhs and Jews. Ceredigion has the highest proportions of Buddhists and people of other religions.
- At the time the Census was carried out, there was an internet campaign that encouraged people to answer the religion question "Jedi Knight". The number of people who stated Jedi was 390,000 (0.7 per cent of the population).
- The religion question was voluntary, and 4,011,000 people chose not to answer it (7.7 per cent).

Background notes

1   Census day was 29 April 2001. Census data give a snapshot picture of the country at this time. Population counts by age and sex for England and Wales, Wales, regions of England and English and Welsh local authorities were published on 30 September 2002.

2   The Office for National Statistics is responsible for the Census in England and Wales. The Census in Scotland and in Northern Ireland is carried out by the General Register Office for Scotland and the Northern Ireland Statistics and Research Agency respectively. Census data for Scotland and Northern Ireland are released separately.

3   There were three Census questions in 2001 on the topic of ethnicity and religion.

- *Country of birth*. This question asked "What is your country of birth?" with tick box options of: England; Wales; Scotland; Northern Ireland; Republic of Ireland and Elsewhere, please write in the present name of the country.

- *Ethnic group*. This question was similar to the one asked in 1991, but with changes in some categories. In particular, people could tick "mixed" for the first time. It asked 'What is your ethnic group? Choose ONE section from A to E, then tick the appropriate box to indicate your cultural background.

  A   *White*. Tick box options of: British; Irish or Any other White background (please write in).

  B   *Mixed*. Tick box options of: White and Black Caribbean; White and Black African; White and Asian or any other Mixed background (please write in).

  C   *Asian or Asian British*. Tick box options of: Indian; Pakistani; Bangladeshi; Any other Asian background (please write in).

  D   *Black or Black British*. Tick box options of: Caribbean; African; Any other Black background (please write in).

  E   *Chinese or other ethnic group*. Tick box options of: Chinese; Any other (please write in).

- *Religion*. This question was new in 2001 and was voluntary. It asked "What is your religion" with tick box options of: None; Christian; Buddhist; Hindu; Jewish; Muslim; Sikh; Any other religion, please write in.

Study probes

1   Compare the 'race' question on the US Census 2000 and the 'ethnic group' question on the Office of National Statistics' (ONS) Census 2001 for England and Wales.

2   Compare the US data for 'two or more races' and the England and Wales data for the 'mixed' category.

3   What historical factors may account for demographic differences between 'mixed' populations in the USA and England and Wales?

Chapter 33

Peter Aspinall

THE CONCEPTUALISATION AND CATEGORISATION OF MIXED RACE/ETHNICITY IN BRITAIN AND NORTH AMERICA: IDENTITY OPTIONS AND THE ROLE OF THE STATE

From *International Journal of Intercultural Relations*, 27 (2003), pp. 289–292.

The recognition of mixed race in the 2000/2001 round of censuses

IN THE 2000/2001 ROUND OF CENSUSES, there has for the first time been some convergence between the state's conceptualisation of race and the way mixed race persons identify themselves, with provision for this population being made in both the USA and Britain. In Canada, a question had been introduced, described in the Census *Guide* as 'population group' or 'visible minority population', in the 1996 Census (asked again in 2001) which allowed for multiple reporting but instructed respondents not to print 'biracial' or 'mixed' in the box provided. However, the way this has been achieved in Britain is substantially different, reflecting different traditions in ethnic/racial data collection.

The 2001 Census for England and Wales, Scotland, and Northern Ireland included a 'Mixed' ethnic group as a pre-designated category for the first time, a change that resulted from unanimous support by census users including government departments and the Commission for Racial Equality in a comprehensive consultation exercise. Although a multiracial social movement did not emerge in Britain in the 1990s – possibly because of the absence of a state-sponsored policy of hypodescent, a more flexible attitude to the classification of the black population, and the smaller absolute numbers of mixed race persons (300,000 vs. 6.8 million in the USA) – focus groups and cognitive tests revealed that mixed race persons were in favour of the category.

In England and Wales, respondents to the question 'What is your ethnic group?' were asked to choose one of five ethnic groups – 'White', 'Mixed', 'Asian or Asian British', 'Black or Black British', and 'Chinese or other ethnic group' – and to indicate their 'cultural background' from a list of options (including a free-text field) given for each group, the 'Mixed' options being 'White and Black Caribbean', 'White and Black African', 'White and Asian', and free text 'Any other Mixed background'. These options clearly encode socially constructed 'race', dominated by White as a co-identity/(even though the 'Other Mixed' group was as large as the 'Asian/White' and 'Black/White' groups combined in the 1991 Census), rather than the concept of 'cultural background' or ethnic origin. Rather than challenging the boundaries of racial groups through a refocusing on ethnic identity, the differentiation of the mixed race/ethnicity group solely along racial lines reinforces dominant racial norms, an approach consistent with the state's racialisation of the concept of ethnicity. Moreover, the combination of two broad racial categories invokes the notion of biological mixing in 'parentage' rather than that of cultural diversity or multiple heritage, the listing of 'White' as the leading group maintaining the historically embedded asymmetries of race relations. Regrettably, one option for the 'mixed' group promoted in the development programme – listing the options of 'Black African and White', 'Asian and White', and a free text 'Any other cultural background, e.g., Chinese and Indian' was eschewed, as was the idea of a two-tier classification of broad groups (including 'Mixed') and detailed ethnic origin categories, with multi-ticking in the latter.

The categorisation is also problematic in the case of the 'White and Asian' option, 'Asian' being defined in the 'Asian or Asian British' cultural background options as relating to the Indian Subcontinent, although substantially higher rates of inter-ethnic unions are found in the Chinese/SE Asian groups, whose off-spring may be unsure which box to tick. The use of White as the dominant group in all the cultural background options (rather than combinations of two 'visible minority' groups) may result in the capture primarily of colloquially defined mixed race rather than other racial mixes exclusive of White, like 'Chinese and Indian'. Further, mixed ethnic origin identities, such as 'Irish and Albanian', 'Somali and Nigerian', or 'Caribbean Asian and Sinhalese', according to ONS's detailed coding frame, will be concealed within the 'other' options of the broad, socially constructed race groups of White, Black, and Asian, respectively. Thus, the England and Wales question fails to satisfactorily allow for hybridised identities representing allegiances to multiple groups as opposed to a method that implies an outcome from two putatively 'pure' categories.

The 2001 Census question for Scotland also included a 'Mixed' ethnic group but with only one cultural background option, a free-text 'Any Mixed background'. In Northern Ireland an ethnic group question ('To which of these ethnic groups do you consider you belong?') was asked for the first time, similar to that used in the 1991 Great Britain Census but including a free-text 'Mixed ethnic group' without reference to cultural background. The terminology of a 'mixed' *group* in all the UK question variants is problematic in that it suggests that everyone of mixed parentage/race, regardless of the type of mixture, is considered part of a single ethnic group. Again, it implies a racialised category in that anyone who is not in a single or 'pure' group is considered out with the conventional classification system and lumped together. Moreover, the use of duplex write-in boxes in all the variants of the 'Mixed' category suggests mixed parentage or dual heritage. While 'mixed race' options offered in the England and Wales question are likely to give a more accurate count of persons for the particular mixes listed (but possibly at the expense of mixes that do not include the White group), respondents in Scotland and Northern Ireland may, without such cues, be more likely to report mixed *ethnic* origins.

The way ONS will tabulate responses to the 'Mixed' group in the United Kingdom has now been finalised. Although there will be no UK-wide standard tables on ethnic group because of the different classifications, all but one of the 15 ethnic tables for England and Wales give the full 'Mixed' breakdown (four categories). Similar ethnic tables in Scotland give 'Any Mixed background' for high area-level output but just five groups excluding Mixed (White, Indian, Pakistani or other South Asian, Chinese, Other) for small area statistics. Comparable ethnic tables in Northern Ireland also report on the 'Mixed' category. Thus, for the first time, information on the mixed group will be available across a wide range of sociodemographic and economic variables and also on health datasets following the Department of Health's decision to adopt the 2001 classification for England and Wales across all its statistical collections.

In the USA a different solution has been adopted. The Interagency Committee rejected the addition of a 'multiracial' category on the grounds that government research had indicated less than 3% of the population identified itself as 'multiracial' and that the term 'multiracial' was frequently misunderstood by respondents to mean multiethnic. In the October 1997 revised standards for the classification of Federal data on race and ethnicity, the OMB agreed that when self-identification is used a method of reporting more than one race should be adopted, taking the form of multiple responses to a single question and not a 'multiracial' category. The recommended forms of instructions for the multiple response option are to 'mark (or select) one or more . . .'. If the criteria for data quality and confidentiality are met, OMB states that provision should be made to report, at a minimum, the number of persons identifying with more than one race and, if possible, greater detail about the distribution of multiple responses. This standard for multiple responses was introduced in the 2000 census race question, the resulting counts providing a selective measure of self-identified mixed race triggered by the question instruction rather than a *full* count of the mixed race population defined by descent. Also, in the 2000 Census free text 'ancestry or ethnic origin' question, the instruction guide informed respondents that 'individuals who think of themselves as having more than one origin . . . are able to write in their multiple ancestry, e.g. German-Irish', as in the 1990 Census (in which a third of the population reported two or more ancestries). This, effectively, brought the US Census in line with the Canadian Census, the 2001 schedule for the latter including questions that permitted multiple reporting of both population group and ethnic origin.

Conclusions

Historically, persons of mixed race have been accommodated in official classifications of ethnicity/race based on the selection of a single option from mutually exclusive, discrete groups. In the United States the stigmatisation of racial mixing and concerns over racial purity led to the adoption of the hypodescent policy which meant that persons of African-American and white heritage were identified as black and the legacy of this policy may continue to influence the identity options of African-Americans. In Canada a different political focus, that of official multiculturalism with its emphasis on ethnic diversity, may be responsible for the saliency of dual heritage identities. Here, the insistence by the state on mutually exclusive categorisation began to give way to more flexible approaches of enumeration from the mid-1980s. The United States followed in the 1990s, the main stimulus in this case being the rise of mixed race/biracial movements seeking recognition as a matter of individual civil rights.

The evidence of research studies in Britain, the United States, and Canada suggests a wide range of identity options available to the mixed race population, including articulating a multiracial identity, embracing a black racial designation, shifting between these options, or adopting more fluid identities including multiple lines of ancestry, depending on situation and social context. Given the role of the state in shaping dominant understandings of race, it is important that classifications respond to this range of racial subjectivities. In the United States and Canada that response has come in the form of multiple reporting on both ethnic origin/ancestry and race questions, while in Britain the dominant response has been the provision of dual heritage options encoding socially constructed race. The challenge is to find ways of allowing for hybridised identities that represent allegiances to multiple groups rather than an outcome from two putatively 'pure' categories. As the findings of the 2000/2001 round of censuses become available, researchers will have an unprecedented opportunity to assess how well the state's conceptualisation of race is meeting the different needs and perspectives of the multiracial population and to provide guidance on the issue of capturing and measuring the increasing racial and ethnic diversity of the populations of Britain, the United States, and Canada.

Study probes

1   What are Aspinall's criticisms of the 'mixed' ethnic question on the 2001 Census for the United Kingdom?
2   Why does he suggest that the question's format is illustrative of the 'state's racialisation of ethnicity'?
3   How does the author compare the official reporting of 'mixed race' in the USA, Canada and the UK?
4   What is his recommendation for the future?

SUGGESTIONS FOR FURTHER READING

Aspinall, Peter(1997) 'The Conceptual Basis of Ethnic Group Terminology and Classifications', *Social Science and Medicine*, 45(5):689–698.

Cose, Ellis (1997) 'Census and the Complex Issue of Race', *Society*, 34 (6): 9–13.

DaCosta, Kimberly McClain (2003) 'Multiracial Identity: From Personal Problem to Public Issue', in L. Winters and H. DeBose (eds) *New Faces in a Changing America*, Thousand Oaks, CA: Sage, pp.68–84.

Fernández, Carlos (1995) 'Testimony of the Association of MultiEthnic Americans Before the Subcommittee on Census, Statistics, and Postal Personnel of the US House of Representatives', in N. Zack (ed.) *American Mixed Race*, London: Rowman and Littlefield, pp. 191–210.

Fernández, Carlos (1996) 'Government Classification of Multiracial/Multiethnic People', in M.P.P. Root (ed.) *The Multiracial Experience*, Thousand Oaks, CA: Sage, pp.15–36

Friedman, Jonathan (1997) 'Global Crises, The Struggle for Cultural Identity and Intellectual Porkbarrelling', in P. Werbner and T. Modood (eds) *Debating Cultural Hybridity*, London: Zed Books, pp.70–89.

Fuchs, Lawrence (1997) 'What Should We Count and Why?', *Society*, 34(6): 24–27.

Kertzer, David and Arel, Dominique (2002) *Census and Identity: The Politics of Race, Ethnicity, and Language in National Censuses*, Cambridge: Cambridge University Press.

Morning, Ann (2003) 'New Faces, Old Faces: Counting the Multiracial Population Past and Present', in L. Winters and H. DeBose (eds) *New Faces in a Changing America*, Thousand Oaks, CA: Sage, pp.41–67.

Nobles, Melissa (2002) 'Racial Categorization and Censuses', in D. Kertzer and D. Arel *Census and Identity: The Politics of Race, Ethnicity, and Language in National Censuses*, Cambridge: Cambridge University Press, pp.43–70.

Phoenix, Ann and Owen, Charlie (2000) 'From Miscegenation to Hybridity: Mixed Relationships and Mixed Parentage in Profile', in A. Brah and A. Coombes (eds) *Hybridity and its Discontents: Politics, Science and Culture*, London: Routledge, pp.72–95.

Root, Maria P.P. (ed.) (1996) *The Multiracial Experience: Racial Borders as the New Frontier*, Thousand Oaks, CA: Sage.

Spencer, Jon Michael (1997) *The New Colored People: The Mixed Race Movement in America*, London: New York University Press.

Waters, Mary (2000) 'Multiple Ethnicities and Identity in the United States', in Spickard, P. and Burroughs, W.J. (eds) *We Are a People: Narrative and Multiplicity in Constructing Ethnic Identity*, Philadelphia, PA: Temple University Press, pp.23–40.

Williams, León (2003) 'Check All that Apply: Trends and Prospectives Among Asian-descent Americans', in L. Winters and H. DeBose (eds) *New Faces in a Changing America*, Thousand Oaks, CA: Sage pp.158–175.

Multiraciality and critiques

Chapter 34

Steven Masami Ropp

DO MULTIRACIAL SUBJECTS REALLY CHALLENGE RACE?: MIXED RACE ASIANS IN THE UNITED STATES AND THE CARIBBEAN

From *Amerasia Journal*, 31 (1) (1997), pp. 1–16.

DO MULTIRACIAL SUBJECTS REALLY CHALLENGE RACE? Although multiracial subjects challenge a biological view of race, the way in which they challenge the social construction of race is limited. Racial meaning and categories of race do not simply disappear when confronted with the multiracial subject. I base this assertion upon three propositions. The first is that although the notion of race as a biological determinant of culture and behavior has been scientifically disproven, more subtle forms of thinking that link culture and race still persist. Second, that the location of multiracial subjects within US racial discourse and an Asian American racial project is constrained by the logic of identity politics. As such, the multiracial subject can pose only a limited challenge to the persistence of race in both the US mainstream culture and the ethnic community. Finally, the assumption that "racial-mixing" leads to a raceless society is inaccurate. Historical and cross-cultural evidence from the Caribbean suggests that there have been other times and places where an Asian immigrant population became predominantly multiracial in character without a subsequent decline in racially assigned meaning.[1] At the convergence of these three areas of inquiry, I examine the degree to which multiracial Asian American subjects effectively challenge notions of race.

I locate my analysis within the contradictory position of being both an object and an objectifier. At the same time that I talk about multiraciality and racial discourses as abstract analytic categories, my own everyday experience is constituted within these fields of social practice. At the same time that I ask what is the nature of cultural behavior and social organization, I also live, practice, and participate in these "abstractions." On a personal level, I draw upon my own lived experience as well as upon the experiences of friends and associates to construct a "multiracial" Asian American subject position with regard to racial discourse. From a different perspective, I draw upon ethnographic fieldwork and my practice as an anthropologist to examine historical and contemporary multiracial Asian experiences in the Caribbean. Going from present-day Belize, to the history of the Chinese in Jamaica and Trinidad, to the experiences of multiracial Asian Americans, this analysis is an attempt to move across national, racial and cultural boundaries to question critically the claims and the practice of multiraciality for Asian-descent peoples. My goal is to distinguish between discourses which simply reinscribe race upon multiracial subjects and the counter-discourses that might actually challenge racial thinking, racial formations, and racism.

The challenge of multiracial subjects

One of the fundamental claims of multiracial subject positionality is that we represent, literally and symbolically, a challenge to racial thinking. Persons of mixed, multiple, or ambiguous racial heritage are presumed to represent a challenge to racial thinking.[2] After twenty-seven years of being one of these people, after eight years of doing research on various aspects of the mixed-race experience, and after four years of involvement with a specific social organization organized around "multiracial" Asian American issues, I increasingly believe that the practice falls far short of the discourse.

One of the more sophisticated and developed theories on race which examines the connection between discourse and practice in a single theoretical concept is Omi and Winant's *racial formation*. By approaching race as a sociohistorical process of categorization, racial formation theory is able to follow the trajectory of specific racial projects over time as they give meaning and justification to practices of social inequality. Processes of racial formation occur "[t]hrough a linkage between structure and representation."[3] Omi and Winant's example of the everyday significance of race is, of course, the encounter with the racially mixed person, for at that moment occurs a temporary "crisis of racial meaning."[4] It is during this critical moment, this disjuncture where racial thinking must come out into the open and account for the discrepancy between existing social categories of race and an individual who doesn't fit these categories, that the supposed challenge of multiraciality exists. The emerging field of multiracial studies[5] is based largely upon the notion that we can intervene in this space at the boundaries and borders of racial meaning and social category and say: See, race is socially constructed, what's wrong with you? In actuality, the response is often less dramatic. Individuals confronted with a temporary crisis in racial meaning generally are able to respond within the existing logic of conventional racial meanings. In the emerging literature on "multiracial" studies, there is this reluctant but almost inevitable use of such terms as multiracial, biracial, and mixed-race even when trying to deconstruct or write against racialized thinking. Even when attempting to transcend race it is necessary to continue to refer to racial categories and racial logic which leads to a reinscription of race albeit in more sophisticated hybrid and multiplied forms.

In terms of racial formation, Omi and Winant point out that there is a tendency to either think about race as some sort of "essence" which is fixed and objective or to subscribe to the opposite tendency which is to view it as an "illusion" which can be eliminated, something not real. They suggest that it is "necessary to challenge both of these positions, to disrupt and reframe the rigid and bipolar manner in which they are posed and debated and to transcend the presumably irreconcilable difference between them."[6] Working from this position, that one of these bipolar positions forms the basis for reaction to the multiracial subject in that "moment of crisis," I suggest that the only way that multiracial subjects actually challenge race is limited to a specific aspect of racial thinking – an essentialized biological determinism. The original use of race was taken from animal biology and taxonomy in the seventeenth and eighteenth century and used the term as a way of accounting for physiological differences among human populations as though these differences represented species level distinctions.[7]

This biologically determined view of race was largely debunked by the 1960s and very few people would explicitly argue such a view today. In this way, the very biological fact of our existence does indeed challenge an essentialized notion of race as a determining factor in shaping sociocultural behavior. However, after having been asked on numerous occasions, "so, what is it like to have two cultures?" as though the fact of my biological blood also accords some sort of cultural competence in not just one culture (read race) but two cultures (read two races) it seems as though some form of determinism is an inevitable part of racial discourse. Expectations about culture, language, and social behavior continue to be connected to categories of race which may be socially constructed, but take form in very real everyday social practice.

Multiracial Asian Americans

The ways in which these discourses of multiraciality play out in terms of everyday practice demonstrate the limitations of the challenge to race. In 1993, while an undergraduate at UC Berkeley, I helped to start a student group called *Hapa Issues Forum*. The original focus of the group was to address specific issues within the Japanese American community such as discrimination against mixed persons through blood-quantum requirements in Japanese American sports leagues and also to provide a "multiracial" voice in debates over issues such as the impact of outmarriage on the future of the community.[8] A common activity for the group is to organize information booths both on the UC Berkeley campus and also for local events such as the annual Cherry Blossom Festival in San Francisco. I bring this up for two reasons. First of all, to demonstrate the persistence of racial practice even in that critical moment where the "racially" ambiguous person is encountered. And second, to demonstrate that the persistence of racial meaning results in the perpetuation of race through two specific discourses which posit either an idealized multiraciality – a new racial category for mixed people, or the denial of race all together. The denial of race takes the form of either the notion that "pretty soon, everyone will be mixed," or "race doesn't matter." These interactions between multiracial subjects and strangers in the specific context of information booths provide concrete examples of the tendency to react to race as either an "essence" or as an "illusion," as Omi and Winant argue.[9]

My assertions here about how people discursively construct multiracial Asian Americans is not necessarily generalizable because a degree of self-selection takes place before a person approaches an information table or even attends an ethnic community event. However, these encounters do capture Omi and Winant's critical moment of disjuncture. The first general category encountered in this context is people who are themselves mixed. The second category consists of those who are "non-mixed" and are generally either in an interracial relationship or have family members who are in interracial relation-ships. Here is the scenario. Interracial couple approaches, looks cautiously at the sign, "Oh, that's interesting. What you are doing is so good!" The best one that I have heard is, "Oh, we just wanted to see what our children will look like." Or the now classic, "I think that mixed people are so beautiful." These are usually the extent of the one-liners and more extended conversations might take the form of inquiries into the novelty of being mixed. "That's really neat, that you can draw upon two different heritages." I am never really sure what that means since both of my parents are pretty distant from any ethnic roots. Beyond being "culturally" American and "biologically" biracial, I cannot figure out how to access those German and Japanese heritages that people keep talking about! Never far behind these types of comments is an everyday discourse based upon the notion that, "pretty soon, everyone will be mixed." Along these lines, *Time* magazine created a computer-generated American of the future based upon a "mixture" of races although the end result still had white facial features with a somewhat darker complexion.[10] Such news magazine stories about what America will be like when "minorities" are the majority feed the popular imagination. If you look at actual intermarriage rates, the groups with high rates, Asian Americans and Native Americans, are statistically small segments of the total population.[11] If all Asian Americans outmarried, being only 3 percent of the total population, that would still leave a significant portion of the white populations as "unmixed." The whole point is not how much a person is actually mixed because racial dynamics adjust for that with one-drop rules where neces-sary. Although academic discourse debunks the notion of race as a biologically determining behavior, race is still part and parcel of everyday common sense and everything and anything must somehow fit into this racialized world. If it's not the idealist denial of race then it's the reinscription of race through the new category of the multiracial.

The construction of the multiracial subject takes place not only through those everyday encounters. In academic fields such as Asian American Studies, race and racial determinism are strongly refuted and yet the construction of multiraciality seems to indicate the continuing centrality of racialized thinking. In academic discourse, multiracial subjects constitute a challenge to that racialized thinking but only to the degree that they can carve out space within the racial logic which, for example, underlies the project of Asian American Studies. Omi and Winant's sociohistorical analysis of racial formation identified the 1960s as a radical point of departure in the US Social movements based upon a new politics of race were able to articulate the demands of various ethnic and racial communities, including Asians. Out of this reconfiguration emerged new forms of race and ethnic-based movements including the project of Asian American Studies. Thus, Asian American Studies has its own "racial project," usually articulated as one of resistance against dominant discourses of exclusion and alienness. Given that a ". . . vast web of racial projects mediate between the discursive or representational means in which race is identified and signified on the one hand, and the institutional and organizational forms in which it is routinized and standardized on the other," where does the multiracial subject fit in?[12] Just as the project of Asian American Studies became one of struggling for inclusion into the larger political and cultural fabric of the US, so too does multiracial studies appear to be about proving that multiracial subjects have legitimate claims to ethnic communities. The need to prove that multiracial subjects have allegiances and feelings of connection to the ethnic community means that racial boundaries which would exclude multiracial subjects are contested but without a significant challenge to the overall system of race itself. An example of this process is a study by Amy Iwasaki Mass in which her findings indicate that multiracial Japanese Americans actually had a higher degree of affiliation and identification with the Japanese American community than mono-racial subjects.[13] This finding was in once sense contradictory to the view of out-marriage as a final step to the complete amalgamation of Japanese Americans into the mainstream. At the same time this study shows how the "multiracial" subject continues to be constructed in relation to predominantly race-based notions of community.

Once these studies are conducted, and the effort is made to demonstrate sufficient allegiance and cultural competency in the ethnic community, where do these studies stand given the racial logic which centers racial and ethnic allegiance often to the exclusion of other aspects of identity (nationality, gender, sexual orientation)? In this context, where identity politics and a notion of ethnic-based community struggle predominate, there are few options for constructing the multiracial subject except as a sub-category of the dominant Asian American experience. Part of the reason why I did not pursue Ethnic Studies or Asian American Studies on the graduate level is because I didn't want to *have* to restrict myself to my "community," that is, I did not want to be limited to doing a study of fourth generation multiracial Japanese Americans who grew up in the Central Valley. With rare exception, subject position largely determines the topic of research. This approach developed from the legitimate and pressing need for Asian Americans to actually engage in research on Asian American communities as a corrective to previous racist and skewed representations. However, taken to an extreme, as in the identity politics of today, this leads to a new form of essentialism whereby only a Japanese American can research and write on Japanese Americans, etc. I recently looked at a list of the approximately thirty MA theses produced in the Asian American Studies program at UCLA and only four are not directly related to the researchers, racial and/or ethnic background. Two of those four were by persons who are white. Within this climate and context, with an almost singular focus on race/ethnicity as the basis for a legitimate and authentic voice, multiraciality becomes subsumed within the racial project of Asian American Studies, thus effectively diffusing any sort of challenge which multiraciality might pose to disrupting the system as a whole. This also explains some of the hesitancy of ethnic/race-based organizations to support the proposed "multiracial category" on the census as they fear that this new category would dilute ethnic numbers and thereby reduce allocated dollars. There is a tremendous investment in race/ethnic based programs by ethnic communities and if multiracial subjects simply opted out of racial identifications as a means of disrupting the process of racial formation then many of these programs would object. Hence, if you want to participate in the program, you must adhere to the underlying logic: "monoracial" Japanese Americans become "multiracial" Japanese Americans.

[. . .]

Effectively challenging race

As can be seen from the Caribbean, the biological fact of being "mixed" does not necessarily reduce the social significance of race. The process of racial formation is a flexible one that adapts to the transgressions of pure racial-boundary logic with new discourses of *mestizaje*, creolization, or multiraciality. A more effective way of developing a critical race theory through the multiracial subject is the engagement of social formations (political, economic, and cultural) as they are constructed along racial lines. Notions of purity and mixing often play central roles in this process and so any discussion of race also implies a multiracial/mixed-race other. Cindy Nakashima, a graduate student in Ethnic Studies at UC Berkeley, employs this kind of engaged multiraciality by questioning taken for granted notions of race and community throughout her course on Asian American history.[14] Although we talk about multiracial studies in terms of a biracial baby boom since the 1960s, there have been multiracial subjects throughout Asian American history. At any given moment in that history, one can effectively examine categories of race and the persons who straddled those boundaries as a means of identifying how racial constructs excluded Asians and eventually shaped Asian immigrants in later generations. For example, Nakashima uses the work of Amerasian author Edith Eaton (who wrote under the pseudonym of Sui Sin Far in the early part of this century) to talk about the Chinese American experience. In this case, multiracial subjects take on a more integrated position in the examination of the history of various Asian communities and in looking at how issues of belonging and difference shaped the social construction and everyday experience of race. Nakashima's approach is an example of how a more critical viewpoint might be taken in the field as a whole through the analysis of the tensions between inclusion and exclusion and the locations of multiracial subjects at these positions.

In conclusion, I reiterate that the denial of race through such notions as "everyone will be mixed," or "race doesn't matter" (and here I would include the proponents of interracial marriage as a cure for racism) is misguided at best and counter-productive at worst. According to Omi and Winant, "[t]oday more than ever, opposing racism requires that we notice race, not ignore it, that we afford it the recognition it deserves and the subtlety it embodies."[15] They argue this based on the presence of "[r]ace in every institution, every relationship, every individual." I concur with this view and suggest that part of the multiracial and ethnic studies project must be a recognition of the persistent and pervasive role of race not only in the form of external white racism but also as it manifests throughout the thinking of all participants in a racialized society.

Study probes

1   What are the three propositions which form the basis of Ropp's critique of 'multiracial' subjectivities?
2   How does he apply Omi and Winant's concept of 'racial formation' to 'multiracial' Asian Americans?
3   Why does the author argue that we must acknowledge rather than ignore the enduring significance of 'race'?

Notes

1   Historical accounts of this history are somewhat limited in that they deal mostly with external push/pull factors such as Persia Campbell's *Chinese Coolie Emigration to Countries within the British Empire* (London: P.S. King & Son, Ltd., 1923). To understand more about settlement and second generation Chinese, I depend upon Walton Look Lai's *Indentured Labor, Caribbean Sugar: Chinese and Indian Migrants to the British West Indies, 1838–1918* (Baltimore, Maryland: Johns Hopkins Press, 1993).
2   See *Racially Mixed People in America*, Maria P. P. Root, ed. (Thousand Oaks, California: Sage Publications, 1992) and her follow-up volume, *The Multiracial Experience: Racial Borders as the New Frontier*, Maria P. P. Root, ed. (Thousand Oaks: Sage Publications, 1996).
3   Michael Omi and Howard Winant, *Racial Formation in the United States: From the 1960s to the 1990s* (New York: Routledge, 1994. Second Edition), 55–56.
4   Omi and Winant, 59
5   The term mixed-race or multiracial studies is used to refer to a particular body of academic research and publication generated by scholars who are themselves of mixed-racial heritage. The edited volumes by Maria P. P. Root as well as *American Mixed Race: The Culture of Micro-diversity*, Naomi Zack, ed. (Lanham, Maryland: Rowman and Littlefield Publishers, Inc., 1995) are examples. See Cynthia L. Nakashima, "Voices from the Movement: Approaches to Multiraciality," in *The Multiracial Experience: Racial Borders as the New Frontier*, 79–97, for an analysis of various discourses within multiracial studies. Also, for a bibliographic attempt at defining this field of study, see *Prism Lives/Emerging Voices of Multiracial Asians: A Selective, Annotated Bibliography*, compilers: Steven Masami Ropp, Teresa Williams, and Curtiss Rooks (Los Angeles: UCLA Asian American Studies Center, 1995).
6   Omi and Winant, 54.
7   George W. Stocking Jr., *Race, Culture, and Evolution: Essays in the History of Anthropology* (Chicago: University of Chicago Press, 1982 [1968]).
8   See Rebecca Chiyoko King and Kimberly McClain DaCosta, "Changing Face, Changing Race: The Remaking of Race in the Japanese American and African American Community" in *The Multiracial Experience: Racial Borders as the New Frontier*, 227–244.
9   Omi and Winant, 55.
10   "Rebirth of a Nation. Computer Style," *Time* 142:21 (September 1993): 66–68. Special Issue. "The New Face of America," Nakashima, "Voices from the Movement: Approaches to Multiraciality," discusses this article and places it within the context of the representations and discussion of multiraciality taking place in the mainstream media.

11   See Harry H. Kitano *et al.*, "Asian-American Interracial Marriage", *Journal of Marriage and the Family* 46:1 (1984), 179–190; and Larry Hajime Shinagawa and Gin Yong Pang, "Asian American Panethnicity and Intermarriage," *Amerasia Journal* 22:2 (1996), 127–152.

12   Omi and Winant, 60.

13   Amy Iwasaki Mass, "Interracial Japanese Americans: The Best of Both Worlds or the End of the Japanese American Community?," in *Racially Mixed People in America*, 265–279.

14   See Teresa Kay Williams, Cynthia L. Nakashima, George Kitahara Kich and G. Reginald Daniels, "Being Different Together in the University Classroom: Multiracial Identity as Transgressive Education," in *The Multiracial Experience: Racial Borders as the New Frontier*, 359–379, for a complete discussion of various teaching strategies and the overall impact of multiracial studies in academic settings.

15   Omi and Winant, 159.

Chapter 35

Cynthia L. Nakashima

SERVANTS OF CULTURE: THE SYMBOLIC ROLE OF MIXED-RACE ASIANS IN AMERICAN DISCOURSE

From T. Williams-León and C.L. Nakashima (eds) *The Sum of Our Parts: Mixed Heritage Asian Americans* (2001). Philadelphia, PA: Temple University Press, pp. 42–47.

A "Cablinasian" in a "color-blind" America

THE 1990S AND THE BEGINNING OF THE TWENTY-FIRST CENTURY have proved to be a watershed period for Americans of mixed race. The discourse on multiraciality is now no longer limited to one-dimensional characters in films and novels, but also includes real people, speaking in their own voices, in what has been called a multiracial movement that has entered the mainstream dialogue on race and ethnicity. But the inclusion of mixed-race people in the dialogue does not mean that they are no longer being used as symbols of cultural dilemmas. On the contrary, the growing voices of multiracials have offered a bounty of representational possibilities for Americans. In fact, these days just about every political and ideological camp utilizes mixed-race people in support of their arguments. The single best illustration of this is golf prodigy Tiger Woods, who in 1996–97 became perhaps the busiest symbolic tool in the history of fictional or nonfictional mixed-race characters. The biggest difference today is that the characters like Tiger can finally participate in the discourse to some extent.

The discussion about race and ethnicity in the 1990s began with one that had started in the latter 1980s, when demographers announced that, by the middle of the twenty-first century, Whites would no longer be the majority racial group in the United States. For the most part, the mainstream media tried to react cheerfully to news of the "browning of America" by stressing that America's strength is in its diverse people, that we are a nation of

272 CYNTHIA L. NAKASHIMA

immigrants, and that we must explore and appreciate our "multicultural" heritage.

People of mixed race were thus presented as a positive version of a multi-cultural America — a new, more colorful sort of "melting pot," where racial groups do not separate and segregate, but marry and have babies.

The representation of mixed-race people as the "children of the future" sporting "global identities" has continued, manifesting itself in advertisements that take advantage of the wide marketing potential of the "W.U.R.E." ("woman of unidentifiable race or ethnicity"), and in fictional and especially science fictional characters that use multiraciality as the racial expression of an Everyman. This juxtaposition of unique and universal is packaged and sold in the Nike television advertisement where faces of young people of a variety of racial phenotypes are flashed, one by one, each of them saying, "I am Tiger Woods."

But shortly after bumper stickers began to remind Americans to "Celebrate Diversity," many expressed the concern that the nation has become "too obsessed" with race, that an emphasis on diversity is "divisive," and that there needs to be a more unified "American" identity. By the early 1990s, the dialogue was driven more and more by social and political conservatives and neoconservative scholars, complaining about the oppressive nature of "politically correct" language and thought.

[. . .]

Also in the university, postmodern and poststructuralist thought has challenged some of the ideas of multiculturalism, although from a very different perspective from the conservative critique. Postmodern discussions of race and ethnicity call attention to the "totalizing" and "essentializing" treatment of racial and ethnic identity, experience, and history that often characterizes multi-cultural discourse. By adhering to the dichotomous categories of African American, Asian American, and so on, multiculturalism tends to place single, unifying definitions around groups of individuals, validating ideas of essential differences. These categories also put certain identities and experiences at the center of the definitions, while those outside of the center are considered marginal and/or inauthentic. People of mixed race, as well as gays, lesbians, and bisexuals, have served as illustrative examples for the postmodern projects of "deconstructing" categories, "problematizing" identities, and "disrupting the master narratives".

The act of deconstructing racial categories is one area of postmodern discourse that has entered into the mainstream dialogue on race and ethnicity. When the highly controversial book *The Bell Curve* by Richard J. Herrnstein and Charles Murray was published in 1994, the question of genetic differences between racial groups was reviewed in the media. The February 13, 1995, issue of *Newsweek* was dedicated to challenging not only *The Bell Curve* but the racial category of "Black." The magazine argued that claims such as Herrnstein's and Murray's are based on outdated notions that view racial categories as scientifically sound, when in fact science itself sees them as mere "social constructs". Indeed, shortly after the *Newsweek* article was published, geneticists at the American Association for the Advancement of Science's annual conference announced that they had confirmed that the racial categories are biologically meaningless.

Newsweek attributed this "assault on racialist thinking" to the growing population of mixed-race people and to the recognition that the traditional categories,
based on the "one-drop rule" of heredity, are no longer acceptable to many
Americans. . . . While operating on the assumption that racism is wrong,[1]
these new proponents of a "color-blind society" argue that race-conscious
policies (i.e., affirmative action) in education, employment, and voting are
discriminatory and violate the civil rights of certain Americans based on race.

Interestingly, those who espouse a color-blind agenda seem especially fond
of arguing that interracial marriage and multiracial people support their
position. They generally do this in one of three ways: (1) the growth of a racially
mixed population is proof that racism is on the decline and that race matters less
and less (which means we don't need affirmative action); (2) the growth of a
racially mixed population makes traditional racial categories outdated and
inaccurate (which means we should stop using categories, especially for programs such as affirmative action); and (3) racially mixed people are able to
manipulate racial categories, thus making race-based policies easily corruptible
(which means we need to dispose of affirmative action).

[. . .]

The debate over racial classification models for the US Census is where all of
these issues – diversity, multiculturalism, the questioning of racial categories,
affirmative action, and color-blindness – have been projected onto the subject of
people of mixed race,[2] or rather onto one particular person of mixed race, Tiger
Woods. Actually, mainstream America and its hero Tiger entered into the debate
quite late. For several years the discussion took place primarily between
organizations representing multiracial families and individuals, and civil
rights organizations such as the NAACP (National Association for the Advancement of Colored People), the National Urban League, the National Council of La
Raza, and the National Asian Pacific American Legal Consortium. The mainstream media mostly stayed out of it, except to report – from an outsider
perspective – this disagreement occurring within the communities of color.

But all of this changed when, in April of 1997, golfer Tiger Woods won the
Master's tournament at the age of twenty-one, signed several multimillion dollar
endorsement deals, and went on the Oprah Winfrey show announcing himself to
be a "Cablinasian" – a neologism referring to his Caucasian-Black-Indian-Asian
heritage. Suddenly, the discussion over racial classification had exploded into a
national debate.[3] On May 5, 1997, both *Newsweek* (Leland & Beals) and *Time*
(White) ran lengthy articles about Tiger and "his multiracial generation." African
American and Asian American periodicals such as *Ebony* and *Asian Week* carefully
scrutinized each of his statements on his ethnic and racial identity. Oprah ran a
second show on Tiger, this time focusing on the controversy over his "Cablinasian" identity. At a summit on volunteerism a few days after the first Oprah
show, Colin Powell was questioned by the media about his reaction to Tiger's
racial/ethnic identity and his opinion on a "multiracial" category on the Census.[4]

With this "mainstreaming" of the debate around multiracial identity, the
mixed-race organizations found that mainstream America was usually sympathetic to Tiger and his "multiracial generation." In fact, the perceived enemy in
this struggle had shifted from the government and its Census to the civil rights

organizations and their greed for numbers and power and set-asides. Positioning themselves as champions of individual rights, many Republican politicians, such as House Speaker Newt Gingrich, came out in favor of a "multiracial" category for the Census. Most of this conservative support, however, including Gingrich's, was undoubtedly motivated by the desire to use the category to upset social programs such as affirmative action by diluting numbers and making tabulation unruly.

[. . .]

Conclusion

Ironically, this country's first Census was supervised by Thomas Jefferson himself in 1790, when the racial categories were "free White males," "free White females," "other persons" (which included free Blacks and "taxable Indians"), and "slaves." We can only wonder if Jefferson was able to recognize the fluidity in these classifications, as reflected in his own family.

On October 29, 1997, the US Office of Management and Budget (OMB) announced the decision to allow Americans to check more than one racial/ ethnic category on the 2000 Census and rejected the option of a separate "multiracial" category, stating that it would "add to racial tension." The OMB's policy was presented as a compromise between those lobbying in the interests of people of mixed race and the traditional civil rights organizations. But in actuality, no compromise was needed: In June 1997, a coalition of mixed-race organizations, such as the Association of MultiEthnic Americans and Hapa Issues Forum, had been in dialogue with the NAACP and the Japanese American Citizens' League and had released a statement that they were *not* in favor of a separate multiracial category, but rather preferred the multiple-check model.

Multiracial people and hybrid identities continue to destabilize racial and cultural boundaries and hierarchies as the dominant society struggles to manage these populations and their identities. Fictional mixed-race characters, under full control of their authors, have served as a site for the exploration and resolution of social dilemmas. But in the drama of the racial classification debate, the attempt to use mixed-race characters to dismantle race-based policies was ultimately thwarted by the real people who can and do speak for themselves.

Study probes

1   Outline Nakashima's argument as it pertains to the 'mainstreaming' of 'multiracial' identity politics.
2   How did Tiger Woods play a pivotal role in this debate?
3   According to Nakashima, what are the three ways in which 'multiracial' subjects are used to defend a 'colour-blind' approach to American race relations?

Notes

1   This is not to say that all Americans agree that racism is wrong. Recent years have also seen a significant rise in White supremacist organizations, who still firmly believe in the genetic superiority of White Christians, and who are very much opposed to interracial marriage, mixed-race people, and a multicultural America.

2   Although I am focusing on the representative role of people of mixed race in mainstream America, multiraciality has played such a role in communities of color as well. In the debate over racial classification, the assertion and exploration of mixed-race identities have been conflated with the movement for a "multiracial" box on the Census, and is often portrayed – by individuals and institutions within the communities of color – as politically naive at best or disloyal at worst.

3   When Tiger Woods objected to such labels as "the great black hope," which recognized only his African American heritage, all of America took a great interest. The fact that he is a mixture of several racial/ethnic heritages, and that he describes himself culturally and ethnically as Asian and Black – two "minority" identities – seems very important. If he, like so many other American athletes and entertainers, were only Black and White or Asian and White, it is doubtful that his identity assertions would have received such an enormous amount of mainstream attention. This is because it was Tiger's Asian heritage (as embodied by his lovingly devoted mother, who is from Thailand and is phenotypically Asian) that was being "denied" to him, a situation that falls outside of America's established tradition of denying "Whiteness" to those who are mixed.

        Societal hypodescent rules did initially label Tiger as "Black," but once he publicly objected to this, the mainstream media seemed to respond positively. It was members of the African American community who were most resistant to Tiger's mixed-race, Black-Asian identity. And it was this resistance that fascinated the mainstream media, and that made him and the "multiracial" Census category an opportunity for social and political conservatives to attack minority interests.

4   It is interesting that reporters would have asked for Powell's opinion on these issues at an event that had nothing to do with the subject of race. Powell has openly admitted to having a multiracial family history, but consistently identifies himself as an African American when questioned by the media, as he did on this occasion.

Chapter 36

George G. Sanchez

Y TÚ ¿QUÉ? (Y2K): LATINO HISTORY IN THE NEW MILLENNIUM

From M.M. Suárez-Orozco and M.M. Páez (eds) *Latinos: Remaking America* (2002). Berkeley: University of California Press, pp. 50–56.

BECAUSE GROWTH IN THE FIELD of Latino history and recognition of the demographic realities of the twenty-first century have much to contribute to changing intellectual understandings of race in the United States, the remainder of this chapter is devoted to these issues of racial formation. In particular, it addresses the question of the 2000 US census and the place of *mestizaje* in contemporary racial discourse in the United States.

During the 1990s, this nation prepared for its decennial census in a unique and important way. Various census officials, academic consultants and racial advocacy organizations debated the efficacy of adding a mixed-race designation to the census form. This debate, although it settled on the solution of allowing Americans to check off more than one racial category, was as important for the various positions taken by the debate participants as for the final resolution. Two multiracial organizations – "Project R.A.C.E.," based in Atlanta and composed of interracial married couples who were worried about their children's designation, and the "Association of Multiethnic Americans," consisting of mixed-race adults – fought for two different census solutions. They were often in conflict with racial advocacy organizations, especially the NAACP and MALDEF, who worried that a "multiracial" category on the census form would dilute the demographic strength of the black and Latino populations, respectively. Most sociologists and demographers involved in this debate agreed that some change in the census form was needed to acknowledge the multiracial population, and they were critical in crafting the final solution.[1]

I am principally concerned not with the actual debate that took place around the census but, rather, with the symbolic value of the multiracial human body around which both popular and academic discussions often revolved. I will argue that the multiracial body has been appropriated for use as a symbol of multi-ethnic America, often representing the nation's hope for the future and its potential for overcoming racial strife. Rather than being a "monstrous" depiction – one has only to think back to literary depictions of the "tragic mulatto" – the multiracial body appeared in the 1990s as an angelic savior for our age. But investing that sort of utopian power in the genetic mixing of our era only serves to heighten a new form of racial essentialism and once again to frame the process of overcoming racial hierarchy as a fundamentally biological one. Moreover, although historians have been among its most avid proponents, this new fascination with multiracial bodies is ahistoric in being unable to look at the particular ways in which racialization occurs *despite* and *alongside* racial mixing.

Probably the most famous interracial image of the 1990s was a virtual person, the computer-generated woman who graced the cover of *Time*'s 1992 special issue on immigration.[2] Abandoning a tradition of magazine covers that had depicted immigration and race by showing a multitude of different faces, *Time* chose to combine the races into one face, a young adult woman of uncertain origins but with striking features and an olive skin tone. This image, rather than evoking concern over the nation's future, as many previous covers had, was supposed to comfort us as Americans. If this is what diversity brings – a multiracial beauty whose own body encompasses all the different strands of newcomers to America – we should embrace this future.

Rather than a virtual image, the male equivalent of this future for the 1990s has been golfing star Tiger Woods, born to African American and Thai parents. Woods broke into the golfing scene when corporations were looking for a new spokesperson for multiracial America. Thus Woods, in his famous Nike commercials, is used to represent the future and becomes almost a Pied Piper among children, encouraging the multiracial legions to join him in taking over one of this nation's whitest of sports. His image, of course, is generally used in this country to stress his black roots. In Asia, however, Nike uses Woods's image to promote golf among that region's middle class, and it is his Asian roots that are played up. The multiracial body, therefore, becomes an excellent vehicle for globalization – an image made to order for multinational corporate capital.[3]

The multiracial body has also become the favorite symbol of a host of liberal and neoliberal writers who call on Americans to move beyond race, ethnicity, and identity politics toward a "new American nation" where difference is minimized and cosmopolitanism and toleration loom large. From historian Gary Nash's call, in his 1995 presidential address to the Organization of American Historians, for a deliberate *mestizaje* to rein in the divisions of contemporary America to social commentator Michael Lind's argument in *The Next American Nation* that the rise of intermarriage will contribute to a new America based on multiraciality, committed liberals have increasingly offered answers to the supposed problems of living in an era of multiculturalism by advocating racial mixing to break down racial difference.[4]

All of these published works point to the increasing rate of interracial marriage since the striking down of antimiscegenation laws in the 1950s and 1960s – and the increase in the numbers of children born to these unions. "Sixty percent of the babies born in Hawaii in 1991 were of 'mixed' race," declares Lind, adding that nearly one of three Hispanics marries a non-Hispanic and that "half of all Asian-Americans born in the United States marry outside of their official racial 'nation.' "[5] Even the numbers of children born to a black and a white parent grew fivefold, to 51,000, from 1968 to 1988. Nash reports that 70 percent of American Indians marry people who are not Indian; that outside the South, 10 percent of all African American males marry nonblack women; and that black–white marriages overall have tripled since 1970. For Nash, this means that "Mestizo America is a happening thing. A multiracial baby boom is occurring in America today."[6]

Both authors point approvingly to the changes that have occurred over the last thirty years, but they also note that these changes are not altogether new. Nash reminds us that the very word *miscegenation* did not appear until the late nineteenth century and that most of the American colonies saw no reason to ban intermarriage with Native Americans. He chronicles a host of "racial boundary jumpers," from John Rolfe and Pocahontas to Sam Houston, who took a Cherokee wife, to fur traders throughout North America, including the fabled Kit Carson. For Nash, US history is awash with folks who illustrate a racial "in-betweenness," including a long history of Indo-Africans such as Crispus Attucks; Spanish mixing with both Indians and Africans to produce individuals like the Spanish-African Pio Pico, the last Mexican governor of California; and the Punjabi-Hispanic couplings of the early twentieth century in agricultural California. According to Nash, "about three-quarters of African Americans today are multiracial, and perhaps one-third have some Indian ancestry. Virtually all Latino Americans are multiracial, so are nearly all Filipino Americans, so are a majority of American Indians, and millions of whites have multiracial roots."[7]

With all this historical intermingling, and with the recent upturn in inter-racial marriage, why is the present moment one in which the products of these unions can be vested with such power? Clearly, for these authors and others it is, as Nash puts it, "the specters of Sarajevo, Sri Lanka, and Somalia" that force us "to ask about the costs of the rigidifying of ethnoracial particularisms." For him, to transcend "America's Achilles' heel of race requires that we embrace hybrid-ity – not only in physical race crossing but in our minds as a shared pride in and identity with hybridity."[8] For Michael Lind, these trends point to the conclusion that "conventional categories promise to become increasingly meaningless, as whites, Asians, and Hispanics intermarry in the Pacific-oriented America of tomorrow." Whereas Lind calls for racial amalgamation and "altogether eliminat-ing race as a category from law and politics," Nash believes that "racial blending is undermining the master idea that race is an irreducible marker among diverse peoples."[9]

Having a background in Chicano history and a working knowledge of Latin American history, I, however, can only respond to these US scholars, "Welcome to the Americas!" Racial mixing has never in itself destroyed racial privilege, as the place of Africans and natives throughout nearly all Latin American countries has proved. Moreover, new racial formations out of mixed-race people, such as the mestizos who make up the vast majority of Mexicans in this country and to the south, are ever-present possibilities that certainly change the meaning of

LATINO HISTORY IN THE NEW MILLENNIUM

race, but not necessarily the privilege of whiteness in our society. If recent work in Asian American, Latino, and Native American studies has shown us anything over the past thirty years, it is that racialization projects can encompass various strategies for assigning difference: outright exclusion, processes of making the native foreign, creating "noble savages" to emphasize the inevitability of (white) progress, the exoticism that creates desire. It has been primarily the white–black binary character of racialization (particularly that created within US slavery with its formal taboo against white–black unions, all the while producing offspring of such illicit unions that would be recategorized as black) that has blinded US scholars to the range of racialization projects that have captured the vivid imagination of Americans in different regions at different times.

Indeed, if recent work in American studies is considered, which encourages us to think of "the cultures of US imperialism," these calls for "positive miscegenation" take on a new and troubling dimension. Many of the historical examples of racial blending occurred in the time of US growth as a continental empire, incorporating Indians and Mexicans through conquest, both territorial and sexual. This is *not* to deny the human emotions involved in individual unions; rather, it is to place these unions in the historical context that enables us to understand their potential for societal transformation. In the twentieth century, many interracial unions were shaped by the US military presence in Asia – from the Philippines, to the occupation of Japan and Korea, to Vietnam. Not only were these unions highly gendered, as in most imperial situations, but they also produced migrations to the United States that gave us the mixed-raced individuals to whom all these authors refer. Our era, at the turn of the twenty-first century, is producing mixed-race individuals in the context of globalization, particularly the hegemonic role played by US military and economic interests, which will help produce international networks of capital and trade without necessarily benefiting those left behind in our inner cities, who, though they too are involved in racial mixing, are left both "darker" and poorer.

Scholars of the imperialism of other nations would not be surprised by an upturn in mixed-race individuals. The histories of Britain and France are full of narratives of new racial formations that have helped perpetuate empires, while at the same time leading to new migrations to the imperial centers, particularly after World War II. Demonstrating, as Nash does, that "human emotions – the attraction of people to each other regardless of race and religion and much else – has run ahead of ideology and has often caused identity confusion and anxiety" does not address the many ways in which desire is structured by our own historical moments.[10] As recent work on "orientalism" has shown us, desire – even when it enjoys state and ideological sanction – can produce as powerful an "othering" process as that which emphasizes separation and containment.[11]

There is more that is troubling to me in this recent fascination with mixed-race unions and individuals than their detachment from our current historical moment. Ironically, the emphasis on biological mixing reinscribes essentialist categories of difference. Indeed, for racial boundary crossings to matter at all, difference has to be consistently maintained so that the act of crossing bears significance to the society. The emphasis on the *unique* role of mixed-race people in challenging America's racial assumptions also makes me wary of returning to biological interpretations linking race and culture. Mixed-race individuals must not only confront our racial assumptions because they exist; they must also act on the basis of their biology. They must serve as bridges and symbols for the rest of us.

No stronger example of this troubling perspective exists than the epilogue to David Hollinger's important book *Postethnic America: Beyond Multiculturalism*. Hollinger emphasizes that the offspring of interracial unions are of critical importance to a society that can move beyond race and ethnicity. "Mixed-race people are a powerful symbol for an opportunity long said to distinguish American society from that of most societies in Europe and Asia: the making of new affiliations . . . Mixed-race people are performing a historic role at the present moment: they are reanimating a traditional American emphasis on the freedom of individual affiliation, and they are confronting the American nation with its own continued reluctance to apply this principle to ethno-racial affiliations."[12] Because his book is a call to move away from affiliations based solely on descent and toward one based on consent (à la Werner Sollors), mixed-race people seem uniquely positioned to have choice in their racial affiliations. But Hollinger's argument also portrays mixed-race individuals as being biologically forced to choose. The reason why their choice is so "historic" is that their mixed gene pool forces them to make a decision about something that other Americans take for granted when they assume that their racial being is shaped by forces out of their control – their skin color and their parents' homogeneous culture.

Of course, the choice available to people of mixed race is also a burden as a consequence of America's racial hierarchy and emphasis on difference. In today's neoliberal, post-civil-rights world, this supposed choice is squandered if individuals do not recognize the duality of their racial position. If they choose solely a white racial position, they reinscribe white racial supremacy; if they choose solely a nonwhite racial position, they reinscribe an ethnic nationalism or a racialized condition that endorses a world where the races live apart. For the world envisioned by Hollinger, Nash, or Lind to exist, these individuals must choose a *dual* existence in which their very bodies serve as a bridge between races and cultures.[13] What a burden for these super-Americans to shoulder! What an abandonment of responsibility by those of us who appear to be bounded by one racial identity!

If this role is starting to sound a lot like a traditional role played by people of color, I think it is. DuBois's double consciousness was an acknowledgment that as long as racial hierarchy exists, as it has throughout the twentieth century he was foreshadowing, both a national and a racial identity would wreak havoc in the consciousness of African Americans. The "choice" of affiliation presented by Hollinger begins to look like the "choice" of African Americans: no choice at all. Others may be reminded of the classic collection of writings by radical women of color, *This Bridge Called My Back*, which in 1981 discussed the highly contested position of radical feminists, particularly lesbian feminists, in serving as bridges for whatever dialogues on race, gender, and sexual oppression arise in the feminist community. In that work, Gloria Anzaldúa spoke for a much more highly conflictual position than that described in the other works I have discussed so far. "I am a wind-swayed bridge, a crossroads inhabited by whirlwinds . . . this task — to be a bridge, to be a fucking crossroads for goddess' sake . . . the pull between what is and what should be . . . the mixture of bloods and affinities, rather than confusing or unbalancing me, has forced me to achieve a kind of equilibrium. Both cultures deny me a place in *their* universe. Between them and among others, I build my own universe, *El Mundo Zurdo*. I belong to myself and not to any one people."[14]

Anzaldúa herself is speaking from a position of multiple identities, but one fully engaged in specific communities of Chicanas, feminists, lesbians, and women of color. Moreover, she continually acknowledges the inner war that affects a *mestiza* consciousness, which sounds so different from the less complicated mestizo world described earlier by Gary Nash. Six years later Anzaldúa writes, "Cradled in one culture, sandwiched between two cultures, straddling all three cultures and their value systems, *la mestiza* undergoes a struggle of flesh, a struggle of borders, an inner war. Like all people, we perceive the version of reality that our culture communicates. Like others having or living in more than one culture, we get multiple, often opposing messages. The coming together of two self-consistent but habitually incompatible frames of reference causes *un choque*, a cultural collision."[15] Mestizo America, I would agree with Anzaldúa, is just as likely to produce cultural conflict as it is to generate individual liberation and collective equality. Whatever symbolic value continues to be placed on multiracial bodies, those bodies will continue to be sites of struggle — places where the visions of America's racial future are contested, both by the individuals who inhabit those bodies and society as a whole.

At one level, these two visions of "*mestiza* America" have a great deal in common. They both celebrate the crossing of racial boundaries and look forward to a time in which race does not determine social condition as much as it does today. But they also have fundamental disagreements that reflect conflicts over the very definitions of race and power in our contemporary and historical United States. One camp believes that the dismantling of racial categorization, in and of itself, will contribute mightily to a more equitable society; this is the vision of racial liberals and conservatives alike, one that links the neoliberals described here with those involved in the dismantling of affirmative action and ethnic studies programs in California. The other camp believes that white racial privilege must be attacked, because it continues to exploit racial difference and the distribution of political and economic power in our society. This attack usually emanates from specific communities whose disempowerment would only delay the elimination of racial privilege in society. Multiracial human bodies, for all their symbolic value in our contemporary world, cannot replace multiracial coalitions of individuals and organizations as the engines that are likely to transform American society. And it is *all* the boundaries that govern privilege in the United States — those shaped by race, class, gender, sexuality, and nation — that must be crossed to bring about a truly equitable society. My hope is that the field of Latino history will contribute mightily, in the next century, to that form of border crossing.

Study probes

1. Compare Sanchez's critique of the ways in which the 'multiracial' body is manipulated as a symbol of 'multiethnic' America to that of Nakashima in the previous extract.
2. Which historical and comparative examples does Sanchez provide which remind us that so-called 'racial' mixing is neither new nor unproblematic?
3. Outline the two visions of '*mestiza* America' the author describes.
4. Compare Sanchez's argument to that put forward in Ropp's extract.

Notes

1   See Juanita Tamayo Lott, *Asian Americans: From Racial Category to Multiple Identities* (Altamira Press, 1999): 99; and Charles Hirschman, Richard Alba, and Reynolds Farley, "The Meaning and Measurement of Race in the US Census: Glimpses Into the Future," *Demography* 37:3 (August 2000): 381–393.
2   *Time*, Special issue on immigration (1992), cover page.
3   See Henry Yu, "How Tiger Woods Lost His Stripes: Post-Nationalist American Studies as a History of Race, Migration, and the Commodification of Culture," in *Post-Nationalist American Studies* John Carlos Rowe, ed. (Berkeley: University of California Press, 2000): 223–246.
4   Gary B. Nash, "The Hidden History of Mestizo America," *The Journal of American History* 82:3 (December 1995): 941–962; Michael Lind, *The Next American Nation: The New Nationalism and the Fourth American Revolution* (New York: The Free Press, 1995).
5   Lind, see note 4: 294.
6   Nash, see note 4: 959.
7   Nash, see note 4: 941–943, 949.
8   Nash, see note 4: 961–962.
9   See note 4: Lind: 294, 295–296; Nash: 960.
10 Nash, see note 4: 959–960.
11 For the classic work on "orientalism," see Edward W. Said, *Orientalism* (New York: Pantheon Books, 1978).
12 David Hollinger, *Postethnic America. Beyond Multiculturalism* (New York: Basic Books, 1995): 166.
13 According to John Womack, in his "Latinos in the twenty-first Century" commentary at the Harvard Conference, the idea that *mestizos* would be natural leaders and the leading missionaries in society comes straight from nineteenth-century positivist and authoritarian notions. This theme surfaces in the work of José Vasconcelos, particularly *Raza Cósmica*, and resonates with anthropologists Franz Boas and Gilberto Friere.
14 Cherrie Moraga and Gloria Anzaldua, eds., *This Bridge Called My Back: Writings by Radical Women of Color* (Watertown, MA: Persephone Press, 1981): 205–209.
15 Gloria Anzaldúa, *Borderlands: The New Mestiza/La Frontera* (San Francisco: Spinsters/Aunt Lute Press, 1987): 78.

Chapter 37

G. Reginald Daniel

THE NEW MILLENNIUM: TOWARD A NEW MASTER RACIAL PROJECT AND EPILOGUE: BEYOND BLACK OR WHITE: A NEW UNITED STATES RACIAL PROJECT

Extract from *More Than Black?: Multiracial Identity and the New Racial Order* (2002). Philadelphia, PA: Temple University Press, pp. 172–175 and 189–194.

Keeping the "one-drop" rule: black essentialism and the Afrocentric idea

NOWHERE IS THE POWER OF THE ONE-DROP RULE for cultural and political mobilization more obvious than in currents of Afrocentrist thought that advance the notion of a primordial African "race" and nation. But the effectiveness of any organizing principle as the basis for essentialized collectives (viewed as if they were "natural," static, and eternal units), is inherently fraught with irreconcilable contradictions. Some of the discourses and practices of radical Afrocentrists are not merely pro-black but anti-white, if not actually "racist" in the strict sociological meaning of the concept. Prior to the late 1960s sociological definitions of racism relied heavily on notions of individual psychological biases and discriminatory attitudes. Since the 1960s racism has been viewed as more than simple antipathy and discrimination toward individuals based on individual racial prejudice. It is now defined as an overarching and more systematic implementation of discrimination based on the desire and power of dominant groups to maintain advantages for themselves at the expense of racialized "others." According to this view, racially subordinate groups – which by definition lack structural power – are not capable of "racism."[1]

This is not to suggest that we should dismiss Afrocentric concerns with identity politics, given the pervasiveness of white racism that has prevented the formation of a radical African diasporic subjectivity or plurality. The strengths of Afrocentric discourse are undeniable, notably the fostering of group pride, solidarity, and self-respect, and an interrogation of the ideology of inegalitarian integration (assimilation) and the perpetuation of differences in the manner of inegalitarian pluralism (apartheid).[2] The contradictions and weaknesses of radical Afrocentrism are, however, also readily apparent. Its exponents often criticize the validity of the concept of "race" on the one hand while reinscribing essentialist notions of black identity on the other.[3] How can they have it both ways?[4]

The "whitening out" of the African participation in the formation of the West is one of many injustices that have been inflicted on individuals of African descent, as well as on the whole of human civilization. It is imperative, therefore, to deconstruct the Eurocentric rendering of history.[5] There now seems to be fairly unanimous agreement on the central African origins of the human species, and few scholars contest the notion that ancient Egyptian civilization was a specialized variant of Nile Valley culture – as well as of a broader continental African type – that contained a largely blended population with strong Africoid geno-phenotypical, ancestral, and cultural components. There is also general acceptance of the fact that Egyptian civilization significantly antedated and influenced Greek civilization and thus ultimately influenced the early formation of the West. Furthermore, Afrocentrists are on solid ground in pointing out that even this more modest African presence in Egyptian civilization, and thus influence on the fountainhead of Western European civilization, has not traditionally been acknowledged by European historians.

The demise of Eurocentrism or Eurocentrism in a new guise?

At the same time, however, radical Afrocentrists' inclusive application of the term "black" to anyone and anything of African ancestry – no matter how remote in space or time – ignores the complex ancestral, genetic, and cultural diversity and blending that has taken place since early humans migrated out of Africa eons ago. At best it perpetuates a gross oversimplification of prehistory and contemporary history, and at worst a new distortion. Despite the legitimacy of the Afrocentric desire to give voice to the shared global disillusionment and alienation embedded in the African diasporic experience, the end result of some strains of Afrocentric revisionism – particularly its more radical variants – is very similar to the oppressive mechanism of the one-drop rule. If Eurocentrism is to be deconstructed, then the "either/or" paradigm that has served as its foundation must also be deconstructed. If anything, the goal should be to move beyond Eurocentrism and radical Afrocentrism in order to embrace a "holocentric" (or postmodern) paradigm based on "both/neither," which would come closer to the actual "truth."

The reluctance of many African-descent Americans to critique the essentialist underpinnings of radical Afrocentrism is rooted in the legitimate fear that this would cause individuals to lose sight of the experience of the African diaspora and the unique sensibilities and culture that have arisen from that experience.[6] bell hooks proposes that we can criticize essentialism while emphasizing the significance of the authority of experience. She argues that there is a significant difference between the repudiation of the idea of an African-derived essence and the recognition that African-derived identity has been forged through the experience of exile and struggle.[7]

The new multiracial identity is part of this process, but it is problematical to many Afrocentrists. Some of their opposition is premised on the belief that a multiracial identity is antithetical and inimical to their goal of forging African Americans into a cohesive political force.[8] Thus they view a multiracial identity as merely one in a series of recent attacks on the integrity of the African American community inspired, however indirectly, by Eurocentric thinking.[9] But this criticism obscures the potential that a multiracial identification may hold for challenging from within and from without the imposition of what Victor Anderson calls a myopic and constricting "ontological blackness."[10]

One of the factors obscuring the compatibility between Afrocentrism and the new multiracial identity is that the term "Afrocentrism" has been used to convey different things, some of which obscure its deeper significance.[11] Although Afrocentrism is significantly related to African history and has emanated from Black Nationalist thought, it is more appropriately described as a paradigm that places African-descent individuals at the center of their analyses. Accordingly, they become subjects rather than simply objects of history. In addition, Afrocentrism is predicated on traditional African philosophical assumptions. Ontologically, Afrocentrism assumes that all elements of the universe are viewed as one and are seen as functionally interconnected. This rejection of clearly delineated boundaries extends to morality, temporality, and the very meaning of reality.[12] Afrocentrism underscores the value of interpersonal relationships. This person-to-person emphasis fosters a human-centered orientation that values interpersonal connections more highly than material objects. Afrocentrists reject Eurocentric dichotomous thinking that divides concepts into mutually exclusive polar opposites.[13] Afrocentricity thus provides a mode through which all individuals can liberate themselves from the restrictive dichotomization and hierarchical concepts of the modern Eurocentric model. It posits a cosmic vision that acknowledges an inheritance that all individuals share as descendants of the first diaspora, when humans migrated out of Africa to populate the globe.

More moderate variants of Afrocentrism *and* of the new multiracial identity both criticize the pathologies of Eurocentrism and also challenge rigid notions of universality and static identity within mass culture and consciousness. They thus provide the occasion for new and more inclusive constructions of self and community absent from more radical Afrocentric discourse. The more inclusive blackness that would emanate from this shift in consciousness would allow African-descent Americans to acknowledge the manner in which the collective African American experience has been altered not only by sex/gender, class, and a host of other categories of experience, but also would take into consideration the empirical conditions of individual lives.[14]

The new multiracial identity rather than imploding African American identity, can potentially forge more inclusive constructions of blackness (and whiteness). This in turn would provide the basis for new and varied forms of bonding and integration that would accommodate the varieties of African-derived subjectivity without at the same time negating a larger African-derived plurality, or maintaining that plurality as a dichotomous space, which is a photographic negative and complete antithesis of whiteness.[15] Furthermore, this discourse would challenge Eurocentric notions of African-derived identity that represent blackness and whiteness in one-dimensional ways in order to reinforce and sustain white domination and black subordination. Part of the struggle for a radical African American collective subjectivity that furthers black liberation must necessarily be rooted in a process of decolonization that continually challenges and goes beyond the perpetuation of racial essentialism and the reinscription of notions of authentic identity. This process should include the search for ways of constructing self and community that oppose any reification of "the blackness that whiteness created" in the manner of the one-drop rule, by recognizing and embracing the multiple experiences of African-descent identity, which are the lived and empirical conditions that make diverse identities and cultural productions possible.[16] Accordingly, the new multiracial identity, with its nonhierarchical and nondichotomous configuration, is quintessentially Afrocentric in the deepest meaning of the word.[17]

. . .

Epilogue

A new United States racial "commonsense": beyond the one-drop rule

THE NEW MULTIRACIAL IDENTITY reflects a fundamental postmodern shift in consciousness premised on the 'Law of the Included Middle,' which seeks to incorporate concepts of 'partly,' 'mostly,' or 'both/neither,' and acknowledges shades of gray. Although embodied in individuals, the new multiracial identity is perhaps best characterized as a cluster of new possibilities in the nation's collective racial consciousness that seeks to transform traditional racial categories and boundaries by expanding definitions of blackness and whiteness.[18] While the new multiracial identity is a flagship for this alternative consciousness, it should not be viewed as the solution, in and of itself, to racism and racial inequality. It remains to be seen how many individuals will actually live out the promise of the new multiracial identity and help create a more egalitarian racial order in the United States. There is no single multiracial voice but many different voices, including those of reactionaries and radical visionaries. Some individuals will reinscribe racial hierarchies associated with previous multiracial identity projects. Those who display the new multiracial identity, however, resist pressures to conform to the existing racial order, with its inequitable power relations. Many will devote their energies to developing institutions that address the needs and interests of multiracial individuals in the manner of egalitarian pluralism, as other groups have done in their ethnogenesis in the United States. At the same time they will seek to build bridges across the racial divide in the manner of egalitarian integration. In the process, these individuals will become part of the larger antiracist struggle for human liberation.

Ethnoempathy and the law of the included middle

As long as public policy deems it necessary to collect data on race and ethnicity – particularly as a means of tracking the nation's progress in achieving social equity – the inclusion of a multiracial identifier, no matter what the format, will not only provide a more accurate picture of contemporary demographics but also help alleviate the psychological oppression imbedded in current methods of data collection, which support and are supported by the one-drop rule. A multiracial identifier is a logical step in the progression of civil rights, with the potential to change social attitudes. The multiracial phenomenon helps deconstruct the notion of racial 'purity' by challenging the notion of mutually exclusive racial categories, which are the very means by which racist ideology and racial privilege are perpetuated in the United States.[19] The option to identify oneself as multiracial should encourage more people to question the artificially fixed and static nature of racial and ethnic categories as they now exist. Ultimately, multiracial identity can initiate a long overdue national conversation about the shared ancestral connections that have been obscured by centuries of racism.

Discussion should not center, however, on multiracial identity, which is not inherently problematic in itself. Being multiracial in a hierarchical system, whether pluralist or integrationist or both, can mean being a little less black, and thus a little less subordinate, but it does not assure equality with whites. The critical challenge is completely to dismantle the Eurocentric underpinnings of the racial order in the United States by deconstructing both the dichotomous and hierarchical relationship between blackness and whiteness and making a genuine socal commitment to affirming the equality of differences in the manner of egalitarian pluralism, while at the same time nurturing the equality of commonalities in the manner of egalitarian integration. This transformative consciousness seeks to achieve equality of similarity without advocating assimilation, to encourage unity without perpetuating uniformity, and to build new kinds of community without promoting conformity.[20]

The acceptance of multiracial identity should in time work in the minds and hearts of European Americans greater sensitivity to the experience of African Americans, or what sociologist John Cruz has called 'ethnosympathy.'[21] Ultimately both African Americans and European Americans would develop a greater level of identification with and appreciation of each other's experiences in the manner of 'ethnoempathy.' Such a development would hold promise for moving race relations beyond the assimilation model toward a new multiracial synthesis, a horizontal process of transracial/transcultural amalgamation. In such a model, Africans American and European American heritage would become relative and complementary rather than absolute and antithetical. Black and white would be extremes on a continuum of blended grays, with no one color or heritage being superior or inferior to another.

A new American revolution: toward a 'declaration of interdependence'

The removal of legal barriers to black equality and the growth of the black middle class have neither eradicated white racism nor achieved the egalitarianism promised by the American creed. Yet the African American struggle for racial equality has been the most powerful assertion in recent times of the American revolutionary tradition embodied in the Declaration of Independence. The success of collective African American resistance provides the nation with a lesson in what political scientist Richard Merelman calls 'supportive interdependence.'[22]

Unlike European American ethnic groups, African Americans have never been permitted to lose what W.E.B. Du Bois calls the 'twoness' of their identity as hyphenated Americans. Despite its painful consequences this twoness has provided African Americans with a shared experience of racial subjugation and a common racial fate — however varied this may be in terms of sex/gender, color, culture, or class — that has historically required blacks to support and depend on each other in the face of white domination.[23] African Americans thus bring to the national conversation on race a sense of bonding that has been forged in isolation, exclusion, and out of the experience of 'Otherness' and difference, but one that can serve as a springboard for a renewed national sense of community.[24] As the United States enters the twenty-first century, European Americans must embrace the supportive interdependence of the African American value sphere.

Racial domination has historically made whites dependent on each other. Unlike blacks, however, many whites are unconscious of their interdependence in a racial collective subjectivity. Unlike African Americans, European American ethnic groups have been largely permitted or encouraged — if not actually forced — to lose the doubleness of their identity as hyphenated Americans in exchange for the benefits of white racial privilege. The apparent 'racelessness' (and 'culturelessness') that seems to have emerged in this process has imbued whiteness with a pervasive and universal status as the hegemonic 'Other' against which all other 'Otherness' is posited. Consequently, whiteness often appears to operate as an unmarked racial category.

But just as African American resistance to racial domination has developed a value sphere premised on supportive interdependence, the practice of racial domination on the part of European Americans has paradoxically imbued them with the values of individualism (or universal particularism). Unfortunately, white racism is deeply embedded in American society and intertwined with the ideas of individualism, merit, and standards of excellence associated with the 'American Dream.' The myth that European Americans achieved their power solely through individual merit and excellence is a powerful one, but it leaves their racial advantage as whites out of the equation. This is not to suggest that individual European Americans have not had to struggle for success, or that all European Americans benefit equally from the advantages of white racial privilege. Nor can individual European Americans be blamed for slavery, Jim Crow segregation, or other racially discriminatory practices and inequities. Yet European Americans as a racial plurality have a structural edge in the pursuit of the American Dream, quite apart from questions of individual merit and excellence. Indeed, one of the privileges of being white is not even having to think about the fact of one's race.[25]

That said, the individualism that whites espouse originates in the idea of universal pluralism and can bring to the national conversation on race a new individualism based on 'supportive independence.' Such a contribution would also provide African Americans with a lesson in the importance of dissent within the African American community. Generally speaking, the experience of oppression diminishes tolerance of internal dissent because subordinate groups must be as unified as possible in order to survive; and nonconformists and dissidents have often been silenced or expelled. Yet receptivity to dissent is a crucial part of fighting domination.[26]

In the European American case, individualism has been allowed to hypertrophy and has consequently degenerated into a pathological sense of disconnection and dissociation that isolates individuals from each other. By contrast, individualism that permits open debate among African Americans would strengthen arguments against outside domination and unite its members in a collective effort to overcome subjugation. By forcing proponents of resistance to make their strongest case, dissident members of subordinate groups play an indispensable role in the struggle for liberation.[27] An openness to internal dissent can disabuse groups of what may be only an illusion of unity – which frequently degenerates into coercion – by replacing it with the more dynamic notion of communion.[28] The European American value sphere's emphasis on individualism in the manner of supportive independence could be an antidote to this dis-ease.[29]

A 'trans-American' value sphere

The United States must, therefore, meld the African American and European American value spheres into a new trans-American value sphere based on supportive independence and interdependence. This new value sphere could serve as the foundation for a new racial contract based on integrative pluralism that would unite European Americans, African Americans, and other Americans of color in a new consciousness.[30] In a system of integrative pluralism, differences become the basis upon which to forge a web of interdependent yet flexibly integrated racial and cultural pluralities.

These dynamics acknowledge the reality of black-white differentiation but maintain porous boundaries that are easily crossed. Group pluralism functions in tandem with individual pluralism that is integrated under a larger national consciousness and identity.[31] A value sphere based on integrative pluralism is greater than the sum of its parts – it exists at a deeper level of organization than either the American creed of individualism or the African American ideal of community alone.[32]

The people of the United States must come together in support of a new consciousness based on the founding principles of individualism while simultaneously making a commitment to a 'Declaration of Interdependence' based on the principles of communion and mutual support. Otherwise, race relations will continue to deteriorate. Cities will become more unlivable, and whites will continue to retreat – psychologically into themselves and physically into the suburbs. The racial divide will widen and the nation will lose both economic power and cultural capital, as both African Americans and European Americans abandon the promise of the American Dream.[33]

From racial dictatorship to racial democracy

The achievement of integrative pluralism will necessarily depend on 'social engineering, constant vigilance, government authority, official attention to racial behavior,' and a willingness by US citizens to relinquish at least some individual rights for the greater national good.[34] Ironically, this presents the United States with a new 'American Dilemma' perhaps even more daunting than the one described by Gunnar Myrdal half a century ago. The very values that are essential to achieving a new racial order run directly counter to some of the nation's deepest and most cherished beliefs about authority, self-determination, and individual rights. African Americans may be more willing than European Americans to compromise these ideals, because they stand to gain. Most whites, on the other hand, are reluctant to give up any authority, self-determination, or rights, and have little to gain from that kind of sacrifice.[35]

Its is doubtful that a majority of European Americans genuinely desire contact with African Americans as equals in more than token numbers. Even if they do, achieving more than token contact would exact a price that most whites are probably not willing to pay.[36] Genuine integrative pluralism is unlikely to be achieved on a large scale until the nation is willing to make a commitment to the social engineering and the sacrifice necessary to achieve it.[37] As long as European Americans refuse to confront notions of white privilege (and lingering beliefs of white supremacy, however subtle), even the best-intentioned efforts to eradicate racial equality will be continually thwarted.[38]

By now, the lessons of history should have taught the nation that neither political reform nor appeals to conscience alone can solve issues of racial inequality in the United States. Yet a new trans-American value sphere based on supportive independence and interdependence would help coordinate political action and public policy. This in turn would serve as a means of building other issue-based coalitions, regardless of racial and ethnic group differences, to work toward an inclusive politics that recognizes the complexity of various types of oppression and how each feeds on the others in order to thrive.[39] This kind of politics would create a constructive and beneficial relationship between the different groups, one marked by mutual respect, interdependence, a balance of power, and a shared commitment to community.[40]

Forging this consciousness will require both blacks and whites to disabuse themselves of the illusions and falsehoods spawned by history.[41] There must be a genuine commitment to undermining hierarchical and dichotomous thinking, particularly in the media and the classroom. The current multicultural curriculum, however – which tends to emphasize differences in the manner of group pluralism – is not likely to meld the African American and European American value spheres into an integrative pluralism. Multiculturalism without a simultaneous commitment to transculturalism could easily harden into a pernicious isolationism, despite its egalitarian premises and goals. What is needed instead is a comprehensive and nationally coordinated curriculum at the pre-school, K-12, and university levels that explores and validates not only racial and cultural diversity (egalitarian pluralism), but also shared racial and cultural commonalities (egalitarian integration). A comprehensive anti-bias curriculum and a program that teaches skills in conflict mediation must buttress this agenda.[42] Both European Americans and Americans of color would be taught to embrace their own 'colorfulness' without internalizing 'white guilt' or 'minority victimization,' respectively.[43]

The new multiracial identity, which seeks to transform traditional racial categories and boundaries, is emblematic of this transformative consciousness. As multiracial-identified individuals climb over the walls, cross the borders, erase and redraw the boundaries that separate them, everyone will be reminded that they actually live most of their lives in the liminal gray space between the extremes of black and white, whether or not they are conscious of that fact.[44] Taken to its logical conclusion, a new national consciousness grounded in integrative pluralism would lead whites and blacks and everyone in between to transcend their separate and hostile worlds.[45] It would ensure that wealth, power, privilege, and prestige were more equitably distributed than has ever been the case before in this country. Such a transformation in thought and behavior would move the United States closer to the ideal of a land of equal opportunity for all.

Study probes

1   How does Daniel define Afrocentrism? Why is he critical of its radical strand's political objectives?
2   Why does he suggest that Afrocentrism and new 'multiracial' identity politics are more compatible than oppositional?
3   In his epilogue, how does Daniel define 'the new multiracial identity'?
4   Compare Daniel's defence of the 'multiracial' Census category and the oppositional arguments put forward by authors in previous extracts.
5   Outline Daniel's recommendations for a 'A New United States Racial Commonsense'.

Notes

1   Others make a distinction between individual racism, which is defined as everyday individual antipathy based on race, and institutional racism, which has larger social structural implications in terms of the distribution of wealth, power, privilege, and prestige. Molefi Asante, *Kemet, Afrocentricity, and Knowledge*, 17–22; Werner Sollors, "The Idea of Ethnicity,"

in *The Truth about the Truth: De-Confusing and De-Constructing the Postmodern World*, ed. Walter Truett Anderson (New York: Putnam Books, 1995), 58–65; Ali Rattansi, " 'Western' Racisms, Ethnicities and Identities in a 'Postmodern' Frame," in *Racism, Modernity and Identity: On the Western Front*, ed. Ali Rattansi and Sallie Westwood (Cambridge: Polity Press, 1994), 57; Christie Farnham Pope, "The Challenge Posed by Radical Afrocentrism: When a White Professor Teaches Black History," *Chronicle of Higher Education* (March 30, 1994), B1; Gerald Early, "Understanding Afrocentrism: Why Blacks Dream of a World without Whites," *Civilization* (July/August 1995), 31–39.

2   hooks, "Postmodern Blackness," 23–31; Marable, *Beyond Black and White*, 121–122; Schiele, "Afrocentricity for All," 27; Nantambu, "Pan-Africanism Versus Pan-African Nationalism," 561–574.

3   Manning Marable, *Beyond Black and White*, 122; Rattansi, " 'Western' Racisms, Ethnicities and Identities," 57; Molefi Asante, *Afrocentricity: The Theory of Social Change*, 105–108; Asante, *Kemet, Afrocentricity, and Knowledge*, 17–22.

4   Marable, *Beyond Black and White*, 122.

5   Mary Lefkowitz, *Not Out of Africa: How Afrocentrism Became an Excuse to Teach Myth As History* (New York: Basic Books, 1996), 161; Molly Myerowitz Levine, "Review Article, The Use and Abuse of *Black Athena*," in *American Historical Review* (April 1992): 440–464; George Will, "Intellectual Segregation: Afrocentrism's Many Myths Constitute Condescension toward African-Americans," *Newsweek* (February 19, 1996), 78.

6   G. Reginald Daniel, "Eurocentrism, Afrocentrism, or Holocentrism?" *Interrace* (May/June), 33; Cornel West, *Beyond Eurocentrism and Multiculturalism*, vol. 1 (Monroe, Maine: Common Courage Press, 1993), 1–30.

7   hooks, "Postmodern Blackness," 23–31.

8   Charles Lemert, *Sociology after the Crisis* (Boulder Westview Press, 1996), 86; Pauline Marie Rosenau. *Postmodernism and the Social Sciences: Insights, Inroads, and Intrusions* (Princeton: Princeton University Press, 1992), 52; John Michael Spencer, "Trends of Opposition to Multiculturalism," *Black Scholar* 23 (1993): 2–5.

9   Spencer, "Trends of Opposition," 2–5.

10   hooks, "Postmodern Blackness," 23–31; Patricia Hill Collins, "Setting Our Own Agenda," 52–55; Anderson, *Beyond Ontological Blackness*, 11–19.

11   Schiele, "Afrocentricity for All," 27.

12   Ibid., 27; Molefi Asante, *The Afrocentric Idea* (Philadelphia: Temple University Press, 1987), 3–18; Linda James Myers, "The Deep Structure of Culture: Relevance of Traditional African Culture in Contemporary Life." in *Afrocentric Visions: Studies in Culture and Communication*, ed Janice D. Hamlet (Thousand Oaks, Calif.: Sage Publications, 1998), 1–14; Norman Harris, "A Philosophical Basis for an Afrocentric Orientation," in *Afrocentric Visions: Studies in Culture and Communication*, ed. Janice D. Hamlet (Thousand Oaks, Calif.: Sage Publications, 1998), 15–26; Terry Kershaw, "Afrocentrism and the Afrocentric Method," in *Afrocentric Visions: Studies in Culture and Communication*, 27–44.

13   Hochschild, *Facing Up to the American Dream*, 137–138; Asante, *The Afrocentric Idea*, 3–18; Jerome H. Schiele, "Rethinking Organizations From an Afrocentric Viewpoint, in *Afrocentric Visions: Studies in Culture and Communication*, 73–88; Linda James Myers, *Understanding an Afrocentric World View: Introduction to an Optimal Psychology* (Dubuque, Iowa: Kendall/Hunt Publishing, 1988), 1–28.

14   Schiele, "Afrocentricity for All," 27; Asante, *Kemet, Afrocentricity, and Knowledge*, 5, 26, 28, 39.

15   hooks, "Postmodern Blackness," 23–31.

16   Ibid., 23–31; Anderson, *Beyond Ontological Blackness*, 9–11; Paul Connolly, "Racism and Postmodernism: Towards A Theory of Practice," in *Sociology after Postmodernism*, ed. David Owen (Thousand Oaks, Calif.: Sage Publications, 1997), 65–80; Rattansi, " 'Western' Racisms, Ethnicities and Identities," 30; Steven Seidman, "Introduction," in *The Postmodern Turn: New Perspectives on Social Theory*, ed. Steven Seidman (New York: Cambridge University Press, 1994), 8–9; Rosenau, *Postmodernism and the Social Sciences*, 5–7.

17   Marable, *Beyond Black and White*, 121.

18   Daniel, 'Beyond Black and White,' 333–41.

19   Paul R. Spickard, Rowena Fong, and Patricia L. Ewalt, 'Undermining the Very Basis of Racism – Its Categories,' *Social Work* 4 (1995): 581–84.

20   John Higham, *Send These To Me: Jews and Other Immigrants in Urban America* (New York: Atheneum, 1975), 242–46.

21   John Cruz, *Culture on the Margins: The Black Spiritual and the Rise of American Cultural Interpretation* (Princeton: Princeton University Press, 1999), 3–4, 68.

22   Richard Merelman, *Representing Black Culture: Racial Conflict and Cultural Politics in the United States* (New York: Routledge, 1995), 284–99.

23   Ibid.

24   Steele, *The Content of Our Character: A New Vision of Race in America* (New York: St. Martin's Press, 1990), 66–68.

25   Hacker, *Two Nations*, 60.

26   Merelman, *Representing Black Culture*, 284–99.

27   Ibid.

28   Ibid.

29   Patterson, *Ethnic Chauvinism*, 154–61.

30   Higham, *Send These To Me*, 242–46.

31   Ibid., 242–46; Steinhorn and Diggs-Brown, *By the Color of Our Skin*, 235; Orlando Patterson, *Ethnic Chauvinism: The Reactionary Impulse* (New York: Stein and Day, 1977), 178–85.

32   Merelman, *Representing Black Culture*, 284–99.

33   Ibid.

34   Steinhorn and Diggs-Brown, *By the Color of Our Skin*, 222–23.

35   Ibid.

36   Ibid.

37   Ibid.

38   Banner-Haley, *The Fruits of Integration*, 55, 67–69.

39   Mark A. Chesler, 'Creating and Maintaining Interracial Coalitions,' in *The Impacts of Racism on White Americans*, (ed.) Benjamin P. Bowser and Raymond G. Hunt (Thousand Oaks, Calif.: Sage Publications, 1981), 217–43; Ervin Laszlo, *Evolution: The Grand Synthesis* (New Science Library: Shambhala, 1987), 133–49; Higham, *Send These to Me*, 242–46; Richard W. Thomas, *Understanding Interracial Unity: A Study of Race Relations* (Thousand Oaks, Calif.: Sage Publications, 1996), 195–211; Merelman, *Representing Black Culture*, 284–99; Loriane Hutchins and Lani Kaahumanu, 'Bicoastal Introduction,' in *Bi Any Other Name: Bisexual People Speak Out* (Boston: Alyson Publications, 1991), xxii–xxiv.

40   Correspondence with Ken Wilber, December 23, 1998; Wilber, *A Brief History*, 188–90.

41   Merelman, *Representing Black Culture*, 284–89.

42   Ibid.; Louise Derman-Sparks, *Anti-Bias Curriculum: Tools for Empowering Young Children* (Washington, D.C.: National Association of the Education of Young Children, 1989), ix–10, 31–38; Yehudi Webster, *Against the Multicultural Agenda*, 5–10, 101–67; Shelby Steele, *The Content of Our Character*, 127–48; Arthur Schlesinger, Jr., *The Disuniting of America: Reflections on A Multicultural Society* (Whittle Direct Books, 1991), 1–3, 20–57; Dinesh D'Souza, *Illiberal Education: The Politics of Race and Sex on Campus* (New York: Free Press, 1991), 1–23, 59–123, 194–228; Wilber, *A Brief History*, 188–90; Diane Ravitch, 'Multiculturalism Yes, Particularism No,' *Chronicle of Higher Education* (October 24, 1990), A44; Martin Cross, *The End of Sanity: Social and Cultural Madness in America* (New York: Avon Books, 1997), 144–73; Sam Allis, Jordon Bonfante, Cathy Booth, 'Whose America?: A Growing Emphasis on the Nation's 'Multicultural' Heritage Exalts Racial and Ethnic Pride At The Expense of Social Cohesion,' *Time Magazine* (July 8, 1991), 12–17; Sharon Bernstein, 'Multiculturalism: Building Bridges or Burning Them?' *Los Angeles Times*, A1; Chester E. Finn, Jr., 'Why Can't Colleges Convey Our Diverse Culture's Unifying Themes?' *Chronicle of Higher Education* (June 13, 1990), A40; Larry Gordon and David Treadwell, 'On Race Relations, Colleges Are Learning Hard Lessons,' *Los Angeles Times*, A1; Peter 1. Rose, *They and We: Racial and Ethnic Relations in the United States*, 5th ed. (New York: McGraw-Hill, 1997), 239–56; John Brooks Slaughter, 'The Search for Pluralism in Higher Education,' keynote address at the eighth annual Naumburg Memorial Lecture, University

of California, Los Angeles (April 18, 1989); William A. Henry, Jr., 'Beyond the Melting Pot,' *Time Magazine* (April 9, 1990), 28–31; Richard Leviton, 'Reconcilable Differences,' *Yoga Journal* (September/October 1992): 50–55, 100.

43   Janet E. Helms, 'An Overview of Black Racial Identity Theory,' in *Black and White Identity: Theory, Research, and Practice*, ed. Janet E. Helms (Westport, Conn.: Greenwood Press, 1990), 9–32; Janet E. Helms, 'Toward a White Racial Identity Development,' in *Black and White Identity: Theory, Research, and Practice*, 49–66; Steele, *The Content of Our Character*, 48–49, 77–109.

44   Hutchins and Kaahumanu, 'Bicoastal Introduction,' xxii–xxiv.

45   Hacker, *Two Nations*, ix–xiii; Wilber, *A Brief History*, 188–90.

Chapter 38

Itabari Njeri

THE LAST PLANTATION

Extract from *The Last Plantation: Color, Conflict, and Identity: Reflections of a New World Black* (1997). New York: Houghton Mifflin, pp. 216–221, 226–229 and 234–236.

> What this current discourse is about is lifting the lid of racial oppression in our institutions and letting people identify with the totality of their heritage. We have created a nightmare for human dignity. Multiracialism has the potential for undermining the very basis of racism, which is its categories.
>
> (G. Reginald Daniel, *The New Yorker*, July 25, 1994)

ILL-INFORMED AND REACTIONARY FORCES have seized an issue that held and still could hold such sanguine possibilities. When I and many others began heeding demands that the mixed ancestry of all Americans be embraced, we hoped it meant a new consciousness was abroad, not the perpetuation of an old one.

A fresh generation of multiethnic children, supported by an older one, and a flood of immigrants for whom a discrete *racial* identity was foreign, were actors on a stage ringing, during the last quarter century, with national rhetoric touting the country's cultural diversity. All this could provide fertile ground for a new view of US identity. A view that could challenge both the polarizing Black - White *racial* bifurcation that exists, as well as the seemingly progressive vision of the US as a cultural mosaic – diverse but carefully bounded. It could offer, instead, the icon of a nation as a tapestry of citizens joined by history, by culture and, yes, *blood*.

G. Reginald Daniel was among those with a similar view; though his belief that *racial* categories are the "very basis of racism," rather than an expression of the ideology of *racism*, misses the mark.

Daniel teaches a course on *multiracial* identity at the University of California at Los Angeles. He shared the stage with Velina Hasu Houston and others at the symposium I organized in 1990, and was among the first of those I interviewed in the 1980s about the emerging *multiracial* issue.

An ordinary-looking Negro, like me, Daniel shares a similar ancestry: African, East Indian, Irish, Native American, and French. In my case, substitute English for Irish (though relatives who have dug deeper into the family's genealogy now speculate that my great-great-grandfather, the pirate Sam Lord, may have been of Black Irish descent – his ancestors trekking from North Africa to the British Isles around the time of the Crusades).

Unlike me, his primary cultural identity is not Black. "I am not a *multiracial* African American. Sometimes I identify with my European ancestry more," Daniel said, and he feels more socially at ease with Whites.

When he says this, I infer that – like too many – the American in "African American" refers merely to geography, not the transformative reality of living in a New World culture.

Those things that he and others may see as distinctly "White" or European, I see as part of my heritage as a Western woman – whether I have any genetic links to that ancestry or not. It is part of, not separate from, my New World identity.

My syncretizing instincts certainly stem, in part, from my family background, but even more, I think, from my experience of music.

I spent childhood days on city playgrounds dancing, till my stomach ached, to "Fingertips," Parts 1 and 2, or mesmerized by opera once I'd been taken to the Met at the age of nine to hear Renata Tebaldi in *La Bohème*. Later, I would wake up to the sound of the shofar from the Orthodox synagogue next door, then rise from bed and look at my autographed picture of Judy Garland. Her likeness occupied a place of honor on my dresser from the time I was ten, when I won a contest for an alarmingly adult rendition of "The Man That Got Away," until I was a teenager. Rushing past Judy, I dressed and went to school to refine what teachers said was an instrument equal to Tebaldi's and just as capable – if I worked really hard – of approaching that of the "Divine One": Sarah Vaughn. She, with Miriam Makeba and Lady Day, became ultimate sources of inspiration – especially the latter two for their understated sensuality.

Of course, some would say that that is how it's supposed to be in the American melting pot. But the end product that metaphor classically insists upon is a homogenized thing, specifically an Anglicized one. You know, the same Big Mac you get here, you get in Oshkosh. The melting pot as ethnic smelter – an idea epitomized during World War I by Henry Ford's Ford Motor Company English School Melting Pot.

Ford – as Werner Sollors recalled in his important book on US identity and culture, *Beyond Ethnicity* – used to have foreign-born employees attend his company's language school, which staged elaborate graduation rituals. With the hull and deck of an ocean steamship docked at Ellis Island as the backdrop, a gigantic cauldron with FORD ENGLISH MELTING POT SCHOOL painted on it stood center stage. The graduates – dressed in native costumes and carrying their Old World possessions tied in a bundle – marched down a gangplank into the cauldron, then emerged wearing American clothes and waving tiny versions of Old Glory.

Assimilation has occurred, will occur, is inevitable and desirable if we are to function as a cohesive society. No truly pluralistic society – large groups of people with completely different languages and cultures – could exist as a nation without extreme coercion; the former Soviet Union is the obvious example of that. But assimilation is not the one-way street too many Americans raised on the melting pot myth believe. In the tapestry of US life I see four-lane boulevards everywhere, with traffic in both directions and stylish cultural jaywalkers always making their mark.

And while none of these categories is discrete, as some might insist, I'd argue that US culture is composed of what is yours, what is mine, and what is ours.

As well as specific cultural practices that may be thought distinct, there is a body of experience that shapes our social perceptions and informs our individual subcultures. The attitudes, more than differing rituals – especially for ethnic groups with long histories in the US – are what define and separate most US citizens from one another, I think. And they constitute a broader definition of culture, not easily overcome.

Further, while polarized opposition exists in every dimension of US life – pro-lifers in combat with pro-choice advocates, environmentalists slugging it out with developers – *race* has been the most intractable source of all our social woes. Though social scientists at the end of the twentieth century assert its declining significance and those in the hard sciences increasingly assail it as an amalgam of prejudice, superstition, and myth, on the whole the national dialogue seems locked in anachronistic rhetoric about its value. Perhaps it is the desperate utterance of a society whose moorings are about to be undone by the loss of a defining myth. I wonder, given the incredible publicity that surrounded Charles Murray and Richard Herrnstem's often spiritually eugenicist tract, *The Bell Curve*.

In it, they attempted to link intelligence – the measure of which is imprecise, often culturally biased, and changeable over time for the same individual – to *race*, a concept that falsely asserts there are pure, discrete divisions of humanity to which intellectual capacity, among other attributes, can be assigned. Having done so, they said that Blacks score lower on intelligence tests than do Whites and that the data they studied indicate the gap is largely genetic rather than environmental.

Even though Murray and the late Richard Herrnstein claimed to reject the pernicious notion of *race*, it's the rotten plank upon which they built their case for nature over nurture in the realm of intelligence.

But to paraphrase the conservative Black economist Glenn C. Loury, for too long, the loudest voices of African American authenticity have insisted on viewing all experience through a *racial* lens. "These racialists are hoisted by their own petard by the arguments and data in *The Bell Curve*." Indeed, these self-lynchings are the strange fruit we've often helped to cultivate.

As Angela Davis reminds us in Anna Deavere Smith's masterly theater piece *Fires in the Mirror*, about the Crown Heights riots, *race* was once synonymous with community for African Americans. But the rope attached to the anchor has become a noose, choking off social growth. It has become an "increasingly obsolete way of constructing community . . . I am convinced," she said, "that we have to find different ways of coming together, not the old coalition in which we anchor ourselves very solidly in our specific racialized communities, and simply voice our solidarity with other people." Though our own communities have to be the base from which we act, the rope attached to the anchor should be long enough to allow us to move into other communities.

"I have been thinking a lot about the need to make more intimate these connections and associations." A way of working with and understanding the "vastness of our many cultural heritages, ways of coming together without rendering invisible all our heterogeneity. I don't have all the answers," said Davis. "[But] what I am interested in is communities that are not static, that can change, that can respond to new historical needs."

As one of the oldest and largest populations of mixed ancestry in the US, and the most politically influential, African Americans, in the debate over *multiracial* identity, have an opportunity to forge an expanded definition of community for ourselves and the nation. But at the national level, African American politicians have been conspicuously absent from the debate, even though their constituencies have a significant stake in the outcome.

[. . .]

Their response to this last accusation, of course, would be that a *multiracial* designation would preclude such hypocrisy, which only brings us back to the lunacy of perpetuating *racial* classification and stratification. And acquiescence to the latter underscores that, ultimately, the last plantation remains the mind – a consciousness unable or unwilling to conceive of a social reality unbound by the calculated politics of ethnic division with which the nation's bloody *racial* history is rife. For despite the bogus rhetoric of a *multiracial* category taking us to the next frontier, the loudest voices addressing the *multiracial* issue prove that the old *racial* order is actually hardening, even as it seems to collapse under the weight of ethnic permutation.

There seems to be a political and psychological need in the US for both the dominator and the dominated to maintain a permanent *racial* caste. One composed of a group taxed with a chronic disability stemming from a historical condition: slavery. As Toni Morrison noted in *Playing in the Dark: Whiteness and the Literary Imagination*: "The concept of freedom did not emerge in a vacuum. Nothing highlighted freedom – if it did not in fact create it – like slavery." Further, she wrote, "in the construction of blackness and enslavement could be found not only the not-free but also, with the dramatic polarity created by skin color, the projection of the not-me." Or, as the late historian Nathan Irvin Huggins put it, "Just as American freedom finds its meaning in American slavery, whiteness and white power found their meaning in the debasement of blacks."

It is, perhaps, this chronic need to stand in juxtaposition to the "not-me" and point a denying finger that compels many *multiracial* Americans, and their families, to demand that their biological truth be acknowledged, and exoticized, while persistently and falsely referring to African Americans as *monoracial*.

Lamely, many of the advocates of a *multiracial* category argue that since African Americans see themselves as *monoracial*, it would be presumptuous to challenge that self-definition. For African Americans, however, constantly under siege, the choices and chances for self-definition have been limited by patterns of dominance and inequality. Holding on to a slavemaster's definition of *race* has seemed a matter of political survival.

But it is possible and politically healthier to construct a strong group identity around the more fluid notion of ethnicity. Picture a very dark, African-looking person standing up at an academic conference in Atlanta in 1968 and saying, " 'Given our diversity, Blacks should consider themselves an ethnic group.' The meeting collectively looked at him as some kind of traitor. What a 'bizarre' idea was the attitude," Ibrahim Sundiata, chairman of the department of African and African American Studies at Brandeis University, told me. People wanted to know, " 'Where is this coming from?' But I think if people had accepted that idea earlier, it would have solved a lot of problems."

"Such as?" I asked.

"We hold on to this idea of pure races. But unless you are an essentialist arguing that the 'true folk' still exist on these shores after three hundred plus years, Blacks are not a race in any old-fashioned biological sense." But an identity constructed around ethnicity gives us much more latitude to accept the complexity of the group. As an ethnic group, people look different but have some commonality in terms of culture and maybe ancestry. We are already there physically, he said, "but psychologically, it requires retooling."

By making Black an ethnic category, he went on, "we can say what Henry Ford said of automobiles. You can have a Ford Model T in any color you want, as long as it's black." This sounded like the Black version of the melting pot as ethnic smelter. And it begged the question of what constitutes a Black identity.

As a child, my Jamaican grandmother never allowed us to move into a new apartment without first anointing the threshold with liquor, nor could one take a drink of rum at a party without first sprinkling a bit on the floor. Both gestures were an offering to our African ancestors. And when I'd tell some tale that seemed outlandish, my grandmother would balk, "Sounds like Anansi story to me." I always thought she was talking about Nancy, some lady I'd never met. I didn't know for years that Anansi was the famed character of West African folklore, the spider who spun tales, his stories still told by the descendants of Africans who'd been brought to Jamaica. Many things we said and did were African, I later learned, and so much a part of me that I took them for granted. But for many of my teen years and beyond, I wasn't Black enough because I sang opera. If my authenticity was questioned, where did somebody who ate sushi instead of grits for breakfast fit in?

Sundiata thought for a moment and then responded obliquely. "There remain a great many essentialists in the Black community espousing ethnocentrism. And African Americans on the whole have all sorts of tests of Blackness which ultimately become [politically] dysfunctional."

One of the things that concerns him about the *multiracial* proposal, should it come into being, is that there will be both a wholesale exodus of Blacks from the category at one end and a refusal to enter it at another. This is the pattern that has occurred elsewhere in the Americas where there are *multiracial* categories, "and I don't think the US would be that different. I'm really concerned that we end up with this residuum," which is both color- and class-based – that darker-skinned brother in the hood standing on the corner who says: I am the true Black. And since color and socioeconomic status are linked in the US to the disadvantage of the darker-skinned, the true Black becomes not only the most African-looking among us, but the poorest – with all the liabilities poverty invites for anybody.

"This person should become even more outraged," Sundiata suggested. And the angrier he gets – because his class position is not improved in this further stratified environment – the more likely he is to spark super-essentialist movements. One immediately thinks of the lure of the Nation of Islam and its successful appeal to the most marginalized of Black folk – convicts, addicts, prostitutes – many of whom can put the prefix *ex-* before these labels because of the salvation they found through the Nation's program of entrepreneurship and self-respect combined with racial chauvinism.

"We would start arguing among ourselves more and more," Sundiata predicted. And other groups, understandably, would go the other way. Potential allies would be loath to align themselves with us, and those who share a similar ancestry would increasingly distance themselves, in Sundiata's scenario, carving out their own social niche.

. . . We should never allow any *multiracial* person – either through ignorance or political calculation – to exoticize his identity at our expense. We should co-opt the position and assert that, as New World Blacks, we are multiethnic people; in doing so, we should make clear to ourselves and others that affirming our multiethnic ancestry and being "Black" are not mutually exclusive. Further, should the day ever dawn when a *multiracial* or multiethnic category appears on the census, Black politicians had better make sure that it is constructed in a way that includes African Americans. If African Americans are not included in the designation – and in a way that ensures our hard-won constitutional protections – there should be no such designation.

Thinking this way, as Sundiata put it, requires psychological retooling, and other groups have done better at accommodating their diversity. "For instance, I am studying the man who popularized the term Hispanics," the Puerto Rican nationalist Pedro Albizu Campos.

Albizu Campos was a complex character who was three *races* in his lifetime. He was a mulatto born under the Spanish in Puerto Rico in 1891. He came to the United States shortly before World War I, lived in Massachusetts for eleven years, went to Harvard to study law, and then joined the US Army. "He was put in a Negro unit for, after all, he was the grandson of a slave and the illegitimate child of a mother who scrubbed floors," said Sundiata. He was thrown into the African American community. And whether he rejected it or vice versa, by the time he returned to Puerto Rico in the early 1920s, he had constructed a new identity for himself and his people.

He did this using the elite ideology of the plantation owners who called themselves *Hispanos*. "The term had a very distinct and limited meaning, referring to people who owned the land," Sundiata explained. But Albizu Campos took that and said no. All of us speak the same language, Spanish. And we are

Catholics. This is the core of our identity, he asserted, the "transcendent power of the Catholic Church and the beautiful Castilian language." Of course the dominant elite laughed at him, Sundiata said. "This little brown man going around saying he was the same as they were. But he joined a party, the Nationalist Party, and continued this compaign – in some ways very violently – until his death, in 1965."

Of course, the term *Hispanic* is a highly contentious one. The Spanish-speaking community in the East is more accepting of it, while in the West, the preferred term is *Latino*. Actually, the preferred term is whatever one's specific national origin is – Nicaraguan, Mexican, Guatemalan. But I am interested here in the larger point: the idea of subsuming the phenotypical aspects of *race* with ethnicity.

Such an idea "would have seemed silly in nineteenth-century Puerto Rico," Sundiata continued. But it has worked out today that Puerto Ricans are an ethnic category. This, he reminded, occurred on an island where slavery was abolished ten years after the Emancipation Proclamation. And for a population that essentially mirrors the polygenetic ancestry of African Americans.

"I am not saying that racism in Puerto Rico is gone. But by emphasizing ethnicity rather than race – when dealing with outsiders, and to a certain extent on the island – ethnicity has triumphed. Politically, culture was exalted over race in Puerto Rico, exactly the opposite of what happened in the US."

While scholars, writers, and artists may be exploring the evolution of Black identity in the United States as the millennium approaches, the Urban League's Billy J. Tidwell lamented that "the rhetoric of the Black leadership in this country is on the whole fifty years behind the times. It is anachronistic in terms of its binary, Black-White construction of race relations, and lacks any serious com-prehension of the place of African Americans in a social landscape transformed by vast demographic changes." The latter is evidenced in part by the emergence of multiethnic Americans of partial African descent who have little or no connection to the traditionally defined Black population – as well as the Black–Korean conflict.

It would be unfair, then, to view the waxen figure of Tom Bradley as singular as he offered political boilerplate standing outside a fire-gutted Korean American market: *"We have to get better mutual understanding of the differences in the cultures of these two racial groups. And we have to stress that courtesy in a market is something that is expected and demanded."* Coming five months after Latasha's death, those were the first words he uttered publicly about the long-standing Black–Korean tensions. Afterward, as he tried to glide to his car, that neighborhood schoolteacher named Desira Ruggles hounded him, accusing him of talking only to the elite, not to the people who patronized the markets daily and felt their lives threatened as much as the Koreans felt theirs were.

But on Bradley's watch, this was the city whose Chamber of Commerce propaganda trivialized multiculturalism as gastronomic tourism, making diver-sity virgins out of visitors who never swallowed a kosher burrito under smoggy L.A. skies. Businessmen and politicians in pre-riot L.A. could pretend that Los Angeles was either a paradise of separate but harmonious ethnic groups or, in an updated version of Anglo-dominated assimilation, a zesty tossed salad served on the American flag. But too late – amidst the smoke that rose from incinerated flesh and bones and wood and steel that was Sa-I-Gu – the Sphinx of City Hall, who took credit for L.A.'s friendly smorgasbord, would say he had never seen an ethnic conflict escalate as quickly and turn so bitter as the one between Koreans and Blacks.

Study probes

1   Why is Njeri critical of Daniel's earlier position on 'race' and cultural identity?
2   Why does the author suggest that African Americans have an important role to play in the 'multiracial' identity politics debate?
3   What does Sundiata, whom Njeri interviews, have to say about the 'multiracial' category? What historical and comparative evidence does he provide to defend his position?
4   Compare Njeri's position on 'multiracial' identity to the argument put forward by Daniel in the previous extract.

Chapter 39

Mark Christian

ASSESSING MULTIRACIAL IDENTITY

Extract from *Multiracial Identity: An International Perspective* (2000). London: Macmillan, pp. 104–107, 111–113 and 115–119.

White supremacy and multiracial identity

IN ASSESSING THE NOTION OF MULTIRACIAL IDENTITY and social grouping it is worth noting how it has been inextricably linked to the ideas of white supremacy. Peter Fryer maintains that the rise of pseudo-scientific racism in the UK was interwoven with that of the British Empire and its dominance of the darker peoples of the 'New World', especially during the eighteenth and nineteenth centuries.[1] With the UK being a nation that espoused the virtue of Christianity via the growth of the British Empire, it needed to excuse itself from the obvious inhumanity that follows in the path of racial dominance and oppression. Put simply, imperial theorists espoused a justification for the enslavement and genocide[2] of Black peoples through an array of pseudo-scientific assumptions expressing the innate superiority of white Europeans over Africans and Asians. Indeed, to have any degree of African ancestry was also to possess, according to European racialist theories, inferior human qualities.[3]

The historian George Fredrickson, in his ground-breaking book *White Supremacy*, suggests that white supremacy refers to the attitudes, ideologies and associated policies connected with the development of white European domination over 'dark' populations. He maintains:

> white supremacy means 'color bars,' 'racial segregation,' and the restriction of meaningful citizenship rights to a privileged group characterized by its light pigmentation.[4]

When examing the issue of multiracial identity it is important to understand the legacy of white supremacy. It is a theory and practice based on the irrational opinion that white Europeans (mainly of Anglo-Saxon and Northern European origin) are inherently superior to non-Anglo-Saxon origin peoples – particularly those of African and Asian ancestry. Moreover, it is also a theory and practice that hover over the subject and analysis of miscegenation. Absurd as it is, we have an approximate 500-year history of European domination and subjugation of African and Asian peoples, yet wherever Europeans have colonised they have sexually intermingled with the indigenous populations. Apart from this obvious paradox, it is a taboo subject that should be exposed, yet rarely does this occur in an academic sense.[5]

Charles Mills, a professor of philosophy, has recently examined how traditional European philosophy refuses to acknowledge its relationship to the development of white supremacy. For Mills, 'White supremacy is the unnamed political system that has made the modern world what it is today.'[6] In other words it is a system that has been developed over centuries of European global expansionism and domination, but in mainstream philosophy and ethics it is taboo subject matter. Mills further contends that the issue of 'race' is segregated from 'the world of mainstream (i.e., white) ethics and political philosophy.'[7] This manifests itself in a number of ways, but specifically it is in the exclusion or offhand dismissal of 'ethnic minority philosophy', for want of a better phrase. It is the manner of legitimating, making 'normal', the inferiority of dark peoples that Mills is alluding to. Without careful consideration of how the 'white world' has been shaped and formed through its intellectual heritage, understanding the various constructions of racial identity will inevitably be that much more complex.

Time and again contemporary studies fail to deal with the history of white supremacy in terms of connecting it to the contemporary sociological aspects of multiracial identities.[8] Yet the notion and practice of white supremacy cannot be dismissed as something ephemeral or superfluous to the history and social construction of multiracial identities. Indeed at the heart of the culture of racism in societies structured in racial dominance is this historical legacy of white supremacy. Take, for example, the view below of the ex-Prime Minister (1979–90) of the UK, Margaret Thatcher, with regard to what Europeans have in common historically:

> Too often the history of Europe is described as a series of interminable wars and quarrels. Yet from our perspective today surely what strikes us most is our common experience. For instance, the story of how Europeans explored and colonised and – yes, without apology – civilised much of the world is an extraordinary tale of talent, skill and courage.[9]

Margaret Thatcher displays an overt notion of white supremacy in her perspective of European colonialism. However, an integral aspect of European expansionism relates to the issue of its miscegenation with, using Thatcher's anaylsis, the 'uncivilised' humanity that it came into contact with. Taking this into account, it would be facile to confine the semantics surrounding multiracial peoples to that of a contemporary phenomenon in suggesting that such persons are, for example, 'new people' and ahistorical.[10] European racist ideology and jingoism, as advocated by Thatcher, is a significant backdrop for appropriate comprehension and analysis of racially mixed international communities.

Therefore, to assess multiracial identity in the UK, US, South Africa and Jamaica in a sociological sense demands both a regional and historically specific analysis. Each nation has its own peculiar social relations when it comes to multiracial populations. With regard to the UK, we have in this study gone beyond the theoretical and provided empirical evidence via in-depth interviews with multiracial respondents of African and European origins. What emerges from the collective views of the mixed origin respondents is that they seem to grasp both a personal and a societal understanding of their multiracial identities. In addition each articulates how they manoeuvre through the incongruity of racial labelling to the reality and relevance it has to their social existence in Liverpool, England.

It is this 'personal' and 'societal' dichotomy that needs to be highlighted when we assess multiracial identity constructs. Despite the fact that many persons could openly claim to have a number of racial origins, from the UK research it was found that the majority of the respondents regarded themselves as 'Black British'. We could take this to mean 'Black *and* British', where 'Black' represents the main aspect of one's social life, and 'British' accounts for the amalgamation and influence of this specific diasporan experience. Or maybe it is a term employed in order to move away from the negative status labels associated with multiracial identity in the UK.

[. . .]

Nomenclature default and multiracial terminology

It is difficult to deny the large effect which racialised labels involving multiracial persons have on the social construction of their identities. Historically, as shown above, we have numerous societies that developed rather offensive nomenclature to describe multiracial persons. Again, in assessing the aspect of multiracial identity in an international context, we need to associate it within the context of white supremacist thought and practice. Indeed, it is out of white European philosophy and intellect that the origin of such labels as 'half-caste', 'half-breed', 'mulatto', and the many more, emerged.

The social fact remains that most of the labels associated with multiracial peoples are in some form problematic. In a sense social analysts often unwittingly fall prey to the racism and mythology by accepting such racialising uncritically. Yet it is rather difficult to navigate through the historical and sociological remnants of specific racialised contexts without being bogged down by imperial nomenclature. Moreover, despite the proliferation of 'identity politics' in the academy, little has been achieved to enhance clarity. It is fair to suggest that there has been an increase in the nebulous aspect of 'Black identities' via the use of ever-confusing terms.

Ifekwunigwe offers a good example of the contemporary confusion in racial labelling theory. Her research is in relation to UK multiracial persons of African and white European origin, yet she prefers to use the term 'metis(se)' (metis, masculine, and metisse, feminine) when defining such persons. Ifekwunigwe states:

> [metis(se)] is the French-African term I have chosen to describe project participants all of whom have British or European mothers and continental African or Caribbean fathers.[11]

The above definition of a specific multiracial group in the UK is somewhat confusing as it comes via a French-African experience. Ifekwunigwe is very critical of Afrocentric scholars for not discussing the relevance of African diasporan experiences in and of themselves. For example, the English-African diaspora in the UK and the US-African diasporan experiences each represent unique communities, even though they both have cultural ties to the African continent. Social researchers, according to Ifekwunigwe, need to acknowledge this complexity and not get drawn into simple anaylses viewing the African diaspora as monolithic. However, in this criticism Ifekwunigwe unwittingly contradicts herself. On one level she states that it is important to understand the experience of multiracial persons within the context of their Black cultural roots, along with the respective 'host nation' experience. While in relation to her research in the UK, she defines the multiracial cohort under French-African terminology! This confusion is typical of a number of contemporary 'identity politics' analyses. It seems that academics are forever searching for nomenclature that is 'new' in order to provide something original in the research output. But often the result is to merely bring forth another syncretic, and obscure, term for describing multiracial persons.

Ifekwunigwe is correct to point out the need to understand each multiracial experience, via the African Diaspora, in its own right. As a matter of fact it is certainly a key theme in this study. Yet, and this is the main problem with Ifekwunigwe's perspective, it is equally important to analyse the links and similarities of international multiracial experiences. If we overlook this interwoven aspect of multiracial identity, then the research findings will be severely lacking – especially in the case of African diasporan experiences.[12] Simply applying 'new names' to multiracial persons in the UK, in the aim of providing an anti-essentialist analysis, fails to adequately deal with the actuality of 'not being white' in a white dominated society. This lived reality usually entails being called a 'nigger' for persons born of mixed African and white European origins. In view of the catalogue of anti-essentialist tracts emanating from postmodern 'Black' theorists, such as Ifekwunigwe, it would be refreshing for them to note this important social fact. Too often the obvious aspects of multiracial identity are ignored for a more evasive, intricate and turgid analysis.

The problem of nomenclature continues to be one of the main aspects of multiracial identity theory. Even though the fact of Blackness goes beyond the realms of skin tone and hair texture, being of 'mixed origin' descent can provide a means of dividing Black peoples.[13] This begs the questions: what's in a name? Is

it a significant aspect of identity? Considering this assessment of how international multiracial communities have emerged and developed, there is little
doubt that 'a name' is very important. Indeed from the perspective of the UK,
US, South Africa and Jamaica, we can see how racial labelling, based primarily
and incongruously on phenotype, has produced various racialised social relations
within these societies.

Naming is therefore central in the assessment of international multiracial
identities. In addition, regardless of the various social circumstances in which
racialised relations have developed, it appears evident that the naming and classification of international multiracial groups is interwoven with upward and
downward social mobility. Societies structured on racialised populations will no
doubt continue to manifest social inequality due to the deep-rooted nature of
racism.

. . . When the taboo surrounding miscegenation is taken into consideration
it is easier to understand why the one drop rule has such potency in US history.
Concomitant with this historical amnesia is the way mainstream American historians often fail to acknowledge or appreciate the contribution African Americans have made to US culture. Yet when African American intellectuals challenge
the narrow view of Anglo-American history they are accused of 'disuniting
America'.[14] At bottom here is a history of social oppression based primarily on
'race' in the US. 'Race-mixing' is an extremely sensitive area to discuss and
debate, and many social researchers find it more useful to ignore rather than
examine. If miscegenation is discussed it is put in the framework of being a
contemporary phenomenon.

A problem with the pressure group calling for a multiracial category in the
US is that they fail to fully take into account the significance and fragility of
African American numbers. The perspective suggesting that there is a 'new'
multiracial group *within* the African American community is both myopic and
ahistorical. Especially in view of the fact that between 75 and 90 per cent of
African Americans could claim to be of multiracial origins. In examining a
multiracial identity, one does not need to have merely a white parent and a Black
parent to be considered 'multiracial'. Indeed, many 'pure Blacks' and so-called
'mulattos' in the US married as 'Blacks' in law. But, using a logical reference,
these are in effect 'mixed marriages'. It is only in a *socially constructed* sense then
that African Americans are 'racially pure'. No doubt there will continue to be
heated debate regarding the issue of 'who is Black?' for many years to come in
the US.

The UK and the city of Liverpool offer a qualitative perspective on multiracial identity and an understanding of a specific nomenclature. This case is also
useful in again indicating how light brown skin does not necessarily mean upward
social mobility. In the city of Liverpool there is a relationship between the
dynamics of widespread social deprivation and Black disempowerment. With the
Black community being in a minority, 'Liverpool-born Blacks' relatively share
the same subordinate position as other Black minorities. There is certainly no
pattern of social privilege given to the light-skinned over dark-skinned Blacks.
However, there does exist an obvious disparity between the rates of employment
among the white and Black populaces.[15] Up to 90 per cent of multiracial Black

youth in some areas of Liverpool are unemployed, that is three to four times more than the figure for whites.[16] Racialised discrimination has an adverse effect on the life chances of multiracial persons in Liverpool. To assess the extent of it would go beyond the confines of this study, but it is fair to suggest that racial discrimination is an everyday occurrence for many designated 'Liverpool-born Blacks'.

Conclusion

To summarise, during the 1990s much debate took place in 'Black cultural studies' academic circles concerning the issue of 'hybridity' and 'diaspora'. In regard to international multiracial identity each of these concepts has specific relevance. However, the majority of theorists who write extensively on hybridity and diaspora tend to view the concepts in correspondence with ethnicity, migration and the postcolonial experience rather than interraciality.[17] To put it another way, these postmodern theorists tend to view hybridity merely in cultural terms and tend to adopt narrow ahistorical perspectives. Writing within a postcolonial frame of reference, Homi Bhabha states:

> the importance of hybridity is not to be able to trace two original moments from which the third emerges, rather hybridity to me is the 'third space' which enables other positions to emerge. This third space displaces the histories that constitute it, and sets up new structures of authority, new political initiatives, which are inadequately understood through received wisdom.[18]

Hybridity is used by Homi Bhabha primarily in theoretical terms to depict the contemporary 'place' of the ex-colonised in the metropolis. It does not necessarily relate to miscegenation; hybridity is more to do with social, cultural and political syncretism. The 'third space' offers a novel way of understanding the age-worn, almost trite, dichotomies: coloniser/colonised or oppressor/oppressed. Instead, out of these dichotomous histories emerges the 'third space' that is somehow 'free' of its parental and historical lineages. It offers a dynamic, postmodern and anti-imperialist, way to contest the power of the powerful. Although Bhabha's writing is rather turgid, even esoteric at times, it does reveal another way of considering the notion of hybridity, certainly beyond the generally negative usage by British Empire apologists and theorists in relation to human hybridity.[19]

A problem with Bhabha's analysis is in the way he assumes we can simply create something entirely 'new' from two histories. It really is ahistorical in perspective and cannot be deemed logical from the perspective of the life experiences of the once 'colonised' – those persons/groups that have migrated from the satellites to the metropoles. In theory Bhabha may well have touched on something worth considering, but when put to the acid test of the social world it fails. Of course history and culture is dynamic and ever-changing, but the pattern or framework of oppression and social exclusion can often remain a constant.

Multiracial persons, for example, cannot simply ignore those histories that created them under the certain sociological dimensions of colonialism. In point of fact more often than not they have had little choice but to side with the 'subordinated history' and social group.

Take the 'coloureds' of South Africa under apartheid: using Bhabha's basic framework, they have emerged primarily via two histories, two peoples – one Black of African descent, one white of European descent – yet it is the connection with their Black/African heritage which has been the source of their collective oppression. Those 'coloureds' who could find a way to deny their Blackness had a chance to enter the 'white world' of social privilege in South Africa. This was the reality of a 'third space people'. They had little choice in the matter of being 'new' or apart from the histories that produced them. Their social world was interwoven with these 'parent histories'. Taking this into account, it is understandable why Bhabha fails to link his 'hybridity theory' directly to the actual social processes of human interaction and experience at ground level. His analysis is unnecessarily abstract and lacking in ethnographic terms.

In addition, Bhabha fails to accommodate the complexity of these various 'colonial-based histories', as each has specific *internal* hybrid formations that also need to be explained. To view 'Englishness' as a monolithic entity, for example, is not to understand its mongrel origins. Therefore and paradoxically, too many theorists, exemplified by Bhabha, construct rather rigid conceptual frameworks to promote 'fluid theories' of cultural hybridity. But they are bound to be proved wanting when examined in relation to what occurs 'on the ground' in the social world.

The concept of the 'African diaspora' is also gaining recognition within the academy. Professor Stuart Hall has written extensively on this subject and is regarded as a *de facto* guru in Black cultural politics in the UK. He can also be situated in the postmodern school of thought linking the concept of 'diaspora' to hybridity and 'difference' in Black culture. Writing in relation to African Caribbean cinematic themes, Hall maintains:

> The diaspora experience . . . is defined, not by essence or purity, but by the recognition of a necessary heterogeneity and diversity; by a conception of 'identity' which lives with and through, not despite, difference; by *hybridity*. Diaspora identities are those which are constantly producing and reproducing themselves anew, through transformation and difference.[20]

Above, Hall is expressing the 'new' in diasporan experiences. In this sense, for persons of African (Caribbean) descent in the diaspora, it is mythical to try and return to a past, to lost origins. They have long gone, and whether one is located in the Americas, the Caribbean or Europe, having fed into a 'new history' is the 'essence' of one's existence. Looking back to a long-lost African civilisation that is devoid of European hegemony may satisfy in a symbolic sense, but it cannot be recaptured. All, in fact, according to Hall, is renewing itself in cultural terms and is forever provisional.[21]

How is this relevant in the assessment of international multiracial identity? Actually it is rather informative and useful in the sense of describing again the fluidity of identity constructs. Yet what Hall suggests is really not novel in regard to an understanding of the development of the 'New World' and its descendants. For example, as we have already discussed, Jamaicans are essentially a 'hybrid' population. Within this population, however, is a hierarchical colour structure. How does Hall explain this? In fact he does not really consider the implications of this implicit white supremacy. He is more interested in explaining away the syncretism of Black culture itself. There is a celebration of 'hybrid forms', but the issue of social privilege via colour stratification is not considered.[22] Moreover, despite this consolidated effort to prove how Black history and culture is interlocked and fused with African, Caribbean, Asian and European forms, Hall *et al.* fail to follow the trail of white supremacy to consider just how this has changed form, but remained constant in terms of hegemonic leadership.

In sum, in our assessment of international multiracial identity, it is important to examine the various forms of Black culture and explain the hybrid elements that make it up. Again, to regard this as something 'postmodern' is to be myopic and ahistorical. To be sure it is well documented, even though at times ignored by white supremacists, that world human civilisation is in essence *hybrid*. This may well be a positive way to promote world harmony and understanding of 'race matters'. However, we must not be content with merely celebrating hybridity *per se*; what we also need to know is how humans have socially demarcated themselves – regardless of their similarities and cultural linkages. Multiracial identity, as maintained throughout this study, is a social construct that has special social consequences for certain groups that are defined as such. The experiences do differ around the globe, but there is a common link in the way each multiracial group has interacted with the social forces of white supremacy. Crucially, this chapter has attempted to assess the complexity of a number of international multiracial identities.

Study probes

1   According to Christian, what is 'white supremacy', and why is it integral to any analysis of 'multiracial' identity?
2   Why is Christian critical of my deployment of *métis(se)* – the term I previously used at one time to highlight the tangle of terminology? *(For my own critique of this term and my rationale for a return to the use of the term 'mixed race', see the 'Notes on terminology' at the beginning of the Reader.)*
3   Using various case studies, how does the author argue for more complex culturally and historically specific analyses of the relationships among 'mixed race', colour, status and power?

Notes

1   See P. Fryer, *Staying Power: The History of Black People in Britain* (London: Pluto, 1984), ch. 7.
2   For example, in relation to the occupation of Tasmania by the British in the eighteenth and

nineteenth centuries and the genocide of the indigenous population, Fryer writes in *Black People in the British Empire: An Introduction* (London: Pluto Press, 1988), p. 38: 'For 30 years black Tasmanians were pitilessly hunted down, tortured and put to death. Men and boys were castrated and otherwise mutilated; women were raped, flogged and burnt with brands; children's brains were dashed out. Some black Tasmanians were tied to trees and used as targets for shooting practice. One old woman was roasted alive. Another woman had her dead husband's head hung round her neck and was driven in front of her captor as his prize. One settler kept a pickle-tub into which he tossed the ears of the black people he shot.

3   Ibid., pp. 66–72.
4   G.M. Fredrickson, *White Supremacy: A Comparative Study in American & South African History* (Oxford: Oxford University Press, 1981), p. xi.
5   One scholar largely overlooked in the analysis of miscegenation is J. A. Rogers (1880–1966). He was a self-educated man and a prolific writer who, among other works, contributed three volumes covering the subject of miscegenation. He provides profound evidence relating to the contradictions of white supremacist thought and practice. Rogers stated in the 1952 edition, and Foreword, of volume 1: 'Racial doctrines as they exist today negate intelligence.' See J.A. Rogers, *Sex and Race*, vols I, II, III (New York: Helga M. Rogers, 1968; first published in 1942 and 1944).
6   C.W. Mills, *The Racial Contract* (Ithaca: Cornell University Press, 1997). p. 1. For another detailed critique of white supremacy in relation to European philosophy see M. Ani, *Yutugu: An African-Centered Critique of European Cultural Thought and Behavior* (Trenton, NJ: African World Press, 1994).
7   Mills, note 6, p. 4.
8   See, for example, M.P.P. Root (ed.), *Racially Mixed People in America* (California: Sage, 1992); and *The Multiracial Experience: Racial Borders as the New Frontier* (California: Sage, 1996). These collaborative works are ahistorical in terms of the analysis of multiracial identities, particularly in the US context.
9   M. Thatcher, *Britain and Europe* (London: Conservative Political Centre, 1988), p. 2.
10 Many authors imply that multitracial persons are a type of 'new people', but this is an erroneous and half-baked perspective that is devoid of the manifold historical evidence pointing to the contrary.
11 J. O. Ifekwunigwe, 'Diaspora's Daughters, Africa's Orphans? On Lineage, Authenticity and "Mixed Race" Identity', in H.S. Mirza (ed.), *Black British Feminism a Reader* (London: Routledge, 1997), p. 147.
12 I have argued this point in relation to the UK and US elsewhere, see M. Christian, 'An African-Centered Approach to the Black British Experience: with Special Reference to Liverpool', *Journal of Black Studies* 28 (3) (January 1998), pp. 291–308.
13 See D. Weekes, 'Shades of Blackness: Young Black Female Constructions of Beauty', in H.S. Mirza (ed.), *Black British Feminism: A Reader* (London: Routledge, 1997), pp. 113–126.
14 See A.M. Schlesinger, Jr., *The Disuniting of America: Reflections on a Multiracial Society* (New York: W.W. Norton, 1992).
15 See A.M. Gifford, W. Brown and R. Bundey, *Loosen the Shackles: First Report of the Liverpool 8 Inquiry into Race Relations in Liverpool* (London: Karia Press, 1989).
16 Information on the contemporary national trend for Black unemployment in the UK can be sought from: 'Race for the Election', c/o Churches Commission for Racial Justice, Inter Church House, 35 Lower Marsh, London SE1 7RL, UK.
17 See H.K. Bhabha (ed.), *Nation and Narration* (London: Routledge, 1990), his *The Location of Culture* (London: Routledge, 1994): and 'The Third Space', in J. Rutherford (ed.), *Identity, Culture, Community Difference* (London: Lawrence & Wishart, 1990), pp. 207–21; P. Gilroy, *The Black Atlantic: Modernity and Double Consciousness* (London: Verso, 1993); S. Hall, 'Cultural Identity and Diaspora', in J. Rutherford (ed.), *Identity, Culture, Community Difference* (London: Lawrence & Wishart, 1990), pp. 222–37.
18 Bhabha, 'The Third Space', p. 221.

19   See R.J.C. Young, *Colonial Desire: Hybridity in Theory, Culture and Race* (London: Routledge, 1995), pp. 6–12.
20   Hall, note 17, p. 235.
21   Ibid., p. 236.
22   Ibid.

Chapter 40

Minelle Mahtani and April Moreno

SAME DIFFERENCE: TOWARDS A MORE UNIFIED DISCOURSE IN 'MIXED RACE' THEORY

From D. Parker and M. Song *Rethinking 'Mixed Race'* (2001). London: Pluto Press, pp. 71–75.

[. . .]

Minelle: We cannot help but observe that non-white 'mixed race' voices are marginalised in current debates, and are not given equal and valuable consideration. We have found that discussions in 'mixed race' circles, as well as public conceptions of 'mixed race', have tended to disregard the experiences of non-white 'mixed race' people. As mentioned before, this is reflected in the common societal perception that the term 'mixed race' is synonymous with a black and white 'mix'. Part of our concern stems from the theoretical assumptions inherent in many writings on 'mixed race.' It is apparent that a privileging of particular voices is taking place. The current discussions in 'mixed race' theory perpetuate a kind of crude asymmetry that has tainted many critical analyses of race theory, where race is a code word for non-white. The binary logic of race, in which the world is perceived in terms of oppositions (white versus non-white) encodes a hierarchy, with the first term of these oppositions superior to the second.

April: It is important, as Judith Butler reminds us, to trouble these categories.[1] As in the changing historical status of Italian and Jewish immigrants to the USA in the early twentieth century (who gradually came to be regarded as 'white'), who qualifies as white or raced changes over time and space. The categorisation of who is permitted to be white and who is marked as non-white fluctuates, and is a highly politicised and contested matter. 'Mixed race' people themselves participate in these dynamics. Yet, in spite of the instability surrounding racial and ethnic categorisation, popular conceptions of 'mixed race' remain predominantly characterised in terms of a white-non-white dichotomy.

Another example of this binary construction and the exclusion it produces can be seen in Amy Iwasaki Mass's study on Japanese-Americans in Southern California. The title of her study is 'Interracial Japanese Americans: The Best of Both Worlds or the End of the Japanese Community?'[2] It is interesting that although she uses the term 'interracial', she does not deconstruct her use of the label. She seems to imply that 'interracial' only refers to people of Japanese and white descent. From personal experience, I have met several Southern Californians who identify as interracial Japanese Americans who do not fit into the category that Iwasaki Mass employs in her article – for example, Japanese-Mexican-Americans. Her use of the term 'interracial' solely to represent Japanese-white-Americans glosses over the differences and demographic diversity characteristic of Southern California.

Minelle: We have no easy answers to these thorny issues, but we hope that by raising them, it will lead to extensive debate. How should 'mixed race' be conceptualised? As discussed in the introduction to this volume, how can we talk about 'mixed race' without reifying the notion that someone who is 'mixed' is descended from two distinct and 'pure' lineages, whatever 'pure' means? Given the common polarisation of white and black heritages (and the accompanying mythologisation of whiteness and white purity in particular), it is vital that we move away from a sole focus on white/black 'mixture'.

We find ourselves at an ironic impasse, because we do not want to dissolve the category of 'mixed race' altogether. We want to acknowledge the wide range of voices, some of which are marginalised within the current 'mixed race' discourse. If we do not begin to assert and give consideration to alternative perspectives on 'mixed race', we fall prey to binary traps of categorisation, where a majority 'mixed race' group (with some white heritage) exists and other minority 'mixes' find themselves silenced or ignored. Other groups should not be negated or overshadowed in the generalised discourse on 'mixed race'.

We believe that there is a lack of interconnectedness among the various groups who study and write about 'mixed race'. At times, discussions at conferences about 'mixed race' seem to disintegrate quickly into a confrontational tone, where a hierarchy of difference emerges among diverse 'mixed race' people. In such meetings, questions such as: 'Are you more "mixed race" than I am?' or, 'Will the real "mixed race" person please stand up?' are raised. At the heart of a productive 'mixed race' theory ought to be a clear articulation of various forms of political subjectivities forging alliances across difference. However, we have yet to contemplate creative alliances and the possibility of creating new collectives.

We find ourselves in good company as there are many other feminists who heed the importance of this call, like Chandra Mohanty, who insists that feminists should develop potential alliances across divisive boundaries in the creation of horizontal comradeship,[3] and Gillian Rose, a feminist geographer, who recognises the importance of alliances in struggle, where the spaces of separatism become spaces of interrelations.[4]

April: So how can we begin to create these new alliances? Our goal is to contemplate ways for 'mixed race' discourse to accommodate the experiences and views of individuals of a whole variety of 'mixes'. It is crucial to begin to address this issue now, as we witness greater partnering and intermarriage not only among black and white peoples, but also between various ethnic minority groups. We have entered into this discussion to see if unity is at all possible in 'mixed race' discourse. We must be able to participate in discussions about 'mixed race', valuing who we are as individuals, while bringing with us a respect for the many and varied experiences of 'mixed race' people. 'Who has it harder in society?' is not a productive question. Instead, we wish to ask: What kinds of oppression, and what kinds of experiences, more generally, have we shared? How can we create more liberating spaces?

Minelle: How can we come together, despite all of our wildly different experiences, as individuals who identify as 'mixed race', or as researchers who wish to delve into further explorations into 'mixed race'? Although it is important to recognise the variable experiences of mixed people, we wish to create some connections across our differences. How can we co-exist and at the same time avoid the potential pitfalls of reified categories? How can we fight stereotypes concerning the experiences of all 'mixed' people?

In approaching these difficult questions we have found the work of 'mixed race' researchers such as Michael Thornton and Cynthia Nakashima particularly compelling. Both authors have tried to open up the discourse on 'mixed race' identity. Thornton, himself of African American and Japanese descent, calls for a broadening of the research agenda to acknowledge that there is no single 'mixed race' experience.[5] Nakashima[6] also highlights the multiplicity within the 'mixed race' movement. She identifies three strands to its political activity. First, the struggle for inclusion within minority ethnic communities. Second, the sharing of a common identity and agenda among 'mixed race' people. Third, the struggle to develop a 'supraracial' discourse which creates connections across racialised boundaries, forging a common humanity. She ends by insisting that we listen attentively to all these voices to 'recognise and reflect the diversity of voices that make up the multiracial movement'.[7] We would emphasise the importance of producing theory and analysis which resonate with the experiences of diverse individuals of various mixes.

April: In order to move toward the generation of productive theorising, however, we must reshape the concept of 'mixed race'. Otherwise, the discourse of 'mixed race' is in danger of deteriorating through division, devaluation, exclusion, sadness and resentment. The title of our chapter is 'same difference' to reflect its dual emphasis. First, we acknowledge the commonality of being 'mixed race' and falling outside the prevailing racialised categories. Second, close reflection on our own experiences calls for a refinement of the emerging discourse on 'mixed race'. There are further dimensions added where one's ancestry is mixed, but not white. These complexities are largely unexplored in existing research which then feeds into a restricted conceptualisation of 'mixed race'.

We need to make further efforts to develop theory where all people who identify as 'mixed race' can contribute and share their experiences within the existing discourse. Although we have each discussed the personal and particular family experiences associated with our dual minority parentage, it would be erroneous to assume any clear-cut categorical differences in our experiences from those of other 'mixed' people. Nor should 'mixed' people conclude that their experiences are wholly different from those of monoracial minorities. In fact, Michael Thornton has questioned how distinct the experiences of 'mixed race' people are from those of monoracial minorities. These questions about areas of commonality and difference are complex and cannot be simply extrapolated from the particularities of individual, personalised accounts (though these are unquestionably important). Rather, such questions need more systematic empirical investigation.

Minelle: There are also many other issues that need further debate and study. For instance, what are the differences and commonalities between 'mixed race' identity and diasporic identity? How questions of nationalism tie in with 'mixed race' identifications also concern us. As North American citizens, April and I came to London to pursue our studies with a very different set of experiences involving particular ethnic and national identities. How does this affect our own interpretation of 'mixed race' in Britain? Future research also needs to interrogate gender differences experienced by 'mixed race' people. All of these questions require that we pay more attention to the specific contexts in which particular 'mixed race' identities are formed and experienced.

April: So although we will refold our map at this juncture, we want to emphasise that there are many more landscapes left to map. We only see this discussion as a point of departure. This map is in a continual state of process. We're constantly revising it, attempting to unveil the contours of 'race' and 'mixed race', emphasising certain roads, establishing landmarks and, most importantly, moving beyond the past discourse on race and 'mixed race' by establishing a new legend. And what would this new legend look like? We propose that it necessitates a new vocabulary – one which shatters the seemingly stable notion of 'race' to describe the varied and diverse terrain of multiracial experiences. This won't be an easy terrain to map, but in doing so, we can work toward revitalising and 'troubling' existing work on 'mixed race' identity.

Study probes

1   What examples do Mahtani and Moreno provide which support their position that binary white/non-white perspectives on 'mixed race' are privileged?
2   How do the authors define 'same difference'? Why is this integral to their 'rethinking' of 'mixed race'?
3   Compare their arguments to the critical perspectives on 'multiraciality' put forward by authors of the other extracts in this section.
4   What does the future hold for 'mixed race' studies?

Notes

1   J. Butler, *Gender Trouble* (London: Routledge, 1990).
2   A. Iwasaki Mass, 'Interracial Japanese Americans: the best of both worlds or the end of the Japanese American community', in M. Root (ed.), *Racially Mixed People in America* (London: Sage 1992).

3   C. Mohanty, 'Cartographies of struggle: Third World women and the politics of feminism', in C. Mohanty, A. Russo and L. Torres (eds), *Third World Women and the Politics of Feminism* (Bloomington: Indiana University Press 1991).
4   G. Rose, *Feminism and Geography* (Minneapolis: University of Minnesota Press 1993).
5   M. Thornton 'Hidden agendas, identity theories and multiracial people', in M. Root (ed.), *The Multiracial Experience* (London: Sage, 1996).
6   C. Nakashima, 'Voices from the movement: approaches to multiraciality', in M. Root (ed.), *The Multiracial Experience* (London: Sage, 1996).
7   Ibid., p. 97.

SUGGESTIONS FOR FURTHER READING

Burroughs, W. Jeffrey and Spickard, Paul (eds) (2000) 'Ethnicity, Multiplicity, and Narrative: Problems and Possibilities', in P. Spickard and W.J. Burroughs (eds) *We Are a People: Narrative and Multiplicity in Constructing Ethnic Identity*, Philadelphia, PA: Temple University Press, pp. 244–254.

Christian, Mark (2000): *Multiracial Identity: An International Perspective*, Basingstoke: Macmillan.

Colker, Ruth (1996) *Hybrid: Bisexuals, Multiracials, and other Misfits under American Law*, London: New York University Press.

Daniel, G. Reginald (2002) *More Than Black?: Multiracial Identity and the New Racial Order*, Philadelphia, PA: Temple University Press.

Dyer, Richard (1997) *White: Essays on Race and Culture*, London: Routledge.

Goldberg, David (1995) 'Made in the USA: Racial Mixing n Matching', in N. Zack (ed.) *American Mixed Race*, London: Rowman and Littlefield, pp. 237–256.

Espiritu, Yen Le (2001) 'Possibilities of a Multiracial Asian America', in T. Williams-León and C. Nakashima (eds) *The Sum of Our Parts: Mixed Heritage Asian Americans*, Philadelphia, PA: Temple University Press, pp. 25–34.

Gilroy, Paul (2000) *Between Camps: Nations, Cultures and the Allure of Race*, London: Allen Lane.

Gordon, Lewis R. (1995) *Bad Faith and Antiblack Racism*, Atlantic Highlands, NJ: Humanities Press.

Hall, Cynthia Iijima (1992) 'Coloring Outside the Lines', in M.P.P. Root (ed.) *Racially Mixed People in America*, Thousand Oaks, CA: Sage, pp. 326–329.

Olumide, Jill (2002) *Raiding the Gene Pool: The Social Construction of Mixed Race*, London: Pluto Press.

Mahtani, Minelle (2001) ' "I'm a Blonde-Haired, Blue-Eyed Black Girl": Mapping Mobile Paradoxical Spaces Among Multiethnic Women in Toronto, Canada', in

D. Parker and M. Song (eds) *Rethinking 'Mixed Race'*, London: Pluto Press, pp. 173–190.

Mahtani, Minelle (2002) 'What's in a Name? Exploring the Employment of "Mixed Race" as Identification', *Ethnicities* 2(4):469–490.

Nakashima, Cynthia (1996) 'Voices from the Movement: Approaches to Multiraciality', in M.P.P. Root (ed.) *The Multiracial Experience*, Thousand Oaks, CA: Sage, pp. 79–100.

Nakashima, Daniel (2001) 'A Rose by Any Other Name: Names, Multiracial/Multiethnic People and the Politics of Identity', in T. Williams-León and C. Nakashima (eds) *The Sum of Our Parts: Mixed Heritage Asian Americans*, Philadelphia, PA: Temple University Press, pp. 111–120.

Papastergiadis, Nikos (1994) *The Complicities of Culture: Hybridity and 'New Internationalism'*, Manchester: Manchester University Press.

Papastergiadis, Nikos (1997) 'Tracing Hybridity in Theory', in P. Werbner and T. Modood (eds) *Debating Cultural Hybridity*, London: Zed Books, pp. 257–281.

Papastergiadis, Nikos (2000) *The Turbulence of Migration: Globalization, Deterritorialization and Hybridity*, Cambridge: Polity Press.

Parker, Richard and Song, Miri (eds) (2001) 'Introduction: Rethinking "Mixed Race" ', in D. Parker and M. Song (eds), *Rethinking 'Mixed Race'*, London: Pluto Press, pp. 1–22.

Rockquemore, Kerry (2002) *Beyond Black: Biracial Identity in America*, London: Sage.

Root, Maria P.P. (ed.) (1996) *The Multiracial Experience: Racial Borders as the New Frontier*, Thousand Oaks, CA: Sage.

Root, Maria P.P. (2003) 'Five Mixed-Race Identities: From Relic to Revolution', in L. Winters and H. DeBose (eds) *New Faces in a Changing America*, Thousand Oaks, CA: Sage, pp. 3–20.

Small, Stephen (2001) 'Colour, Culture and Class: Interrogating Interracial Marriage and People of Mixed Racial Descent in the USA', in D. Parker and M. Song (eds) *Rethinking 'Mixed Race'*, London: Pluto Press, pp. 117–132.

Spencer, Jon Michael (1997) *The New Colored People: The Mixed Race Movement in America*, London: New York University Press.

Spickard, Paul (2001) 'The Subject is Mixed Race: The Boom in Biracial Biography', in R. Parker and M. Song (eds) *Rethinking 'Mixed Race'*, pp. 76–98.

Spickard, Paul (2003) 'Does Multiraciality Lighten? Me-too Ethnicity and the Whiteness Trap', in L. Winters and H. DeBose (eds) *New Faces in a Changing America*, Thousand Oaks, CA: Sage, 289–300.

Spickard, Paul and Burroughs, W. Jeffrey (eds) (2000) *We Are a People: Narrative and Multiplicity in Constructing Ethnic Identity*, Philadelphia, PA: Temple University Press, pp. 244–254.

Texeira, Mary Thierry (2003) 'The New Multiracialism: An Affirmation of or an End to Race As we Know It', in L. Winters and H. DeBose (eds) *New Faces in a Changing America*, Thousand Oaks, CA: Sage, pp. 21–38.

Thornton, Michael (1996) 'Is Multiracial Status Unique? The Personal and Social Experience', in M.P.P. Root (ed.) *Racially Mixed People in America*, Thousand Oaks, CA: Sage, pp. 321–325.

Velasco y Trianosky, Gregory (2003) 'Beyond *Mestizaje*: The Future of Race in America', in L. Winters and H. DeBose (eds) *New Faces in a Changing America*, Thousand Oaks, CA: Sage, pp. 176–193.

Ware, Vron and Back, Les (2002) *Out of Whiteness: Color, Politics and Culture*, Chicago, IL: University of Chicago Press.

Weisman, Jan (2001) 'The Tiger and his Stripes: Thai and American Reactions to Tiger Woods's (Multi) "Racial Self" ', in T. Williams-León and C. Nakashima (eds) *The Sum of Our Parts: Mixed Heritage Asian Americans*, Philadelphia, PA: Temple University Press, pp. 231–244.

Williams, Kim (2003) 'From Civil Rights to the Multiracial Movement', in L. Winters and H. DeBose (eds) *New Faces in a Changing America*, Thousand Oaks, CA: Sage, pp. 85–98.

Williams, Patricia J. (1997) *Seeing a Colour-Blind Future*, London: Virago.

Williams-León, Teresa and Nakashima, Cynthia (eds) (2001) *The Sum of Our Parts: Mixed Heritage Asian Americans*, Philadelphia, PA: Temple University Press.

Winters, Loretta (2003) 'Epilogue: The Multiracial Movement: Harmony and Discord', in L. Winters and H. DeBose (eds) *New Faces in a Changing America*, Thousand Oaks, CA: Sage, pp. 373–380.

Winters, Loretta and DeBose, Herman (eds) (2003) *New Faces in a Changing America: Multiracial Identity in the 21st Century*, Thousand Oaks, CA: Sage.

Zack, Naomi (ed.) (1995) *American Mixed Race*, London: Rowman and Littlefield.

Zack, Naomi (1995) 'Life After Race', in N. Zack (ed.) *American Mixed Race*, London: Rowman and Littlefield, pp. 297–307.

Index

Himmler, Heinrich 84
Hindus/Hinduism 68, 253
Hispanics 16, 153, 201, 225–8, 229, 241–2, 293–4
history, Eurocentric rendering of 284
Hitler, Adolf 13, 80, 98
Hodes, Martha 5, 9–10
Hoffman, Paul 3
Ho-lattos 207
Hollinger, David 280
Holmes, Samuel J. 105
Holocaust 89, 98
holocentrism 284
Holzhauzer, Thomas 87
homosexuals 13, 98
hooks, bell 285
Houston, Sam 278
Hudson, Nicholas 3
Hudson's Bay Company 60
Huggins, Nathan Irvin 291
Hughes, Langston 212
Huhndorf, Shari 5, 10
Human Genome Diversity Project (HGDP) 15, 18
Human Genome Project (HGP) 15, 18
Huntington, Samuel 5
Huxley, Julian 109–10, 111–12
Hyam, Ronald 12
hybrid degeneracy theory 33
hybridity 8, 11, 42–6, 301–3; unilateral 11
hypodescent 12, 144, 145, 192, 220, 221–2, 258; see also 'one drop rule'

'Iamism' xx, 8
identity 143–6, 150, 151–2, 168, 173, 184–94; ethnic 143–4; genetic 116–122; linear models of 144, 145; multidimensional models of 145
identity crisis 143–4
identity politics 4, 137–97, 201, 263, 267, 299
Ifekwunigwe, Jayne 1–29, 183–94, 306
Ignatiev, Noel 5
immigration: Britain 77–8; quotas and blood quantum 146; United States 43, 62–3, 70
imperialism 5, 7, 100, 279, 303, 304
in-between individual 70
inclusion 267, 268
India 6, 66, 67
Indian population, England and Wales 251
inequality, racial 68, 98, 99

intelligence 100–1, 103, 105, 106, 112, 113, 290
Interrace magazine 211, 212
Interracial Voice 247
Irish 77–8, 250
Islam 68

Jackson, Michael 1–2, 162
Jacobson, Keith 5
Jacquinot 45, 49
Jaimes, M. Annette 9, 10
Jamaica 66, 105–6, 303
Jamestown Colony 59
Japanese American Citizens' League 274
Japanese population, US 6, 62–3, 146, 265, 267, 314
Java, Indo-Europeans 66, 67
Jefferson, Thomas 274
Jenks, A.E. 60
Jennings, Herbert Spencer 106–7
Jensen, Arthur 113
Jewlattos 206
Jews 108, 118, 119, 152 n.2, 165 n.6; in Britain 77, 253; in Nazi Germany 13, 81, 82, 87, 98, 113
Jim Crow segregation 13
Johnson, Keith 4, 8
Johnson, Roswell H. 102–3
Jones, Donald F. 103
Jones, Lisa 201, 209–13
Jones, Steve 3
Justice, David 211

Kant, I. 49
Katz, William Loren 10
Kelsey, Henry 60
Kelves, Daniel Jo 13
Kempadoo, Kamala 7
Knight, Chris 3
Knox, Robert 37–8
Kohn, Marek 13
Kolreuter, Joseph Gottlieb 50 n.6
Korean-Black conflict 301–2
Koubaka, Henri-Pierre xix
Kravitz, Lenny 206
Kroeber, Karl 172
Krupat, Arnold 10

labelling, racial *see* language, racial
Labour Force Survey 246, 247
language, racial 153–7, 305–7